WEEKS PUBLIC LIBRARY
GREENLAND, N. H

Profiting Without Producing
How Finance Exploits Us All

D0807837

Profiting Without Producing
How Finance Exploits Us All

Costas Lapavitsas

VERSO

London • New York

First published by Verso 2013
© Costas Lapavitsas 2013

All rights reserved

The moral rights of the author have been asserted

1 3 5 7 9 10 8 6 4 2

Verso
UK: 6 Meard Street, London W1F 0EG
US: 20 Jay Street, Suite 1010, Brooklyn, NY 11201
www.versobooks.com

Verso is the imprint of New Left Books

ISBN-13: 978-1-78168-141-1 (pbk)
ISBN-13: 978-1-78168-246-3 (hbk)

British Library Cataloguing in Publication Data
A catalogue record for this book is available from the British Library

Library of Congress Cataloging-in-Publication Data

Lapavitsas, Costas, 1961–
    Profiting without producing: how finance exploits us all / Costas Lapavitsas.
        pages cm
    ISBN 978-1-78168-246-3 (hardback)
1. Finance. 2. Economic policy. 3. Financial crises. 4. Economics–Political aspects.
I. Title.
    HG173.L37 2013
    332–dc23
                    2013024705

Typeset in Minion Pro by Bibliosynergatiki, Athens, Greece
Printed and bound by CPI Group (UK) Ltd, Croydon, CR0 4YY

*To Elektra and Maria in the hope that they will
excuse my prolonged self-absorption.*

CONTENTS

LIST OF FIGURES

LIST OF TABLES

PREFACE

The 2000s were an extraordinary period for finance in terms of prices, profits, and volume of transactions, but also in terms of influence and arrogance. By the middle of the decade a vast bubble had been inflated in the US and the UK, the bursting of which could not be reliably timed but whose aftermath was likely to be devastating. Trivial as this point might seem in 2013, it was almost impossible to convey it at the time to specialists and students of finance, and even to activists and socialists. Public perceptions were dominated by the so-called expert skills of the financial system in 'slicing and dicing' risk, and by the putative wisdom of the 'Great Moderation' in inflation policy. Structural crises were a thing of the past, or of the developing world, not of mature countries, where institutions were strong and economists well trained. It seemed that finance had discovered the *perpetuum mobile* of profit making.

By the middle of the first decade of the new century, it was also apparent that the processes under way amounted to more than financial excess. The bubble reflected profound changes in the conduct of non-financial enterprises, banks, and households. After years of financial ascendancy, the agents of capitalist accumulation assigned to financial operations a weight that was historically unprecedented. Finance was pivotal to profit making and to organizing everyday life, but also to determining economic policy as a whole. Mature capitalism had become financialized.

This book was initially conceived in that context, and its aim was to analyse the ascendancy of finance and the concomitant financialization of capitalism. By bringing to bear previous work on money and finance, the intention was to develop a theoretical analysis of financialization with clear Marxist characteristics. It was to be a book that would draw on Anglo-Saxon political economy and Japanese Uno Marxism, while being familiar with mainstream theory of money and finance. It would thus contribute to filling the hole still gaping in political economy in this field.

As is often the case with plans of this sort, reality intervened. In August 2007 the US money market had a heart attack, and in August–September 2008 the global financial system had a near-death experience. The bubble had indeed burst and a catastrophe was in the offing. The destructive influence of finance on the rest of the economy had become evident, as had the role of the state in supporting and promoting financiali-zation. More than that, however, it soon became clear that this was a structural crisis that would not go away quickly. The bursting of the bubble had ushered in a crisis of financialization that cast fresh light on the historic transformation of mature capitalism during the preceding decades. It became necessary to re-examine the underlying tendencies of financialization, focusing in particular on the sources of financial profit. The book would have to be delayed.

And then in 2010–2012 the crisis took an even more dangerous turn. States had become perilously exposed to debt because recession had reduced tax revenues, while rescuing finance had imposed fresh costs on the exchequer. A bubble inflated by private capital had resulted in a crisis of public finance. Rising state indebtedness created turmoil of extraordinary ferocity in the eurozone, bringing into sharp relief the split between core and periphery, pushing several peripheral countries toward default, and threatening a break-up of the monetary union. The spectre of a gigantic crisis hung over the world economy. It became clear that financialization would have to be rethought still further in view of its monetary dimension, particularly the precariousness of its domestic and international monetary underpinnings.

The crisis was far from over at the time of writing this book. However, the temptation had to be resisted to delay publication still further in the expectation that other important features of financialization would emerge. It was time to submit to the public sphere the analysis of the structural and historical content of financialization, even if that meant trying to hit a moving target. The monetary and financial aspects of the transformation of capitalism during the last four decades have been increasingly discussed by political economy, particularly its Marxist strain. This book has a distinctive argument to make regarding financialization, including particularly the predatory and expropriating character of financial profit and its implications for social stratification. Light could thus be shed on the tendency to crisis that has characterized financialization since its inception.

In offering thanks for help with preparing this book, I must first acknowledge that too many debts are owed to too many people to thank them all by name. Still, Makoto Itoh must be thanked personally, not so much for helping directly but for his unstinting intellectual support over many years. If only other senior political economists shared his generosity of spirit. I must also thank Tomohiko Sekine for sparing the time to discuss with me difficult issues of capitalist accumulation on several occasions. The finer points of Unoist Marxism were far easier to grasp with such teachers. Thanks should also be addressed to many other Japanese political economists who have been friends, colleagues and interlocutors to me over long years. *Iroiro to osewa ni narimashite, hontou ni arigatou gozaimashita.*

It is also necessary to thank members of Research on Money and Finance to whom I owe intellectual and practical debts. RMF came to life when the bubble of the 2000s burst, and I am proud to say that its input in international debate has been significant. Back in 2010, it was impossible to imagine the full extent of the storm hitting Europe, but we gave a good account of ourselves despite having very few resources. Without the lively spirit of inquiry of RMF members, the analysis of financialization would have been much harder to undertake. In this respect I should single out Iren Levina whose persistent intellectual curiosity and facility with data helped shape the arguments of this book. Special thanks are also due to Eugenia Pires, Jeff Powell, Juan Painceira and Jo Michell for help with the bibliography and the data despite heavy pressures of life and work.

One of the few positive outcomes of financialization has been the resurgence of Marxist analysis of money and finance. It is not so long ago that these issues were a minority pursuit among Marxist political economists, particularly in the Anglo-Saxon tradition. Things are now very different as a new generation is entering the lists. Things are still more different as activists and socialists have come to realize the specific gravity of finance in contemporary capitalism. There are growing political and social demands for an effective response to the disasters created by financialization. This book is intended as a theoretical contribution to the debate in the hope that it would also contribute to confronting financialization in practice. The opposition to contemporary capitalism will only gain if Marxist theory continues its resurgence.

London
January 2013

Part 1 FINANCIALIZATION: THEORETICAL ANALYSIS AND HISTORICAL PRECEDENTS

1. INTRODUCTION: THE RISE AND RISE OF FINANCE

A peculiar crisis

In the summer of 2007 several mature capitalist economies entered a period of instability of historic proportions. The first intimations of economic malfunctioning had appeared in the US in the summer of 2006, as the housing market started to fall, demand weakened, and profitability took a turn for the worse. But actual crisis conditions emerged only in August 2007, after a spasm had traversed the international money markets, making liquidity hard to obtain among banks. During the following twelve months, financial conditions became progressively worse, while production, consumption, and trade essentially marked time. And then, in August–September 2008, a ferocious financial storm broke out: international banks failed, credit disappeared, and money became almost impossible to obtain on a private basis.

Collapse of much of the US financial system, and by extension much of global finance, was avoided only through state intervention supplying banks with liquidity and capital, all drawn from public resources. Nonetheless, the world economy entered a sharp recession in 2008–2009, at the end of which conditions of rapid accumulation failed to be restored across developed countries. On the contrary, the tightness of public revenue due to recession, as well as the public expenditures required to rescue finance and forestall economic collapse, created large fiscal deficits in several countries.

The result was the emergence of a crisis of public debt after 2010, which assumed a particularly severe form in Europe. The crisis of public debt has had two implications, both pregnant with risks for capitalist accumulation across the world. First, it has menaced banks holding the public bonds of states that have had difficulties in meeting their obligations; hence, the crisis has threatened to return to the financial system whence it has emanated. Second, and far more dangerously, the crisis of public debt has directly affected the cohesion of the European Monetary Union. If the common currency created by the European Union collapsed, it is likely that there would be an unprecedented global disturbance.

The crisis of the 2000s will prove fertile ground for economic historians for decades to come with regard to both its causes and consequences. However, the crisis has already had one definite outcome: it has finally lifted the curtain on the transformation of mature and developing capitalist economies during the last three decades, confirming the pivotal role of finance, both domestically and internationally. Financial capital permeates economic activity, and interacts with financial markets in ways capable of generating enormous profits but also precipitating global crises. In terms that will be used throughout this book, contemporary capitalism is 'financialized' and the turmoil commencing in 2007 is a crisis of 'financialization'.

The economic processes – and the social relations – characteristic of financialization represent a milestone in the development of capitalism. The catalyst of crisis in 2007 was speculative mortgage lending to the poorest workers in the US during the 2000s, the loans being subsequently traded in 'securitized' form in global financial markets. It is hard to exaggerate what an extraordinary fact this is. Under conditions of classical, nineteenth-century capitalism it would have been unthinkable for a global disruption of accumulation to materialize because of debts incurred by workers, including the poorest. But this is precisely what has happened under conditions of financialized capitalism, an economic and social system that is much more sophisticated than its nineteenth-century predecessor.

Financialization has emerged gradually during recent decades, and its content and implications are the focus of this book. To be sure, capitalist economies are continually restructured due to pressures of competition and to the underlying drive to maintain profitability. However, some transformations have a distinctive historical significance, and financialization is one of those. The change that has taken place in mature capitalist economies and societies since the late 1970s requires appropriate attention to be paid to finance. Consider the following features of financialization to substantiate this claim.

Context and structural aspects of financialization

Mature capitalism has been historically marked by deep transformations of economy and society. Toward the end of the nineteenth century, for instance, there emerged new methods of production in heavy industry, accompanied by the rise of monopolistic, joint-stock enterprises. The change coincided with a long depression, 1873–96, and led to a rebalancing of global productive power away from Britain and toward the US and Germany. Similarly, at the end of the Second World War, mass consumption emerged across several developed countries based on methods of mass production. A long boom occurred, lasting until 1973–74, during which production became increasingly dominated by transnational monopolistic enterprises, while finance operated under a system of controls domestically and internationally. For nearly three decades, the US was the dominant economic force in global production and trade.

The transformation represented by financialization is of a similar order of importance. Since the 1970s, there have been profound changes in production methods deriving from information and telecommunications technologies. Transnational enterprises have become dominant over global production and international trade. The centre of gravity of global productive capacity has partly shifted from mature economies in the West toward rising economies in the East, primarily China. Meanwhile, the institutional framework of capitalist activity has been altered as deregulation has prevailed in important markets, above all, for labour and finance. Throughout this period, accumulation has lacked dynamism in mature countries, inequality was exacerbated, and crises have become sharper and more frequent.

The most striking feature of the period, however, has been the rise of finance, the start of which can be usefully placed in the late 1970s. The financial sector had become progressively larger in the 1950s and 1960s, while still operating within the regulatory framework characteristic of the long post-war boom. However, even by the late 1970s, the domestic and international importance of finance remained modest. The three decades that followed have witnessed unprecedented expansion of financial activities, rapid growth of financial profits, permeation of economy and society by financial relations, and domination of economic policy by the concerns of the financial sector. At the same time, the productive sector in mature countries has exhibited mediocre growth performance, profit rates have remained below the levels of the 1950s and 1960s, unemployment has generally risen and become persistent, and real wages have shown no tendency to rise in a sustained manner. An asymmetry has emerged between the sphere of production and the ballooning sphere of circulation.

The rise of finance has been predicated on a radical alteration of the monetary framework of capitalist accumulation, both internationally and domestically. International monetary conditions have been stamped by the collapse of the Bretton Woods Agreement in 1971–73. Bretton Woods had enforced the convertibility of the US dollar into gold at $35 to the ounce, thus fixing exchange rates during the long boom. Its collapse led to the gradual emergence of alternative international monetary arrangements based on the US dollar functioning as inconvertible quasi-world-money. The new arrangements have generated considerable instability of exchange and interest rates, thereby spurring the growth of international financial markets. Growth of international capital flows during the same period, partly in response to exchange and interest rate instability, has led to financialization in developing countries. Domestic monetary conditions, in contrast, have been marked by the steady accumulation of power by central banks as controllers of credit money backed by the state. Central banks have emerged as the dominant public institution of financialization, the defender of the interests of the financial sector.

The ascendancy of central banks is hardly surprising, since financialization in general would have been impossible without active and continuous intervention by the state. Financialization has depended on the state to deregulate the financial system with regard to prices, quantities, functions and cross-border flows of capital. Equally, financialization has depended on the state to regulate the adequacy of own capital, the management of risk, and the rules of competition among financial institutions. Even more decisively, financialization has depended on the state to intervene periodically to underwrite the solvency of banks, to provide extraordinary liquidity and to guarantee the deposits of the public with banks.

Ultimately, however, the rise of finance has resulted from changes deep within capitalist accumulation. Three characteristic tendencies of accumulation in mature countries have shaped financialization as a structural transformation of contemporary capitalism. First, non-financial enterprises have become increasingly involved in financial processes on an independent basis, often undertaking financial market transactions on own account. The financialization of industrial and commercial enterprises has affected their profitability, internal organization, and investment outlook. Non-financial enterprises have become relatively more remote from banks and other financial institutions. Second, banks have focused on transacting in open financial markets with the aim of making profits through financial trading rather than through outright borrowing and lending. At the same time banks have turned toward individual and household income as a source of profit, often combining trading in open markets with lending to households, or collecting household savings. Third, individuals and households have come increasingly to rely on the formal financial system to facilitate access to vital goods and services, including housing, education, health, and transport. The savings of households and individuals have also been increasingly mobilized by the formal financial system.

The transformation of the conduct of non-financial enterprises, banks and households constitutes the basis of financialization. Examining these relations theoretically and empirically, and thus establishing the deeper content of financialized capitalism, is the main task of this book. The concepts and methods deployed for the purpose derive from Marxist political economy. To summarize, the capitalist economy is treated as a structured whole that comprises different spheres of activity – namely production, circulation, and distribution – among which production is dominant. Both production and circulation possess their own internal logic, even though the two spheres are inextricably linked. Production creates value; its motive is profit (surplus value) deriving from the exploitation of labour; its aim is the accumulation of capital. Circulation does *not* create value; it results in profits, but these derive mostly – though not exclusively – from redistributing surplus value. Finance is a part of circulation, but also possesses mechanisms standing aside commodity trading and its corresponding flows of money. The traded object of finance is loanable money capital, the cornerstone of capitalist credit. Production, circulation and distribution give rise to class relations, pivoting on the ownership of the means of production, but also determined by the appropriation of profits.

Financialization reflects a growing asymmetry between production and circulation – particularly the financial component of the latter – during the last three decades. The asymmetry has arisen as the financial conduct of non-financial enterprises, banks and households has gradually changed, thus fostering a range of aggregate phenomena of financialization. A telling aspect of the transformation has been the rise of profits accruing through financial transactions, including new forms of profit that could even be unrelated to surplus value. This process is summed up as 'financial expropriation' in subsequent chapters. New social layers have emerged as financial profit has burgeoned.

Financial markets and banks

It might seem paradoxical at first sight to associate financialization with the conduct of banks, given that the rise of finance has had far more extravagant aspects. Financialization, for instance, appears to relate more to the global spread of financial markets, the proliferation of traded financial instruments, and the emergence of novel, market-related financial transactions, rather than to the behaviour of banks. Compared to the expanding and rapidly changing world of financial markets, banks seem old-fashioned and even staid. And yet, as is shown in the rest of the book, banks have been a decisive factor in the financialization of capitalism. Banks remain the cornerstone of contemporary finance and several of the most visible market-related features of financialization emanate from banks. It is not accidental that the crisis of financialization in the late 2000s has revolved around banks rather than other financial institutions.

To establish the importance of banks in the course of financialization consider some general features of the derivatives markets, arguably the most prominent financial markets of recent years.[1] Simply put, a derivative is a contract that establishes a claim on an underlying asset – or on the cash value of that asset – which must be executed at some definite point in the future. The underlying asset could be a commodity, such as wheat; or another financial asset, such as a bond; or a financial price, for example the value of a currency; or even an entirely non-economic entity like the weather. The units of the underlying asset stated on the contract and multiplied by the spot price define the notional value of the derivative. Historically, derivatives have been associated with agricultural production: a forward or a futures contract would specify the quantity and price of an agricultural commodity that would be delivered at a definite point in the future. A forward contract would be a private agreement between two parties agreeing to trade some specific output at a certain price and time (e.g., the wheat produced by one of the contracting parties); a futures contract would also be a private agreement between two parties but the commodity traded would be generic (e.g., any wheat of a certain type and quality).

Capitalist farmers could use derivatives to hedge against unforeseen fluctuations in the price of output. In addition to hedging, derivatives could also be used to speculate on the future movement of prices, or to arbitrage among different markets exhibiting

---

1 Derivatives are also discussed in subsequent chapters but mostly in the context of the crisis of the 2000s and not in and of themselves. There is scarce theoretical and empirical work on derivatives in the tradition of political economy, including Edward LiPuma and Benjamin Lee, 'Financial Derivatives and the Rise of Circulation', *Economy and Society* 34:3, 2005; Dick Bryan and Michael Rafferty, *Capitalism with Derivatives*, Basingstoke: Palgrave Macmillan, 2006; Duncan Wigan, 'Financialisation and Derivatives: Constructing an Artifice of Indifference', *Competition and Change* 13:2, 2009; some of this work will be discussed in subsequent parts of this book. Jan Toporowski's work in the post-Keynesian and Kaleckian tradition has analysed derivatives as an integral element of the financial inflation of the period (*The End of Finance*, London: Routledge, 2000). Among economic sociologists Donald MacKenzie has shed light on risk management, valuation theory, and derivatives as instruments boosting exchangeability (*An Engine, Not a Camera*, Cambridge, MA: MIT, 2006; see also Donald MacKenzie and Yuval Millo, 'Constructing a Market, Performing Theory', *American Journal of Sociology* 109:1, 2003).

unwarranted price divergences in the underlying asset. Thus, the standard way of introducing derivatives in textbooks is as instruments that make for hedging, speculation or arbitrage among market traders.[2] Derivatives markets are typically perceived as spontaneously emerging entities which supplement the services offered by the markets in underlying assets, and hence improve the efficiency of the capitalist economy.

Even with this simple definition of derivatives, a key distinction is apparent – one between a contract that meets the specific conditions of two counterparties (a forward) and a contract that is more generic and could be traded freely in open markets (a future). The former is similar to an over-the-counter derivative, the latter to an exchange-traded derivative. They represent two different ways of undertaking the trading process – the forward depends on the specific decisions of the trading parties, the future depends on the impersonal and 'third' institution of the 'exchange' which organizes the trading. The 'exchange' standardizes futures contracts, steps between buyers and sellers to clear purchases and sales by the counterparties and, critically, demands a daily 'margin' in cash as protection from failure to meet contracted obligations at maturity.

The most important development in the evolution of derivatives trading in recent years has been the move to cash settlement of the contract, thus freeing the counterparties from the need to deliver the underlying asset.[3] On this basis, derivatives have become essentially a punt on the future direction of the price of the underlying asset that is subsequently settled in cash. Consequently, the trading of derivatives has come to include underlying assets that could never be delivered, such as a stock market index. In effect, the derivative has become what could be called a contract-for-differences – an agreement between buyer and seller to exchange the difference between the current value of a share, currency, commodity, or index and its value at maturity of the contract. If the difference is positive, the seller pays the buyer; if it is negative, the buyer is the one who loses money. Profit, in this context, depends on the difference between a fixed financial parameter and its uncertain value in the future.[4]

Spurred by cash settlement, the growth of derivatives markets in the years of financialization has been breathtaking: from practical irrelevance in the 1980s, their notional sum in 2011 was in the vicinity of 700 trillion US dollars for over-the-counter and probably a similar sum for exchange-traded derivatives.[5] Yet, at the core of the enormously expanded derivatives markets lie a few international banks, which have also been one of the driving forces of financialization. Banks are the pillar of contemporary

2 Shelagh Heffernan, *Modern Banking in Theory and Practice*, New York: Wiley, 1996.

3 MacKenzie, *An Engine, Not a Camera*.

4 Toporowski, *The End of Finance*, p. 96.

5 Bank for International Settlements (BIS), 'Triennial Central Bank Survey of Foreign Exchange and Derivatives Market Activity in 2010 – Final Results', December 2010; and BIS, 'Semiannual OTC Derivatives Statistics at End-June 2011', 2011.

derivatives markets both as market-makers – as agents who stand ready to buy and sell at all times – and as organizers of the basic structure of derivatives markets, as is shown in the following section.[6]

Expanding derivatives markets, dominant banks

At the end of 2010 both exchange-traded (ETD) and over-the-counter (OTC) derivatives markets had become enormous, as is shown in table 1.

TABLE 1 Derivatives markets and global output, US $tn, end of 2010

Indicator	US $	Stock/flow
Global GDP	63 tn/annum	Flow
Global stock market capitalization	55 tn	Stock
OTC notional outstanding	601 tn	Stock
OTC IR and FX turnover	4.5 tn/day	Flow
ETD turnover	8.1 tn/day	Flow
ETD outstanding	83 tn	Stock

Source: Adapted from Lindo (2013); IMF (2011); BIS (2010b, 2011)

Indicators of the size of derivatives markets are difficult to construct and even more difficult to compare against other magnitudes.[7] Table 1 measures the size of derivatives markets in terms of the notional outstanding amounts for both over-the-counter and exchange-traded derivatives, the former being much greater than the latter mostly because the 'exchange' regularly terminates offsetting trades, while termination does not generally take place in the over-the-counter market. The table also shows turnover, which is a further indicator of the size and the importance of these markets. Turnover in the over-the-counter market is shown only in terms of interest-rate (IR) and foreign-exchange (FX) derivatives because of data availability. For comparison the table also shows global GDP as well as global stock market capitalization.

It is apparent that notional and turnover figures in derivatives markets absolutely dwarf the rest, even bearing in mind that some indexes are of stocks while others are of flows and cannot be compared directly. The exceptional magnitude of the derivatives markets is the result of astounding growth during the last two decades. The rate of growth for the over-the-counter market, in particular, has been startling: from the end

---

6 This fundamental point is developed with exemplary acuity by Duncan Lindo, 'Political Economy of Financial Derivatives: The Role and Evolution of Banking', unpublished PhD dissertation, School of Oriental and African Studies, University of London, 2013.

7 Ibid., for a discussion of the figures, the nature of the data and the problems involved.

of the 1980s to the end of the 2000s the notional outstanding appears to have doubled every two or three years for most of the period.

Consider now the role of banks in these enormous markets. The importance of banks is most apparent in the over-the-counter market, which naturally lacks the organizing role played by the 'exchange' in the exchange-traded market. Banks function as market-makers, that is, as agents that stand ready to buy and sell in the over-the-counter market; they are the dealers that are integral to market functioning. Banks also provide the necessary market infrastructure through vital market institutions such as the International Swaps and Derivatives Association (ISDA). Table 2 classifies over-the-counter transactions in terms of the counterparties, which are split into dealer banks, other financial institutions, and non-financial customers.[8]

TABLE 2 Over-the-counter derivative nominal outstanding amount by counterparty, US $tn, June 2011

Counterparty type	Reporting dealers	Other financial institutions	Non-financial customers
Reporting dealers	206 tn 29%	401 tn 57%	51 tn 7%
Other financial institutions		Assumed negligible	Assumed negligible
Non-financial customers			Assumed negligible

Source: Adapted from Lindo (2013); BIS (2011). Approximately US $50tn is not allocated either because it refers to commodity derivatives, or because it represents adjustments in BIS statistics.

In practice, over-the-counter derivatives function as banking instruments. Almost a third of the trading in over-the-counter derivatives in 2011 took place in dealer-to-dealer transactions, while all transactions had at least one dealer bank as a counterparty. There were, perhaps, seventy sizeable dealer banks in about twenty countries transacting with many thousands of end users of derivatives; indeed, concentration appears to have been even greater than that, and perhaps fifteen to twenty dealers controlled the overwhelming bulk of over-the-counter trading across the world.[9] These dealers were large global banks that were also fundamental to financialization. The same banks were among the largest participants in the exchange-traded markets, though data is hard to obtain for the latter. There is no doubt, however, that the large dealer banks were heavily involved in the management of the 'exchanges', including determination of risk management procedures and 'margin' levels.

Given the dominant presence of banks in the derivatives markets, it is hardly

---

8   Ibid., for further discussion of methodology and data.

9   Ibid.

surprising that banks have encouraged the broadening of derivatives trading to include underlying assets with which they are most familiar – financial securities. Table 2 shows that less that 10 percent of over-the-counter transactions actually involved non-financial enterprises: the great bulk comprised transactions that took place among financial institutions, and thus referred mostly to financial derivatives. In fact, growth in the derivatives markets has generally been dominated by inter-est-rate and foreign-exchange derivatives; since the early 2000s the strongest growth has been in credit default swaps (CDS), which are briefly discussed in Part III of this book.[10]

The price of financial derivatives depends, among other factors, on the rate of interest, and the rate that is typically used to value most financial derivatives is the London Interbank Offered Rate (LIBOR). The LIBOR is determined by a com-mittee comprising several of the banks that dominate the derivatives markets; its determination involves the simple averaging of interest rates (excluding outliers) submitted by LIBOR committee banks daily. These are rates at which the LIBOR banks think that they can borrow from each other, although no LIBOR bank is obliged to undertake borrowing at the submitted rate. The LIBOR acts as a rate of interest that determines the value of derivatives, but it is not a rate of interest in the normal sense since no actual transactions need to take place at the rates declared by the committee banks.

In short, the banks that dominate derivatives trading are also the banks that set the interest rate at which derivatives are traded and valued, although the banks are not obliged to trade at the declared rate. No wonder, then, that one of the most egregious scandals of financialization appears to be the manipulation of the LIBOR by large deal-er banks, a matter which has been under police investigation since 2010. The problem is not a few 'rotten apples' amidst the LIBOR committee, criminally colluding with each other and with brokers to influence the LIBOR. Rather, a deeply flawed structure has

---

10   Note that the term 'financialization' has been increasingly deployed in relation to global commodities markets, including agricultural commodities (for instance, Annastiina Silvennoin-en and Susan Thorp, 'Financialization, Crisis and Commodity Correlation Dynamics', Research Paper 267, Quantitative Finance Research Centre, University of Technology Sydney, 2010). The meaning of financialization is quite vague in this context, but it seems to refer to the extraor-dinary weight of financial institutions using speculative derivatives strategies in commodities markets. By implication, price distortions have emerged as commodities futures prices became increasingly correlated with capital market indexes and other financial asset prices (Ke Tang and Wei Xiong, 'Index Investment and Financialization of Commodities', Princeton University, March 2011; David Biccheti and Nicolas Maystre, 'The Synchronized and Long-Lasting Structur-al Change on Commodity Markets', MPRA Paper No. 37486, UNCTAD, 2012). In 'financialized' commodities markets prices tend to reflect the profit-making activities of financial institutions and other derivatives players, rather than underlying 'real' factors.

allowed dealer banks to dominate derivatives markets while effectively manipulating the terms of derivatives trading.[11]

Banks are at the heart of the derivatives markets which have been such a prominent feature of financialization. Derivatives markets rely on banks, in particular on the price-making skills and general organizational capabilities of banks. Indeed, banks are so dominant in derivatives markets that they are even capable of manipulating the key rate on the basis of which derivatives prices are formed. The vast growth of derivatives markets reflects in part the turn of banks toward trading in open financial markets, which is one of the fundamental tendencies of financialization. In sum, at the root of financialization lie the vast banks of mature and other economies. The theoretical and empirical analysis of financialization in the rest of this book, therefore, focuses on banks as well as non-financial enterprises and households.

Organizing the analysis

Part I of this book lays out the broad parameters of financialization and develops an appropriate theoretical framework for its analysis by drawing on Marxist political economy. Specifically, Chapter 1 introduces the topic, following which Chapter 2 reviews the literature on financialization by going back to Paul Sweezy, Harry Magdoff and the *Monthly Review* current as well as discussing other Marxist approaches, including Giovanni Arrighi, and the French Regulation School. The literature reviewed also covers post-Keynesian, sociological and political approaches to financialization. The aim of the review is to substantiate a theoretical approach to financialization, also outlined in Chapter 2, which focuses on the previously mentioned fundamental tendencies – namely the involvement of non-financial enterprises in financial transactions, the turn of banks toward trading in open markets and transacting with households, and the increasing implication of households in the operations of the formal financial system.

Chapter 3 then considers the historical antecedents of financialization by discussing the first major period of financial ascendancy in mature capitalism which took place in the late nineteenth and early twentieth century. To be precise, Chapter 3 examines the classical Marxist literature on finance capital and imperialism that emerged at the turn of the twentieth century. Drawing on the work of Rudolf Hilferding, it is argued that the premises and method of classical Marxist theory are capable of sustaining the analysis of contemporary financialization. Some of the concepts deployed in the older

---

11   For an outstanding analysis of the processes involved – of 'endogenous deception' emerging as banks make LIBOR bids on the basis of what they expect other banks to bid – see Alexis Stenfors, 'LIBOR as a Keynesian Beauty Contest: A Process of Endogenous Deception', Discussion Paper no. 40, Research on Money and Finance, 2012; and Alexis Stenfors, 'LIBOR Games: Means, Opportunities and Incentives to Deceive', Discussion Paper No. 39, Research on Money and Finance, 2012.

Marxist debates, including that of finance capital, are not directly applicable to current conditions, but the analytical approach of classical Marxism remains of decisive importance.

On this basis, Part II develops the analysis of financialized capitalism both theoretically and empirically. Chapter 4 discusses the monetary basis of financialization in line with the distinctive feature of Marxist political economy to treat the theory of money as a foundation for the theory of credit and finance. Particular attention is paid to the evolution of the form of money in the course of financialization, including the emergence of electronic money. The dominant contemporary form of money is credit money that also incorporates fiat money issued by the state; this form of money is the basis for the ascendancy of central banks in financialized capitalism. Chapter 4 also pays close attention to the peculiar form taken by world money in conditions of financialized capitalism, exemplified, above all, by the US dollar.

Chapter 5 considers capitalist finance from first principles by examining the relationship of borrower to lender, the concept of loanable capital, the character of banking capital, and the structure and role of the financial system in capitalist accumulation. The approach to finance adopted in this book draws on three strands of economic thought: classical Marxism, contemporary Anglo-Saxon political economy, and Japanese Marxism.

Chapter 6 then turns to the problem of financial profit. This form of profit has grown enormously in the years of financialization, but it has not been explicitly analysed by Marxist or other political economy. Drawing on Hilferding's notion of 'founder's profit' the chapter shows that financial profit derives primarily from surplus value but could also originate in any money flow or stock associated with finance. In this vein, financial profit could arise from financial expropriation relating to households but also to holders of loanable capital in general. More broadly, it is argued that financial profit reflects the ancient predatory dimension of finance which, far from disappearing, has been re-strengthened in financialized capitalism.

Part III subsequently turns to empirical and historical analysis of financialization, above all, to its emergence, characteristic features, tendency to crisis and reliance on state intervention. Chapter 7 lays out the historical terrain of financialization by reviewing literature and empirical evidence on the transformation of capitalist economies since the 1970s. The focus is exclusively on the domestic economies of the US, Japan, Germany and the UK, a group of countries that also allows for conclusions to be drawn regarding the traditional distinction between capital market–based and bank-based financial systems. Particular attention is paid to productivity, profitability, and inequality, as well as to the role of the state in supporting financialization, above all, through the central bank.

Chapter 8 examines more closely the financialization of productive capital and the financialization of household income in light of the transformation of banks. Empirical evidence is mobilized to demonstrate the changing relations among industrial and commercial capital, banks, and households in financialized capitalism. It is further shown that the sources of profitability have changed, shifting toward the sphere of circulation and raising the prominence of financial profit. Finance has been able to extract profits directly and systematically from salaries and wages, thus shaping financial expropriation. Finally, the extension of financialization to developing countries is also briefly considered in the context of international capital flows and the entry of foreign banks into developing countries. The result has been a different form of financialization in developing countries, subordinate to that in mature countries.

On this basis, Chapter 9 considers to the tendency to crisis that has marked financialization. It is shown that a pure financial bubble occurred in 2001–2007, with limited impact on real accumulation. Growing personal indebtedness and the extraction of investment banking profits characterized the bubble. Moreover, the crisis that broke out in 2007 represents a systemic failure of private banking in terms of liquidity, solvency, information gathering and risk management. Potentially the most serious twist in the crisis, however, has been the threat to the European Monetary Union once public finance had come under pressure. Financialization in Europe has entailed the introduction of the euro as a competitor to the dollar for the role of world money. The result has been the emergence of a division between core and periphery in the eurozone – the latter bearing the brunt of the crisis. If default and exit from the eurozone occurred for peripheral states, the monetary union would receive a body blow with severe implications for financialization across the world.

Finally, Chapter 10 considers the regulation of finance and the role of state intervention in the course of financialization. Finance was systemically regulated in the 1950s, 1960s and much of the 1970s in terms of prices, quantities and functions of the financial institutions, but these regulations were lifted in the years that followed. Extensive re-regulation of finance has taken place in the decades of financialization, but it has been regulation of financial institutions rather than of the financial system as a whole. Regulation has generally focused on the liability side of the balance sheet, particularly on the own capital of banks, typified by the three Basel Accords. This mode of regulation has manifestly failed to protect banks and to prevent instability. Still, state intervention in the form of liquidity provision, deposit guarantees and implicit guarantees of the solvency of financial institutions has prevented a generalized collapse of finance in the late 2000s. The crisis and the failure of existing regulation have posed afresh the issue of reintroducing systemic regulation of finance as well as re-establishing public banks as a foundation for contemporary finance. With transparency and democratic accountability, public intervention in the realm of finance could begin to turn the tide against financialization.

2. ANALYSING FINANCIALIZATION: LITERATURE AND THEORY

The term 'financialization' has been widely deployed in political economy, sociology, geography, political science, and increasingly in popular debate, since the late 1990s. Its prominence evidently reflects the ascendancy of finance for more than three decades. And yet, there is no universally accepted notion of financialization within social science; the term might be increasingly used, but its meaning remains elusive.

In this respect, financialization is reminiscent of 'globalization', another term that began life modestly in the 1990s but has subsequently had a meteoric career in academic and popular discourse. Broadly speaking, globalization refers to the growth of the world market, the expansion of international financial markets, the increasing interpenetration of economies via foreign direct investment, the rise of global flows of lending, and a host of related phenomena in the world market during the last three decades. Nonetheless, the content of globalization has never been precisely defined, even though the term has been widely deployed in the realm of political theory, international relations, cultural theory, and so on.[1]

It would facilitate discussion of financialization in the rest of this chapter if three broad points regarding its relation to globalization were established at the outset. First, the concept of globalization has emerged outside the broad terrain of Marxist political economy and was initially viewed with considerable scepticism by Marxist theorists.[2]

---

1   The literature on globalization is vast and has a natural overlap with the debates on imperialism, see note 1 in Chapter 3. Several of the tropes of the mainstream can be found in Kenichi Ohmae (*The Borderless World*, 1990), including the notion of an interlinked world economy that is pushing the nation state toward irrelevance. At about the same time David Harvey (*The Condition of Postmodernity*, 1989) argued, from a Marxist perspective, that a post-modern, fragmented capitalism had emerged, based on the 'compression of time-space' according to the dictates of global capital. Anthony Giddens (*The Consequences of Modernity*, 1991) also put forth an influential sociological formulation for the rather pedestrian idea that globalization links distant localities and makes local happenings depend on faraway events. Manuel Castells (*The Rise of the Network Society*, 1996; *The Power of Identity*, 1997; *End of Millennium*, 1998; *The Internet Galaxy*, 2001) on the other hand, emphasized the importance of new technologies for globalization, stressing the role of network relationships in creating a new sociality that can also oppose the effects of globalization. Note, finally, that Paul Hirst and Grahame Thompson (*Globalization in Question*, Cambridge: Polity, 1999) have directly challenged the notion that globalization represents a qualitatively new phase of development for mature capitalist countries, and have criticized the mainstream for ignoring power and inequality in the global economy.

2   Ben Fine makes this point in a wide-ranging review of the uses and meanings of globalization at a time when the term was heavily influential ('Examining the Ideas of Globalisation and Development Critically', *New Political Economy* 9:2, 2004). Fine contrasts David Harvey's critical dismissal of globalization in the middle of the 1990s to Harvey's recognition that the

Financialization, in contrast, has Marxist origins and its birthmarks have remained evident even when the term has been deployed by different intellectual traditions, as is shown below.

Second, despite its enormous general popularity, globalization has never gained more than limited acceptability within mainstream economics. Similarly, financialization has so far made negligible inroads into mainstream economics. This is perhaps not surprising given that the dominant paradigm of neoclassical economics remains extremely conservative in approach, outlook and methods. Both globalization and financialization are by nature systemic concepts that do not easily admit of technical formalization within the framework of individual rational choice, which is the preferred method of neoclassicism.

Third and perhaps most important, several key features of globalization relate to finance, including flows of lending becoming global, financial institutions engaging in global operations, and capital markets attaining global reach. At the core of the period of globalization can be found the ascendancy of finance, i.e., exactly the phenomenon that financialization aims to capture. Interestingly enough, financialization admits of a far more precise theoretical definition than globalization, as is shown in the rest of this book. The deeper character of the transformation of capitalism during the last three and more decades can be more easily captured by focusing on financialization rather than globalization.

---

term had become hegemonic a few years later (Harvey, *Justice, Nature and the Geography of Difference*, Blackwell, 1996; Harvey, *Spaces of Hope*, Edinburgh University Press, 2000). In the 2000s globalization became common coin among Marxist theorists, without necessarily gaining in precision. However, several writers in the radical and Marxist traditions have been critical of both the notion and the phenomena of globalization. Werner Bonefeld and John Holloway have stressed the importance of class and exploitation in explaining globalization (*Global Capital, National State and the Politics of Money*, London: Macmillan, 1995). Others have insisted that the nation state remains vital to capitalism and has indeed shaped globalization; thus, Eric Helleiner related both globalization and the rise of finance to the role of the state (Helleiner, *States and the Re-emergence of Global Finance*, Cornell University Press, 1994); Linda Weiss argued that the nation state has transformed itself to adapt to the conservative agenda of globalization in the social and economic fields ('Globalization and the Myth of the Powerless State', *New Left Review* 225, 1997); Louis Pauly focused on legitimacy slipping away from the state toward unelected economic actors as globalization and the rise of finance have proceeded ('Capital Mobility, State Autonomy and Political Legitimacy', *Journal of International Affairs* 48:2, 1995; *Who Elected the Bankers? Surveillance and Control in the World Economy*, Cornell University Press, 1997); Cox also stressed the retreat of democracy in the face of globalization ('Globalization, Multilateralism, and Democracy', in *Approaches to World Order*, ed. Richard Cox and Timothy Sinclair, Cambridge University Press, 1996; 'Democracy in Hard Times' in *The Transformation of Democracy?*, ed. Anthony McGrew, Blackwell, 1997).

Note, finally, that there is also a positive side to the lack of a generally agreed theoretical content for financialization in the literature. For, by exploring the differences among the various approaches to financialization, light can be thrown on the multiple aspects of financial ascendancy, as well as on the evolution of finance in recent decades. Reviewing the relevant literature in the rest of this chapter provides the foundations for a theory of financialization from the perspective of political economy.

Thus the following section considers several approaches to financialization and the general rise of finance, on the basis of which a theoretical view of financialization drawn on Marxist political economy is put forth on pages 36, 43. To be more specific, and as was already mentioned in Chapter 1, financialization amounts to a systemic transformation of advanced capitalist economies pivoting on changes in the underlying conduct of non-financial enterprises, banks, and households. First, non-financial enterprises have become broadly involved in the realm of finance, often undertaking financial transactions independently. Financialization represents the opening of more space between non-financial enterprises and banks, with a lessening of mutual dependence among the two. Second, banks have directed their activities toward trading in open financial markets and dealing with households. Third, individuals and households have become heavily implicated in finance in terms of both borrowing (such as for housing and general consumption) and holding assets (such as for pensions and insurance). In chapters 7 and 8, this theoretical argument is considered in further detail and submitted to empirical investigation.

Roots in Marxist political economy

The concept of financialization is closely associated with Marxist political economy, whether implicitly or explicitly, as even a cursory glance at the literature would reveal. First, it hints at an epochal change of capitalism, and the latter has traditionally invited Marxist analysis. Second, it suggests systemic, or aggregate, transformation of economy and society, which has similarly attracted Marxist interest. Third – and here things become much more complex – it carries a whiff of disapproval by tacitly suggesting a problematic relationship between finance and the rest of the economy. This is, again, broadly consistent with Marxist theoretical predilections, but considerable care is required not to lapse into treating finance as a parasitical or speculative set of activities, thus assigning to financialization a purely pathological character that would be misleading.

Monthly Review *and the absorption of surplus*

Close association of financialization with Marxism goes back at least to the insights advanced by the current of *Monthly Review*.[3] For these Marxist authors, financializa-

---

3   Discussion of the approach to financialization by *Monthly Review* in this section draws on the theoretical analysis in Harry Magdoff and Paul M. Sweezy, *Stagnation and the Financial Explosion*, New York: Monthly Review Press, 1987; John Bellamy Foster, 'The Financiali-

tion is a characteristic trend of mature capitalism ultimately deriving from the production of a 'surplus' that cannot easily be absorbed. Paul Baran and Paul Sweezy in
Monopoly Capital, the work that is the theoretical cornerstone of the current, argued
that as capitalism matures it becomes dominated by monopolies.[4] Under conditions of
monopoly capitalism, the exploitation of labour results in an ever-expanding surplus
of value. An intractable problem is thus created because the surplus cannot be easily
re-absorbed through consumption and investment by the productive sector, or via
wasteful activities associated with sales, or even through state spending, including for
armaments.

The idea of problematic 'surplus absorption' is clearly related to the more standard
Marxist theory of the tendency of the rate of profit to fall as a result of rising productivity and technical progress, but there are also important differences. The tendency
of the rate of profit to fall, as proposed by Marx, contains both a secular and a cyclical
aspect; equally, for Marx, there are ('countervailing') tendencies that raise the rate of
profit operating as necessarily and automatically as the tendencies that depress the rate
of profit.[5] The capitalist economy is thus caught in the ceaseless swing of a pendulum
that moves between high and low profitability for reasons arising from the intrinsic
nature of production, circulation and distribution.

In contrast, surplus absorption is a tide that flows but rarely ebbs: the normal state
of the monopolistic capitalist economy is to be overwhelmed by surplus.[6] It follows
that methods must emerge through which the surplus would be absorbed, either in
production or in consumption, because it would otherwise lead to stagnation of the
productive sector. For this reason, monopoly capitalism is characterized by unproduc-

---

zation of Capitalism', *Monthly Review* 58:11, 2007; John Bellamy Foster, 'The Financialization
of Accumulation', *Monthly Review* 62:5, 2010; John Bellamy Foster and Robert W. McChesney,
'Monopoly-Finance Capital and the Paradox of Accumulation', *Monthly Review* 61:5, 2009. For
a related analysis of the crisis of 2007, see John Bellamy Foster, 'The Financialization of Capital
and the Crisis', *Monthly Review* 59:11, 2008; and John Bellamy Foster and Fred Magdoff, *The
Great Financial Crisis: Causes and Consequences*, New York: Monthly Review Press, 2009. For
a briefer presentation of Sweezy's own thought see Paul M. Sweezy, 'The Triumph of Financial
Capital', *Monthly Review* 46:2, 1994; Paul M. Sweezy, 'More (or Less) on Globalization', *Monthly
Review* 49:4, 1997. The importance of the early contribution of *Monthly Review* to the development of radical approaches to financialization can also be gauged by Robert Pollin's short piece
on Sweezy's legacy ('The Resurrection of the Rentier', *New Left Review*, 46, 2007).

4 Paul A. Baran and Paul M. Sweezy, *Monopoly Capital*, New York: Monthly Review Press, 1966.

5 See Karl Marx, *Capital*, vol. 3, London: Penguin/NLR, 1981, Part 3, Ch. 13, 14.

6 For Baran and Sweezy, the 'law of rising surplus' is clearly not the same as the 'law of the
tendency of the rate of profit to fall' (*Monopoly Capital*, p. 72). The former reflects the monopolistic structure of advanced capitalism, and hence the manipulation of price by monopolies; the
latter belongs to the competitive capitalism of Marx's time.

tive consumption, including advertising, military expenditure, and even pure waste, that absorb the surplus.[7] This argument has evident affinities with the Keynesian analysis of deficient aggregate demand, as has been openly acknowledged by Baran and Sweezy.[8]

From the perspective of *Monthly Review*, the theory of surplus absorption offers a ready explanation for the epochal events of the mid-1970s and the subsequent emergence of financialization: by the 1970s, surplus absorption had become problematic, crisis had burst out, and the spectre of stagnation hung over mature capitalist countries. As a result, capital began to search for refuge in the sphere of circulation and, above all, in the speculative activities of finance. Financialization has emerged as a decisive way of absorbing the investible surplus that inundated the sphere of production by chanelling it to the realm of finance. More broadly, financialization is one of three epochal trends of capitalist accumulation in the twentieth century, together with the slowing down of the rate of growth and the rise of monopolistic multinational corporations.[9]

The approach of *Monthly Review* to financialization has several remarkable strengths. The expectation that the structure of mature capitalist economies would shift in favour of finance in the final decades of the twentieth century was strikingly prescient, particularly in view of the relative absence of financial analysis in Sweezy's work, or in the output of the current as a whole.[10] Equally striking is the attempt to connect financialization to an underlying malaise of the capitalist economy, which *Monthly Review* has claimed to be the failure of surplus absorption. Finally, *Monthly Review* has presented financialization as flight, or escape by capital from the malfunctioning productive sector. This particular aspect of *Monthly Review*'s formulation of financialization can be found in several other approaches, irrespective of whether the latter accept 'surplus absorption'.

However, *Monthly Review* has not fully examined the causes of financialization at the level of capitalist enterprises and financial institutions, other than to develop the well-established Marxist argument of monopolization. The closest that the *Monthly Review* current has come to specifying the changing financial conduct of productive capital has been to argue that financial asset prices tend to become inflated as non-financial enterprises direct surplus to finance, thus creating a speculative environment.[11] Yet, if non-financial capital has indeed been seeking escape from stagnation by engaging in the speculative activities of finance, it follows that industrialists, merchants and bankers must have had economic reasons to change their conduct, which have to be

---

7   Marx, *Capital*, vol. 3, ch. 6, 7.

8   Baran and Sweezy, *Monopoly Capital*, p. 143.

9   Paul M. Sweezy, 'More (or Less) on Globalization', *Monthly Review* 49:4, 1997.

10 On the other hand, Sweezy was one of the few Anglo-Saxon economists to be familiar with Hilferding's work already from the interwar years, as is shown in more detail in Chapter 3.

11 Magdoff and Sweezy *Stagnation and the Financial Explosion*, p. 104.

specified accordingly. The tendency toward monopolization is important in this regard, but also far too general to account for the specific character of the financial transformation commencing in the 1970s.

Monthly Review has broken an innovative path by claiming that financialization reflects an epochal shift in the balance between the spheres of production and circulation, in favour of the latter. This is an appropriate point of departure for a theory of financialization. The next step, however, ought to be an analysis of the altered conduct of the agents of the capitalist economy – productive capitalists, bankers, and workers – which has produced the changed balance between the two spheres. For, if financialization is not explicitly related to the operations of the fundamental agents of the capitalist economy, its content will remain unclear. Unfortunately, the output of the *Monthly Review* current does not offer the requisite analysis, and the same holds for other Marxist work that treats financialization as the flight of capital from a stagnating productive sector. For this reason, the examination of non-financial enterprises, banks and households takes up much of the rest of this book.

Arrighi and the epochal trajectory of capitalism

The epochal aspect of financialization is even more prominent in the work of Giovanni Arrighi, which also has strong affinities with Marxist political economy. The original insight in connection with Arrighi's theory, however, goes back to Fernand Braudel's analysis of the *longue durée* of capitalism. In the second volume of *Civilization and Capitalism*, Braudel proposed a pattern of recurrent historical rise of finance based mostly on examining the expansion of capitalist world trade since the early modern era.[12] On each occasion that finance has emerged as the ascendant capitalist activity, the 'sign of autumn' has marked the state power that took the lead in financial development. From this perspective, the financialization of a social formation is an omen of its decline.

In his *Long Twentieth Century*, Arrighi adopted Braudel's insight on the recurrent rise of finance, turning it into an argument about the financialization of contemporary capitalism. Arrighi's true interest, nonetheless, lay in elaborating a theory of historical hegemony in the evolution of capitalism, as is apparent from his last major work, *Adam Smith in Beijing*, in which discussion of financialization plays only a marginal role. In the *Long Twentieth Century*, Arrighi claimed that the capitalist world economy tends to contain a hegemonic power that evolves in a cyclical pattern. Hegemonic powers succeed each other as their prowess in production and trade declines, while the sphere of finance grows. Financialization thus represents autumn in the cyclical trajectory of a particular hegemonic power. The historical path of hegemony has traversed Genoa, the

---

12   Fernand Braudel, *Civilization and Capitalism, 15th–18th Century*, trans. Sian Reynolds, Berkeley: University of California Press, 1982, p. 246.

Netherlands, Britain and the US.[13] On each occasion the newly dominant power has emerged partly through availing itself of the financial resources of the declining – and financializing – hegemon. In this light, contemporary financialization, including the global crisis that began in 2007, are aspects of the long-term decline of US hegemony.

A degree of caution is necessary at this juncture, particularly in view of the discussion of world money and the world market in the present and subsequent chapters of this book. Braudel's work, whence Arrighi's insight originates, is on a gigantic scale, casting light on the evolution of capitalism over several centuries and outlining networks of trade across continents. However, from the perspective of theoretical political economy, global commerce is one thing, the world market quite another. International commercial transactions are a feature of capitalism from its inception since capital is inherently international. But the world market as a set of institutions, mechanisms, practices, and customs is a creation of industrial, commercial and financial capitals which have become dominant in their respective national economies. The logic of theoretical analysis ought to run from the national economy to the world market and not vice versa. This is without denying that the tendencies emanating from the world market could decisively impact on the national economy, as is shown in subsequent chapters.

The point is far from trivial or abstruse, and has a direct bearing on the analysis of financialization. For Marxist political economy, the world market is the outcome of interactions among advanced capitalist enterprises but also among capitalist states. It retains a strongly anarchical element despite the systematic presence of states capable of acting as coordinating forces within their respective national economies. The true coordinating presence in the world market is world money. However, the manner in which world money acts as coordinating force in the world market depends on the form that world money takes. A characteristic feature of the world market in the twentieth century has been the emergence of non-metallic (and inconvertible) world money issued by particular nation states. Financialization is inherently bound up with the US dollar operating as the dominant form of world money since the 1970s.

With these provisos in mind, two analytically important points stand out in Arrighi's theory. The first is the association of financialization with declining productive vigour and thus waning hegemonic power. Arrighi's theoretical point of departure is different from Sweezy and Baran's 'absorption of surplus', but the outcome is similar: the productive sector has lost the fire to accumulate as financialization has burgeoned. The epochal turn of the capitalist economy toward finance reflects a malaise in the realm of accumulation, while at the same time exacerbating the weakness of production and trade.

The second point – and again similarly to *Monthly Review* – is that Arrighi's analy-

---

13   See also Giovanni Arrighi and Beverly J. Silver, *Chaos and Governance in the Modern World System*, Minneapolis: University of Minnesota Press, 1999.

sis of financialization encourages attention to be paid to the returns to capitalist activity: financialization is reflected in high profits from financial transactions compared to other activities.[14] Arrighi's work does not clearly spell out the mechanisms and patterns through which profit derives from finance, but has motivated the path-breaking empirical studies by Greta Krippner.[15] In *Capitalizing on Crisis* Krippner is reluctant to treat financialization as an epochal transformation of capitalism, preferring to focus specifically on the rise of finance in the US, which she associates with the response of the state to crisis conditions in the 1970s and 1980s. The innovative aspect of her work, however, is explicitly to link financialization to the growing weight of financial profit, including for the non-financial sector. Her work is the first systematic attempt to give empirical content to the claim by *Monthly Review*, Arrighi and others that financialization is about capital seeking profits in the realm of finance.

It is important, therefore, to draw attention to a theoretical issue regarding financial profit, which is further discussed in Chapter 6 of this book. The category of financial profit is hard to establish, both conceptually and empirically: it is not an accident that the concept barely exists either in classical political economy, or in Marxist economics. The source of financial profit in terms of the aggregate flows of value in a capitalist economy is far from obvious once theoretical analysis moves beyond the simple statement that a 'surplus' is available which seeks investment in finance. To demonstrate both the nature and the sources of financial profit, it is necessary theoretically to examine the activities of non-financial corporations, banks and individuals – precisely the agents whose conduct defines financialization. Much of the rest of this book is concerned with this task.

The last point to mention is that Arrighi's theory of financialization suffers from the intractable problem of identifying a replacement for the current hegemon, the US. In the Epilogue to *The Long Twentieth Century* Arrighi suggested that Japan might play this role; in *Adam Smith in Beijing*, he has indicated that China might inherit the mantle.[16] However, neither suggestion works particularly well from the perspective of Arrighi's theory of financialization. A remarkable feature of the last two decades has been the emergence of the US as a net borrower, not lender, while much of its

---

14   See particularly Giovanni Arrighi and Jason W. Moore, 'Capitalist Development in World Historical Perspective', in *Phases of Capitalist Development*, ed. Robert Albritton et al., London: Palgrave Macmillan, 2001.

15   See Greta Krippner, 'The Financialization of the American Economy', *Socio-Economic Review* 3, 2005, pp. 173–208; and, with a broader theoretical discussion, Greta Krippner, *Capitalizing on Crisis*, Cambridge, MA: Harvard University Press, 2011.

16   Note that Michel Aglietta, also inspired by Braudel's work, argues that China is the emerging hegemon, the US having been brought to its knees by successive financial crises. China's presumed strength derives from productivity growth, the result of technological advance and urbanization. Michel Aglietta, 'Into the New Growth Regime', *New Left Review* 54, 2008, pp. 61–74.

borrowing has been precisely from Japan and China. The autumn of US hegemony, whether due to financialization or not, has coincided with substantial capital inflows to the US including, remarkably, from some of the poorest countries in the world. This paradoxical outcome is largely due to the role of the US dollar as world money, which has imposed costs on developing and poor countries. It is also an aspect of subordinate financialization examined in various places in the rest of this book.

Regulation of capitalism through finance
There are further theoretical approaches of Marxist origin that similarly associate the rise of finance with a secular transformation of the capitalist economy, often noting decline or stagnation of the sphere of production. This outlook can be found, for instance, in the work of the Regulation School which discussed financialization already in the 1990s. The regulationist approach to financialization has resulted partly from the search for the new 'regime of accumulation', on the assumption that the old regime of 'Fordism' came to an end in the 1970s.[17] By the second half of the 1990s, Chesnais had already proposed the term 'regime of accumulation with financial dominance', a term that he deployed within a Marxist framework, briefly discussed below.[18] The Regulation School appropriated the term and deployed it extensively within its own theoretical framework.

For regulationists the crisis of the 1970s and the ensuing period of turbulence have resulted from the exhaustion of the elements characteristic of the period of 'Fordism' in the decades following the Second World War: mass production, rising productivity, and rising real wages. Thus, a new regime of accumulation might have begun to emerge based on finance. Frédéric Lordon has proposed that a 'financialized regime of accumulation' has perhaps begun to form around the ascendant realm of finance, replacing the lost material basis of Fordist regulation.[19] Orléan more clearly proposed the notion of regulation occurring through the trading of capital in financial markets, an idea that Boyer has attempted to model in relation to the operations of the stock

---

17   For an early and balanced review of Regulationist analysis of financialization see John Grahl and Paul Teague, 'The *Régulation* School, the Employment Relation and Financialization', *Economy and Society* 29:1, 2000, pp. 160–78. An analysis of the emergence of the idea among regulationists from the inside, as it were, has been given in François Chesnais, 'La théorie du régime d'accumulation financiarisé: contenu, portée et interrogations', Forum de la regulation, Paris, 11-12 Octobre 2001.

18   François Chesnais, 'Mondialisation du capital et régime d'accumulation à dominante financiére', *Agone* 16, 1996.

19   See Frédéric Lordon, 'Le nouvel agenda de la politique economique en régime d'accumulation financiarisé', in *Le triangle infernal*, ed. Gérard Duménil and Dominique Lévy, Paris: PUF, 1999; and more fully, Frédéric Lordon, *Fonds de pension, piège à cons?*, Paris: Raisons d'Agir, 2000.

exchange.[20] Regulation through finance can have problematic effects for the performance of accumulation, including rates of growth, output and so on.[21] In subsequent work Michel Aglietta and Antoine Rebérioux have further developed the notion of 'patrimonial capitalism' whereby income accrues through shareholding and could compensate for stagnant real wages.[22]

The theoretical core of regulation theory, including the very notion of 'regime of accumulation', is at some distance from Marx's perception of capitalist accumulation occurring within a framework of social, juridical, political and other relations which ultimately reflect the material realities of production. More significantly, it is debatable that the notion of 'Fordism' ever accurately captured the character of accumulation in leading advanced countries, including in the US.[23] It is important to bear in mind the doubts surrounding the notion of the 'Fordist regime', since the economy of the US is standard reference for the regulationists when it comes to financialization. While there is no doubt that regulationism was quick to appreciate the systemic importance of the rise of finance in recent decades, the specification of the 'financialized regime' is even less clear than that of the 'Fordist regime'. It is questionable whether the regulationist view goes beyond a reworking of theories of shareholder value and of the dominance of stock markets, briefly discussed below.

---

20   André Orléan, *Le pouvoir de la finance*, Paris: Odile Jacob, 1999; Robert Boyer, 'Is a Finance-Led Growth Regime a Viable Alternative to Fordism? A Preliminary Analysis', *Economy and Society* 29:1, 2000. Note that Boyer discussed further the notion of shareholder's profit as the organizing principle of non-financial enterprises in the US and the UK which has contributed to the subprime crisis; Robert Boyer, 'Feu le régime d'accumulation tiré par la finance: La crise des subprimes en perspective historique', *Revue de la régulation* 5, Spring 2009. Boyer is certainly right to treat the upheaval that began in 2007 as a crisis of financialization, but its ambit has turned out to be far broader than merely the economies of the US and the UK. By the same token, financialization is a far broader phenomenon than the regulation of non-financial enterprises through the stock market. Lordon similarly sees the crisis as the result of a confluence of forces characteristic of financialization, and proposes a list of deep reforms to control finance; Frédéric Lordon, 'Après la crise financière: "regular" ou refondre?', *Revue de la regulation* 5, 2009.

21   Michel Aglietta, 'Shareholder Value and Corporate Governance: Some Tricky Questions', *Economy and Society* 29:1, 2000, pp. 146–59; see also Michel Aglietta and Régis Breton, 'Financial Systems, Corporate Control and Capital Accumulation', *Economy and Society* 30:4, 2001, pp. 433–66.

22   Michel Aglietta and Antoine Rebérioux, *Dérives du capitalisme financier*, Paris: Albin Michel, 2004. For a sharp critique of the validity of this idea, see Michel Husson, 'L'ecole de la regulation, de Marx à la Fondation Saint-Simon: un aller sans retour?', in *Dictionnaire Marx Contemporain*, ed. Jacques Bidet and Eustache Kouvélakis, Paris: PUF, 2001.

23   A powerful argument to this effect has been put forth in Robert Brenner and Mark Glick, 'The Regulation Approach: Theory and History', *New Left Review* 188, 1991, pp. 45–119.

Note, however, that the Regulation School places emphasis on the concrete aspects of the regime of accumulation, and is therefore capable of producing typologies of financialization; this feature is important to the discussion in the rest of this book. Thus, Joachim Becker and Johannes Jaeger have distinguished among, first, productive/financialized accumulation determined by the sectoral direction of investment; second, extensive/intensive accumulation, determined by whether wage earners consume goods that are obtained primarily in the market; third, introverted/extroverted accumulation, determined by the orientation of output toward domestic or international markets.[24] Along these lines Becker et al. have postulated four types of financialization: i) based on 'fictitious' capital, by which is meant inflation of financial prices; ii) based on interest-bearing capital, meaning expansion of banks; iii) 'elite', implying the involvement of the bourgeoisie and the upper middle class; iv) 'popular', indicating that workers have also been drawn into financial operations. Irrespective of the validity of these categorizations, distinguishing among varieties of financialization is vital to analysing the phenomenon in its totality.[25]

Theories of perpetual crisis

The perception that the rise of finance has been associated with secular stagnation, or malfunctioning, of capitalist accumulation is also apparent among Marxist approaches that have retained an ostensible allegiance to the theory of the tendency of rate of profit to fall. Generally speaking, the underlying assumption of this type of Marxism is that the sphere of production in recent decades has been characterized by low and unstable profitability for a variety of reasons, including overaccumulation. Capital has therefore sought profits in the realm of finance, often through speculative and other transactions. However, the relief afforded by financial profit has been at best temporary, the underlying problems in the sphere of production have reasserted themselves, and economic crisis has tended to re-emerge.

This fundamental outlook is frequently found among Marxist currents with a strong political outlook, and which often do not realize their affinities with the tradition of *Monthly Review*. Strikingly, they have helped to establish the notion that the normal state of contemporary capitalism is to be in crisis emanating from the sphere of production, which is merely ameliorated by measures typically involving the state. A sophisticated version of this view has been advanced by Robert Brenner in a series of influential publications.[26] Summarily put, Brenner's argument links putative stag-

---

24 Joachim Becker and Johannes Jaeger, 'Development Trajectories in the Crisis in Europe', *Debate: Journal of Contemporary Central and Eastern Europe* 18:1, 2010, pp. 5–27.

25 Joachim Becker et al., 'Peripheral Financialization and Vulnerability to Crisis: A Regulationist Perspective', *Competition and Change* 14:3/4, 2010, pp. 225–47.

26 Brenner's output on this issue has been consistent and systematic over a period of years; see Bibliography.

nation in the sphere of production to Marx's theory of the tendency of the rate of profit to fall. From his perspective, there has been sustained overcapacity in production since the 1960s which has exacerbated competition and therefore lowered profit rates. Incumbent enterprises, however, have not exited the sphere of production, a move that would have destroyed capital and eventually led to a resurgence of profit rates. Consequently, advanced capitalist economies have been lodged in permanent, if latent, crisis emanating from the sphere of production. The actual outbreak of crisis, nonetheless, has been evaded through a variety of measures adopted at different points in time, including exchange rate manipulation and the advance of cheap credit by central banks. When the potency of these interventions ran out, as happened for instance in 2007, the underlying reality of production manifested itself and the world was again plunged into crisis.

For the purposes of this book, three aspects of Brenner's analysis merit further attention. First, Brenner's extensive references to the tendency of the rate of profit to fall should not obscure the fact that his theoretical explanation of falling profitability relies on the pressure of competition on active capitalists, rather than on the changing organic composition of capital; in this regard, Brenner's theory of profit differs decisively from Marx's and is reminiscent of Smith's. Linked to this point is that the putative fall in profitability in Brenner's theory is also associated with a fall in real wages, once again distancing it from Marx's theory of the tendency of the rate of profit to fall.[27]

Second, Brenner's view that contemporary capitalism suffers from chronic overaccumulation is similar to the approach of *Monthly Review*. The difference is that Brenner has relied on an idiosyncratic interpretation of the tendency of the rate of profit to fall which, as was mentioned above, stresses persistent over-capacity among functioning capitalists. Sweezy, in contrast, postulated 'surplus absorption' which is openly different from Marx's tendency of the rate of profit to fall. A further difference is that *Monthly Review* has explicitly adopted – indeed proposed – the notion of financialization, while Brenner has avoided the term, even if he has stressed the role of finance as temporary palliative for low profitability.[28]

Third, and again similarly to *Monthly Review*, Brenner has not analysed the financial sector as a separate field of capitalist activity with its own internal logic and practices. Brenner's discussion of banks and other financial institutions does not even

---

27   Anwar Shaikh, 'Explaining the Global Economic Crisis', *Historical Materialism* 5, Winter 1999, pp. 103–44; John Weeks, 'Surfing the Troubled Waters of "Global Turbulence": A Comment', *Historical Materialism* 5, Winter 1999. For a detailed discussion of Brenner's theory see Ben Fine, Costas Lapavitsas, and Dimitris Milonakis, 'Analysing the World Economy: Two Steps Back', *Capital and Class* 67, Spring 1999, pp. 21–47.

28   Note that Arrighi's main criticism of Brenner is that he has ignored financialization as a structural transformation of US capitalism that has led to instability. Giovanni Arrighi, 'The Social and Political Economy of Global Turbulence', *New Left Review* 20, 2003.

approach the complexity of his analysis of industrial and commercial enterprises. For Brenner, the cheap credit that has presumably staved off stagnation on several occasions in recent decades has essentially originated in arbitrary decisions by the state operating through the black box of finance.

The basic outlook of Brenner has been shared by several other Marxist writers, even without accepting his core theoretical analysis. Chris Harman and Alex Callinicos, for instance, believe that overaccumulation is a chronic condition of contemporary capitalism, without subscribing to Brenner's theory.[29] Both defend a version of Marx's tendency of the rate of profit to fall that stresses the rising organic composition of capital, which presumably cannot be lowered because modern corporations can successfully resist failure and thus the destruction of capital. Financial expansion and credit provision are able to create periods of prosperity, but as soon as credit growth runs its course, the underlying stagnation manifests itself. Unlike Brenner, however, both Harman and Callinicos accept that financialization is a notable trend of contemporary capitalism, even if they do not offer a systematic definition.

Marxist analyses of the transformation of finance
There has also been much Marxist work on the rise of finance that does not necessarily relate it to malfunctioning production, but which remains important for the analysis of financialization. Several French Marxists, for instance, have traced the rise of finance without necessarily subscribing to what might be called the 'stagnationist' or 'permanent crisis' approach. Chesnais was one of the first to study financialization in conjunction with globalization and international capital flows, stressing the advancing integration of national financial systems.[30] Chesnais draws his analytical categories directly from Marx's analysis, but has also paid particular attention to the role of rentiers in mature capitalist economies. Thus, he has emphasized the dominance of financial interests – the 'dictatorship of creditors' – over industrial and other capital which has given to globalization the character of 'rentier capitalism'.[31] The influence of Chesnais's work on the analysis of financialization in this book can be easily detected; however, it is argued below that relations between industrial and financial capital are not permeated by rentier processes, and the dominant role of finance does not amount to the 'dictatorship of creditors'.

Gérard Duménil and Dominique Lévy, in a series of empirically based works, have related the growth of finance to the rise of neoliberalism, the latter representing a sec-

29 Chris Harman, *Zombie Capitalism*, London: Bookmarks, 2009. Chris Harman, 'Not All Marxism Is Dogmatism: A Reply to Michel Husson', *International Socialism Journal* 125, Winter 2010. Alex Callinicos, *Bonfire of Illusions*, New York: John Wiley, 2010.

30 François Chesnais (ed.), *La mondalisation financière: Genèse, enjeux et coûts*. Paris: Syros, 1996.

31 Chesnais, 'Mondialisation du capital et régime d'accumulation à dominante financiére'.

ular transformation of the capitalist system.[32] From this perspective, financialization has meant higher profit rates for the financial sector, while also contributing to greater instability, above all, in the form of the crisis that broke out in 2007. However, for Duménil and Lévy, financial capital does not dominate industrial capital in the neoliberal era, unlike the first period of financial ascendancy at the start of the twentieth century; these writers also make the contentious claim that neoliberal capitalism has witnessed a transformation of class structure such that a class of owners hold property through financial assets, while a larger managerial class draws profits in the form of wages and salaries.[33]

The relationship between industry and finance, or more specifically, the financialization of non-financial corporations has been a major concern of Claude Serfati. It is particularly relevant for our purposes that Serfati rejects the notion of financial interests dominating industrial interests in contemporary capitalism. For Serfati, Hilferding's notion of finance capital should be understood more broadly to encompass industrial enterprises that undertake financial transactions.[34] A similar view has been developed by François Morin who has examined the transformation of French enterprises and shown the emergence of a financial level of governance within large industrial capitals.[35] The financialization of non-financial enterprises is an aspect of the structural transformation of contemporary capitalism that is considered in some detail in Chapter 8 of this book.

Finally, among French Marxists, Dominique Plihon has proposed the term 'shareholding capitalism' to capture the rise of finance and the concomitant transformation of capitalism in recent decades.[36] Plihon has suggested that, at least for France, non-fi-

---

32   See, for instance, Gérard Duménil and Dominique Lévy, *Capital Resurgent*, Cambridge, MA: Harvard University Press, 2004; Gérard Duménil and Dominique Lévy, 'The Real and Financial Components of Profitability (United States, 1952–2000)', *Review of Radical Political Economics* 36:1, 2004, pp. 82–110; Gérard Duménil and Dominique Lévy, *The Crisis of Neoliberalism*, Cambridge, MA: Harvard University Press, 2011.

33   Gérard Duménil and Dominique Lévy, 'Finance and Management in the Dynamics of Social Change (Contrasting Two Trajectories: United States and France)', 26 June 2006.

34   Claude Serfati, 'Le role actif de groupes à dominante industrielle dans la financiarisation de l'économie', in *La mondialisation financière : genèse, coût et enjeux*, ed. François Chesnais, Paris: Syros, 1996. Claude Serfati, 'Financial Dimensions of Transnational Corporations, Global Value Chains and Technological Innovations', *Journal of Innovation Economics* 2:2, 2008. Claude Serfati, 'Transnational Corporations as Financial Groups', *Work Organisation, Labour and Globalisation* 5:1, 2011, pp. 10–38.

35   François Morin, 'A Transformation in the French model of Shareholding and Management', *Economy and Society* 29, 2000. François Morin, 'Le capitalisme de marché financier et l'asservissement du cognitif', Cahiers du GRES, May 2006.

36   Dominique Plihon, *Le nouveau capitalisme*, 3rd edition, Paris: Éditions La Découverte, 2009.

nancial enterprises have been instrumental to the transformation, including through reliance on retained profits to finance investment, issuing financial assets in open markets, and fostering the pre-eminent role of institutional investors in contemporary finance. Banks have also been transformed by turning to financial markets. Plihon's arguments, even if exclusively focused on France, have strong affinities with the core thesis of this book regarding the nature of financialization.

French writers aside, some of the most pertinent Marxist analysis of the rise of finance in recent years has been produced in India, even though these writers have meticulously avoided the term 'financialization'.[37] The work of Prabhat Patnaik, in particular, has been concerned with the macroeconomic dimension of the rise of finance and the role of world money, an issue that is extensively discussed in the rest of this book. For Patnaik, the ascendancy of finance has been associated with the centralization of capital, but has not led to the re-emergence of Hilferding's finance capital – that is, to a coalescence of industrial with financial interests. Globalized finance is directed to financial markets and has been largely speculative.[38]

This approach has implications for the classical Marxist theory of imperialism, since the global ascendancy of finance has drawn into its orbit poor and developing countries, primarily through debt and financial liberalization. For Patnaik, imperialism necessarily entails developed countries encroaching on a pre-capitalist periphery and drawing benefits in terms of obtaining new markets and keeping wages low.[39] International stability is predicated upon maintaining the value of world money, namely the US dollar. However, the rise of finance has upset the management of domestic demand within the imperialist countries, thus enhancing instability. Moreover, the accumulation of debt by the US, partly due to lack of direct colonial control, has created additional difficulties in holding the value of world money stable. In this context, C.P. Chandrasekhar has examined the mechanisms through which a small number of international financial enterprises have intermediated global capital flows, while Jayati Ghosh has argued in favour of regulating the domestic financial systems of developing countries.[40]

---

37   Prominent among them are Prabhat Patnaik, C.P. Chandrasekhar, and Jayati Ghosh.

38   Prabhat Patnaik, *The Value of Money*, New York: Columbia University Press, 2009. Prabhat Patnaik, 'The Economics of the New Phase of Imperialism', paper presented at IDEAS conference on The Economics of the New Imperialism, 22–24 January 2004, Jawaharlal Nehru University, New Delhi, 2005.

39   See Prabhat Patnaik, 'The Theory of Money and World Capitalism', paper presented at IDEAS conference on International Money and Developing Countries, Muttukadu, Tamil Nadu, India, 19 December 2002; and more fully Prabhat Patnaik, *The Value of Money*, New York: Columbia University Press, 2009.

40   C.P. Chandrasekhar, 'Global Liquidity and Financial Flows to Developing Countries', G24 Discussion Paper Series No. 52, UNCTAD, 2008; Jayati Ghosh, 'The Economic and Social Effects

From a still different Marxist perspective, Harvey has sought the origin of financial expansion in blockages of productive accumulation, which might then be resolved through a 'financial fix' as capital seeks profits in the realm of finance.[41] Peter Gowan, on the other hand, has put forth the argument that the rise of finance masks a bid for US dominance undertaken by the 'Dollar–Wall Street Regime'.[42] The merit of Gowan's analysis is its emphasis on the role of the dollar as world money, though Gowan's view that financial expansion and crisis are primarily phenomena of North Atlantic economies – put forth in one of his final works – carries little conviction in view of the crisis spreading to the eurozone after 2010.[43]

A similar point can be made about Leo Panitch and Sam Gindin, who have produced a series of works claiming that globalization is a reassertion of US empire in the face of intra-imperialist rivalries.[44] For these writers, financialization is the 'Americanization' of finance, which has strengthened and universalized US power. Panitch and Gindin stress the importance of the dollar in shaping financialization as well as arguing that the dollar will not be easily supplanted by another currency; both of these insights are extensively discussed in subsequent chapters of this book. However, financialization represents much more than the 'Americanization' of finance, and it is far from obvious that financialization has strengthened the hegemonic position of the US.

In sum, Marxist political economy, broadly understood, has cast considerable light on financialization, although the concept has remained unclear. Other radical currents in social science have brought out still further dimensions of financialization, as is shown in the next section. Before briefly engaging with non-Marxist approaches to financialization, however, it is important to mention one significant conceptual issue which has a bearing on the analysis in the rest of this book.

It is notable that Marxist writings on finance are frequently laced with references to Marx's concept of fictitious capital.[45] At its core, this is a technical idea amounting to net present value accounting – that is, to ideal sums of money that result via discounting streams of future payments attached to financial assets. These ideal sums correspond to financial prices that could fluctuate independently of the

---

of Financial Liberalization', DESA Working Paper No. 4, October 2005.

41 David Harvey, *The New Imperialism*, New York: Oxford University Press, 2003; David Harvey, *The Limits to Capital*, 3rd ed., Oxford: Blackwell, 2007.

42 Peter Gowan, *The Global Gamble: Washington's Faustian Bid for World Dominance*, London: Verso, 1999.

43 Peter Gowan, 'Crisis in the Heartland', *New Left Review* 55, 2009, pp. 5–29.

44 See Leo Panitch and Sam Gindin, *Global Capitalism and American Empire*, London: Merlin Press, 2004; 'The Current Crisis: A Socialist Perspective', *Studies in Political Economy* 83, 2009; 'Finance and American Empire', in *American Empire and the Political Economy of Global Finance*, ed. Leo Panitch and Martijn Konings, New York: Palgrave Macmillan, 2009.

45 Marx, *Capital*, vol. 3, p. 567.

money capital originally expended to purchase the financial asset in question. In that obvious sense, financial prices, particularly those in the stock market, represent fictitious capital.[46]

The notion of fictitious capital is capable of offering insights into the operations of capitalist finance and to this purpose it will be deployed in chapters 5 and 6; but it can also lead to extraordinary flights of fancy when analysing financial activities. The huge nominal values associated with some financial markets – for instance, the derivatives markets discussed in Chapter 1 – could give the false impression that the state lacks the resources for effective intervention in the realm of finance. Alternatively, bloated nominal values might lead to the equally false impression that the rising profits of the financial sector during the years of financialization have been fictitious. The result would be to divert attention from precisely the point that needs explaining: the existence and the source of enormous financial profits.

Even worse confusion potentially surrounds the relationship between fictitious capital and interest-bearing or loanable money capital, the latter being yet another innovative idea by Marx in this field.[47] Loanable capital is a special type of capital available for lending and remunerated through the payment of interest, as is discussed at length in chapters 5 and 6. The trading of loanable capital could give rise to fictitious capital, but loanable capital itself is anything but fictitious. Rather, it emerges from investment and consumption processes attached to capitalist accumulation, and initially takes the form of idle money. Loanable capital is a hard reality of the capitalist economy and affords to its holders direct claims to value and output. At the root of financialization lies loanable, not fictitious, capital. This distinction is fundamental to the analysis in the rest of this book.

Other approaches to financialization

The only other systematic theoretical approach to financialization in the field of economics has been put forth by post-Keynesians; in important ways it is similar to Marxist analysis, but there are also decisive differences. Post-Keynesianism, needless to say, is a broad current with many different strains, a point of some importance in assessing post-Keynesian views on financialization.[48]

It is interesting to note that the post-Keynesian approach to financialization has not originated with Hyman Minsky, whose work is the cornerstone of post-Keynes-

---

46   Marx actually used the term to denote several distinct cases of financial price or traded value, but no generality is lost by considering fictitious capital as simply net present value.

47   Marx, *Capital*, vol. 3, part 5.

48   For a wide-ranging review of regulationism and post-Keynesianism that is sharply aware of the empirical aspects of financialization and also appreciates the significance of Marxist concepts, see Robert Guttmann, 'A Primer on Finance-Led Capitalism and Its Crisis', *Revue de la régulation* 3/4, Autumn 2008.

ian financial analysis. The bulk of Minsky's output is concerned with developing his path-breaking treatment of financial instability that postulated destabilizing balance sheet behaviour by large capitalist enterprises over the cycle as optimism became increasingly unbridled and led to excessive debt accumulation.[49] Minsky's empirical knowledge of the US financial system also made him aware of the risks of financial innovation, including securitization. However, there is little discussion in his work of the long-term balance between finance and the rest of the economy. To be precise, there are brief references to 'money manager capitalism' in some very late work.[50] Nonetheless, the characteristic features and broader implications of 'money manager capitalism' were not examined in depth by Minsky.

Post-Keynesian analysis of financialization is generally based on the concept of the rentier, and in particular of the moneylender as rentier. For this reason it has found common ground with Marxist analyses, for instance, with the work of Chesnais. The affinities with Marxist theory are evident in the writings of Crotty, Pollin, and Epstein, although the strongest influence has come from Keynes rather than Marx.[51] In Keynes's *General Theory* the rentier is a parasitical economic entity that extracts profits due to the scarcity of capital, and might thus depress investment and profitability for active capitalists.[52] Successful capitalism requires the 'euthanasia of the rentier' that could be attained through low interest rates. In Marx's writings, the rentier makes only fleeting appearances, and there are no clear references to a social stratum of rentiers. However, Marx discusses extensively the character and functioning of 'monied' capitalists, a category that is strongly reminiscent of rentiers, as is shown in detail in Chapter 5. Specifically, 'monied' capitalists form a section of the capitalist class that does not invest capital in production but prefers to lend it to others. Productive capitalists use the loanable capital of 'monied' capitalists, and the latter are repaid by receiving a portion of the resulting surplus value in the form of interest. By this token, there is tension and opposition between productive and 'monied' capitalists.[53]

---

49 See, in particular, Hyman Minsky, *John Maynard Keynes*, New York: Columbia University Press, 1975; *Can "It" Happen Again? Essays on Instability and Finance*, Armonk, NY: M.E. Sharpe, 1982; *Stabilizing an Unstable Economy*, New Haven, CT: Yale University Press, 1986.

50 Hyman Minsky, 'Uncertainty and the Institutional Structure of Capitalist Economies', Working Paper No. 155, Levy Economics Institute of Bard College, April 1996; Hyman Minsky and Charles Whalen, 'Economic Insecurity and the Institutional Prerequisites for Successful Capitalism', Working Paper No. 165, Levy Economics Institute of Bard College, 1996.

51 See, for instance, James Crotty, 'Owner–Manager Conflict and Financial Theory of Investment Stability', *Journal of Post Keynesian Economics* 12:4, 1990; Robert Pollin, 'The Resurrection of the Rentier', *New Left Review* 46, 2007; and Gerald Epstein (ed.), *Financialization and the World Economy*. Cheltenham: Edward Elgar, 2005.

52 John Maynard Keynes, *The General Theory of Employment, Interest and Money*, London: Macmillan, 1973, ch. 24.

53 Note that another and quite different approach to finance can also be found in Marx's work,

For post-Keynesians, financialization represents the ascendancy of the rentier due to neoliberal economic policies adopted by the state in the last few decades.[54] The ascendancy of rentiers has strengthened financial at the expense of industrial profit, and therefore financialization has induced poor performance of investment and output in mature countries. In short, post-Keynesians recognize the analytical connection between, on the one hand, stagnating or declining production and, on the other, booming finance in the period of financialization; however, contrary to the Marxist approaches reviewed above, post-Keynesians consider that the poor performance of the real sector has been caused in good measure by the expansion of the financial sector. The root cause of the growth of finance, in turn, is inappropriate economic policy in the US, the UK, and elsewhere.

The characteristic feature of post-Keynesian analysis of financialization has, therefore, been extensive empirical work seeking to show the deleterious impact of financial activities on the economy as investment has been directed to finance rather than production.[55] The underlying logic of much of this work is that the ascendancy of the rentier has had a depressing effect on the real sector, typically by constraining available investment funds and/or lowering the returns of industrial capitalists.[56]

---

as is shown in chapters 5 and 6. Namely, capital for loan does not belong to a separate group of 'monied' capitalists, or rentiers, but rather emerges spontaneously through the operations of industrial (and other) capital by taking the form of idle money in the first instance. On this basis, the financial system is a set of markets and institutions that mobilizes loanable capital and supports capitalist accumulation. This approach to finance is naturally averse to treating financialization as the triumph of the rentier over the productive capitalist.

54   Toporowski relates saving to the middle class as well as to rentiers, though neither term is specified in sufficient detail. Financialization from this perspective is the channelling of middle class and rentier saving to the stock market inducing asset price inflation and fostering the growth of institutional investors. Jan Toporowski, 'The Economics and Culture of Financial Inflation', *Competition and Change* 13:2, 2009.

55   For instance, James Crotty, 'Owner–Manager Conflict and Financial Theory of Investment Stability', *Journal of Post Keynesian Economics* 12:4, 1990; Engelbert Stockhammer, 'Financialization and the Slowdown of Accumulation', *Cambridge Journal of Economics*, 28, 2004; Engelbert Stockhammer, 'Some Stylized Facts on the Finance-dominated Accumulation Regime', *Competition and Change* 12:2, 2008; Gerald Epstein and Arjun Jayadev, 'The Rise of Rentier Incomes in OECD Countries: Financialization, Central Bank Policy and Labor Solidarity', in *Financialization and the World Economy*, ed. Gerald Epstein, Cheltenham: Edward Elgar, 2005; Özgür Orhangazi, 'Financialization and Capital Accumulation in the Non-Financial Corporate Sector', *Cambridge Journal of Economics*, 32, 2008. The work of Dutt is also notable since his models relate financialization to consumption, individual debt and saving; Amitava Krishna Dutt, 'Maturity, Stagnation and Consumer Debt: A Steindlian Approach', *Metroeconomica* 57, 2005.

56 Skott and Ryoo develop models to test the macroeconomic effects of putative changes in

This is also broadly the outlook of the 'finance-dominated capitalism' current, a strain of post-Keynesianism that has focused on demonstrating the poor macroeconomic performance caused by the ascendancy of finance, while also exhibiting affinities with Marxism.[57] Rising shareholder power that commands increasing returns – interpreted as the ascendancy of rentiers – has squeezed investment and led to unstable accumulation of household debt. Important in this regard are also the distributional effects of financialization, perceived as a worsening balance for labour versus capital. The conclusion is apparent: policy intervention is required to regulate finance with the aim of improving output, employment and income. Policies could, for instance, regulate the liquidity reserves of banks, force credit in pre-determined directions, impose limits on investment banking activities, and so on.[58]

For the purposes of this book, it is important to note that post-Keynesian work is aware of the specific features of financialization in particular countries. Stockhammer has argued that capitalist accumulation has become slow and fragile as investment has declined and income distribution has worsened, thus leading to a bifurcation of

---

financial behaviour and, unsurprisingly, find that the results depend on the specification of labour constraints, accumulation tendencies, and household behaviour; Peter Skott and Soon Ryoo, 'Macroeconomic Implications of Financialization', *Cambridge Journal of Economics* 32:6, 2008. For empirical measurements of the impact of rentier income on aggregate demand in the US, see also Özlem Onaran, Engelbert Stockhammer, and Lucas Grafl, 'Financialization, Income Distribution and Aggregate Demand in the USA', in *Cambridge Journal of Economics* 35, 2011. Dallery on the other hand, develops a microeconomic analysis of rentier interests influencing negatively the investment decision of enterprises; Thomas Dallery, 'Post-Keynesian Theories of the Firm under Financialization', *Review of Radical Political Economics* 41:4, 2009.

57 Prominent among them are Eckhard Hein et al. (eds), *Finance-Led Capitalism?*, Marburg: Metropolis Verlag, 2008; Eckhard Hein, 'A (Post-)Keynesian Perspective on Financialisation', IMK Working Paper No. 01-2009; Eckhard Hein, *The Macroeconomics of Finance-Dominated Capitalism – and Its Crisis*, Cheltenham: Edward Elgar, 2012; Eckhard Hein and Till Van Treeck, 'Financialisation and Rising Shareholder Power in Kaleckian/Post-Kaleckian Models of Distribution and Growth', *Review of Political Economy* 22, 2010; and Trevor Evans, 'The 2002–7 of US Economic Expansion and Limits of Finance-Led Capitalism', *Studies in Political Economy* 83, 2009.

58 Similar arguments in more standard post-Keynesian mould can be found in James Crotty, 'Profound Structural Flaws in the US Financial System That Helped Cause the Financial Crisis', *Economic and Political Weekly* 44:13, 2009; James Crotty, 'Structural Causes of the Global Financial Crisis', Political Economy Research Institute Working Paper 180, 2008; James Crotty and Gerald Epstein, 'Proposals for Effectively Regulating the US Financial System to Avoid yet Another Meltdown', Political Economy Research Institute Working Paper 181, 2008; James Crotty and Gerald Epstein, 'Regulating the US Financial System to Avoid Another Meltdown', *Economic and Political Weekly* 44:13, 2009.

the process of financialization.[59] One group of countries has gone through a credit-fuelled consumption boom on the back of a property bubble; another has fostered the growth of exports mostly because institutional constraints have blocked the path of credit-fuelled consumption. The two groups are complementary since the current account deficits and capital inflows of the former correspond to the current account surpluses and capital outflows of the latter.

Still other – but not necessarily economic – approaches to financialization have been produced by economic geographers and sociologists who have traced the social impact of the rise of finance, including the implications for the spatial development of capitalism. This literature is often consciously eclectic, examining key features of contemporary capitalism almost as 'thick description' rather than by developing general theoretical explanations. The output is large and shifting, while not easily admitting of thematic classification.[60]

It is notable that there has been sustained interest in the institutional, cultural and political aspects of the ascendancy of finance since the late 1990s.[61] Significant work has been produced regarding the power of financial markets, particularly the role of institutional investors in transforming practices, outlook and ideology in finance.[62]

---

59   Engelbert Stockhammer, 'Neoliberalism, Income Distribution and the Causes of the Crisis', RMF Discussion Paper No. 19, 2010

60   For an extensive review of recent output see Roger Lee et al., 'The Remit of Financial Geography – Before and After the Crisis', *Journal of Economic Geography* 9, 2009, pp. 723–47; see also Ewald Engelen, 'The Case for Financialization', *Competition and Change* 12, 2008. Andy Pike and Jane Pollard suggest that economic geographers have approached financialization from the perspective of, first, the existence of several types of financial institutions; second, the instability of financialized capitalism; and third, the spreading of financialization, including geographically; see 'Economic Geographies of Financialization', *Economic Geography* 86:1, 2010.

61   Andrew Leyshon and Nigel Thrift, 'The Capitalization of Almost Everything', *Theory, Culture and Society* 24, 2009, pp. 97–115; Ron Martin, *Money and the Space Economy*, London: Wiley, 1999.

62   Gordon L. Clark, *Pension Fund Capitalism*, Oxford: Oxford University Press, 2000. Ewald Engelen, 'The Logic of Funding European Pension Restructuring and the Dangers of Financialiation', *Environment and Planning A* 35, 2003, pp. 1357–72. There have also been several studies of institutional investors in specific contexts, for instance, on Swiss pension funds, see José Corpataux, Olivier Crevoisier, and Thierry Theurillat, 'The Expansion of the Finance Industry and Its Impact on the Economy', *Economic Geography* 85:3, 2009. Note that Robin Blackburn was one of the first Anglo-Saxon Marxists systematically to deploy the term financialization and to examine it in relation to the rise of pension funds. For Blackburn, functioning capitalists have come to terms with institutional investors accepting shareholder value. Power has been devolved to the 'shady' areas of the financial system, partly through financial innovation. See Robin Blackburn, *Banking on Death, or Investing in Life: The History and Future of Pensions*,

Paul Langley has discussed the financialization of individual life and the penetration of financial practices in the realm of consumption and saving.[63] In this regard, the rise of finance has also had profound cultural implications for personal values, customs, and relations examined in the growing literature on cultural economy.[64] Note that Manuel Aalbers has focused on the financialization of housing, a topic that is discussed in subsequent chapters of this book; Andrew Leyshon and Nigel Thrift, finally, have been aware of the transformation of personal income flows into profit via the mechanisms of securitization.[65]

Eclecticism is also present in the illuminating output on financialization produced by the UK Centre for Research on Socio-Cultural Change (CRESC). Researchers at CRESC have posited financialization as 'coupon pool' capitalism whereby the income drawn from claims on financial markets becomes the regulator of macroeconomic behaviour.[66] Financialization is associated with the transformation of banks, seeking profits out of trading rather than lending, and the emergence of new elites that have the power to direct flows of income in their favour.

Among economic sociologists, Paul Thompson has argued that financialization has prevented employers from treating workers as 'stakeholders' in the enterprise. Capital has become 'disconnected' from established institutions and systems of business, thus making employment short-term and precarious. Ian Clark has developed the argument further by stressing the advantages of financialization for private equity holders.[67] These arguments have drawn on the voluminous literature on 'sharehold-

---

London: Verso, 2002; and Robin Blackburn, 'Finance and the Fourth Dimension', *New Left Review* 39, 2006, pp. 39–70.

63   Paul Langley, *The Everyday Life of Global Finance*, Oxford: Oxford University Press, 2008; Paul Langley, 'Financialization and the Consumer Credit Boom', *Competition and Change* 12:2, pp. 133–47, 2008.

64   Randy Martin, *Financialization of Daily Life*, Philadelphia: Temple University Press, 2002; Michael Pryke and Paul du Gay, 'Take an Issue: Cultural Economy and Finance', *Economy and Society* 36:3, 2007.

65   Manuel B. Aalbers, 'The Financialization of Home and the Mortgage Market Crisis', *Competition and Change* 12:2, 2008; Andrew Leyshon and Nigel Thrift, 'The Capitalization of Almost Everything: The Future of Finance and Capitalism', *Theory, Culture and Society* 24, 2009.

66   See, selectively, Julie Froud et al., 'Shareholder Value and Financialization: Consultancy Promises, Management Moves', *Economy and Society* 29, 2000; Julie Froud et al., *Financialization and Strategy: Narrative and Numbers*, London: Routledge, 2006; Ismail Erturk et al. (eds), *Financialization at Work*, London: Routledge, 2008; Mike Savage and Karel Williams (eds), *Remembering Elites*, London: John Wiley and Sons, 2008.

67   Paul Thompson, 'Disconnected Capitalism', *Work, Employment and Society* 17, 2003, pp. 359–78; and Ian Clark, 'Owners and Managers: Disconnecting Managerial Capitalism?', *Work, Employment and Society* 23: 2009, pp. 775–86.

er value' and corporate governance, which has been a permanent subtext in the financialization debates, as is clear from the survey above. The issue of corporate governance and control is of long standing in economic theory, and will be considered in chapters 6 and 7 in connection with capital markets, shareholding and income distribution. Influential in the financialization literature has been the work of William Lazonick and Mary O'Sullivan arguing that the ideology of 'shareholder value' has led to company 'downsizing' and thus to problematic investment outcomes among US corporations. The financialization of US corporations in particular has also been examined empirically by others seeking to show that shareholder value has contributed to deficient investment.[68]

This literature has affinities with the 'varieties of capitalism' approach, briefly discussed on pages 38–43. An important contribution in this field has been made by Masahiko Aoki who has stressed the nature of information flows in horizontally structured Japanese enterprises compared to vertically structured US enterprises, further associating the differences with the frequently superior performance of Japanese enterprises.[69] Suffice it to note, at this point, that the institutional and organizational structure of capitalist enterprises, important as it is for explaining performance, is not an appropriate criterion for defining financialization. Shareholder value might contribute to explaining differences in behaviour among US and Japanese enterprises, but financialization has to do with systematic access to funds and acquisition of financial assets, both of which are more fundamental processes than shareholder value. From this perspective, and as is shown in subsequent chapters, Japanese enterprises are also financializing, even if differently from US enterprises.

---

68   William Lazonick and Mary O'Sullivan, 'Maximizing Shareholder Value: A New Ideology for Corporate Governance', *Economy and Society* 29:1, 2000. See also William Milberg, 'Shifting Sources and Uses of Profits: Sustaining US Financialization with Global Value Chains', *Economy and Society* 37:3, 2008; and William Milberg and Deborah Winkler, 'Financialisation and the Dynamics of Offshoring in the USA', *Cambridge Journal of Economics* 34, 2010.

69   Masahiko Aoki, *Information, Incentives and Bargaining in the Japanese Economy*, Cambridge: Cambridge University Press, 1988; Masahiko Aoki, 'Toward and Economic Model of the Japanese Firm', *Journal of Economic Literature* 28, 1990; Masahiko Aoki, 'The Japanese Firm as a System of Attributes: A Survey and Research Agenda', in *The Japanese Firm: Sources of Competitive Strength*, ed. Mashiko Aoki and Ronald Dore, Oxford: Clarendon Press, 1994. For a comparison and contrast of US and Japanese corporations, see William Lazonick, 'Innovative Business Models and Varieties of Capitalism: Financialization of the US corporation', *Business History Review* 84, 2010. A reference point for economic analysis of the organizational structure of US corporations is the work of Milgrom and Roberts: 'The Economics of Modern Manufacturing: Technology, Strategy and Organization', *American Economic Review* 80, 1990; and *Economics, Organization and Management*, Englewood Cliffs, NJ: Prentice Hall, 1992.

An approach that draws on classical Marxism

The approach to financialization in this book draws heavily on the theories reviewed in the previous sections, but its analytical backbone derives from work on Marxist theory of finance that has been developed since the early 1980s.[70] It also draws on the characteristic features of the crisis of 2007, a systemic upheaval that has cast light on the path of social and economic development of contemporary capitalism.[71] The crisis is a product of financialized capitalism, the culmination of contradictory tendencies that have unfolded for more than three decades, as is shown in Chapter 9. The approach, finally, draws on classical Marxist debates on finance capital and imperialism, particularly Hilferding's *Finance Capital* and Lenin's *Imperialism*, even if the specific conclusions of both belong to a different era and do not necessarily apply to financialized capitalism. Its broad features are as follows.

Financialization as systemic transformation of capitalist economies

The theoretical and empirical point of departure is that financialization represents a structural transformation of advanced capitalist economies, and its roots must therefore be sought within the fundamental relations of non-financial enterprises, financial enterprises, and workers. It is pointless to attempt to define financialization without first examining its foundations: the conduct of non-financial capitals, the operations of banks, and the financial practices of workers. Only on this basis it is possible to examine the articulation of financial markets and institutions with each other and with the rest of the economy, as well as the interventions of the state in the financial sphere. In short, the content of financialization becomes clear only after demonstrating the financialization of non-financial enterprises, banks, and households, subsequently considering the implications for mature capitalist economies as a whole.

It is misleading to interpret financialization as the escape of capital to the realm of finance in search of higher (and possibly speculative) profits. Financialization has indeed been characterized by rapid growth of circulation compared to production, but this asymmetry is the outcome of 'financialized' interactions among the fundamental agents of the capitalist economy. The emerging social phenomena are highly complex, and cannot be interpreted as the outcome of non-financial capitalists escaping low profits in the sphere of production. Note that it is particularly problematic to assume that financialization reflects higher profitability in the realm of finance compared to

---

70   The theoretical framework is based on Makoto Itoh and Costas Lapavitsas, *Political Economy of Money and Finance*, London: Macmillan, 1999; and Costas Lapavitsas, *Social Foundations of Markets, Money and Credit*, London: Routledge, 2003.

71   See Costas Lapavitsas, 'Financialised Capitalism: Crisis and Financial Expropriation', *Historical Materialism* 17:2, 2009, pp. 114–48 – but, more broadly, the work of the network Research on Money and Finance. See also Costas Lapavitsas (ed.), *Financialisation in Crisis*, Leiden: Brill, 2012.

the sphere of production. As is shown in chapters 5 and 6, this assumption would run counter to the basic tenets of Marxist political economy regarding the determination of the rate of profit, but more particularly regarding the remuneration of financial capital. There is no doubt that rising financial profits have been a prominent feature of financialization, but the causes of this phenomenon should not be confused with the relative profitability of finance.

Finance is a well-defined field of capitalist economic activity, not a nebulous realm into which capital seeks to escape when, and if, profitability is low in production. The processes of finance should be analysed in their own right, rather than being treated as surface phenomena sitting atop the 'real' economic activities of production and exchange. More specifically, the financial system is a set of ordered economic relations, comprising markets and institutions with characteristic profit-making motives which are necessary to support capitalist accumulation. The rational and social basis for the extraction of financial profit derives from the role played by the financial system in the context of accumulation. At the same time, finance is a relatively autonomous field of capitalist profit making with its own rules and internal life. For this reason, financial profit also has a predatory aspect setting it apart from profit in the sphere of production. The predatory dimension of finance has placed its mark on financialization.

Financialization, moreover, represents a historically specific transformation of capitalist economies. The interaction between finance and the rest of the economy is mediated by a complex set of institutional structures that often reflect historical, political, customary and even cultural factors. A major source of difficulty in analysing financialization lies in identifying the necessary mediations in a historically specific way. Financialization does not readily lend itself to abstract theorization because it represents epochal change resting on financial phenomena that are inherently institution-specific. Consequently, the theoretical approach of this book focuses on the fundamental tendencies that define financialization at the level of non-financial enterprises, financial enterprises, and households. It subsequently considers the concrete ways in which these tendencies have been deflected through the historical and institutional peculiarities of core capitalist countries. Financialization by nature lacks a homogeneous form valid across the world; rather, it varies among mature countries, as is shown with reference to the US, Japan, Germany and the UK throughout this book. Moreover, financialization also varies between developed and developing countries, taking a subordinate form in the latter.

There are similarities but also differences between financialization and the first bout of financial ascendancy in advanced capitalism which took place at the end of the nineteenth and the start of the twentieth century. Both Hilferding and Lenin sought the origins of the historic transformation of capitalism of their era in fundamental interactions occurring within capitalist accumulation. Hilferding associated the transformation with the rise of finance capital – an amalgam of industrial and banking capital created as monopolistic corporations come increasingly to rely on banks for investment finance. Finance capital 'organizes' the economy to suit its own interests, thus resulting in exclusive trading blocs and the export of money capital. Consequently, it seeks to establish territorial empires by mobilizing the political and military help of the state. Lenin adopted Hilferding's analysis, added to it 'parasitical rentiers' and greater emphasis on monopoly, and produced the definitive Marxist theory of imperialism in the twentieth century. Hilferding's and Lenin's diagnoses and conclusions hardly fit the current period of financial ascendancy. However, their analytical and methodological approach is vital to examining financialization theoretically.

Tendencies and forms

Three underlying tendencies characterize financialization, as was mentioned in Chapter 1 and is more fully analysed in chapters 7 and 8. First, although monopolization remains a characteristic feature of mature contemporary economies in terms of both trade and foreign direct investment, monopoly capitals have become 'financialized'.[72] Large multinational corporations are typically able to finance the bulk of their investment without relying heavily on banks and mostly by drawing on retained profits. Insofar as they require external finance they are able to obtain significant volumes in open financial markets, relatively independently of banks. Even the wage bill of large non-financial corporations is frequently financed through the issuing of commercial paper in open markets. Successive waves of takeovers, furthermore, have led to corporations becoming heavily involved in bond and equity trading in stock markets, thus developing skills in independent financial operations and trading.

Second, banks have restructured themselves, partly reflecting the altered conduct of non-financial enterprises. Specifically, banks have moved toward mediating in open markets to earn fees, commissions, and profits from trading; they have also turned toward individuals (and households in general) to obtain profits from lending but also from handling savings and financial assets. The transformation of banks has been in line with the enormous growth of open financial markets in recent decades, further fostered by state legislation. Banking capital has benefited from successive waves of mergers and acquisitions among non-financial enterprises; from channelling personal savings to stock markets at the behest of the state; and from lifting of controls on interest rates and capital flows that has encouraged growth of financial markets.

Third, perhaps the most striking aspect of the recent period has been the financialization of the personal revenue of workers and households across social classes.[73] This

---

72   On the role of multinationals in foreign direct investment and trade see, for instance, Carlos Morera Camacho and Jose Antonio Rojas Nieto, 'The Globalisation of Financial Capital, 1997–2008', RMF Discussion Paper 6, 2009.

73   Workers and households are, of course, not the same category. However, both terms indicate economic agents that are associated with capital but whose revenues also have non-capitalistic aspects. The availability of flow of funds data for households has allowed for empirical analysis in subsequent chapters of this book.

phenomenon refers both to increasing debt (for mortgages, general consumption, education, health) and to expanded holdings of financial assets (for pensions, insurance, money market funds). Household financialization is associated with rising income inequality but also with the retreat of public provision across a range of services, including housing, pensions, education, health, transport, and so on. In this context, the consumption of workers and others has become increasingly privatized and mediated by the financial system. Banks and other financial institutions have facilitated household consumption but also the channelling of household savings to financial markets, thus extracting financial profits.[74]

Note that relations between banks and households are qualitatively different from relations between banks and industrial capitalists. Financial transactions between banks and households do not refer directly to the creation of profit (surplus value) in the sphere of production. Generally speaking, workers seek finance to acquire use values; in contrast, financial institutions and industrial capitalists engage in financial transactions aiming at profit extraction. Moreover, workers are typically disadvantaged compared to banks with regard to economic information and power. Thus, the systematic extraction of financial profits out of the revenue of workers and other social layers constitutes a new set of relations that has been called financial expropriation.[75] It is shown in subsequent chapters that financial expropriation is a characteristic feature of financialization and represents the re-strengthening of the predatory outlook of finance toward economy and society.

The three underling tendencies of financialization have emerged within the historical and political context of neoliberalism, including financial liberalization and labour market deregulation. Moreover, the epochal features of financialization have been conditioned by the historical and institutional specificities of particular countries, reflecting the shifting balance of class forces between capital and labour. Financialization has thus necessarily varied across different times and among different countries. By this token, the aim of theoretical analysis cannot be to produce a generally valid abstract model of financialization but rather to specify its underlying tendencies and to ascertain the particular form and content it acquires in different contexts.

It cannot be overemphasized that historical and institutional variation is a necessary feature of financialization. The first bout of financial ascendancy at the end of the nineteenth century was also characterized by considerable historical and institutional

---

74 An innovative Marxist analysis of the crisis of the 2000s, fully aware of the independent significance of finance, has been put forth by Photis Lysandrou focusing on hedge funds as wealth pools of the rich. For Lysandrou, profit making via securitized securities draws on generalized relations of exploitation prevalent in contemporary markets. However, the nature of these relations remains unclear in his work. Photis Lysandrou, 'Global Inequality, Wealth Concentration and the Subprime Crisis: A Marxian Commodity Analysis', *Development and Change* 42:1, 2011.

75 See Lapavitsas, 'Financialised Capitalism'.

variation. Hilferding's *Finance Capital* focused heavily on Germany and Austria, both of which had very prominent bank-based practices in finance, thus lending a misleading air of universality to his analysis. In contrast, Lenin's *Imperialism* stressed that finance capital acquired a different form depending on the economic structure, on the political system and on the institutional mechanisms of particular countries. Imperialism was significantly different between, say, Germany and France.

It is established in chapters 7, 8 and 9 that financialization is different among mature countries, as is shown with reference to the US, Japan, Germany and the UK. Non-financial corporations have generally become less reliant on banks, but there are major differences in financial practices between, on the one hand, US and UK and, on the other, Japanese and German enterprises. Banks, on the other hand, have moved away from lending for productive activities and toward lending to other financial corporations and households in all four countries. Nonetheless, significant variation is still present and often of unexpected form; German banks, for instance, have a strong tendency to transact with other financial institutions. Households, finally, exhibit a general trend to move savings away from bank deposits and toward other financial assets that could be traded in open markets, including pension funds and equities. Also notable is the increase in household indebtedness, typically associated with housing, though local practice can still be very different, as in relatively low household indebtedness in Germany.

There are parallels in this respect between the analysis of financialization and the long-standing debate on bank-based versus market-based (or German–Japanese versus Anglo–US) financial systems in the course of capitalist development.[76] John Zysman has provided fresh focus for this debate within political theory by examining the interaction between governments and markets in the context of the industrial development in Japan.[77] Closely related is also Michel Albert's influential depiction of Rhineland capitalism, pivoting on banks, in contrast to Anglo-Saxon capitalism, pivoting on stock markets.[78] The implicit or explicit assumption in much of this literature is that finance plays a central – if not the central – role in determining the content and form of a capi-

---

76 Historically associated with Alexander Gerschenkron, *Economic Backwardness in Historical Perspective*, Cambridge, MA: Harvard University Press, 1962. For a more recent – mainstream – approach see Franklin Allen and Douglas Gale, 'Comparing Financial Systems', Cambridge, MA: MIT Press, 2000.

77 John Zysman, *Governments, Markets and Growth*, Ithaca: Cornell University Press, 1983. It is important to note that the notion of Japan possessing a peculiar type of (bank-based) financial system that makes it distinct from other developed capitalist countries has not emanated from within the country but has come from abroad. Indeed, the term 'main bank', which presumably characterizes the close relationship between banks and industry, does not even exist in Japanese; a transliteration of the English term is used in practice.

78 Michel Albert, *Capitalism vs. Capitalism*, New York: Four Walls Eight Windows, 1993.

talist economy. Thus, bank-based finance allows for more sustained state intervention, makes room for longer-term investment planning, and might also allow for greater social solidarity. The perception is, however, that market-based finance has been on the ascendant during the last two decades, despite its weaknesses.[79]

There are also parallels with the 'varieties of capitalism' approach, named after the seminal book by Peter Hall and David Soskice that has proposed the distinction between 'liberal market economies', represented by the US and the UK, and 'coordinated market economies', represented by Germany.[80] The distinction is based on the relationship between enterprises and the financial system: short-term finance relying on the open market characterises the former, long-term finance relying on banks characterizes the latter. For these authors, four institutional domains define firms' incentives and constraints: financial systems and non-financial governance, industrial relations, education and training systems, and the inter-company system.[81] Along similar lines, Amable has suggested a typology of capitalisms depending on institutional make-up and geographical location.[82] A variety of criticisms have been levelled against these attempts to categorize capitalism according to its institutional features.[83] Nevertheless,

---

79   Ronald Dore believes that the rise of market-based finance that is characteristic of financialization is in part due to the dominance of the ideology of shareholder value. Dore, 'Financialization of the Global Economy', *Industrial and Corporate Change* 17:6, 2008, pp. 1097–1112.

80   Peter A. Hall and David Soskice (eds), *Varieties of Capitalism*, Oxford: Oxford University Press, 2001. The affinity between financialization and 'varieties of capitalism' has been noted by Engelen, Konings, and Fernandez, who have suggested that the two approaches should be combined; Martijn Konings, Engelen Ewald and Rodrigo Fernandez, 'Geographies of Financialization in Disarray: The Dutch Case in Comparative Perspective', *Economic Geography* 86:1, 2010, pp. 53–73.

81   Gregory Jackson and Richard Deeg, 'From Comparing Capitalisms to the Politics of Institutional Change', *Review of International Political Economy* 15, 2008, pp. 680–709.

82   Bruno Amable, *The Diversity of Modern Capitalism*, Oxford: Oxford University Press, 2003.

83   The most sustained critique has been by Jamie Peck and Nik Theodore ('Variegated Capitalism', *Progress in Human Geography* 31:6, 2007), rejecting the bipolar classification of capitalism and pointing out that there are common underlying tendencies in capitalist restructuring. Others have cautioned against over-emphasizing national boundaries, suggesting that there is a much wider scope for 'hybridization' across national boundaries; see Masahiko Aoki and Gregory Jackson, 'Understanding an Emergent Diversity of Non-Financial Governance and Organizational Architecture', *Industrial and Non-Financial Change* 17, 2008; and Gregory Jackson and Richard Deeg, 'From Comparing Capitalisms to the Politics of Institutional Change', *Review of International Political Economy* 15, 2008. Höpner (2005) has criticized the idea of institutional complementarity. For a collection of critical positions, see Bob Hancké, Martin Rhodes, and Mark Thatcher (eds), *Beyond Varieties of Capitalism*, Oxford: Oxford University Press, 2007. For a Marxist critique, mostly focusing on the absence of class analysis from the

the 'varieties of capitalism' approach remains relevant to analysing financialization as well as to determining the empirical issues examined in subsequent chapters.

The Marxist approach adopted in this book differs significantly from the approach of bank-based versus market-based finance as well as from the 'varieties of capitalism' approach, not least by stressing the exploitative and contradictory character of all forms of capitalism. Financialization is neither finance- nor enterprise-driven; rather, it emerges due to the spontaneous interactions among non-financial enterprises, banks and households. These interactions occur within an institutional context influenced by state policymaking, resulting in systemic change that reflects the peculiarities of each country. The form of the capitalist economy necessarily varies, and often in ways that are related to the financial system. This insight is vital to analysing financialization as well as to navigating among the empirical data examined in the rest of this book. Financialization has a systemic outlook that still reflects the peculiarities of each country.[84]

The final point in this section is that financialization also varies systematically between developed and developing countries. Formal imperialism has become practically irrelevant in contemporary capitalism, but mature capitalist countries have retained a dominant role in economic activity across the world. At the same time, the mode of integration of developing countries into the world market has changed profoundly in recent decades. Financialization in developing countries is associated with the financial liberalization that began in the 1970s, lifting price and quantity controls in domestic financial systems. Financial liberalization has gradually acquired further features, including the establishment of stock markets. By the late 1980s financial liberalization had morphed into an integrated pro-market development strategy, the Washington Consensus.[85]

A fundamental component of the Washington Consensus has been to open domestic economies to international capital markets, typically on the grounds that capital would flow from rich to poor countries, thus promoting development. However, in the 2000s, as developing countries became more closely integrated with world capital markets, precisely the opposite has taken place, as is shown in more detail in Chapter 8. The

literature, see David Coates (ed.), *Varieties of Capitalism, Varieties of Approaches*, Basingstoke: Palgrave Macmillan, 2005.

84   There is a growing perception within economic geography that financialization varies among developed countries; see Claude Dupuy, Stéphanie Lavigne, and Dalia Nicet-Chenaf, 'Does Geography Still Matter? Evidence on the Portfolio Turnover of Large Equity Investors and Varieties of Capitalism', *Economic Geography* 81:1, 2010.

85   For further analysis of the Washington Consensus from a Marxist and heterodox standpoint see Ben Fine, Costas Lapavitsas, and Jonathan Pincus (eds), *Development Policy in the Twenty-first Century*, London: Routledge, 2001; and Costas Lapavitsas and Makoto Noguchi (eds), *Beyond Market-Driven Development: Drawing on the Experience of Asia and Latin America*, London: Routledge, 2005.

peak years of financialization have been characterized by reverse net flows of capital as developing countries have accumulated reserves of international means of payment – mostly US dollars. The accumulation of reserves has acted as catalyst for the growth of domestic finance in developing countries, spurring the emergence of financialization but with a subordinate character. Entry of foreign banks in developing countries has further fostered the evolution of subordinate financialization.

Financialization in developing countries, in short, has been driven by the opening of capital accounts, the accumulation of foreign exchange reserves, and the establishment of foreign banks. More fundamentally, it has been directly connected to the functioning of world money in recent decades, particularly the US dollar. There is a monetary basis to financialization in developing countries, which has determined its subordinate character relative to financialization in developed countries. However, the monetary basis of financialization has also been important for developed countries, and nowhere more so that in Europe, as is shown in Chapter 9.

3. THE FIRST WAVE OF FINANCIAL ASCENDANCY: MARXIST THEORETICAL RESPONSES

The rise of finance at the end of the nineteenth century

Financialization represents the second bout of financial ascendancy in the history of mature capitalism, the first spanning the last quarter of the nineteenth century and lasting until the interwar years. During that period giant monopolistic corporations emerged as the pre-eminent units of production, often organized as cartels operating in exclusive trading zones. Moreover, capital export and international financial markets grew powerfully, typically associated with monopolistic banks that dominated global finance. At the same time British predominance in the productive sphere – and correspondingly in world trade – was decisively challenged by Germany and the US. The political counterpart to these underlying economic trends was militarism and imperialism among the main capitalist powers.

Financialization has clear similarities with the first bout of financial ascendancy.[1] Multinational corporations dominate global economic activity; global banks play a leading role in international finance; capital exports have grown substantially; a certain type of political and military imperialism has reasserted itself, led by the US but facing powerful challenges from other powers. However, there are also significant differences between the two periods. Financialization has not resulted in exclusive trading zones

---

1 The similarities between the two periods, particularly with regard to the question of imperialism, can be gauged from the debates on globalization. Clear and empirically founded parallels between the two periods can be found in Paul Bairoch, *Economics and World History*, Harvester Wheatsheaf, 1993; and Paul Bairoch and Richard Kozul-Wright, 'Globalization Myths: Some Historical Reflections on Integration, Industrialization and Growth in the World Economy', UNCTAD Discussion Papers No. 113, March 1996. Political and economic aspects of post-imperial relations in developing countries have been examined in David Becker et al., *Postimperialism: International Capitalism and Development in the Late Twentieth Century*, Boulder: Rienner Publishers, 1987; David Becker and Richard Sklar, *Postimperialism and World Politics*, London: Praeger, 1999; David Fieldhouse, *The West and the Third World*, Oxford: Blackwell, 1999; Ankie Hoogvelt, *Globalisation and the Postcolonial World*, Palgrave, 2001. Leslie Sklair has put forth a theory of transnational capitalist class corresponding to the globalization of capital (*Capitalism and Its Alternatives*, Oxford: Oxford University Press, 2002; *The Transnational Capitalist Class*, Oxford: Blackwell, 2001). Leo Panitch and Sam Gindin, from a Marxist perspective, have developed the view that globalization and the rise of global finance have been driven by the US state and US capital; US imperialism in the modern era has entailed the reshaping of other states according to the dictates of globalization and ascendant finance; see 'American Imperialism and EuroCapitalism', *Studies in Political Economy* 71/72, 2003; *Global Capitalism and American Empire*, London: Merlin Press, 2004; 'The Current Crisis: A Socialist Perspective', *Studies in Political Economy* 83, 2009; *The Making of Global Capitalism*, London: Verso, 2012.

associated with territorial empires, and banks are not dominant over non-financial enterprises. Nonetheless, there has been heavy interpenetration between the realm of finance and the sphere of production, while financial relations have proliferated in the economic life of workers and households in general.

The first period of financial ascendancy led to intense debate among Marxist theorists, briefly summed up in the rest of this chapter. The outstanding contribution was Rudolf Hilferding's *Finance Capital*, which is also the natural point of departure for a Marxist analysis of financialization as well as a Marxist theory of finance. The conclusions drawn by Hilferding more than a century ago do not apply directly to the conditions of financialized capitalism. But the issues he raised, the theoretical concepts he deployed, and the connections he drew between the economic, social and political phenomena of his day are invaluable for the analysis of financialization.

Hilferding sought the causes of the great transformation of his time in the underlying relations of accumulation, rather than in stagnating production, institutional change, or policy choices. His fundamental claim, discussed further in the following sections of this chapter, was that as the size of capitalist production grows monopolies come to depend heavily on investment credit provided by banks. A close relationship thus ensues between banks and industry, eventually leading to the emergence of finance capital. Hilferding was fully aware of the organizational implications of this development, which would be called today 'corporate governance'. Finance capital is supposed to rest on dense links between finance and industry through interlocking appointments, exchange of information, and joint decision making. Note that Hilferding largely ignored the putative opposition between 'active' industrialist and 'idle' financier. There was no suggestion of rentiers imposing their interests on industrial capitalists and lowering investment rates, or rates of growth. Rather, finance capital was seen as an amalgam of banking and industrial capital, and hence the latter took a direct interest in the profitability of financial operations.

Hilferding also identified a new form of profit for the capitalist class as finance capital emerged. In stock markets future profits are discounted at the rate of interest, but the capital that is actually invested in production or trade earns the rate of profit. Since the rate of interest tends to be below the rate of profit, the price paid for shares exceeds the capital actually invested, if expected returns are translated into net present value. The difference between the two is 'founder's profit', which accrues as a lump sum to those who issue shares. Banks also obtain parts of 'founder's profit' as payment for investment banking. Hilferding's concept of 'founder's profit' remains fruitful in analysing contemporary financial profits, including capital gains, as is shown in Chapter 6.

Lenin built the theoretical core of his analysis of imperialism by borrowing the concept of finance capital from Hilferding. He placed greater emphasis on the tendency toward monopoly for both industrial and banking capitals, though Hilferding was certainly aware of monopolization. The main theoretical innovation by Lenin was to introduce rentiers as an important social group within the capitalist class in the period of imperialism. This notion, which Lenin borrowed from the British radical Hobson, who was not a Marxist, is certainly powerful but could also lead to considerable confusion in analysis of finance, as is shown in several sections of this chapter and in following chapters. Lenin, furthermore, also stressed the importance of the re-division of the world by countries dominated by finance capital, hence leading to imperialist rivalries and war. Finally, Lenin had no truck with Hilferding's view that finance capital 'organizes' the capitalist economy and could thus ameliorate the tendency to crisis.

Neither Hilferding nor Lenin sought to explain the ascendancy of finance as the result of capital escaping to the sphere of circulation in search of speculative financial profits. After all, both Hilferding and Lenin – indeed most of the leading Marxists of their time – treated crises as complex and multifaceted phenomena that could not be reduced to a simple theory of the rate of profit to fall. The notion that the normal state of capitalist production is to malfunction due to a persistently excessive organic composition of capital, or even due to failing 'surplus' absorption, would have been alien to classical Marxists. Both Hilferding and Lenin, moreover, would have been surprised at the idea that the ascendancy of finance represents the 'autumn' of capitalist hegemonic power. On the contrary, Germany, the paradigmatic country of finance capital, was the rising imperial power representing the cutting edge of advanced capitalism. It is true that Lenin thought of imperialism as 'parasitic' and 'decaying', but this referred to the capitalist mode of production as a whole rather than to the sphere of production in countries where finance capital was at its strongest.

The rest of this chapter discusses concepts and theoretical conclusions deriving from the classical Marxist debates on the first bout of financial ascendancy with a view to developing the theoretical analysis of financialization. Attention naturally focuses mostly on Hilferding's work, but Lenin and other leading Marxist theorists are also considered in some detail.

The intellectual and political context of Hilferding's analysis of capitalist transformation

Rudolf Hilferding belonged to the remarkable Austro-German generation that embraced and shaped Marxism at the end of the nineteenth century. He enrolled at the University of Vienna in 1894 to study medicine but in practice studied political economy, not least in debate with Austrian neoclassicism. In 1896 the prominent Austrian theorist Eugen Böhm-Bawerk published *Karl Marx and the Close of his System* claiming to have found a damning inconsistency between the first and third volumes of Marx's *Capital*.[2] While, in the first volume, Marx assumes commodities to exchange at value – in line with his theory of value as abstract human labour – in the third volume he assumes that commodities are exchanged at prices of production diverging from value. This is, of course, the well-known problem of 'transformation' of values into prices, of which Marx was fully aware. For Böhm-Bawerk the broader significance of

---

2   Paul M. Sweezy (ed.), *Karl Marx and the Close of His System*, New York: A.M. Kelley, 1949.

this apparent contradiction in Marx's work is that it shows the labour theory of value to be inferior to neoclassical subjective value theory. By the same token, Marx's theory of worker exploitation in production is rendered incoherent.

Hilferding responded with an essay that stressed the social basis of commodity exchange, an issue that is typically ignored by neoclassical theory. For Hilferding, Marx's theory of value aims at capturing the social and historical underpinnings of commodity exchange, rather than simply explaining relative prices of commodities. In contrast, subjective value theory focuses on the psychological predilections of the individual and cannot grasp the social constituents of economic activity. Marx's value theory, therefore, is a powerful instrument that seeks to throw light on society as a whole, rather than simply providing foundations for a theory of price.

Hilferding submitted his essay to *Die Neue Zeit*, edited by Karl Kautsky in Germany, who was impressed by the quality of the work but actually turned it down. It was eventually published in Vienna in 1904 as *Böhm-Bawerk's Marx Kritik* and its impact was immediate.[3] By then, Böhm-Bawerk was professor at Vienna and in 1905 initiated a celebrated seminar which soon became a forum of debate between the rising stars of Austrian neoclassicism and Austro-Marxism. The most prominent participant was Joseph Schumpeter but the group also included Ludwig von Mises. Among the Marxists, Otto Bauer had a strong presence, and he probably invited Hilferding to take part in the debates, thus developing a lasting relationship with Schumpeter.[4]

The broader impact and significance of Hilferding's reply to Böhm-Bawerk becomes clear only in the context of the 'revisionism' debate within the German Social Democratic Party. In 1899, Eduard Bernstein had published *Evolutionary Socialism* rejecting the prospect of revolutionary transition to socialism. Bernstein was very influential within Social Democracy partly because he had had personal relations with Marx and Engels. In his book, he declared himself unable to 'believe in a final aim of socialism' and emphasized the 'step by step' transformation of society toward 'real democracy'.[5]

For the leadership of German Social Democracy, weaned on Marx's and Engels's revolutionary politics, Bernstein's arguments were unacceptable. Rosa Luxemburg attacked Bernstein in print, and began to draw around her the revolutionary left of Social Democracy.[6] Her critique forced Kautsky also to reject Bernstein's revisionism, thus gradually giving shape to the Kautskyite centre of Social Democracy, which defended the idea of revolutionary transition to socialism and set the tone for Marxist orthodoxy within the Second International. The centre welcomed Hilferding's strong

3   Ibid.

4   Minoru Kurata, *Wakaki Hirufadingu* (The Young Hilferding), Mitaka: Okashobo, 1984, pp. 88–90.

5   Eduard Bernstein, *Evolutionary Socialism*, New York: Schocken, 1961, p. xxii.

6   Rosa Luxemburg, 'Reform or Revolution', in *Rosa Luxemburg Speaks*, New York: Pathfinder Press, 1970.

defence of Marx's economics and in particular his theory of value, while Bernstein rejected it out of hand.[7] Kautsky encouraged Hilferding to write for *Die Neue Zeit* and eventually persuaded him to move to Berlin in 1906.

In Berlin, Hilferding taught political economy at the Party School for a short while but could not keep the post as he did not have German citizenship, and was replaced by Rosa Luxemburg. He then assumed editorial responsibilities for *Vorwärts* – the party's main daily paper – a post he kept until 1914. During this period he produced *Finance Capital*, published in 1910 but in large part ready by 1906. The book was an instant and enormous success for reasons discussed in the rest of this chapter. *Finance Capital* appeared in English only in 1981, seventy one years after the original was published in German. For nearly three-quarters of a century, this key work of Marxist economics was known to Anglo-Saxon Marxists mostly through its impact on Lenin's *Imperialism*. However, things have changed drastically since 1981 and Hilferding's classic is now widely read and cited in English, even within mainstream economics.[8]

Following the book's publication, Hilferding emerged as a leading economist of the Second International. His broader theoretical views also took definitive shape during this period, resulting in several publications in *Die Neue Zeit*, including essays on the question of the mass strike and on imperialism.[9] Hilferding saw Marxism as a dispassionate scientific endeavour that establishes the laws of motion of capitalism and provides a superior theory of society. Political conclusions must be based on scientific research that seeks to demonstrate how capitalism lays the ground for socialism through a process of advancing 'socialization' of the economy; the eventual arrival of socialism depends on working class revolution. Elements of this approach are to be found throughout *Finance Capital*.

During the First World War, Hilferding took a principled anti-war position, unlike much of German Social Democracy, including Kautsky. He returned to Berlin from the front in 1918 and kept his distance from the Social Democrats, including Rosa Luxemburg and her group. In 1922, however, he rejoined the party and became a stalwart of the Weimar Republic. As Keynes had predicted in *The Economic Consequences of the Peace*, Germany faced continuous economic problems in large part due to the scandalous reparations imposed by the treaty of Versailles. Hilferding served twice as finance minister – in 1923 and 1928–29 – as Germany struggled to cope with the aftermath of war.

Hilferding's activities during the Weimar period drew on the concept of 'organized

---

7   F. Peter Wagner, *Rudolf Hilferding: Theory and Politics of Democratic Socialism*, Atlantic Highlands, NJ: Humanities Press, 1996, pp. 38–9.

8   For instance, Steven Horwitz, 'Complementary Non-Quantity Theory Approaches to Money', *History of Political Economy* 26:2, 1994; and James A. Gherity, 'The Evolution of Adam Smith's Theory of Banking', *History of Political Economy* 26:3, 1994.

9   Wagner, *Rudolf Hilferding*, ch. 3, 4.

capitalism' which he developed in several party political publications. Theoretical foundations for it can be found in *Finance Capital*, including the notion that 'socialization' proceeds inexorably under capitalism and lays the ground for rational organization of economy and society. Particularly striking in this connection is his remark that the German economy could be publicly controlled by taking over 'six large Berlin banks'.[10] However, Hilferding properly formulated the concept of 'organized capitalism' in the 1920s, a long time after completing *Finance Capital*.[11]

'Organized capitalism' assumes that the centralization of capital leads to the formation of gigantic cartels which suppress competition. Centralization also occurs among banks similarly suppressing competition and preventing sudden swings of credit. Banks and industry form giant amalgamations of finance capital that can plan their activities – reducing the anarchy of the capitalist economy – and in conjunction with the state prevent the emergence of classic capitalist crises. Consequently, economic stability could prevail in general, if disruptions caused by war, such as the reparations, were eliminated. In this context, socialists had to struggle for greater democracy and economic reform, rather than for revolutionary change. It is worth noting that Hilferding's view stood in contrast to that of Bukharin in *Imperialism and World Economy*. Bukharin, despite proposing an even stronger notion of 'organized' nation-states competing in the world market, was careful to argue that economic and political stability could not last for long in a capitalist economy.

The crisis of the 1930s brought Hitler to power and Hilferding was forced to flee because the Nazis saw him as one of the Jews that personified the failure of Weimar. After the fall of France the Vichy regime handed him over to the Gestapo in February 1941 and within days he was dead, probably after committing suicide. He died a broken man – lonely, disillusioned, and a political failure. But his legacy is *Finance Capital*, a path-breaking work that continues to shed light on the inner workings of capitalism.

The structure of Hilferding's theoretical analysis
The aim of *Finance Capital* is to show that an epochal transformation of capitalism took place toward the end of the nineteenth and the beginning of the twentieth century, associated with the remarkable rise of finance during the same period. The term 'finance capital' conveys the sense of a historical change, while remaining rooted in the analysis of Marx's *Capital*. Hilferding's book attempted to capture this putative change in theoretical terms, and by going back to first principles. To this purpose, the book comprises five analytical parts: i) money and credit, ii) the mobilization of capital; fictitious capital, iii) finance capital and the restriction of free competition, iv) finance capital and crises, and v) the economic policy of finance capital.

The order of Hilferding's theoretical analysis is certainly coherent, rising from high-

---

10   Rudolf Hilferding, *Finance Capital*, London: Routledge & Kegan Paul, 1981, p. 368.

11   Wagner, *Rudolf Hilferding*, ch. 5.

ly abstract economic categories to more concrete issues of crisis and economic policy. This order is in itself a guide to analysis of contemporary financialization, but it is also vital to realize that the structure of Hilferding's book involves omissions and leaps.[12] The most important omission has to do with the analysis of production, the labour process and the labour market. These fundamental aspects of the capitalist economy are not discussed throughout Hilferding's book, with the insignificant exception of the penultimate chapter on the 'Conflict Over the Labour Contract'.

If, however, an epochal transformation of capitalism has indeed taken place, its roots are likely to be found in the forces of production and in the labour process. Hilferding does not discuss these issues in any depth, and offers practically no relevant empirical evidence throughout *Finance Capital*. The reasons for his approach are not clear but the result is to weaken his overall analysis. To be more specific, instead of concretely examining the development of production in key capitalist countries, Hilferding makes general assumptions based on the outlook of German capitalism, as is shown in more detail in the following sections of this chapter. Unfortunately, the subsequent path of development of German capitalism proved far less typical of capitalism in general than Hilferding had assumed.

Furthermore, Hilferding's exposition involves a leap from the first three parts of the book (comprising analysis of finance that goes back to first principles) to the last two (comprising analysis of crisis and imperialism). In line with Marx's dialectical approach in *Capital*, proper analysis of the last two topics would require the introduction of further levels of mediation substantiating the historical evolution of both crises and capitalism in general. The mediations would be related to the sphere of production, but also to the institutional outlook characteristic of each historical era. Hilferding offers little in this respect.

These weaknesses have an evident importance for the analysis of contemporary financialization. First, and rather obviously, they limit the direct relevance of Hilferding's conclusions to the current era; second, and more significantly, they indicate that analysis of financialization ought to be rooted in the sphere of production as well as in the institutional framework of markets. Theoretical focus on money and finance – fundamental as it is – could never capture the gist of financialization by itself. Financialization is a complex phenomenon that involves changes in both production and circulation, and not merely in the relations between the financial system and real accumulation. Nevertheless, the logical structure of Hilferding's theory is vital to the theoretical analysis of financialization, as is clear from the five analytical building blocs mentioned above. By considering them closely, it becomes possible to establish a theoretical approach to financialization in the rest of this book.

---

12   As pointed out long ago in M. Takumi, 'Hilferding', in *Marukusu Keizaigaku Kogi* (Discourses in Marxian economics), ed. K. Suzuki, Tokyo: Seirinshoin-shinsa, 1972.

The importance of starting with a theory of money and credit

Hilferding started his analysis from first principles, that is, by developing initially a theory of money and subsequently one of credit. The order in which he approached these issues is in line with Marx's own discussion in the first volume of *Capital*, and that is also the order adopted in this book in chapters 4 and 5.[13] Marx put forth a 'monetary theory of credit', to use Schumpeter's terminology in the *History of Economic Analysis*. The importance of this approach is examined in detail in Chapter 4; suffice it to state here that it rests on money being a more fundamental – a prior – category compared to credit. For Marx, the category of money must have been already established in theory (and reality) for the category of credit to have theoretical (and real) content. By the same token, Marx stressed that capitalist crises typically involve the collapse of the system of credit into the system of money which lies at the foundations of the system of credit.[14] Monetary famine is a typical feature of credit crises, reflecting the prior and fundamental character of money compared to credit.

This analytical order is a distinguishing feature of Marxist theory of money and credit, setting it apart from 'credit theories of money' – theories that essentially presuppose the prior existence of credit to derive a concept of money. Schumpeter's *Theory of Economic Development* is typical of this approach, also adopted by much of contemporary sociology and anthropology of credit money, as is shown in Chapter 4. Ultimately 'credit theories of money' dispute the fundamental idea that money is a spontaneous outgrowth of commodity exchange, thus setting themselves apart from classical political economy but also from neoclassical and Marxist economics.[15]

Although Hilferding organized his analysis of money and credit in a standard Marxist way, his theory of money attracted severe criticism from Marxist theorists. In *Imperialism*, Lenin called it 'mistaken', but without explaining his remark.[16] It is instructive, consequently, to consider Hilferding's theory of money in some detail, first, to establish what is problematic with it and, second, to identify the fundamental

---

13   See Karl Marx, *Capital*, vol. 1, London: Penguin/NLR, 1976, ch. 1, 3.

14   Ibid., ch. 3.

15   For further discussion of the issues involved, see the debate carried out in the following texts: Ben Fine and Costas Lapavitsas, 'Markets and Money in Social Science: What Role for Economics?', *Economy and Society* 29:3, 2000; Viviana Zelizer, 'Fine Tuning the Zelizer View', *Economy and Society* 29:3, 2000; Viviana Zelizer, 'Pasts and Futures of Economics Sociology', *American Behavioral Scientist* 50:8, 2007; Geoffrey Ingham, 'Fundamentals of a Theory of Money: Untangling Fine, Lapavitsas and Zelizer', *Economy and Society* 30:3, 2001; Geoffrey Ingham, 'Further Reflections on the Ontology of Money: Responses to Lapavitsas and Dodd', *Economy and Society* 35:2, 2006; and Costas Lapavitsas, 'The Social Relations Of Money as Universal Equivalent: A Response to Ingham', *Economy and Society* 34:3, 2005.

16   V.I. Lenin, *Imperialism, the Highest Stage of Capitalism*, in *Collected Works*, vol. 22, Moscow: Progress Publishers, 1964, p. 195.

elements of a theory of money necessary for the analysis of financialization, fully discussed in Chapter 4.

Money

Hilferding first established the 'necessity' of money by postulating two generic types of society: those organized consciously, through traditional practices or planning, and those organized unconsciously, through market exchange.[17] The latter must evidently possess some means of impersonally validating each producer's efforts; for Hilferding, this is the defining aspect of money. There is certainly support for this argument in Marx's general discussion of money in the *Grundrisse*, as is shown in Chapter 4. However, Hilferding's argument bears little relation to Marx's derivation of money as the independent form of value (or the universal equivalent) through analysis of the contradictory nature of the commodity and the form of value.[18] His theory of the necessity of money is ideally abstract and does not offer an integral connection between commodity value and money.

Nonetheless, Hilferding's analysis of the circulation of money and money's forms has several strengths. Following Marx, Hilferding laid out the principles of determination of the quantity of money required in circulation.[19] He differentiated between commodity money and fiat paper money, associating the latter with money's function as means of circulation. His analysis of fiat money was also in standard Marxist mould, since he argued that overissue of fiat money would lead to inflation. His writings, finally, were characterized by an underlying tendency to treat gold as an indispensable aspect of the capitalist monetary system.

Hilferding was also careful to distinguish between fiat and credit money, associating the latter with money's function as means of payment.[20] Again following Marx, he argued that credit money emerges in credit transactions among capitalists which give rise to private instruments of debt, or bills of exchange. When Hilferding subsequently discussed money's function as means of hoarding, he actually improved on Marx.[21] By bringing together Marx's comments scattered across the three volumes of *Capital*, Hilferding put forth a systematic theory of money hoard formation as industrial capital

---

17 Hilferding, *Finance Capital*, ch. 1.

18 See Karl Marx, *A Contribution to the Critique of Political Economy*, Moscow: Progress Published, 1970, pp. 42–6; Karl Marx, *Grundrisse*, London: Penguin/NLR, 1973, pp. 142–5; Karl Marx, *Capital*, vol. 1, London: Penguin/NLR, 1976, ch. 1, sec. 3. For a recent treatment of the issue, drawing on Marx, see Costas Lapavitsas, 'The Emergence of Money in Commodity Exchange, or Money as Monopolist of the Ability to Buy', *Review of Political Economy* 17:4, 2005, pp. 549–69.

19 Marx, *Capital*, vol. 1, ch. 3; and Rudolf Hilferding, *Finance Capital*, London: Routledge & Kegan Paul, 1981, ch. 2.

20 Hilferding, *Finance Capital*, ch. 3.

21 Ibid., ch. 4.

goes through its normal, circular motion. The fundamental insight he offered – again originating in Marx – was that money hoards are subsequently mobilized by banks to be advanced as credit.

In sum, three aspects of Hilferding's discussion of money are important to analysis of contemporary financialization, all deriving from Marx's theory of money. First and foremost, Hilferding considered money to be the cornerstone of the structure of credit and finance. Second, he differentiated clearly (and theoretically) among the key forms of money in mature capitalism: commodity, fiat, and credit. Third, he located the structural sources of credit in money hoards systematically created in the normal operations of the circuit of capital.

But Hilferding's treatment of money, particularly of its forms and functions, also has notable deficiencies for the purpose of analysing financialization. Hilferding appeared implicitly to assume that gold is an indispensable form of money for advanced capitalist monetary systems, and in this respect he was perhaps typical of Marxist theorists of his day. Consequently, he left little room for analysing the displacement of gold by valueless credit money and, more significantly, for the conscious management of credit money by the state throughout the twentieth century. Both of these features of money are vital to financialization.

To a degree this absence is surprising for a theorist who came later to believe in 'organized' capitalism. For, if there is one element of 'organized' capitalism that has become progressively stronger throughout the twentieth century it is precisely the management of domestic credit money. Monopoly control over domestic money by the central bank has countermanded the tendency toward 'disorganization' that financialization has brought on its wake mostly through deregulation of various markets. The state management of domestic credit money has been essential to financialization, particularly in confronting the crises to which financialization has led.

The theory of money required for the analysis of financialization should take Marx's and Hilferding's analysis as point of departure, but also seek to develop the insights of both in line with the profound monetary changes in the intervening decades. For one thing, it is important to account for the forcible exclusion of gold from domestic and international transactions, which has become the practical reality of capitalist circulation in the twentieth century. For another, it is necessary to analyse the progressive domination of contemporary monetary processes by various forms of credit money. Chapter 4 discusses these topics by placing Marxist analysis of money within the broader context of monetary theory and paying particular attention to the following two issues.[22]

---

22   Makoto Itoh and Costas Lapavitsas, *Political Economy of Money and Finance*, London: Macmillan, 1999, ch. 1, 2, 3; Costas Lapavitsas, 'The Theory of Credit Money: A Structural Analysis', *Science and Society* 55:3, 1991, pp. 291–322. Costas Lapavitsas, 'The Banking School and the Monetary Thought of Karl Marx', *Cambridge Journal of Economics* 18:5, 1994, pp. 447–61; Costas

First, the monetary basis of financialization has been created by the gradual emergence of domestic money monopolistically issued by the central bank and backed by state instruments of debt. This is a form of valueless legal tender that combines aspects of credit and fiat money and rests on the power of the modern state, including the ability to intervene in the economy. It is also a form of money that draws heavily on the conventions, customs, and legal practices that sustain social and individual trust in its 'moneyness'.[23] This form of domestic money has allowed the capitalist class to manipulate monetary processes to protect the extraction of profit, including from the financial sphere.

Second, the monetary basis of financialization has been created by the international function of money – that is, by world money. This is probably the most distinctive function of money discussed by Marx though Hilferding largely ignored it. The gist of Marx's argument is that, in the world arena, the commodity aspect of money is fully restored, fiat and credit forms of money are marginalized, and gold once again reigns supreme.[24] Impersonal (and non-national) commodity money is called upon to act as world money – as international means of hoarding, payment, and transfer of value.

Marx's view of world money was developed when gold dominated international monetary transfers, while Hilferding's book was written when the gold standard was at its peak, shortly before being abandoned in 1914. Briefly put, for most of the second half of the nineteenth century, sterling (freely convertible into gold) acted as reliable means of hoarding and payment internationally; London provided clearing and lending facilities to the rest of the world; the bill on London financed world trade; and the gold hoards of the Bank of England were the ultimate source of world money. Transfers of gold (gold drains) among nations characterized the international dimension of economic crises, while access to gold dictated a nation's ability to confront the external pressures of crisis. It is striking that neither Hilferding nor Lenin made much of the purely monetary aspects of the world market in their respective analyses of imperialism.

Lapavitsas, 'Money and the Analysis of Capitalism: The Significance of Commodity Money', *Review of Radical Political Economics* 32:4, 2000, pp. 631–56; and Lapavitsas, 'The Emergence of Money in Commodity Exchange'.

23   There is scant Marxist literature on this issue. For the elements of an approach, though from different perspectives, see Duncan Foley, 'Marx's Theory of Money in Historical Perspective', in *Marx's Theory of Money: Modern Appraisals*, ed. Fred Moseley, London: Palgrave Macmillan, 2004; Costas Lapavitsas, 'The Classical Adjustment Mechanism of International Balances: Marx's Critique', in *Contributions to Political Economy* 15, 1996; Costas Lapavitsas, 'Money as Monopolist of the Ability to Buy', in *Marx's Theory of Money: Modern Appraisals*, ed. Fred Moseley, London: Palgrave Macmillan, 2004; and Costas Lapavitsas, 'Power and Trust as Constituents of Money and Credit', *Historical Materialism* 14:1, 2006.

24   Marx, *Capital*, vol. 1, pp. 240–4.

The role of world money is very different under conditions of financialization. World money has had no clear connection with gold since the collapse of the Bretton Woods system in 1971–73. The US dollar is the form of money closest to world money under present conditions; but the dollar is valueless legal tender (in the US) that combines aspects of credit and fiat money. It evidently lacks the impersonal, value-containing character of gold. At best the dollar is quasi-world-money, and as such it relies on trust and customs present in the world market, but also on the political and military power of the US as the dominant imperialist power. Precisely this aspect of the dollar has allowed the transfer of value from the rest of the world to the US as financialization has spread its tentacles across the world. The dollar has lent a monetary aspect to contemporary imperialism that was absent in Hilferding's and Lenin's day. It has also considerably exacerbated the tensions and instabilities of the world market, particularly in connection with the global flows of loanable capital.

Credit

Hilferding's analysis of credit is on firmer ground than his analysis of money, and reveals the true strengths of his theory. In the spirit and letter of Marx, Hilferding produced an analytical layering of capitalist credit relations according to their intrinsic character.[25] This fundamental ordering of credit relations characterizes the theoretical treatment of the credit system put forth in Chapter 5 below to support the analysis of financialization.

More specifically, Hilferding first discussed commercial (or trade) credit, which arises spontaneously between capitalist enterprises and takes the form of bills of exchange.[26] This is the most elementary form of credit that does not presuppose the existence of financial institutions. The innovative element of Hilferding's analysis in this respect was to associate commercial credit with 'circulation credit'; commercial credit was assumed to be advanced typically to finance the needs of non-financial enterprises for circulating capital.

Monetary (or banking) credit is a more advanced form of credit which involves the lending of money and is mediated by financial institutions. Furthermore, banks intervene and centralize the flows of commercial credit by replacing bills with their own credit. Matching the institutional reality of Hilferding's day, banks were assumed to discount bills with their own banknotes which circulated as an advanced form of credit money. Banks were also assumed to collect idle money hoards generated in the circuits of industrial capital, which they turned into loanable money capital and made available to functioning capitalists through lending. This is 'capital or investment credit' that earns the rate of interest.

The critical step subsequently taken by Hilferding was to associate the supply of

---

25   Marx, *Capital*, vol. 1, ch. 3; and *Capital*, vol. 3, part 5.
26   Hilferding, *Finance Capital*, p. 83.

investment credit with the formation of fixed capital by industrial enterprises, ultimately allowing him to construct the concept of finance capital.[27] Hilferding observed that investment credit necessarily generates a close link between banks and enterprises since it finances fixed capital investment and its repayment takes a long time. Consequently, banks are obliged to collect information and to monitor enterprise operations. This penetrating insight was advanced decades before neoclassical banking theory began to appreciate the importance of monitoring and 'commitment' relations between banks and enterprises, briefly discussed in Chapter 5 of this book. Unlike contemporary mainstream theory, moreover, Hilferding was alive to power relations and indicated that the monitoring activities of banks allowed them to control industrial capital.

However, Hilferding went astray by asserting that, as the scale of capitalist production and fixed investment grew over time, industrial enterprises would be forced increasingly to rely on investment credit, thus finding themselves under the tutelage of banks. For Hilferding, this is an underlying, secular tendency of capitalism that ultimately leads to the emergence of finance capital. This aspect of his argument is clearly incorrect, as Sweezy noted already in the 1940s in *The Theory of Capitalist Development*.[28] There is no secular tendency toward greater reliance of industrial enterprises on bank loans to finance investment. On the contrary, since the end of the Second World War the requirements of investment in developed countries have been met increasingly through retained profits. This trend underpins financialization.[29]

In this respect, Hilferding paid a hefty price for not undertaking a concrete analysis of the financing of investment in the leading capitalist countries of his time. Instead, he relied on the abstract argument that as the scale of production grows so must the reliance of enterprises on external funds to finance fixed investment. This argument appears plausible but there is little empirical support for it as a secular trend of advanced capitalism. It is likely that Hilferding generalized unduly from credit transactions between German and Austrian corporations and banks at the end of the nineteenth century, which he interpreted as the future of advanced capitalism. In contrast, financialization is characterized by increasing distance between enterprises and banks, rising relative autonomy of finance and a turn of finance toward households, shown empirically in chapters 7 and 8.

---

27 Ibid., pp. 94–6.

28 Paul M. Sweezy, *The Theory of Capitalist Development*, New York: Monthly Review Press, 1942.

29 Not a little ink has been spilled on this issue by Marxists seeking – in vain – to show that banks have remained in control of non-financial enterprises. For a perspective on US banks and corporations that is directly critical of Sweezy's view, see for instance, David M. Kotz, *Bank Control of Large Corporations in the United States*, Berkeley: University of California Press, 1978. However, for the opposite view, see Edward S. Herman, 'Do Bankers Control Corporations?', *Monthly Review* 25:2, 1973; and for a telling response to Kotz, see Edward S. Herman, 'Kotz on Banker Control', *Monthly Review* 31:4, 1979.

Stock markets

Hilferding subsequently turned his attention to joint-stock capital, the stock market, the futures market, and banks as capitalist enterprises. His analysis of these topics again rested on Marx, but was also highly original, representing an advance over Marx's disorganized and largely incidental remarks in *Capital*. His discussion of joint-stock capital, in particular, stressed the separation of ownership from control of capital. Consequently, Hilferding was led to examine the character of the shareholder as capitalist, including the differences between shareholder and classical capitalist entrepreneur. Following Marx, Hilferding treated investment in shares as akin to moneylending.[30] Funds invested in shares come from society's great pool of loanable money, given that shares can be easily sold and the shareholder could secure return of capital without much trouble.

Separation of ownership from control turns the shareholder into an agent who advances money capital in the expectation of earning interest-like returns while maintaining liquidity; effectively, the shareholder is a rentier. Always keeping an eye on power relations, Hilferding stressed that the main beneficiaries of the separation of ownership from control are the large shareholders, who end up controlling huge enterprises with a relatively small capital outlay. The emergence of joint-stock capitalism brings a shareholding oligarchy, not a shareholding democracy.[31]

Hilferding's focus on the specific character of joint-stock capital is one of the strengths of his book, and provides a key element for the analysis of financialization. The separation of ownership from control, the transformation of capitalist owners into shareholders, and the emergence of giant, impersonally run enterprises have been fundamental to the transformation of capitalism throughout the twentieth century. They are also, in large measure, characteristic of financialization, as is shown in Chapter 6 of this book. However, for Hilferding, these phenomena were also constitutive elements of the advancing socialization of the economy. He considered joint-stock giants to have some capacity to plan the future as well as taking action to lessen the anarchy and instability of markets. There is no reason to accept this assumption, even though it marked the approach of Hilferding to mature capitalism.

The transformation of the active capitalist into a shareholder, moreover, has implications for profits and financial asset prices. In this connection, Hilferding offered the first thorough-going Marxist analysis of share price determination as discounted future profits.[32] This is an innovative part of his book and includes the concept of 'promoter's profit', *Gründergewinn*, better translated as 'founder's profit', which is not to be found in Marx's work. 'Founder's profit' is a pivotal concept for the analysis of financial profit in general, and of capital gains in particular. Its importance to financialization is intui-

---

30 See, for instance, Marx, *Capital*, vol. 3, pp. 567–8; and Hilferding, *Finance Capital*, pp. 108–9.

31 Hilferding, *Finance Capital*, pp. 118–20.

32 Ibid., pp. 110–16.

tively obvious, but applying it to contemporary capitalism is far from straightforward, as is shown in detail in Chapter 6.

The core of Hilferding's argument regarding 'founder's profit' is that the expected return on shares tends to be equal to the rate of interest (plus a risk premium) given that shareholders are similar to lenders of money. Marx's analysis of finance, furthermore, claimed that the average rate of interest is normally below the average rate of profit, a view that was accepted by Hilferding.[33] The implications are profound since share prices result from discounting an enterprise's expected profits. Furthermore, the actual capital invested in the enterprise is equivalent to the discounted value of the expected profits. However, the rate of discount used in the former case (shares) would be the rate of interest (plus risk premium) while in the latter case (actual capital) it would be the (higher) rate of profit. Consequently, the total value raised through a share issue would be greater than the amount of capital actually invested in the enterprise, the difference being founder's profit. For Hilferding, founder's profit amounted to capitalized future profit of enterprise, that is, to profit that remains to the functioning capitalist after payment of interest. The issuers of shares – but also the banks that manage the issuing of shares – are able to obtain the future profit of enterprise in one fell swoop. Thus, 'founder's profit' is a further element contributing to the emergence of finance capital.

Hilferding's concept opens a path to analysing the gigantic financial profits characteristic of financialization. The relationship between loanable capital advanced in financial markets, financial asset prices, expected flows of surplus value and capital gains is integral to determining financial profit. Furthermore, the theoretical link between future profit of enterprise and capital gains would necessarily draw on differences in rates of remuneration among the various agents involved in handling loanable capital. With these points in mind, the concept of founder's profit could contribute to developing a theory of financial profit and capital gains, as is shown in Chapter 6.

Finally, Hilferding asserted that bank profits from transactions in financial markets also represent a share of the future profits of enterprise.[34] He claimed that these profits accrue to the banks because of committing money capital to share transactions while maintaining the confidence of society in the stock market. This is not a strong argument since investment bank profits accrue for a variety of services provided by banks to agents trading in financial markets. Furthermore, a prominent area of bank profitability in financial markets in the course of financialization has been trading on own account in financial markets, which has certainly involved making profits out of other people's loanable capital. The analytical path opened by Hilferding in this respect needs to be further developed, if Marxist theory of finance is more fully to account for contemporary financial profit.

---

33   Marx, *Capital*, vol. 3, p. 482; and Hilferding, *Finance Capital*, pp. 198–12.
34   Hilferding, *Finance Capital*, pp. 127–9.

Finance capital and trading blocs

Hilferding subsequently put forth his main theoretical innovation – the concept of finance capital.[35] Put briefly, as capitalism matures, the scale of production expands, bringing an increase in fixed capital requirements. Consequently, capital mobility is reduced and the equalization of profit rates is hampered due to persistent over-capacity. Industrial sectors that have large volumes of capital sank into fixed investment find it difficult to raise the rate of profit. Hence capitalists in these sectors are led to merge and to acquire each other's enterprises, thereby eliminating competition, cyclical fluctuations and commercial middlemen. In short, the centralization of capital is exacerbated, thus raising profitability.

Joint-stock companies are particularly suitable for the centralization of capital since they facilitate control of enterprises via relatively small shareholdings. Crucially, centralization also spreads to banks. The emergence of huge joint-stock banks encourages further reduction of industrial competition in order precisely to protect bank profits. Thus, mature capitalism is dominated by centralized capital that consciously restricts competition to protect profitability. Hilferding offered a detailed discussion of the organizational forms of centralized capital, including cartels and trusts.[36] Sweezy was sufficiently impressed to state that Hilferding's discussion could be accepted with 'few reservations'.[37]

For Hilferding, finance capital was a new form of capital that emerged on the basis of centralized industrial and banking capital. Indeed, it was an amalgam of the two: large banks and industrial corporations were drawn together as corporations borrowed to finance fixed capital formation and as banks took a leading role in floating shares in the stock market. Banks became closely involved with the running of enterprises and made large gains in the form of founder's profit, while retaining much of their own capital in liquid, money form. Consequently, banks had a significant power advantage over industrial capital – they were the senior partners in finance capital dictating its actions and behaviour.

Hilferding's concept of finance capital has played a tremendously important role in the development of Marxist thought. It was widely accepted by his contemporaries, above all, by Lenin in his theory of imperialism.[38] In the course of the twentieth century, finance capital often became synonymous with monopoly capital in Marxist literature, mostly due to Lenin's influence. Its relevance has sometimes been asserted in conditions that barely resemble those of Hilferding's day – such as the post-war boom of the 1950s and 1960s – and even by writers who have otherwise adopted a critical perspective on Lenin's theory of imperialism.[39]

---

35 Ibid., p. 225.

36 Ibid., ch. 11, 12.

37 Sweezy, *The Theory of Capitalist Development*, p. 266.

38 Lenin, *Imperialism, the Highest Stage of Capitalism*, p. 226 Note though that Luxemburg avoided the concept of finance capital in her classic *Accumulation of Capital*.

39 See, for instance, the works of Michael Barratt-Brown. The effort to coax Hilferding's notion

Hilferding's concept should be treated with considerable caution. The tendency toward monopolistic competition has been present throughout the twentieth century, including since the 1970s. However, in practice, a broad range of relations has prevailed among contemporary industrial and financial capitals, often with national characteristics. Moreover, as was noted above, there is no universal long-term tendency for industrial capital to rely on bank loans to finance fixed capital formation.

In short, finance capital does not adequately capture the complexity and range of relations between industrial and banking capital in the course of the twentieth century. Nevertheless, the concept is still important because it focuses attention on the organic and institutional links that have emerged between these two types of capital in the course of capitalist development. Links of this nature were merely incipient when Marx wrote *Capital*, but have become characteristic of capitalism since the end of the nineteenth century and exhibit a variety of forms across particular countries.

Banks are not the dominant partner in bank–industry relations under conditions of financialized capitalism. Even in provision of external finance to industry, banks compete against other financial institutions, including pension funds, money trusts and insurance companies. Furthermore, industrial and commercial capitals systematically engage in financial activities on own account. These include independent issuing of debt in open markets (commercial paper, bonds, warrants, and so on) supplying consumer and trade credit, engaging in foreign exchange markets as well as transacting in forward, futures and derivatives markets. Evidence for the altered practices of both enterprises and banks under conditions of financialization is adduced in chapters 7 and 8.

Crises

Hilferding ascribed crises primarily to disproportionalities between the departments of the total social capital. In the great Social Democratic debate on capitalist economic crises, he thus broadly sided with Mikhail Tugan-Baranovsky's approach in *Les Crises industrielles en Angleterre*. He certainly rejected underconsumptionism which was soon to receive its developed form by Luxemburg in *The Accumulation of Capital*. While Hilferding believed that crises were an integral part of the behaviour of the capitalist economy, he dismissed the notion that capitalism would inevitably collapse of its own

---

into service for analysis of contemporary capitalism has not abated. Bülent Hoca, for instance, discusses Hilferding's notion with considerable sensitivity, but then seeks to link it to a putative general tendency of capital to 'financialize'. The result is to render finance capital devoid of all specificity, and hence not very meaningful for theoretical and empirical analysis. See Bülent Hoca, 'A Suggestion for a New Definition of the Concept of Finance Capital Using Marx's Notion of "Capital as Commodity"', *Cambridge Journal of Economics* 36: 2012.

accord, as Schumpeter has noted approvingly.[40] He also discussed the role of credit and money capital in exacerbating the business cycle.

Of greater significance, however, was his analysis of the changed form of crises due to the emergence of finance capital, hinting at his later concept of 'organized capitalism'. Cartels and large banks make banking crises less likely as well as less severe by suppressing competition. Since cartels and banks operate on an enlarged scale of accumulation, they can guarantee a minimum volume of production and circulation, thus also reducing the disruption of credit in a crisis. Furthermore, joint-stock corporations can rationally assess the prospects of production and profitability. Finally, large banks are able to take a more rational view of the credit requirements of the economy, thus reducing the speculative use of credit characteristic of the early days of capitalism.

For Hilferding, these factors ameliorated crises as capitalism developed, although he also thought that crises could not be finally eliminated by finance capital. In this connection, Hilferding claimed that Germany and the US were the paradigmatic countries of advanced capitalist relations, dismissing England for her 'backward' credit system.[41] This view was pivotal to his analysis of imperialism, considered below.

Imperialism

Hilferding's theory of imperialism has been fundamental to the classical Marxist analysis of imperialism largely because of its influence on Lenin. The issue of imperialism is, of course, relevant to the analysis of financialization and aspects of it are considered in subsequent chapters. Suffice it at this point briefly to revise key arguments from the classical Marxist debates at the turn of the twentieth century which will help specify the content of subordinate financialization in subsequent chapters.

Discussion of imperialism inevitably turns on Lenin's work, the standard reference point for Marxist analysis since the end of the First World War.[42] Lenin's theory, moreover, has left its imprint on political practice in developed and developing countries throughout the twentieth century. Examining the large literature attached to these phe-

---

40   Joseph A. Schumpeter, *Imperialism and Social Classes*, New York: Augustus Kelly, 1951, p. 108; Joseph A. Schumpeter, *Capitalism, Socialism and Democracy*, 5th ed., London: George Allen & Unwin, 1976, p. 41.

41   Hilferding, *Finance Capital*, p. 293. An early and incisive critique of Hilferding reliance on German/Austrian phenomena was made by Kozo Uno (*Keizai Seisakuron*, Tokyo: Kobundo Shobo, 1936, part 3, ch. 2), who suggested that finance capital actually takes several forms, and British finance capital is heavily dependent on stock markets. Uno was fully aware of the importance of joint-stock capital for Hilferding's analysis (part 3, ch.1). The specific character of joint-stock capital was vital to Uno defining the stage of 'imperialism' in contrast to the stages of 'liberal' capitalism and 'mercantilism'.

42   Lenin's view of imperialism was developed in a variety of writings during 1915–17; see Bibliography.

nomena would require a separate volume. Thus, Lenin's work is considered exclusively from the perspective of its differences and similarities with Hilferding's analysis with a view to establishing a theoretical framework for financialization. The importance of Hilferding's *Finance Capital* in this respect lies in providing economic foundations for Lenin's theory, including the core concept of finance capital.

The classical Marxist debates on imperialism were concerned with the sudden surge of European imperial expansion during the last quarter of the nineteenth century, rather than with imperialism as a general historical phenomenon. It should be stressed that this is a merit, in view especially of mainstream theories that have often defined themselves in opposition to the Marxist approach.[43] By and large, classical Marxist theories avoided bland historical generalizations and related imperialism to well-defined economic processes of their era. They typically sought to account for phenomena such as the 'scramble for Africa' and the rise of militarism among European powers at the end of the nineteenth century.

These events had a shocking novelty for societies that had not known a major European war since 1815 and were pervaded by the ideological belief that capitalism meant rational progress in human affairs. It is also worth mentioning that classical Marxist explanations of imperialism shared common ground with the theory advanced by the liberal Hobson in *Imperialism*, for whom imperialism resulted from underconsumption at home that created the need to send capital abroad. Note further that Marxist theories were far more soundly based than Schumpeter's view of imperialism as an unfortunate 'atavistic' aspect inherited from feudalism by a fundamentally peaceful capitalism.[44]

Not surprisingly, there were substantial differences among the classical Marxist theories of imperialism. Thus, Kautsky linked imperialism to the need to secure markets internationally as well as to the tendency of agriculture to lag behind industry as capitalism developed. To ensure an adequate supply of agricultural commodities, industrial countries colonized agrarian countries.[45] For Kautsky, imperialism was an international policy chosen by the bourgeoisie, which could also be altered in a peaceful direction. In contrast, Luxemburg, in part three of her *Accumulation of Capital*, argued that the capitalist economy faced an insuperable problem in securing sufficient domestic demand to realize rising volumes of surplus value. This led to a search for foreign markets as capitalism matured, involving violence and political domination of one country by another. Imperialism, for Luxemburg, was not a matter of policy but a process that sprang from the deep core of capitalist accumulation.

---

43 See, for instance, John Gallagher and Ronald Robinson, 'The Imperialism of Free Trade', *Economic History Review* 6:1, 1953; and David Fieldhouse, *The West and the Third World*, Oxford: Blackwell, 1999.

44 Joseph A. Schumpeter, *Imperialism and Social Classes*, New York: Augustus Kelly, 1951, p. 84.

45 Patrick Goode, *Karl Kautsky: Selected Political Writings*, London: Macmillan, 1983, pp. 74–96. See also Karl Kautsky, 'Ultra-imperialism', *New Left Review* 59, Jan–Feb 1970.

Hilferding treated imperialism as a policy of the bourgeoisie, but the true strength of his theory came from his focus on the historical inevitability of imperialism, particularly for Germany which had developed late. To establish his thesis, Hilferding drew directly on the concept of finance capital as well as on ideas that were common currency among Viennese Austro-Marxists. His point of departure was the aggressive tariff policies that were generally adopted in the last quarter of the nineteenth century. This phenomenon had already been examined from a Marxist perspective by Bauer, who related imperialism to a shift from the protective tariffs of early capitalism (seeking to shield domestic industry) to the aggressive tariffs of mature capitalism (seeking to destroy foreign industry).[46] It is important to stress this point in view of today's not infrequent – and erroneous – association of nineteenth-century capitalism with 'free trade'. In practice international capitalism was characterized by increasing restrictions on trade from the 1870s to the outbreak of the First World War, with the exception of Britain.[47] Classical imperialism was closely associated with high and rising trade barriers.

Hilferding gave theoretical depth to the analysis of aggressive tariff policy by relating it to finance capital.[48] Cartels favoured aggressive tariffs because these resulted in an exclusive territory that shored up profitability and stabilized domestic combinations of enterprises. Therefore, competition among finance capitals took place via creation of exclusive, tariff-protected territories, instead of merely selling commodities. On this basis, Hilferding developed an argument explaining the export of money capital. The creation of exclusive territories limited the scope for other cartels to increase commodity exports, thus encouraging the export of money capital. Hilferding took capital export to mean capital invested abroad which remained under domestic control and whose profits were repatriated, that is, a type of foreign direct investment. He evidently thought that export of capital took place toward less developed countries that offered lower wages and other advantages to corporations.

Hilferding concluded that the imperialist policy of finance capital represented a major rupture with the laissez-faire policies characteristic of mid-nineteenth-century Britain. The model countries of finance capital were Germany and the US. Finance capital – joint-stock capital in association with banks – made possible the mobilization of Germany's scattered resources allowing the country to catch up. Late development also meant weaker social opposition to advanced technology. As Germany overtook

---

46 Otto Bauer, *The Question of Nationalities and Social Democracy*, Minneapolis: University of Minnesota Press, 2000, pp. 370–81.

47 See Paul Bairoch, *Economics and World History*, Hemel Hempstead: Harvester Wheatsheaf, 1993; and Paul Bairoch and Richard Kozul-Wright, 'Globalization Myths: Some Historical Reflections on Integration, Industrialization and Growth in the World Economy', UNCTAD Discussion Papers No. 113, March 1996.

48 Hilferding, *Finance Capital*, ch. 21.

Britain, its finance capital came to rely on the state, particularly on military power to sustain the creation of exclusive territories. Imperialism inevitably led to competition in armaments, to constant threat of war among the imperialist countries, and to racism toward the dominated.

To recap, Hilferding related imperialism to the epochal transformation of capitalism represented by finance capital. Imperialism sprang from the transformed mechanisms of capitalist competition and accumulation. It thus had a specific economic content that gave rise to phenomena such as the emergence of giant cartels and banks, aggressive tariffs, and export of capital. At a stroke, Hilferding was able to account for key political phenomena, such as militarism and the threat of war, while also arguing that the working class had to oppose imperialism.

It is hardly surprising that Hilferding's theory appealed to Lenin, who adopted the concept of finance capital as well as the view of territorial (imperial) exclusivity through tariffs and the consequent export of capital. From Hilferding also came the notion of rising militarism as well as of finance capital deploying the state in order to succeed in international competition. Reliance on Hilferding, finally, is apparent even in the subtitle of Lenin's main work on imperialism (the 'highest' or 'latest' or 'new' stage of capitalism) which echoes the subtitle of Hilferding's book ('the latest phase of capitalist development').

Nevertheless, Lenin placed his own stamp on the theory of imperialism, thus turning it into standard reference for Marxists. Lenin produced, above all, a political pamphlet that was concerned with the outbreak and likely outcomes of the First World War. To be sure, the work rested on voluminous research on the major capitalist economies, plus a theoretical analysis of the periodization of capitalism. Lenin, furthermore, was concerned to provide empirical substantiation for his claims, and his short book carried far more factual data than Hilferding's tome. But it remained primarily a political intervention, as is evidenced by its emphasis not only on territorial exclusivity among cartels but also on the territorial re-division of the world as a cause of imperialist war.

In terms of its theoretical underpinnings, moreover, Lenin's work differed from Hilferding's in two respects. First, while accepting the concept of finance capital, Lenin presented it as the outcome of rising monopoly tendencies within industry and finance.[49] There is no doubt that Hilferding had also stressed monopolistic (and cartels), but Lenin's emphasis was of different order of significance. He placed enormous importance on the intrinsic tendency in capitalist economies for laissez-faire competition to be replaced by monopolistic competition dominated by giant enterprises and giant banks. Thus, finance capital resulted from the coming together of enterprises and banks, with the latter holding the upper hand. Note also that while Lenin's argument rested on a theoretical understanding of capitalist competition, it lacked Hilferding's analysis of the forms of credit and the financial requirements of industrial

---

49   Lenin, *Imperialism, the Highest Stage of Capitalism*, ch. 2, 3.

corporations. Bukharin's *Imperialism and World Economy*, incidentally, also relied on rising monopolies and finance capital, though – going well beyond Hilferding – Bukharin claimed that the world economy comprised competing national units resembling gigantic enterprises.

Second, and more significant, Lenin admired the liberal Hobson and borrowed several of his arguments. Hobson, in Chapter 4 of his *Imperialism*, had stressed underconsumption and capital export, believing that imperialism entailed the emergence of 'parasitical' capitalism that exported loanable capital and lived off bond coupons. Lenin adopted much of Hobson's view, claiming that the leading imperialist countries systematically absorbed interest payments from poorer countries across the world.[50] These 'rentier' countries, furthermore, contained a 'labour aristocracy', a thin layer at the top of the working class that was bought off with some of the coupon clippings. Hilferding kept aloof from such ideas. This was probably related to his theoretical analysis of the credit system as a mechanism for the reallocation of idle sums of money within the capitalist class. The implications of this point for the analysis of financialization are profound, as is shown briefly below but also in chapters 5 and 6 of this book.

What is the relevance of these theories for the analysis of financialization and the evolution of capitalism in late twentieth century?[51] It is worth noting at the outset that classical Marxist theories of imperialism offer stronger insights into contemporary capitalism than the dependency theories of the 1960s and 1970s. The vast literature on 'underdevelopment', for instance, has become rapidly dated in the face of financialization and global deregulation. It is true that dependency theorists have focused far more than the classical Marxists on the form taken by capitalism in the countries of the 'periphery'. But, even in this respect, the emergence of dynamic industrial capitalism in the 'periphery' – above all, in East Asia – hardly fits with 'the development of underdevelopment'.[52] Similarly, the emphasis of classical Marxist theories on political economy is a strong advantage compared to much contemporary theorizing on 'global' capitalism. The latter often focuses on the political, sociological, military, ethical and moral aspects of modern imperialism, rather than its connection to capitalist accumu-

---

50 Ibid., pp. 276–85.

51 A summary of Marxist theories of imperialism, which still repays reading, was put forth by in Anthony Brewer, *Marxist Theories of Imperialism*, London: Routledge, 1990; see also Ernest Mandel, *Marxist Economic Theory*, London: Merlin, 1968; and Roger Owen and Bob Sutcliffe (eds), *Studies in the Theory of Imperialism*, London: Longman, 1972. For a broader work that also discusses development issues, see Albert Szymanski, *The Logic of Imperialism*, New York: Praeger, 1981.

52 Most clearly seen in the loss of relevance of the work of Andre Gunder Frank, but also Samir Amin.

lation.[53] But even explicitly Marxist work on contemporary imperialism has generally been short of foundations in political economy.[54]

The classical Marxist theory of imperialism has an immediate relevance to several of the key features of financialization. Thus, it stresses the centralization of capital as a typical trend of mature capitalism; mergers and acquisitions have been a salient feature of global economic activity since the 1970s, providing scope for the extraction of financial profits. By the same token, multinational corporations dominate the world market, as is shown in subsequent chapters. Furthermore, the theory identifies the export of capital as integral to imperialism, but also as an aspect of fundamental transformation of capitalist economies. The world market since the late 1970s has been characterized by successive waves of capital exports that have shaped global financialization, discussed in chapters 8 and 9.

But there are also aspects of the classical Marxist theory of imperialism that are currently irrelevant, or highly specific to the first bout of financial ascendancy. Thus, while contemporary imperialism seeks territorial control, there is no dominant tendency toward aggressive tariffs or exclusive territorial rights, much less toward formal colonial empires. Furthermore, the tendency toward capital export is not the result of territorial exclusivity, and nor is it characteristic merely of relations between developed and developing countries. The greatest capital flows have occurred among developed countries; more poignantly, in the 2000s there have also been reverse net flows of capital from developing to developed countries. This is a striking aspect of financialization connected to the contemporary role of world money, which is absent from the classical Marxist theories of imperialism.

It is remarkable in this respect that the dominant imperialist power, the US, has become a huge borrower, relying on inflows of loanable money capital even from

---

53 This is evident in the influential work of Michael Hardt and Antonio Negri (*Empire*, Cambridge, MA: Harvard University Press, 2000), which is devoid of political economy. See the devastating critique of Atilio A. Boron, *Empire and Imperialism: A Critical Reading of Michael Hardt and Antonio Negri*, London: Zed Books, 2005; see also Finn Bowring, 'From the Mass Worker to the Multitude: A Theoretical Contextualisation of Hardt and Negri's *Empire*', *Capital and Class* 83, Summer 2004; and Paul Thompson, 'Foundation and Empire: A Critique of Hardt and Negri', *Capital and Class* 86, Summer 2005, pp. 73–98.

54 As in the influential offerings by David Harvey (*The New Imperialism*, New York: Oxford University Press, 2003) and Ellen Meiksins Wood (*Empire of Capital*, London: Verso, 2003). The relative absence of political economy is in sharp contrast to earlier work by Bill Warren but also by Prabhat Patnaik, both of whom have been concerned with the economics of imperialism, even if drawing very different conclusions from each other. See Bill Warren, *Imperialism Pioneer of Capitalism*, London: Verso, 1980; Prabhat Patnaik (ed.), *Lenin and Imperialism*, London: Sangham, 1986; and Prabhat Patnaik, 'Globalization of Capital and the Theory of Imperialism', *Social Scientist* 24:11/12, 1996, pp. 5–17.

developing countries to finance domestic consumption. This phenomenon fits badly with classical Marxist perceptions of dominant imperialist countries as world lenders, not to mention the notion of 'parasitical' imperialists living off coupon clippings from lending abroad. At the same time, command over world money has allowed the US to extract benefits directly from even the poorest countries in ways that would have been impossible in the classical era, as is shown in Chapter 8. This is a key aspect of global domination as well as of subordinate financialization.

These observations point to an underlying weakness in Hilferding's overall analysis of capitalist transformation and imperialism. As was mentioned at the beginning of this chapter, Hilferding sought to establish structural, 'endogenous' reasons for the emergence of finance capital but without analysing the evolution of production and the labour market; moreover, throughout his exposition, he focused mainly on Germany and Austria. Yet, the structure of the capitalist financial system and the connection between banking and industrial capital do not easily admit of 'endogenous' theorization, as is obvious with a century's hindsight.

Relations between production and finance tend to be historically specific, and subject to institutional and political factors that shape the financial system. The links between industrial capital and the credit system in the period of financialization have been far more variable than the simple picture of increasing reliance of industry on banks which Hilferding assumed. Moreover, financialization has witnessed the rising involvement of workers in the workings of the financial system in ways that would have been unthinkable to classical Marxists. While the classical Marxist debates on the first bout of financial ascendancy remain indispensable to analysing financialization, the current period is qualitatively different.

Part 2 POLITICAL ECONOMY OF FINANCIALIZATION

4. THE MONETARY BASIS OF FINANCIALIZED CAPITALISM

Monetary features of financialization

The first step in building a theoretical framework to analyse financialized capitalism is to establish the monetary underpinnings of the rise of finance. For Marxist political economy, money is an integral part of capitalist economies that provides both real and theoretical foundations for finance. In dialectical terms, money is the initial category, while credit and finance derive from the further unfolding of the category of money (and capital). Marxist theory of credit and finance is inherently monetary in the sense that it rests analytically on the theory of money.[1] The rise of financialized capitalism has depended on particular forms of money and monetary practices, the importance of which is demonstrated at various places throughout this book. Summarily put, there are three salient monetary features to financialization, which are further examined in this chapter.

First, the monetary terrain of financialization has been determined by the absence of commodity money from domestic monetary transactions, including from the operations of banking. Since the early 1970s – indeed for most of the twentieth century – commodity money (gold) has been a hoard of last resort held by central banks with minimal monetary functioning in practice.[2] The retreat of commodity money from monetary circulation has been accompanied by the complete domination of the monetary sphere by credit money. This is money that is normally generated by private financial institutions (banks) and comprises private promises to pay backed by a variety of financial assets, both private and public. It is the dominant form of money in advanced capitalism sustained by the corresponding development of the credit system. However, despite the dominance of credit money, the form of money has continued to evolve in the course of financialization, including the emergence of electronic money that differs qualitatively from credit money.

---

1   This fundamental theoretical point is often not appreciated even by Marxists who engage in analysis of finance. The appearance in English of Suzanne de Brunhoff's path-breaking work on Marx's theory of money has been important to establishing the primacy of monetary analysis (*Marx on Money*, New York: Urizen Books, 1976). However, the tendency toward credit-based theories of both money and finance has hardly gone away, as is shown below.

2   The largely passive holding of enormous gold hoards by contemporary central banks continues to be seen as an enigma by mainstream literature; see Joshua Aizenman and Kenta Inoue, 'Central Banks and Gold Puzzles', NBER Working Paper No. 17894, 2012.

Second, crucial to the ascendancy of private credit money has been its legal convertibility into state-backed money created by central banks. The latter is a hybrid form of money: it is partly credit since it is created through credit mechanisms (mostly lending by the central bank to private banks); it is partly fiat since it is inconvertible legal tender that normally rests on the state's promises to pay. This hybrid form of money is the ultimate lever of state power in the realm of finance because it allows the state to provide liquidity and to make payments at critical junctures. Financialization has been stamped by the conscious management of state-backed central bank money through various mechanisms of the state. Central banks have emerged as a leading public institution, typically under a façade of independence. The command exercised by states over central bank money has made sustained intervention in the field of finance possible throughout the period of financialization. The importance of control over state-backed credit money was made clear in the course of the global crisis of the 2000s, discussed in chapter 9.

Third, even more important for the emergence of financialization has been the evolution of the form and functioning of money in the world market. Gold has played a very minor role in international payments following the collapse in 1971–73 of the Bretton Woods Agreement which had stabilized exchange rates by fixing the convertibility of the US dollar into gold. Since then, commodity money has functioned as an international hoard of last resort, while the functions of international means of payment and means of hoarding have been taken over largely by the US dollar. The functioning of the dollar as quasi-world-money during the last four decades has been a development of paramount importance for the global spread of financialization. However, the world role of the dollar has also been contradictory and destabilizing, not least by affecting the international transfers of value and leading to flows of capital from poor to rich countries. It is shown in chapters 8 and 9 that accumulation of dollar reserves has contributed to financialization in developing countries as well as to the gigantic crisis of the 2000s.

It should also be mentioned, even if only for completeness, that money has placed its mark on the social outlook of financialized capitalism. Communal and associative bonds have shrunk; public provision has generally retreated and money has been re-strengthened as the pivot of a broad range of social interactions. The moral and ethical development of individuals in financialized capitalism has reflected the enhanced presence of money. After all, an integral feature of financialization has been the spreading of monetary relations in areas that were previously relatively aloof from monetary mechanisms, including health, education, transport and housing. The financialization of individual income has enabled money to penetrate deeply into the economic, social, moral, and customary life of households in financialized capitalism.

By no means, however, has the hold of money over society been inexorably strengthened in the decades of financialization. Often the ascendancy of money has been consciously opposed through collective action in several areas of social life. Associative forms of exchange, such as Local Exchange Trading Systems, or 'green' and 'time' money have created networks functioning without the organizing presence of ordinary, commercial money.[3] Furthermore, technological, institutional and organizational changes across the economy have also restricted the role of money in several areas of social interaction. Services and other goods associated with the internet, for instance, have been partially detached from the power of money, at times becoming nearly free at the point of consumption, including newspapers and music. The trend of distancing some areas of individual life from the power of money has had important implications for electronic money, briefly considered below.

In sum, the monetary underpinnings of financialization have been determined by institutional and historical changes occurring in the monetary sphere during the last four decades. To grasp the full significance of these changes analysis should start from the fundamental questions of what money is and how it functions in capitalist economy and society. The following section undertakes a brief sojourn into first principles, focusing on Marxist monetary theory and recapping Marx's own work on money.

Marxist monetary theory in relation to contemporary money

The significance of Marx's monetary writings

Marx's monetary writings are very extensive, ranging from early discussions of philosophical and cultural aspects of money, to mature analysis of monetary phenomena of industrial capitalism, to asides on monetary events in newspaper articles and correspondence. Marx considered monetary theory to be a weighty part of his intellectual output.[4] However, it has remained a relatively underdeveloped part of Marxist economics.[5]

Mainstream economic theory generally acknowledges Marx's stature as a great thinker, but dismisses outright his monetary theory, or is even unaware of it. There is an unjustified perception of Marx as a 'metallist' of little relevance to contemporary monetary phenomena. The prevalence of this view owes much to Schumpeter, whose frequently unjustified assertions about the history of economic thought can befuddle those unfamiliar with the original texts.[6] It is also due to Marx's – admittedly copious – references

---

3 For an excellent discussion particularly in the British context, see Peter North, *Alternative Currencies as a Challenge to Globalisation?*, London: Ashgate, 2006; and Peter North, *Money and Liberation*, Minneapolis: University of Minnesota Press, 2007.

4 Already in 1858, while completing *A Contribution to the Critique of Political Economy*, Marx wrote in a letter to Engels: 'If I'm wrong, so is the whole history of the monetary theory'. *Karl Marx and Frederick Engels: Collected Works*, vol. 40, *Correspondence, 1856–1859*, London: Lawrence and Wishart, 1983, p. 396.

5 This is certainly true for the currently dominant Anglo-Saxon Marxism, but less so for German and Japanese Marxism.

6 See, for instance, Joseph A. Schumpeter, *History of Economic Analysis*, New York: Oxford University Press, 1954, p. 290.

to gold, which have frequently misled Marxist and heterodox economists.[7] Some Marxist monetary theorists have, moreover, continued to search for an active role of gold in contemporary monetary phenomena, particularly in relation to the function of money as measure of value.[8] The presumption is that, unless money was shown to retain a commodity form – a value-containing form – Marx's monetary theory, not to mention the labour theory of value, would be rendered obsolete.

The dismissal or one-sided reading of Marx's monetary writings is also due to the inherent difficulty of the material itself. Much of Marx's advanced monetary work lies in chaotic form in part five of volume three of *Capital*. It was actually a jumble of notes found by Engels in Marx's papers after his death, and brought to publishable form through a true labour of love. At first sight it appears as a medley of theoretical points, empirical observations, long quotes and comments on others. To appreciate its depth it is necessary to persevere and, above all, to place it in the appropriate institutional context, including the development of monetary thought. This is often lacking among those who comment on Marx's theory of money.

Even the monetary theory that Marx actually prepared for publication, however, presents daunting problems. At its core lies very dense analysis of the dialectics of value and money, coupled with critical discussion of an enormous range of monetary theorists. For those familiar with Marx's method, these monetary writings can offer startling insight. For those trained in neoclassical economics, the prevalence of dialectics as well as Marx's systematic references to the history of economic thought pose insurmountable challenges.

The cornerstone of Marx's published analysis of money can be found in volume one of *Capital*. Relevant points are also available in the *Grundrisse*, though strictly speaking the latter was not prepared for publication by Marx and appeared long after his death.[9] Equally important is *A Contribution to the Critique of Political Economy*, Marx's first systematic foray into political economy, which was published almost a decade before *Capital*. In that work Marx put forth one of the earliest surveys of the history of monetary theory, while placing his own monetary analytics in appropriate context. Command over *the Contribution* – and of the work of the theorists surveyed within – is a sine qua non for appreciating Marx's monetary theory.

Marxist theorists have pored over volume one of *Capital* and the *Grundrisse* (but much less *the Contribution*) for several decades, typically with the aim of develop-

---

7   A characteristic example is Don Lavoie, 'Marx, the Quantity Theory, and the Theory of Value', *History of Political Economy* 18:1, 1986.

8   See, for instance, Claus Germer, *The Commodity Nature of Money in Marx's Theory*, London: Routledge, 2004.

9   Rosdolsky's account of the place of the *Grundrisse* in Marx's writings is outstanding, and much of it focuses on Marx's analysis of money. Roman Rosdolsky, *The Making of Marx's 'Capital'*, London: Pluto Press, 1977.

ing the labour theory of value. In recent years, for instance, a stream of writings has emerged which treats value as abstract labour that necessarily has a monetary expression – that is, it necessarily appears as money. The origin of this literature is ultimately Rubin's *Essays on Marx's Theory of Value* published in the Soviet Union in the 1920s. This work has had a strong influence on contemporary writings on value, for instance, through the 'value-form' current.[10] It has also been influential in the recent resurgence of monetary interpretations of Marx's value theory, often with a neo-Hegelian tinge.[11]

Concern with the relationship between value and money is a characteristic aspect of the revival of interest in monetary theory among Marxist economists in recent years.[12] The output produced has created fresh openings for Marxist political economy, but the bulk of it has remained fundamentally concerned with value rather than money. That is, it has rarely offered a specific understanding of monetary phenomena as an integral aspect of the capitalist economy.[13] In contrast to Marx's own monetary writings, this work almost never engages with non-Marxist monetary analysis, and nor does it place Marxist analysis within the broad evolution of monetary theory. Last but not least, much of it suffers from a surfeit of Hegelian argumentation at the expense of economics.[14]

Marx's monetary writings should be critically assessed in terms of both their internal coherence and their relationship to classical and other monetary theory. Ultimately, however, the standing of Marxist monetary theory depends on the insight it offers on

---

10   Geert Reuten and Michael Williams, *Value Form and the State*, London: Routledge, 1989.

11   For instance, Christopher J. Arthur, 'Money and the Form of Value', in *The Constitution of Capital*, ed. Riccardo Bellofiore and Nicola Taylor, New York: Palgrave Macmillan, 2004; and Patrick Murray, 'Money as Displaced Social Form: Why Value cannot be Independent of Price', in *Marx's Theory of Money: Modern Appraisals*, ed. Fred Moseley, London: Palgrave Macmillan, 2004.

12   The collection by Moseley admirably sums up much of the current state of play in this field; Fred Moseley (ed.), *Marx's Theory of Money: Modern Appraisals*, London: Palgrave Macmillan, 2004.

13   The outstanding exception is Foley, whose insights have been vital to developing Marxist monetary theory, as is also mentioned in other places in this book. See Duncan Foley, 'The Value of Money, the Value of Labour Power and the Marxian Transformation Problem', *Review of Radical Political Economics* 14:2, 1982; and Duncan Foley, 'On Marx's Theory of Money', *Social Concept* 1:1, 1983, pp. 5–19. Nonetheless, Foley's concept of the Monetary Expression of Labour, developed in connection with his solution to the transformation problem, has limited explanatory power over the value of money; see Ben Fine, Costas Lapavitsas, and Alfredo Saad-Filho, 'Transforming the Transformation Problem: Why the "New Interpretation" is a Wrong Turning', *Review of Radical Political Economics* 36:1, Winter 2004, pp. 3-19.

14   A characteristic example is Christopher J. Arthur, for whom Hegel-type dialectics entirely replace monetary theory and economics ('Money and Exchange', *Capital and Class* 30:3, 2006); for a telling response see Thomas Sekine, 'Arthur on Money and Exchange', *Capital and Class* 33:3, 2009.

contemporary monetary phenomena. Relevance is the prime requirement, particularly in view of the remarkable monetary features of financialized capitalism. Marx's own writings were, of course, produced under very different conditions of capitalist monetary development. But they can still provide powerful guidance, if their intellectual and historical context is kept firmly in mind, as is shown in the following section.

Marxist theory of money relative to neoclassicism and chartalism

The relevance of any monetary theory to actual monetary phenomena derives in part from the answer it gives to the question: What is money and how does it emerge? At first sight, the question appears trivial, or highly abstruse, yet, on closer inspection, its true complexity and significance begin to emerge. Money has the ability to buy commodities, but is itself never bought; money is universally held by market participants, but is not directly consumed; money's typical state is to be in motion, but it is also kept static in hoards; and so on, and so forth. Why is such an extraordinary economic entity present in markets, and how does it emerge?

Marx offered a distinctive answer to this question, the significance of which can be fully appreciated only in the context of other monetary theories.[15] It is notable, for instance, that classical political economy offers little guidance on this issue. Classical economists were certainly concerned with the peculiarity of money, but approached the issue instrumentally, so to speak. The standard view was put forth by Adam Smith in *The Wealth of Nations* while analysing 'primitive' exchange.[16] In short, if money was absent, direct commodity exchange would prevail; however, direct exchange would be prone to constant breakdowns since the commodities held by traders would frequently be incompatible in terms of quantities, quality, time of exchange, and so on. Hence, a 'prudent' trader would have to keep a commodity desired by all to facilitate exchange. This commodity is money.

Smith was thus fully aware of the inherent economic awkwardness of direct exchange, and associated money with it. But he did not confront the most difficult part of the problem: why should there be a commodity desired by all? And how could such a commodity emerge, if it was not already money? In short, what is the essence of 'moneyness' and how does it come about? Answers to this question began to appear only after the Classical School had gone into decline, and were produced almost simultaneously by Neoclassicism, the German Historical School, and Marxism.[17] The first

---

15 Discussion in this section draws heavily on Costas Lapavitsas, *Social Foundations of Markets, Money and Credit*, London: Routledge, 2003, ch. 3.

16 Adam Smith, *The Wealth of Nations*, ed. Edwin Cannan E, London: Methuen, 1904, vol. 1, ch. 5.

17 This point is often missed by anthropologists, sociologists and other social scientists who discuss the origin of money and criticize 'economic theory' for relating money to direct exchange. Thus, David Graeber makes a typically withering attack on Smith for assuming a

major economist to confront the issue was Marx, though his views remain the least known within economic theory. However, the power of Marx's answer can be fully appreciated only in the context of the other two schools.

Neoclassicism contains two theoretical strains on this issue. The dominant strain is closely associated with Leon Walras's formulation of General Equilibrium in *Elements of Pure Economics* in which money appears as abstract measure of value and means of exchange. Despite being aware of the fundamental place of money in commodity exchange, this approach offers no explanation for the endogenous emergence of money.[18] General Equilibrium models, purporting to be the most advanced theoretical formulation of capitalist markets, ultimately treat capitalist trading as direct exchange.

The minor neoclassical strain, originating with the Austrian School and in particular Carl Menger, has more to offer on this issue.[19] Avoiding mathematical formulations of market operations, Menger focused on individual choices and actions. His argument, brutally simplified, is as follows: Commodities are, by assumption, differentially 'marketable'; gifted individuals identify and demand commodities with better 'marketability', thereby facilitating their own transactions; other individuals learn by example and hence also demand commodities with better 'marketability'; consequently the 'marketability' of one commodity increases until it dominates all others, thus becoming money.

Menger's argument is logically powerful, but its coherence derives from overwhelming focus on money as means of exchange, paying much less attention to more complex functions of money, such as means of hoarding. This was probably related to Menger's narrow approach to economic theorizing, based on extreme methodological individualism. Nonetheless, the Austrian tradition still offers the best argument that neoclassical theory can muster on the issue of money's emergence. In recent years

---

'primitive' society and an imaginary state of barter out of which money presumably emerges (*Debt: The First 5000 Years*, New York: Melville House, 2011, ch. 2). There is, of course, little doubt that Smith's image of barter among 'primitives' is fallacious and a product of its time. However, engaging in the abstraction of barter, even if crudely, is hardly the main problem with Smith's analysis, particularly as this abstraction allowed him to capture the economic difficulties of direct exchange in exemplary fashion. Rather, the problem is that Smith's abstraction does not provide a logical foundation for the emergence of money out of the difficulties of direct exchange. Contemporary 'economic theory' is fully aware of this weakness and has attempted to answer it by developing a variety of further abstractions, briefly mentioned in the text below. Graeber, and other critics from anthropology and related disciplines, appear unaware of this aspect of modern monetary theory.

18   As was explicitly acknowledged in Frank Hahn, *Money and Inflation*, Blackwell: Oxford, 1982.

19   Carl Menger, 'On the Origin of Money', *Economic Journal* 2, 1892, pp. 239–55. Carl Menger, *Principles of Economics*, New York: New York University Press, 1981.

there have been attempts to incorporate Menger's argument within Walrasian General Equilibrium, adding considerable formalism but not much further substance.[20]

The German Historical School – locked in debate with the Austrians – rejected Menger's individualist economic theorizing, favouring instead analytical descriptions of economic processes that drew on accumulated historical evidence. Consequently, it has produced no theory of money's emergence. However, it has generated a body of analysis that places money in a wider social context, further associating it with non-market and non-economic forces. Its legacy among social sciences other than economics has been enormous and its prominence has increased in recent years.

The most influential approaches to money broadly belonging to this current appeared as the German Historical School entered its terminal decline.[21] One prominent view associates money with non-economic forces of a communal character, deriving from ancient practices of recompense for damage inflicted on others, commonly known as *wergeld*. This approach has had considerable influence among social scientists, though not among economists, for obvious reasons.[22] Another influential view, known as chartalism, identifies the origin of money with the state. The best-known exponent is Georg Friedrich Knapp in *The State Theory of Money*, for whom money is a legal convention of value imposed by the state. Unlike the wergeld approach, chartalism has always maintained a toehold in economics.[23] The argument that money is essentially an arbitrary construct which measures commodity values on the basis of legal and customary conventions has been revived in recent years by Post-Keynesians.[24]

---

20 The original contribution in this literature is Robert A. Jones, 'The Origin and Development of Media of Exchange', *Journal of Political Economy* 84, 1976. For further discussion of this issue as well as of further views on the emergence of money see Lapavitsas, *Social Foundations of Markets, Money and Credit*, ch. 3, 6.

21 Probably the last systematic echo of the German Historical School on the issue of money's emergence can be found in Max Weber, *Economy and Society: An Outline of Interpretive Sociology*, New York: Bedminster Press, 1968.

22 In recent years the wergeld approach has been forcefully restated by the erudite numismatist Philip Grierson. Note that Karl Polanyi and his followers, for instance, George Dalton, have put forth penetrating arguments about money and markets that resonate with those of the German Historical School as well as Marxism. Some of these views – for example, the distinction between 'general purpose' and 'special purpose' money – have been very influential within anthropology and sociology. However, they do not constitute theoretical analysis of the emergence of money, and hence they are not directly relevant to our concerns.

23 Even attracting Keynes's attention. John Maynard Keynes, *The General Theory of Employment, Interest and Money*, London: Macmillan, 1973, p. 3.

24 See L. Randall Wray, *Money and Credit in Capitalist Economies*, Aldershot and Brookfield: Edward Elgar, 1990; Wray, *Understanding Modern Money*, Cheltenham: Edward Elgar, 1998; Wray, 'Modern Money', in *What is Money?*, ed. John Smithin, London: Routledge, 2000;

Chartalism has an obvious appeal under conditions of financialized capitalism since the monetary sphere is permeated by valueless credit money convertible only into state-backed legal tender: it is easy to assume that the measure of value results from the say-so of the state.

Both the wergeld and the chartalist approaches to money's emergence are broader than neoclassical analysis, encompassing several of money's functions instead of focusing mainly on means of exchange. Moreover, both incorporate a wealth of non-economic factors to account for the emergence of money, and hence have a special appeal for anthropologists and economists. The approach of the German Historical School, furthermore, appears to fit naturally with evidence from Sumerian and Babylonian history regarding the ancient emergence of money and credit in societies that were based on royal and priestly prerogative.[25] On this score, money's origin seems unrelated to commodity exchange.

The putative historical connection between money and the credit practices of ancient Middle Eastern societies has offered further possibilities to develop alternative theories of the origin of money. In this connection mainstream economic theory has been useful to alternative theorists, even if mainstream analysis has not always been acknowledged by critics who are not economists. Thus, both Joseph Schumpeter and John Hicks have put forth credit-theories of money.[26] Despite differences, both

---

and Wray (ed.), *State and Credit Theories of Money*, Cheltenham: Edward Elgar, 2004; see also Geoffrey Ingham, *The Nature of Money*, Cambridge: Polity Press, 2004. Both Wray and Ingham attribute some of their insights to Alfred Mitchell-Innes; see Mitchell-Innes, 'What Is Money?' and 'The Credit Theory of Money', both reprinted in Wray, *State and Credit Theories of Money*.

25   See Geoffrey Ingham, "'Babylonian Madness'", in Smithin (ed.), *What Is Money?*; and Ingham, *The Nature of Money*. Note that the search for historical evidence to support the view of money emerging as abstract unit of account long predates the recent preoccupation with Sumeria and Babylonia. Luigi Einaudi, whose views are strangely ignored by contemporary chartalists, has argued that medieval European money was originally an imaginary unit of account ('The Theory of Imaginary Money from Charlemagne to the French Revolution' in *Enterprise and Secular Change*, ed. Frederic Lane and Jelle Riemersma, 1953; and 'The Medieval Practice of Managed Currency', in *The Lessons of Monetary Experience*, ed. Arthur David Gayer, London: George Allen & Unwin, 1970). Unfortunately, this view holds no water for historians, who have shown that medieval money was a very real means of exchange; see Hans Van Werveke, 'Monnaie de Compte et Monnaie Réelle', *Revue Belge de Philologie et d' Histoire* 13: 1–2, 1934. This is perhaps one reason why contemporary chartalists seek refuge in the fields and deserts of Mesopotamia.

26   Joseph A. Schumpeter, *The Theory of Economic Development*, Cambridge, MA: Harvard University Press, 1934; John Hicks, *Critical Essays in Monetary Theory*, Oxford: Clarendon Press, 1967. Schumpeter's theory is harder to access in his writings and less known; see Marcello Messori, 'Credit and Money in Schumpeter's Theory', in *Essays in Honour of Augusto Graziani*, ed. Richard Arena and Neri Salvadori, Aldershot, Hants: Ashgate, 2004.

postulate that the fundamental interaction among economic agents is characterized by credit relations based on promises to pay, rather than by the give-and-take of exchanging equivalents. From this perspective, money is fundamentally a promise to pay that might be based on relations of trust, power, social custom, and so on. To critics of mainstream economics, treating money as a promise to pay appears to augment the scope for alternative analysis: money does not have to be a commodity and its origin can be sought in non-commercial social relations typically found in non-capitalist historical societies.[27]

A number of critical points can be made about the approaches to money spawned by the German Historical School. First, it is notable that their strength is also the source of their weakness. By emphasizing the role of non-economic forces in the emergence of money, theorists are led to seek the origins of money outside the process of exchange, and even outside the sphere of the economy altogether. This is deeply unsatisfactory for a phenomenon that is overwhelmingly economic and closely associated with markets. It is one thing to acknowledge that money has non-economic dimensions, quite another to argue that it derives independently of economic processes. Second, the chartalist view that money is a measure of value determined arbitrarily by the state is itself an arbitrary assertion. The state certainly intervenes in the functioning of money, but that does not mean that money is logically anchored on the state. An extra-market authority would need to possess extraordinary omniscience and power arbitrarily to determine the basis of commodity value measurement. Third, credit-based theories of money suffer from the telling weakness that commodity forms of money are not promises to pay since they incorporate value. Advanced capitalism is indeed based on money that comprises promises to pay, but only a leap of logic would equate gold with a promise to pay – that is, with a debt.[28] Fourth, and more generally, credit-based theories of money offer a slender foundation for explaining the collapse of financial relations and the corresponding rise of monetary relations that is characteristic of capitalist crises.

It is instructive to note, incidentally, that some aspects of the chartalist view go back to classical political economy. Sir James Steuart proposed a well-developed version of abstract value measurement shortly before Adam Smith wrote *The Wealth of Nations*.

---

27 On this basis, Ingham has even erected a complex sociological argument regarding money as a social relation; Geoffrey Ingham, *The Nature of Money*, Cambridge: Polity Press, 2004. However, the most recent, and by far the most ambitious, attempt to develop the various strains of the approach of the German Historical School, while mobilizing anthropological insight, was made in Graeber, *Debt: The First 5000 Years*. Both Ingham and Graeber are dismissive of Marx's theory of money, even though both have a limited appreciation of it.

28   A leap attempted with aplomb by Graeber, who confuses the trust on which all money must be based – that is, trust to accept money as representative of value – with the trust that is the essence of credit – that is, trust to accept the validity of a promise to pay later. Graeber, *Debt: The First 5000 Years*, ch. 3.

In his *Inquiry into the Principles of Political Economy*, Steuart suggested that 'money of account' is an abstract numeraire that establishes ideal prices, which are then approximated in practice by 'material money'.[29] Marx, despite the high regard in which he held Steuart's monetary analysis, rejected this view and offered fresh insight into money originating in commodity exchange.[30]

The gist of Marx's objection to Steuart's theory of the abstract numeraire was that it obfuscates the relationship between ideal prices (established abstractly by money on paper, or in the mind) and actual prices (established in practice by money through regular commodity exchanges). The distinction between the two is valid and characteristic of commodity exchange, but actual prices are not practical approximations of ideal prices. Rather, actual prices reflect local, particular and incidental factors; hence they do, and must, diverge from ideal prices. The divergences do not arise from putative disparities between an ideal measure of value and its material approximation, but rather from the universal determination of value in the abstract compared to the particular determination of value in practice. The actual operations of commodity exchange render the abstraction of value into a real phenomenon, but they do so in specific circumstances. Furthermore the process of reconciling actual and ideal prices often involves violent economic episodes, including monetary crises. The measure of value, however, has nothing ideal and abstract about it since it arises spontaneously out of the operations of commodity exchange.

Marx's own analysis of 'moneyness' predates those of Neoclassicism and German Historicism. It is profoundly theoretical, though not in the individualist manner of Menger, while incorporating the broad array of money's functions and relations that concerned the Historical School. Its finished form is found in Chapter 1 of the first volume of *Capital*, where Marx proudly claimed to have been the first to have solved the riddle of the 'dazzling money-form'.[31] *A Contribution to the Critique of Political Economy* had prepared the ground by examining the dialectics of use value and exchange value, while the *Grundrisse* explored the historical and social role of money.

---

29 James Steuart, *An Inquiry into the Principles of Political Economy*, vol. 2, part 3, ch. 1, 2; in *Works, Political, Metaphysical, and Chronological, of the Late Sir James Steuart*, London: Routledge, 1995.

30 Karl Marx, *A Contribution to the Critique of Political Economy*, Moscow: Progress Publishers, 1970, pp. 79–81. See also Lapavitsas in debate with Ingham: Geoffrey Ingham, 'Fundamentals of a Theory of Money: Untangling Fine, Lapavitsas and Zelizer', *Economy and Society* 30:3, 2001; Costas Lapavitsas, 'The Social Relations Of Money as Universal Equivalent: A Response to Ingham', *Economy and Society* 34:3, 2005; Geoffrey Ingham, 'Further Reflections on the Ontology of Money: Responses to Lapavitsas and Dodd', *Economy and Society* 35:2, 2006, pp. 259–78. For an earlier analysis that deals with money as measure of value in Ricardian as opposed to Marxist theory, see Costas Lapavitsas, 'The Classical Adjustment Mechanism of International Balances: Marx's Critique', *Contributions to Political Economy* 15:1, 1996, pp. 63–79.

31 Marx, *A Contribution to the Critique of Political Economy*, p. 139.

Summarily put, money is a commodity that emerges spontaneously as the 'universal equivalent' or the 'independent form of value'. For Marx, the emergence of money occurs necessarily in commodity exchange due to the contradictory unity of use value and exchange value. As use values, commodities are imperfectly divisible, available at specific places and times, perishable, and so on – they are particular. As exchange values, they are the opposite – general. In direct exchange, therefore, the two sides continually contradict each other, leading to breakdown of exchange. The emergence of money is necessary in order to resolve (or, rather, pacify) the contradictions. Money resolves the contradictions by being the independent form of value, thus disentangling the two sides: commodities can be use values as themselves, while becoming exchange values as money. In short, monetary exchange overcomes and transcends direct exchange.

The logical necessity of money's emergence also has a historical and social dimension, most clearly discussed by Marx in the *Grundrisse*. To reproduce themselves, all societies must engage in internal exchange of products. However, societies in which production is organized primarily on communal and associative principles need not necessarily turn products into commodities. Customary, hierarchical, moral, political, and other mechanisms can facilitate product exchange, thus excluding money. Marx did not subscribe to Adam Smith's fallacious abstraction of 'primitive' trade. Treating money as the outcome of relations of commodity exchange has nothing to do with assuming that money emerges out of a primordial state of barter.

For Marx, societies in which production is run by autonomous and private owners of the means of production necessarily turn products into commodities. Such societies rely on markets to organize the flow of commodities and to allow reproduction to take place: they require money as a social organizer, and none more so than capitalist society. However, the historical origin of money does not lie within the internal organization of communities; money does not emerge as a curative for a malfunctioning barter economy. Rather, money emerges where communities come into contact with each other and commodity exchange occurs.[32] When communities come into contact, relations of 'otherness' and 'foreignness' are dominant; thus room is provided for commodity exchange allowing money to emerge as the independent representative of value. This is an insight of astonishing power in view of anthropological and sociological research that has broadly confirmed its validity during the following century and more.[33]

For Marx, however, it was not enough simply to show that money must necessarily emerge in commodity exchange. The real theoretical difficulty is to demonstrate the

32   Karl Marx, *Capital*, vol. 1, London: Penguin/NLR, 1976, pp. 182; Karl Marx, *Capital*, vol. 3, London: Penguin/NLR, 1981, pp. 447–8; Karl Marx, *Grundrisse*, London: Penguin/NLR, 1973, p. 223.

33   Emphasis on this point is one of the great merits of the treatment of money by the Uno School; see also Lapavitsas, *Social Foundations of Markets, Money and Credit*, ch.3.

process through which money emerges spontaneously; put differently, the problem is to specify the essence of 'moneyness'. Marx's answer was given in Chapter 1 of volume one of *Capital* in analysis of the 'form of value' (to be precise, the analysis was added by Marx in the second edition). Money is shown to emerge through the dialectic of the relative and the equivalent forms of value, both of which are inherent to commodity exchange. The relative form stands for the active element, the side which commences the act of exchange; the equivalent form stands for the passive element, the side that responds.[34]

The form of value goes through four stages as the dialectic of relative and equivalent is played out: the accidental, the expanded, the general, and the money stage. At each of these stages, a transformation occurs of both the relative and the equivalent until, at the money stage, the equivalent becomes firmly associated with a single commodity. This happens because all other commodities act collectively as relatives and therefore place the isolated commodity in the position of universal equivalent – money. Thus the money commodity acquires what Marx called a 'formal use value' – that is, being able directly to exchange with (buy) all the others, which is the foundation of its 'moneyness'.[35]

There are loose ends to Marx's argument – and even unwarranted assertions – particularly regarding the dialectics of the transition among the various stages.[36] However, his analysis has formidable power for several reasons. For one thing, it shows that money emerges spontaneously as well as necessarily in commodity exchange. Further, it posits the emergence of money as the outcome of the actions of the other commodities; the universal equivalent is created by the collective relative. Even more crucially, Marx's analysis pivots on the 'formal' aspect of 'moneyness'. The latter is an essence that arises within the process of exchange without which no theoretical account of money's emergence would be possible. Commodities are identical qua commodities; if one is to stand aside from all the others, it must possess some extra dimension. For Marx, the extra dimension arises solely and necessarily because of the conduct of other commodities (that is, of commodity owners). 'Moneyness', in other words, is

---

34   This approach to Marx's treatment of money's emergence has been further developed in the spirit – though not necessarily the letter – of the Uno School, in Lapavitsas, 'The Emergence of Money in Commodity Exchange'; see also Makoto Itoh, 'A Study of Marx's Theory of Value', in *Value and Crisis*, London: Pluto, 1980; and Thomas Sekine, 'Marxian Theory of Value: An Unoist Approach', *Chiiki Bunseki, Aichi Gakuin* 37:2, 1999, pp. 99–136. The original insight regarding the opposition between the active ('*to poioun*') and the passive ('*to paskhon*') in commodity exchange comes from Aristotle (for instance, *Nicomachean Ethics*, Cambridge, MA: Harvard University Press, 1926, pp. 280–1), whose views on money and profit are discussed in more detail in Chapter 6.

35   Marx, *Capital*, vol. 1, p. 184.

36   Discussed more fully in Lapavitsas, 'The Emergence of Money in Commodity Exchange'.

not invented by the state or some other non-economic agency: it is a social construct emerging spontaneously out of commodity interactions, and therefore containing an irreducible economic content.

To recap, for Marx, money is the universal equivalent, or the independent form of value. It arises spontaneously and necessarily in commodity exchange as a result of the development of the form of value, and spurred by the contradictions between use value and exchange value. Money has a profound historical and social role in societies that engage in commodity exchange. The money form tends to be exclusively associated with one commodity, typically gold. Commodity money is thus the original and fundamental form of money.

These conclusions are a sound foundation for Marxist monetary theory, but could also be a source of concern since they ostensibly contradict the prevalence of valueless money in contemporary capitalism. Is Marx's theory of money capable of casting light on the salient monetary aspects of financialization – the ascendancy of private credit money, the pivotal role of state-backed central bank money, and the emergence of the dollar as quasi-world-money? The answer is in the affirmative provided the functions of money are brought to the fore.[37] In this vein, the next two sections discuss private credit money and state-backed central bank money; the chapter turns to world money on pages 101–5, laying the ground for discussion of the monetary phenomena of financialization in chapters 8 and 9.

Contemporary valueless domestic money: Fiat money, private credit money, and state-backed central bank money

Fiat money

For Marxist monetary theory the original form of money is a commodity, typically taken to be gold.[38] Yet, there has never been a unique form of commodity money, but rather a range of commodities serving as money, including salt, hides, cattle, slaves, tobacco, metals, and so on. Even though Marxist analysis demonstrates the tendency for one money commodity to dominate the rest as the independent form of value, in practice such a unique occurrence has never taken place. The precious metals have certainly overshadowed other forms of the money commodity in the course of history; however, even gold and silver functioned concurrently as money until the second half of the nineteenth century, with gold having the paramount role.

Multiple and concurrently existing forms of the money commodity are a natural

---

37 Further theoretical discussion can be found in Costas Lapavitsas, 'The Theory of Credit Money: A Structural Analysis', *Science and Society* 55:3, 1991, pp. 291–322; and Makoto Itoh and Costas Lapavitsas, *Political Economy of Money and Finance*, London: Macmillan, 1999, ch. 1.

38 This view is consistent with historical evidence as well as with the conventional association of money with precious metals, particularly gold; see Pierre Vilar, *A History of Gold and Money, 1450–1920*, London: Verso, 2011.

outcome of commodity exchange, and do not negate the tendency toward a single universal equivalent. The reason is that the economic and social forces that lead to the emergence of the universal equivalent are continually replicated across the sphere of exchange. These forces reflect local conditions with specific features, which therefore give rise to local and partial equivalents. At any moment in time, there are likely to be several commodities that strive for the position of the universal equivalent.[39] Moreover, the privilege of being the universal equivalent, or the independent form of value, is continually contested among commodities, even if one has in practice risen above the rest. Success depends partly on the physical features of the commodity that seeks to be money and partly on the economic and social factors that generate trust in its use – the broader factors that sustain 'moneyness'. By the same token, the commodity that acts as the universal equivalent must continually reassert its dominance over the rest.

Fiat money represents a form of money that arises primarily due to the tension between the function of commodity money as measure of value and its function as means of exchange.[40] The actual use of the money commodity as means of exchange inevitably results in wear and tear (exacerbated by fraud and counterfeiting). It follows that the function of measure of value cannot be delivered adequately since commodity values are rendered into one set of prices when measured by the intact (and abstract) money commodity, and into quite another (and higher) when measured by the degraded (and circulating) money commodity. In other words, the intrinsic operations of commodity exchange generate a (degraded) form of money that symbolizes itself. Thus, room is spontaneously created for fiat money – a proper symbol of commodity money – to emerge.

The tension between measure of value and means of exchange inherent to commodity money could be partly assuaged if the money commodity was standardized by the state. Transforming commodity money into metallic coin strengthens its social acceptability by associating money with the power of the state.[41] Coin also stabilizes the measurement function by fixing the unit of account across the sphere of exchange, particularly if the state succeeds in limiting other types and denominations of coin within its territory.[42] But coining does not eliminate the problem of wear and tear

39   The economic logic of this phenomenon is discussed in detail in Lapavitsas, 'The Emergence of Money in Commodity Exchange'.

40   Marx, *A Contribution to the Critique of Political Economy*, p. 110.

41   Coin most likely appeared first in ancient Asia Minor but, in historical terms, it was essentially a Greek invention, as has been shown in David Schaps, *The Invention of Coinage and the Monetization of Ancient Greece*, Ann Arbor: The University of Michigan Press, 2004. It probably arose independently of state authority yet, at least in the ancient Greek world, its minting and use were inextricably connected to state power.

42   Historians of Medieval Europe have shown that significant accounting costs used to result when coins of different state denominations were in concurrent circulation; see Frederic Lane

through actual circulation. Indeed, it could make the problem worse since the state could corrupt coin to lessen the burden of its debts and other obligations.

Fiat money replaces commodity money with valueless and inconvertible symbols issued by the state. It ultimately rests on social trust in the ability of the state to enforce payments in this form of money; it competes with commodity money and restricts the presence of the latter in the sphere of exchange; it also provides a standard unit of account for prices. Fiat money can take several forms varying from cheap metallic coin, to crude paper monies with forced circulation, to sophisticated legal tender issued by central banks and backed by state debt. The dominant form of fiat money in the period of financialization overlaps with credit money, as is shown below.

The various forms of fiat money thus have two fundamental functions: means of exchange and unit of account for prices. The adequacy with which they deliver these functions depends on the institutional framework of circulation, but also on the quantities in which fiat money is issued by the state. If fiat money was overissued, it would obviously translate value into rising prices, thus malfunctioning as unit of account; if overissue persevered, fiat money would also fail as means of circulation. Inflation and hyperinflation are thus constant threats to the validity of fiat money. In principle, however, there is no reason why some forms of fiat money could not function indefinitely in the sphere of exchange. Fiat coin, for instance, obviates the need to cut precious metals in tiny amounts; it is also cheaper than issuing very small denominations of credit money, or even of e-money, as is discussed in the rest of this chapter. Fiat coin has adapted remarkably well to the small end of commodity circulation across a huge range of social relations and institutions in the course of history. Contemporary coin would not have been entirely unfamiliar to Venetian citizens, or even to Roman plebeians.

Private credit money and state-backed central bank money
In contrast to commodity and fiat money, credit money is a privately issued form of money that results from credit relations among agents of circulation. It is inherently a promise to pay in the future, a liability of the issuer. Credit money is normally created as financial institutions issue liabilities to finance the loans they make. By the same token, credit money returns to its issuer as loans mature (liabilities drain away).[43] Final settlement requires either cancellation against another promise to pay, or the intervention of commodity or fiat money.

Credit money is rooted in money's function as means of payment and arises as a

---

and Reinhold Mueller, *Money and Banking in Medieval and Renaissance Venice*, vol. 1, Baltimore: Johns Hopkins University Press, 1985.

43   The return of credit money to its issuer is the 'law of the reflux' that was noted by Steuart and became a defining feature of the Banking School in Britain; see Costas Lapavitsas, 'The Banking School and the Monetary Thought of Karl Marx', *Cambridge Journal of Economics* 18:5, 1994, pp. 447–61.

by-product of the development of credit in capitalist economies.[44] In its original form it is a promise to pay an amount of commodity money. Consequently, credit money springs from the very essence of credit relations. A promise to pay is capable of functioning as money ultimately because of trust in the ability of the issuer to fulfil the promise made. Unlike fiat money, credit money is a specifically capitalist form of money insofar as it is created spontaneously and according to the demand for credit among capitalist enterprises.[45] Typically, banks advance loans to industrial and commercial enterprises, funded through the expansion of bank liabilities, and thus credit money dominates large-scale transactions. The extent to which credit money displaces other forms of money in circulation depends on the holders' trust in the issuer's promise to pay. In turn, trust derives from the quality of the issuer's assets as well as from the issuer's social and economic power. Furthermore, trust depends on the overall stability of the credit system within which issuers make loans and create credit money.[46]

It follows that the specific form of credit money depends critically on the institutional structure and the practices of the credit system. Credit money has changed substantially as capitalism has developed, ranging from clumsy circulating trade credit instruments, to private banknotes, to ever-multiplying deposits issued by financial institutions (primarily banks). The evolution of credit money has continued apace under financialized capitalism, even giving rise to electronic forms, discussed below.

The state intervenes in the realm of credit money on terms that are dictated by the spontaneous evolution of the credit system itself. The operations of the credit system tend to isolate one bank among the others by turning it into the bank of banks – the central bank. Specifically, banks tend to concentrate their reserves in one bank and, consequently, favour its liabilities in settling promises to pay among themselves.[47] Room is thus created for the state to declare the liabilities of the bank of banks to be legal tender, making acceptance obligatory in settlement of debts and obligations. State action profoundly alters privately created credit money by turning it into a promise to pay the liabilities of the central bank rather than the money commodity.

The state thus plays a decisive role in the ascendancy of credit money as well as in excluding commodity money from the sphere of circulation. However, considerable analytical care is needed to avoid misconceptions on this issue. Credit money comes spontaneously to dominate large-scale transactions in mature capitalism, but never

---

44   Marx, *Capital*, vol. 1, p. 238.

45   This is a fundamental insight of the post-Keynesian tradition that is in broad agreement with Marxist monetary theory.

46   These issues are more fully discussed in Lapavitsas, *Social Foundations of Markets, Money and Credit*, ch. 4.

47   Some elements of this development are discussed in Chapter 5; see also Itoh and Lapavitsas, *Political Economy of Money and Finance*, ch. 1, 2, 3; and Lapavitsas, *Social Foundations of Markets, Money and Credit*, ch. 4.

completely eliminates commodity money from the sphere of circulation, and not even from the circulation of personal income. The liabilities of the bank of banks tend to remain promises to pay the money commodity. The precious metals have obvious advantages as both coin and bullion (intrinsic value, portability, durability, and so on) which allow them to continue serving as money among enterprises and in the circulation of personal income. Tellingly, and running ahead of the following section, the precious metals persist as world money and states keep hoards of commodity money for payments and value transfers.

The umbilical cord between commodity money and capitalist circulation can only be finally cut by the state. The typical way would be for the state to lift the convertibility of the liabilities of the central bank into the money commodity. In the modern era the decisive action in this respect was taken by the British state in 1914 at the outbreak of the First World War.[48] Since that time, gold has not functioned in the domestic circulation of advanced capitalist countries in any significant way. However, gold retained a strong presence in the world market after the Second World War, buttressed by the Bretton Woods Agreement of 1944. The link of credit money with the money commodity was finally severed in 1971–73, when the US reneged on its promise to exchange a troy ounce of gold for $35. Gold became a hoard of last resort, jealously held and managed by central banks and other state authorities.

Severing the link between credit money and the money commodity has had profound implications for both domestic and international circulation. The impact on international circulation is discussed in the next section; in domestic circulation, cutting the gold anchor has made it possible, already since the interwar years, for the state to manage private credit money on the basis of a form of state-backed credit money. To be specific, in contemporary capitalism bank-created credit money ultimately promises to pay central bank credit money (banknotes and bank reserves) while the state has declared the latter to be inconvertible into anything else. This development has afforded enormous scope for economic intervention and, together with the lifting of the gold anchor internationally, has been fundamental to financialization.

Central bank money that is inconvertible into the money commodity while simultaneously being legal tender is a peculiar hybrid of fiat and credit money. On the one hand, it is credit money created as loans are advanced and drain away as debt is repaid, even if these operations relate to the central bank. On the other, it is fiat money because it rests on the authority of the state and is supported by central bank assets that typically include state instruments of debt. Such hybrid money has two specific forms:

---

48   Convertibility of sterling into gold was also suspended in 1797 as the Napoleonic Wars began in full earnest but the period of the 'Restriction' came to an end in 1819, after giving rise to the Bullion Controversy that ushered Ricardo into political economy. At the time neither the British, nor the world economy possessed sufficiently mature credit mechanisms to allow circulation to thrive on inconvertible credit money.

banknotes issued by the central bank and bank reserves held at the central bank; both are fundamental to financialization but function differently from each other. Their differences are considered in more detail in the following section; suffice it here to note the following.

Banknotes are in practice absent from large-scale transactions among enterprises and are rarely used to pay wages and salaries. They function primarily as means of exchange and hoarding at the tail end of individual income circulation.[49] The trust required for banknotes to function as money – their social acceptability – is generated through the backing of the state as well as through the norm of daily use. Banknote use differs significantly among advanced countries depending on the institutional mechanisms of banking but also on the customs and habits of personal income expenditure. Central banks supply banknotes passively since they consider banknotes to be largely irrelevant to the management of credit money and of credit flows more generally.[50]

Bank reserves, on the other hand, are the primary means of hoarding and payment among large financial institutions; they also provide the ultimate means of redemption for privately created credit money. Thus, bank reserves are a vital lever used by the state to manage domestic money but also to influence credit flows. The deployment of bank reserves depends on, first, the trust that private banks have in the central bank and, second, the cost of holding reserves. Trust in the central bank, in turn, depends on state backing but also on the quality of the assets of the central bank. A complex game of institutional rules and practices is continually played between the central bank and private banks to ensure that bank reserves remain the preferred form of settlement for privately created credit money among financial and other institutions. This inevitably results in differences in the use of reserve deposits in practice among developed capitalist countries, discussed in the following section.

Domestic valueless money in the course of financialization: Electronic money

It is apparent from the preceding discussion that valueless money poses no problems for Marxist monetary theory – there is no crippling 'metallism' in Marx. Valueless money arises necessarily and spontaneously, and takes the form of both fiat and credit money. As the former, it is a symbolic replacement of commodity money; as the latter, it is a promise to pay commodity money, or a state-backed unit of money that is itself valueless. Both forms function and intervene in capitalist circulation according to the economic and institutional relations that support their emergence.

---

49   Banknotes also function in criminal, illicit or 'grey' transactions, and large volumes are typically held outside their country of issue; for evidence on the largest countries, see Kenneth Rogoff, 'Blessing or Curse? Foreign and Underground Demand for Euro Notes', *Economic Policy* 13:26, April 1998. This issue is also briefly considered in the following section.

50   As is clearly established in Charles Freedman, 'Monetary Policy Implementation: Past, Present and Future', *International Finance* 3:2, 2000.

In the course of financialization both private credit money and state-backed central bank money have continued to evolve, particularly by adopting electronic forms. Moreover, forms of electronic money have emerged that are qualitatively different from credit money, a rather unusual phenomenon in capitalist circulation. Closer empirical examination of these developments can cast further light on the underlying relations of financialized capitalism. The discussion below relates to US, Japan, Germany and the UK, the four countries that are more broadly considered throughout this book in empirical terms. Data comes from the Bank of International Settlements (BIS) and refers to the 1990s and 2000s, the decades during which financialization reached a peak.

Private credit money takes electronic form

It is instructive to start the analysis by briefly describing the dominant forms taken by monetary transactions in recent years. The BIS classifies transactions as 'cash' (completed with banknotes and coin) and 'cashless' (completed with credit or debit cards, direct debits, cheques, and credit transfers). In terms of the preceding analysis, the former are transactions using fiat or state-backed central bank money, while the latter are credit money transactions.

Among credit money transactions, there is little substantially to differentiate cheques from direct debits or credit transfers. Cheques are written payment orders transferring credits among bank accounts, while direct debits or credit transfers are similar payment orders that typically take an electronic form. The difference is that cheques alter money entries mostly in paper form, while transfers do the same electronically.[51] Debit cards are yet another way of transferring funds already existing in bank accounts. Credit cards, on the other hand, typically provide the holder with credit, that is, with a loan made by the card supplier. However, debit cards could also allow for overdrafts on existing bank accounts, blurring the difference between already possessing a sum of money and obtaining fresh funds from a lender. Both types of card shift money entries electronically among transacting parties.

In this light, consider the evolution of cashless transactions from the middle of the 1990s to the middle of the 2000s. Figures 1, 2, 3 and 4 show credit/debit cards, cheques, credit transfers, and direct debits as a share of the total number of cashless transactions.

There has been considerable variation in the dominant forms of credit money across the four countries during this period. Japan has consistently used cards more heavily than the rest, while Germany has lagged significantly behind the others; cheques have never had much weight either in Germany or Japan, while they have been strongly

---

51 This essential similarity creates technical problems of classification and presentation of figures, which are apparent, for instance, in the sudden jumps of the time series for Japan in figures 4 and 5. Even more violent jumps occur in the US data, though they are not reported here. However, these classification problems do not affect the gist of the analysis.

FIG. 1 Credit/debit cards as percentage of total volume of cashless transactions

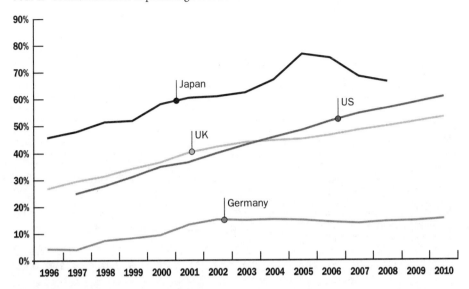

Source: BIS, Statistics on payment, clearing and settlement systems in the Committee on Payment and Settlement Systems countries, 2012, 2011, 2007, and 2002. Data for Japan in 2009–2010 and for the US in 1996 are not available.

FIG. 2 Cheques as percentage of total number of cashless transactions

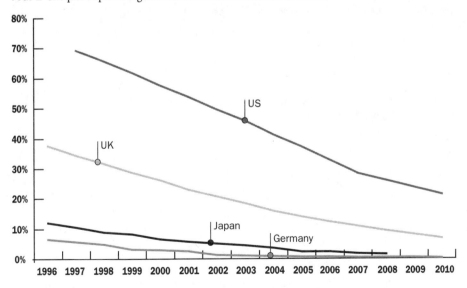

Source: BIS, Statistics on payment, clearing and settlement systems in the Committee on Payment and Settlement Systems countries, 2012, 2011, 2007, and 2002. Data for Japan in 2009, 2010 and for the US in 1996 are not available.

FIG. 3 Credit transfers as percentage of total number of cashless transactions

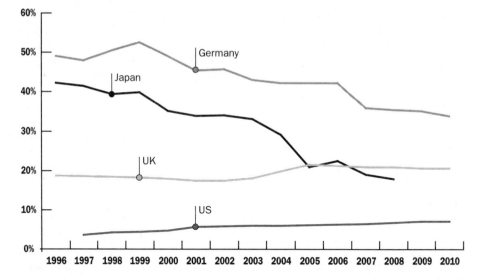

Source: BIS, Statistics on payment, clearing and settlement systems in the Committee on Payment and Settlement Systems countries, 2012, 2011, 2007, and 2002. Data for Japan in 2009–2010 and for the US in 1996 are not available.

FIG. 4 Direct debits as percentage of total number of cashless transactions

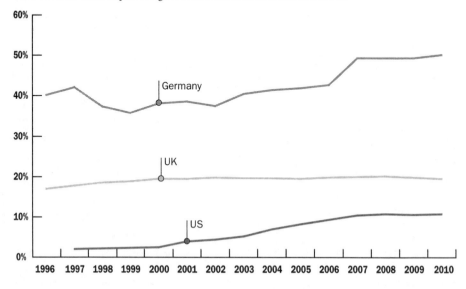

Source: BIS, Statistics on payment, clearing and settlement systems in the Committee on Payment and Settlement Systems countries, 2012, 2011, 2007, and 2002. Data for the US in 1996 and for Japan are not available.

FIG. 5 Credit/debit cards as percentage of total value of cashless transactions

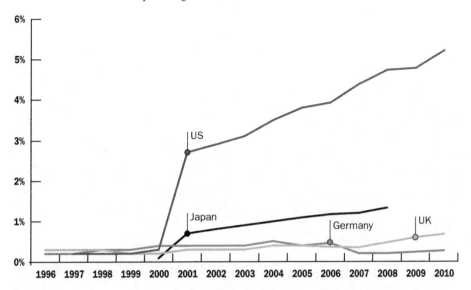

Source: BIS, Statistics on payment, clearing and settlement systems in the Committee on Payment and Settlement Systems countries, 2012, 2011, 2007, and 2002. Data for Japan in 1996–1999 and 2009–2010 and for the US in 1996 are not available.

used in the US. Apart from these variations that reflect institutional, legal and even cultural differences, it is notable that the use of cards has risen across the sample, while cheques have been in retreat. The decline of cheques is most apparent in the US, which has traditionally relied on cheques for a large part of the total number of transactions.[52]

Consider now credit/debit cards, cheques, credit transfers, and direct debits in relation to the total value of cashless transactions, shown in figures 5, 6, 7, and 8. There has been much less variation across the four countries in this respect (the sudden jumps in the US data reflect changes in classification rather than actual shifts in money use). The vast bulk of the value of cashless transactions has been mediated by payment orders among bank accounts, the US retaining its predilection for written orders in the form of cheques; nonetheless, the use of paper orders has still gone into decline. Meanwhile, the use of cards has risen, even if the value mediated has been a small fraction of the total.

Extrapolating from both total number and total value of transactions, it appears that credit transfers, direct debits, and cheques have been the money of large-scale

---

52   See also Federal Reserve Bulletin, 'The Use of Checks and Other Noncash Payment Instruments in the United States', December 2002; Federal Reserve Bulletin, 'Trends in the Use of Payment Instruments in the United States', Spring 2005; Federal Reserve, 'The Future of Retail Electronic Payments Systems: Industry Interviews and Analysis', Staff Study 175, December 2002.

FIG. 6 Cheques as percentage of total value of cashless transactions

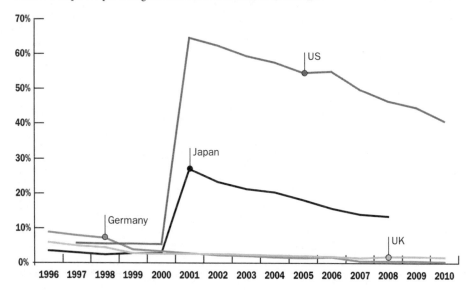

Source: BIS, Statistics on payment, clearing and settlement systems in the Committee on Payment and Settlement Systems countries, 2012, 2011, 2007, and 2002. Data for Japan in 2009–2010 and for the US in 1996 are not available.

FIG. 7 Credit transfers as percentage of total volume of cashless transactions

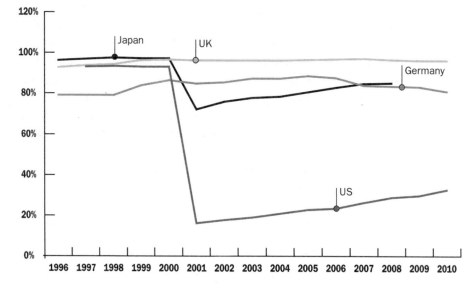

Source: BIS, Statistics on payment, clearing and settlement systems in the Committee on Payment and Settlement Systems countries, 2012, 2011, 2007, and 2002. Data for Japan in 2009–2010 and for the US in 1996 are not available.

FIG. 8 Direct debits as percentage of total value of cashless transactions

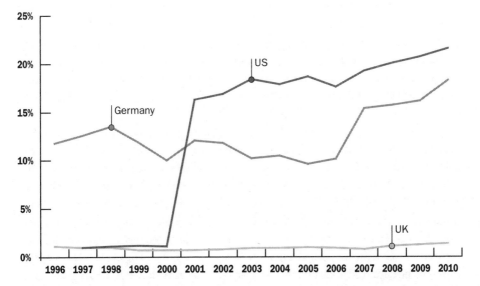

Source: BIS, Statistics on payment, clearing and settlement systems in the Committee on Payment and Settlement Systems countries, 2012, 2011, 2007, and 2002. Data for the US in 1996 and for Japan are not available.

transactions during this period. It is reasonable to suppose that these have been trans-actions among enterprises, while debit and credit cards have been used primarily to circulate private income. The evidence also shows that electronic forms of transferring bank account entries have been increasingly deployed compared to paper-based forms.

The electronic form of credit money that has been on the ascendant in the years of financialization can be called 'access electronic money', or 'access e-money'. This is an envelope term that captures several means of transferring conventional credit money electronically. Typical examples are debit and credit cards but also other forms of payment that have been increasingly 'electronified', such as credit transfers, and direct debits.[53] Access e-money presents no theoretical challenges since it involves little more than altering the corporeal form of credit money from paper to electronic signals. International commercial banks have been using electronic forms of money transmission in the clearing process since the interwar years. It appears, however, that financialization has been marked by stronger use of access e-money both among cor-porations and in the circulation of personal income.

The spread of access e-money is related to the transformation of banks in the course of financialization. The introduction of new information and telecommunications

---

53   See European Central Bank, 'Electronification of Payments in Europe', *Monthly Bulletin*, May 2003.

technology which has contributed to changes in the lending practices of banks has also lowered the costs of completing transactions electronically compared to sorting and processing paper orders. On the other hand, introducing electronic transaction processing capacity, including automated teller machines (ATMs) has imposed substantial investment costs on banks, including changes in organization and requisite labour skills.[54] The spread of access e-money in the course of financialization, thus, reflects the introduction of new technology but also the altered internal organization and even the branch structure of banks.

The growth of access e-money has probably had a significant effect on aggregate profitability during this period, though it is hard to assess its extent. For banks, it has facilitated cheaper and easier settlement of transactions in 'real time'. By implication it has probably speeded up the turnover time of industrial and commercial capital, thus boosting profitability. Other things equal, enterprises would also have kept lower money reserves, hence also boosting profitability. More generally, access e-money has probably accelerated the operations of financial institutions, thus encouraging financialization. Nonetheless, the ascendancy of access e-money within cashless transactions has not induced a decline in cash transactions, as is shown in figure 9 depicting the use of banknotes and coin.

Again, there has been significant variation across the four countries reflecting historical, institutional and cultural factors. Japan and Germany have been generally heavier users of cash than the US and the UK, though the figures for Germany also reflect the replacement of the Deutschmark by the euro. The striking feature of figure 9, however, is the persistence of cash across all countries throughout this period. In Japan the use of cash has actually increased substantially, though this has probably been related to the long period of financial instability in the 1990s and 2000s and the associated policy of quantitative easing by the central bank, which is further discussed on pages 100–1 and in subsequent chapters.

Why has the spread of access e-money failed to generate a decline in the use of banknotes and coin? This issue has also concerned mainstream economists, who have generally expected the use of cash to decline.[55] Paradoxically, the persistence of cash

---

54   For further analysis of this point, see Costas Lapavitsas and Paulo Dos Santos, 'Globalization and Contemporary Banking: On the Impact of New Technology', *Contributions to Political Economy* 27, 2008, pp. 31–56.

55   Some replacement has of course taken place, though the extent of it remains empirically unclear; see Willem Boeschoten and Gerrit E. Hebbink, 'Electronic Money, Currency Demand and Seignorage Loss in the G10 Countries', De Nederlandsche Bank, 1996; Sheri Markose and Yiing Jia Loke, 'Network Effects on Cash-Card Substitution in Transactions and Low Interest Rate Regimes', *Economic Journal* 113, April 2003; Helmut Stix, 'How Do Debit Cards Affect Cash Demand?', Working Paper 82, Oesterreichische Nationalbank, 2003; Gene Amromin and Sujit Chakravorti, 'Debit Card and Cash Usage: A Cross-Country Analysis', WP 2007–04, Federal

FIG. 9 Banknotes and coin as percentage of GDP

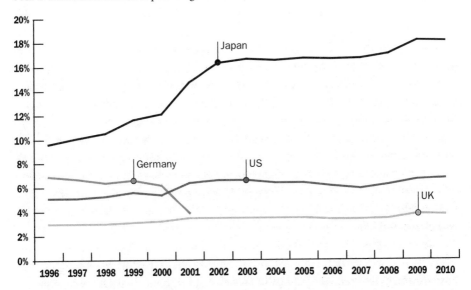
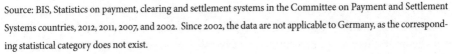

Source: BIS, Statistics on payment, clearing and settlement systems in the Committee on Payment and Settlement Systems countries, 2012, 2011, 2007, and 2002. Since 2002, the data are not applicable to Germany, as the corresponding statistical category does not exist.

is in part an unintended consequence of the spread of access e-money. For, as banks have developed extensive ATM networks facilitating the use of debit and credit cards, cash has also become more readily available in small sums that could be obtained more frequently. The question then properly becomes, why did the demand for banknotes and coin in circulation remain strong? The following three factors are important, and shed light on the role of money in financialized capitalism.

The first is the risk of fraud attached to access e-money since the account details of the buyer might become known to the seller, or to a third party, thus allowing for fraudulent charging, especially over the internet. The holder might also fraudulently add units to e-money vehicles. Both types of fraud have been major concerns of access e-money issuers, users and regulators, thus necessitating substantial investment in encryption technology.[56]

The second is that most forms of access e-money provide information about hold-

Reserve bank of Chicago, 2007.

56   There is much official concern about this issue, see, selectively, BIS, 'Security of Electronic Money', August 1996; BIS, 'International Convergence of Capital Measurement and Capital Standards', July 1988; and European Central Bank, *Electronic Money System Security Objectives*, May 2003.

ers, though anonymous forms also exist. In contrast, banknotes normally leave no trail of use, thus being suitable for illegal and 'grey' transactions.[57] Banknote anonymity also protects users against the attentions of a prying state.

The third is that access e-money has limited ability to deal with very small payments. The difficulties involved can be gauged from the internet where it has proven very difficult to introduce a reliable system of e-money 'micro-payments' (a fraction of the unit of account). There are transactions costs – including plain inconvenience – to using access e-money for tiny purchases, leading internet users simply to avoid the latter.[58] Beyond the internet, coin appears to be superior to access e-money in dealing with very small payments: it is easy to carry; it can be readily supplied in sufficiently small denominations; there is negligible profit from counterfeiting it; the cost is generally small if it is lost; it is also relatively cheap to produce and to put in circulation. Coin might be an ancient form of money but it is still capable of dominating the tail end of the circulation of personal income in financialized capitalism.

Electronic forms of credit money, in short, have come to dominate circulation in the years of financialization but without rendering obsolete either banknotes or coin, both of which have remained robustly present in the circuits of personal income and elsewhere. Technological change and the associated transformation of banks have sustained the ascendancy of access e-money. In turn, access e-money has had an impact on the operations and probably the profitability of banks as well as industrial and commercial capital. During the same period, however, a further form of e-money has emerged which is qualitative different from access e-money and which reveals further important aspects of financialization.

E-money proper: A new form of money in financialized capitalism
E-money proper is a novel form of money that has emerged in the course of financialization. Summarily put, it is money that is issued privately and its units are stored on electronic devices; units are purchased by advancing ordinary money at par value; the holder subsequently using these units to pay for commodities sold by agents other than the issuer.[59]

---

57   See Mathias Drehmann et al., 'Challenges to Currency', *Economic Policy*, April 2002.

58   The possibility of introducing micro-payments has led to lively exchanges often revealing strong ideological opposition to the rule of money on the internet; see, for instance, Clay Shirky, 'Fame vs Fortune: Micropayments and Free Content', 5 September 2003, at shirky.com; and Scott McCloud, 'Misunderstanding Micropayments', 11 September 2003, at scottmccloud.com.

59   See Article 1(3) of the European Monetary Institute's Directive 2000/46/EC, which regulates the issuing of e-money in the European Union. The British Financial Services Authority (FSA) uses a slightly different description which excludes the condition that e-money should be exchanged at par for ordinary money (article 3.1 of *The Regulation of Electronic Money Issuers*, Consultation Paper 117, December 2001). This is to prevent institutions from issuing e-money

Rapidly growing forms of e-money proper are prepaid cards, or prepaid software programmes used on the internet, often called server-based e-money.[60] E-money proper can be 'single-function', capable of buying particular commodities at particular locations, for instance, department store cards and transport cards. It can also be 'multi-function' allowing for a broader range of payments as, for instance, for so-called smartcards or transport cards with broader applications. As the use of e-money proper has spread, it has become possible to carry its units on the same card as access e-money, on bank debit and credit cards.

E-money proper is a liability of the issuer, but nevertheless differs qualitatively from ordinary credit money (and thus from access e-money). Credit money is typically issued against debt, and entails advancing the credit of the issuer which the holder accepts on trust. Credit money is typically more liquid than the assets held by the issuer against it, and drains away from the issuer as these assets mature. In contrast, e-money proper can only be issued against ready money (typically ordinary credit money) at par. The issuer can either hold the received funds as regular deposits with other financial institutions, or use the funds to purchase financial assets.

In effect, the issuers of e-money proper receive credit from its holders which lasts until the issued units of e-money are converted back into ordinary money by the holders. In contrast to credit money, e-money proper drains away from its issuer only when it is converted into ordinary money. The issuers are thus obliged to hold large reserves of ordinary money, or of financial assets that could be quickly converted into ordinary money. Issuers make a profit be earning returns on the assets that exceed the costs of issuing and managing the units of e-money proper. It is notable, and provides a further contrast with ordinary credit money, that e-money proper typically has less 'moneyness' than the ordinary money paid for it; it is less liquid. However, its 'moneyness' has a specific and local character which makes it preferable to the holder, for instance, in the case of transport cards.

The functioning of e-money proper is shaped by the regulatory framework supporting it, which naturally varies among countries.[61] However, certain features of reg-

---

below par and thus formally placing themselves outside the FSA's regulations.

60   Analytical descriptions of these and other forms of e-money can be found in BIS, 'Survey of Developments in Electronic Money and Internet and Mobile Payments', March 2004; Helen Allen, 'Innovations in Retail Payments: E-Payments', *Bank of England Quarterly Bulletin*, Winter 2003; European Central Bank, 'Issues Arising from the Emergence of Electronic Money', *Monthly Bulletin*, November 2000, pp. 49–60; and EMI Report, 'Report to the Council of the European Monetary Institute on Prepaid Cards by the Working Group on EU Payment Systems', May 1994.

61   In Europe these are determined by Directive 2000/28/EC, which amended Directive/2000/12/EC (EMI 2000), as well as Directive 2000/46/EC (EMI 2000). Regulation in the US is far less centralized and relies on existing legislation regarding money transmission at State level. Malte Krueger is of the opinion that US regulation is 'lighter', but the European Commis-

ulation are common and have shaped the character of e-money proper. Thus, e-money proper can only be issued in exchange for ordinary (typically credit) money at par; it must also be redeemed at par; issuers face severe restrictions on the capital they must hold; issuers can only invest in a narrow range of very liquid securities – mostly public financial assets. Regulation, therefore, prevents issuers from operating as ordinary banks since e-money proper cannot be issued to make loans or buy securities. The normal state of affairs is indeed the opposite of a bank: since the holder has to pay ready money to acquire e-money proper, as long as the latter is not immediately spent, the holder is giving credit to the issuer.

This complex regulatory framework has strengthened the acceptability of e-money proper by supporting trust in its use. Nonetheless, in developed countries the spread of e-money proper has been limited, not even meriting reference in the quantitative description of circulation given by the figures above. Limited spread is also due to the stipulation that e-money proper must be initially purchased at par with ordinary money, which makes it unsuitable for large transactions among enterprises. Regulation has forced e-money proper to remain small-scale money, functioning primarily as means of exchange and hoarding in the circulation of individual income. In that domain it has been heavily constrained by the strength of incumbent forms of money, particularly banknotes and coin.

Recapping, e-money proper differs qualitatively from credit money since it does not emerge from the advance of credit but comprises private liabilities obtained in exchange for existing money at par. Its emergence is an instance of the inherent tendency of capitalist circulation spontaneously to generate new forms of money. In the years of financialization industrial and commercial enterprises have re-strengthened this tendency by issuing e-money proper. At the same time, in developed countries, e-money proper has remained confined to the circulation of personal income leaving large-scale transactions untouched. Regulation and the residual strength of incumbent forms of credit money have limited its spread. Even in this respect, however, the emergence of e-money proper has reflected the peculiar importance of the circuits of personal income in financialized capitalism, briefly discussed in Chapter 2 and more fully explored in the rest of this book.

Remarkably, the potential for spontaneous money creation represented by technological and institutional changes within financialized capitalism has been more fully apparent in developing countries. E-money proper has come into its own in a swathe of countries in Africa and Asia based particularly on telecommunications enterprises. The spread of mobile telephony has provided the underpinnings of acceptability, and

---

sion argues strongly that US regulation is in practice equally restrictive. See Krueger, 'E-Money Regulation in the EU', in *E-Money and Payment Systems Review*, ed. Pringle R. and Robinson M., London: Central Banking, 2002; and European Commission, 'Evaluation of the E-Money Directive (2000/46/EC)', 2006.

thus of 'moneyness', for e-money in developing countries. Typically, mobile phone users purchase e-money proper by advancing ordinary money; hold it as electronic units; and transfer it by simple messages. Related forms of e-money include 'scratch' cards, that is, electronic units purchased in cards with a code number, which can then be transferred by mobile phone message. Telecommunications companies have also started to allow mobile phones holders to use prepaid airtime units to make a variety of payments unrelated to telephony.[62]

Vital in this respect has been the relative weakness of financial systems in developing countries, particularly their limited geographical and economic penetration across the economy, which has reduced the strength of incumbent forms of credit money. In developing countries access to formal bank accounts is often restricted by physical absence of bank branches, high setting up costs and prohibitive minimum balances. Furthermore, for low-income countries that rely on emigrant remittances, the costs of money transmission through formal financial channels can be prohibitive. Informal mechanisms, on the other hand, could entail significant risks and social obligations.

In this context e-money proper is capable of thriving by acting as means of exchange and hoarding for personal income and for small enterprises. E-money proper based on mobile phones, or 'scratch cards' also offers the potential to remit money to remote areas at little cost. Thus, privately issued money and associated monetary innovations have created the possibility of bypassing formal financial institutions in low-income countries and expanding monetary circulation at the lower end.[63]

The further spread of e-money proper in developing countries might be hampered by the lack of mutual convertibility of different issues at par. This is a weakness common to all e-money, but its importance becomes more apparent when such money spreads widely. All e-money units have to be converted into ordinary money before they can be turned into each other. It is conceivable that mutual convertibility could be

---

62 Academic work on these very recent developments is scarce. For a brief description see Helen Allen, 'Innovations in Retail Payments: E-Payments', *Bank of England Quarterly Bulletin*, Winter 2003. For further descriptions and analysis see David Porteous, *The Enabling Environment for Mobile Banking in Africa*, DFID, 2006; and Gautam Ivatury and Mark Pickens, *Mobile Phone Banking and Low-Income Customers*, Consultative Group to Assist the Poor, 2006. More recent and broadly based work examining trust and the mechanics of the Kenyan M-PESA in particular can be found in Olga Morawcynski and Gianluca Miscione, 'Examining Trust in Mobile Banking Transactions, in *Social Dimensions of Information and Telecommunications Policy*, ed. Chrisanthi Avgerou et al., New York: Springer, 2008; and William Jack and Tavneet Suri, 'The Economics of M-PESA', NBER Working Paper No. 16721, 2011.

63 Leading even to the far-fetched argument that electronic finance might allow developing countries to 'leapfrog' stages of financial development; see Stijn Claessens et al., 'Electronic Finance: Reshaping the Financial Landscape Around the World', *Journal of Financial Research* 22: 2002.

FIG. 10 Reserve deposits at central banks as percentage of GDP

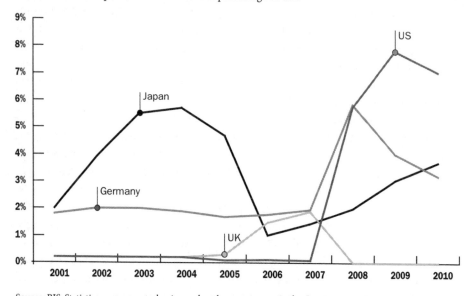

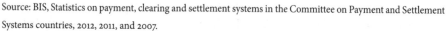

Source: BIS, Statistics on payment, clearing and settlement systems in the Committee on Payment and Settlement Systems countries, 2012, 2011, and 2007.

instigated in the future, thus further broadening the range of e-money proper. For this to arise, however, it would be necessary to introduce a system of mutual clearance of e-money liabilities, entailing significant costs for issuers. It remains to be seen whether such a development is feasible in developing countries.

State-backed central bank money at the peak of financialization

The final part of domestic valueless money that calls for closer examination comprises bank reserves held with the central banks. Bank reserves, as was mentioned on pages 101–5, are the most important component of state-backed credit money and the pivot of state intervention in the realm of finance. The fluctuations of bank reserves in the four countries during the period preceding the crisis of 2007 are briefly discussed below on the basis of figure 10. Only limited analytical mileage can be gained at this point in view of the complexity of the processes involved. Nonetheless, a foundation can be provided for further discussion of central banking and state intervention in subsequent chapters.

There have been significant differences in the use of bank reserves among the four countries, Japan and Germany initially surpassing the other two. These differences reflect variations in the institutional structure of the domestic credit system, particularly in the interaction between private banks and the central bank in the money market. But more fundamentally, they reveal differences in state intervention in the monetary sphere.

The sudden bulging of Japanese bank reserves after 2001 is the outcome of 'quantitative easing' – the policy of partly forcing, partly encouraging commercial banks to accumulate reserves in the hope of inducing commercial lending. A similar policy was adopted by the US and the UK central banks in 2008–2009 as the crisis hit the financial sector. The proportionate size of bank reserves in the US in 2009–2010 has exceeded the peak of the Japanese bulge. This represents a dramatic change from US policy during the preceding period, which basically maintained reserves at very low levels. During that time banks in the US and the UK were able to generate liquid funds in open markets; banks were also less inclined to hoard means of payment for reasons discussed in Chapter 9.

Bank reserves have been vital to state intervention in the monetary sphere, even when their absolute size has been typically small relative to both output and other forms of money. Needless to say, state intervention in the realm of money and finance reflects a far broader set of actions than merely managing bank reserves, and includes determination of interest rates. In the years of financialization state intervention has been driven by the express concern to limit the propensity of valueless money to generate inflation, and thus to perform inadequately as measure of value. Since the 1990s monetary policy has been set within the institutional regime of 'central bank independence' and has been summed up as 'inflation targeting', both of which are discussed in Chapter 5. The crisis of the 2000s has delivered a major blow to inflation targeting, but at the same time reaffirmed the power of the state to intervene in the financial sphere, pivoting on state-backed central bank money.

Contemporary valueless world money: The dollar as quasi-world-money

The severing of the link of credit money with gold after the collapse of Bretton Woods has had more severe repercussions in the international rather than the domestic monetary sphere for two fundamental reasons. First, there is no global credit system capable of generating a form of international credit money that could adequately operate as replacement for gold. Second, there is no state that could replicate the prevalent domestic monetary arrangements of financialized capitalism by generating state-backed credit money at the international level. The world market contains a range of sovereign states that operate within it and thus comprises a qualitatively different phenomenon to the domestic market that is normally supported by a single nation state.

The US dollar has in practice functioned as a valueless replacement for gold in the world market. But it has been a problematic substitute for gold resulting in unstable and exploitative arrangements that have placed their stamp on financialized capitalism. The theoretical parameters of this development are discussed below by briefly considering Marx's theory of world money, an undeveloped but integral part of his monetary theory. Empirical aspects of the role of the dollar as world money in the course of financialization are examined in chapters 8 and 9.[64]

---

64   For a fuller analysis of the functioning and the form of world money in contemporary capitalism see Costas Lapavitsas, 'Power and Trust as Constituents of Money and Credit', *His-*

Marx discussed the concept of world money briefly in the first volume of *Capital*, treating it as part of the composite function of money 'as money' which also comprises means of hoarding and means of payment. In his own words, 'World money serves as the universal means of payment, as the universal means of purchase, and as the absolute social materialization of wealth as such (universal wealth). Its predominant function is as means of payment in the settling of international balances'.[65]

Several points stand out in this definition. First, world money possesses the fundamental attribute of all 'money as money': to stand aloof from the regular grind of capitalist circulation while remaining capable of intervening decisively to transfer value, or settle balances. Second, and related to the first, the agents that operate in the world market are obliged to hold world money to be able to act in the market at required moments. There is an element of external compulsion to holding world money and not merely choice. Third, by this token, holding world money is an instrument of power for participants in the world market. Its possession affords the opportunity to pay and transfer value at critical junctures thereby shaping the underlying processes of value creation and circulation. Fourth, compulsion and power jointly reassert the fundamental 'moneyness' of world money, that is, its ability to dominate commodities and to emerge as the absolute form of value in the world market.

The function of 'money as money' is characteristic of Marx's monetary theory and sets it apart from the corpus of classical political economy. The hoarding function, for instance, inherently contains the possibility of crisis, since money stops buying commodities and lies idle. 'Money as money' thus represents a potential theoretical break with the notion of spontaneous market equilibrium. Consequently, classical political economists were troubled by money's hoarding function. David Ricardo, for one, could not readily accept the importance of money hoards, particularly because of the implication of insufficient demand and thus crisis. He had a well-known debate with Thomas Robert Malthus on this issue, including on the international role of money.[66] A few decades later, the Banking School in Britain, locked in debate with the Currency School, stressed that there could be external compulsion to holding money as, for instance, when economic agents had obligations to meet.[67]

In this light, Marx's stress on 'money as money' reveals the influence of mercantilism on his thought. For the mercantilist tradition, money was much more than simply

---

torical Materialism 14:1, 2006, pp. 129–54; and Costas Lapavitsas et al., *Crisis in the Eurozone*, London: Verso, 2012.

65   Marx, *Capital*, vol. 1, p. 242.

66   See, for instance, David Ricardo, *Letters*, in *The Works and Correspondence of David Ricardo*, vol. 6, ed. Piero Sraffa and Maurice Dobb, Cambridge: Cambridge University Press, 1951, pp. 64–5.

67   This view was clearly, and sharply, articulated by Thomas Tooke, *An Inquiry into the Currency Principle*, London: LSE Reprint Series, 1959.

a 'veil' on harmonious markets, and constituted the embodiment of wealth capable of reshaping economic activity and delivering political power. The legacy of mercantilism in this respect can be found across much heterodox monetary theory and not only Marxism. Heterodox theorists have often been forced to acknowledge the unique role of money when analysing capitalist crises and disruptions of circulation. Even Keynes discovered the continuing validity of elements of mercantilism when he examined the monetary phenomena of the inter-war crisis in *General Theory*.[68]

The mercantilist strain in Marx's monetary thought is clear with regard to world money for two reasons associated with the functioning of the world market. First, the world market lacks the legal, conventional, practical and customary mechanisms which provide homogeneity to national markets. It is inherently less homogeneous than national markets, also reflecting the absence of a world state that could have imposed conditions analogous to national markets. The world market is the terrain over which international private capitals meet the system of nation states. Private capitals have to deal with a range of legal, customary, practical, and even cultural specificities in the world market. At the same time, nation states must use the mechanisms of the world market to settle balances, transfer value, make payments, and borrow.

Second, the world market lacks the coordinating presence of an integrated credit system analogous to the credit system of national economies. Credit and finance certainly permeate the world market, but do not amount to a structured credit system comprising ordered layers of credit relations, typically including commercial, banking and money market credit.[69] By extension, there is no world central bank that could act as lender of last resort and issuer of legal tender.

For these reasons, world money is obliged to act as the coordinator (or organizer) of the world market. In other words, it must be a generally accepted means of hoarding (reserve) and means of payment for both international capitals and national states. In order to deliver these tasks, it must also be a commonly agreed measure of value that could apply to both commodities and past obligations. Finally, it must facilitate the exercise of inter-state political and military power, thus reflecting the conscious intervention of states in the world market.

The complexity of the role of world money becomes clear in Marx's analysis of the concrete monetary and commercial conditions of his era, found in several chapters of part five of the third volume of *Capital*.[70] Briefly put, the world market systematically generates disequilibria in the balance of trade, which are violently readjusted through crisis and necessitate forced flows of world money. In this context, the ability of a

---

68   John Maynard Keynes, *The General Theory of Employment, Interest and Money*, London: Macmillan, 1973.

69   The logical ordering of credit relations is examined in Itoh and Lapavitsas, *Political Economy of Money and Finance*, ch. 4, and is discussed in ch. 5.

70   See, for instance, Marx, *Capital*, vol. 3, ch. 30, 31, 32.

state to access reserves of world money is an element of global power. There is strong evidence of mercantilist influence on this part of Marx's work, particularly due to Sir James Steuart, who insisted that there is no automatic equilibration of trade balances through spontaneous flows of money.[71] Marx explicitly approved of Steuart's term 'money of the world' in his own brief discussion of world money.[72]

The form of world money presents complex problems, particularly when taken in conjunction with its functioning. For Marx, world money assumes the commodity form, typically gold, thus reasserting the essential 'moneyness' of world money.[73] The money commodity that is gradually sidelined by valueless forms of money in domestic circulation re-emerges triumphant at the world level. The intrinsic value of gold generated in production acts as the anchor of international value measurement. The reserves and flows of gold forcibly provide order to international transactions of commodities and money capital.

Unfortunately, Marx's assertion that world money must take the form of a commodity has not fared well historically, and is at odds with the severing of the link with gold in 1914. For most of the twentieth century world money has taken a variety of valueless, non-commodity forms, all of which have been managed by the state. The functioning of money in the world market has been typically performed by credit money domestically created and resting on the fiat of national governments, above all, the US dollar. This development is of paramount importance for financialization. The Bretton Woods Agreement of 1944 maintained a degree of convertibility of the US dollar with gold but, as was noted above, the link was snapped in the early 1970s. Since then, international reserve formation and payments – underpinned by the international measurement of values – has depended on state intervention in ways that are unprecedented in the history of capitalism. World money has become even more clearly an instrument of state power, particularly of hierarchical, imperial power in the world market. For these reasons, contemporary world money has been called 'quasi-world-money' in Marxist literature.[74]

The benefits to the US of the dollar functioning as world money have been substantial in terms of its ability to exercise monetary policy domestically, to maintain foreign trade deficits and to import and export capital. Use of the dollar internationally has also spurred financialization in developing countries and systematically transferred value to the US, as is discussed in Chapter 8. However, the function of world money

---

71—See, for instance, Steuart, *An Inquiry into the Principles of Political Economy*, vol. 3, book 4, part 2, ch. 8; and vol. 3, book 2, ch. 28.

72—Marx, *Capital*, vol. 1, p. 243.

73—Ibid., pp. 240–1.

74—See, for instance, Costas Lapavitsas, 'Power and Trust as Constituents of Money and Credit', *Historical Materialism* 14:1, 2006, pp. 129–54. The term has been borrowed from Makoto Itoh. In the rest of this book the simpler term 'world money' will be used to refer to national currencies competing to deliver the function of world money.

has continued to be contested terrain among the national currencies of the major capitalist powers. The most serious challenge to the dollar has come from the euro, a peculiar form of world money created collectively by several European powers. The euro has had a complex and contradictory role in the development of financialization, contributing to the crisis of the 2000s, as is shown in Chapter 9.

5. THE FLUID TERRAIN OF FINANCIALIZATION:
FINANCE AND THE CAPITALIST ECONOMY

The underlying tendencies of financialization as well as the variation in its form and content, even if they have monetary foundations, derive primarily from the interaction between finance and the rest of the economy. This chapter draws on Marxist political economy to examine how and why finance comes to form a distinct system influencing the pace and direction of capitalist accumulation as a whole. The financial system is neither a minor adjunct, nor a parasitical excrescence of the capitalist economy, but an integral part of it sustaining accumulation. At the same time, its functioning is determined by the historical and institutional framework within which financial activities occur. Finance remains relatively independent from the rest of economic activity, and could even become predatory and destructive toward it.

The emergence of a system of finance requires capitalist social conditions
At first sight, the realm of finance appears to be a chaotic collection of institutions, markets, assets, practices, laws and regulations. However, on closer inspection, a certain analytical order can be imposed on finance; institutions, for instance, could be categorized into financial intermediaries of various types, markets could be split into short-term and long-term, and assets could be divided into tradable and non-tradable. On this basis common patterns of financial practice could emerge, which could even allow for the theoretical determination of financial rates of return, or of financial prices. This is indeed the typical way for mainstream economics to approach finance.[1] Much mainstream theory consists of highly analytical treatments of particular financial activities and is concerned with determining financial prices in different contexts and institutional settings.

However, when finance is analysed by observing regularities and commonalities among particular financial phenomena, the resulting theoretical distinctions remain essentially partial, or even *ad hoc*. Mainstream economics does not offer a theoretical approach to finance as a system – as an ordered set of relations that contain regular interactions connected to production and circulation of goods and services. Despite the sophistication of the models determining financial price, the mainstream approach to the realm of finance as a whole retains an arbitrary dimension.

A greater sense of systemic coherence could, and does, emerge when finance is considered institutionally in particular countries. Analytical description is capable of establishing commonalities of practice among institutions (for instance, commercial or investment banks) among markets (such as the interbank or the bond market) and

---

1   See, for instance, Arnold Boot and Anjan Thakor, 'Financial System Architecture', *Review of Financial Studies* 10:3, 1997; and Anjan V. Thakor, 'The Design of Financial Systems: An Overview', *Journal of Banking and Finance* 20, 1996.

among assets (for example, futures and forward contracts). More significantly, analytical description could begin to show that integral relations exist among particular sets of institutions, markets, and assets. Coupled with descriptions of customary practices, of the relevant legal framework, and of the mechanisms of intervention by public authorities, institutional analysis could convey the impression of systemic functioning of finance.[2]

By definition, however, analytical description does not provide a theoretical explanation for the emergence of systemic behaviour. The US, for instance, would appear to possess a financial system, if an institutional description was given of the main agents, markets, assets, laws and practices. But description alone fails to establish the reasons for the ordered and regular interaction of the elements comprising the US system of finance. If systemic financial behaviour exists, it must ultimately rest on fundamental relations that bind together the elements of the financial system. Demonstrating these relations requires arguments based on economic theory.

It is also notable that analytical description fails to convey even the impression of systemic financial behaviour as soon as its focus moves onto international finance. The realm of global finance presents a picture of transactions and markets that is irreducibly chaotic and disorderly. The term 'global financial system' is in practice a misnomer: global finance amounts to a jumble of financial flows, often undertaken by institutions that have global reach. There is ultimately no sense of ordered and regular interaction among the many global financial agents. Thus, there is a distinct contrast between national finance, which can take the appearance of a system through mere description, and global finance, which is inherently far more chaotic. To account for this disparity it is again necessary to have a theoretical explanation of how finance becomes a system.

Political economy has distinct advantages compared to mainstream economics in demonstrating the systemic content of finance, not least because it typically searches for systemic integrity. Nonetheless, finance presents a paradox, which creates complex problems even for political economy in this respect. In a nutshell, the key economic relations that provide systemic content to finance do not lie within the realm of finance, but within the rest of the economy. The paradox is that the processes of finance, even when they attain great complexity, cannot by themselves create a system. The emergence of a financial system is ultimately derivative of relations characteristic of the spheres of production, exchange and distribution of goods and services.

---

2   There is no shortage of books that do precisely this for particular countries and in different historical contexts. US banking, for instance, is well served by a variety of works, including the magisterial account of Fritz Redlich, *The Molding of American Banking*, New York: Johnson Reprint Corporation, 1951; but see, for example, Larry Schweikart, *Banking in the American South: From the Age of Jackson to Reconstruction*, Baton Rouge: Louisiana State University Press, 1987; and Naomi Lamoreaux, *Insider Lending*, NBER, Cambridge: Cambridge University Press, 1994.

It is not hard to ascertain the derivative nature of the system of finance, both theoretically and practically. When finance is shorn of its institutional particulars, it essentially amounts to advancing monetary value either against a promise to pay it back, or against a title of ownership over the economic activities that would deploy the advanced value. Financial institutions, markets and assets can be understood as methods of issuing, collating, exchanging, and clearing promises to pay as well as titles to ownership. There is no doubt that some of these methods possess sufficient institutional coherence to attain a high degree of regularity under a broad variety of social and economic conditions. Banking activity, for instance, has been observed under greatly varied social conditions across historical time, often reaching remarkable complexity.[3]

However, for financial practices – including banking – to become integrated into a system, there must already be regularity in creating and augmenting monetary value in the rest of the economy. Without such regularity, the augmentation and return of value that has been mobilized in financial transactions would depend exclusively on the specific and particular conditions of the recipient as well as on the legal framework surrounding the transactions. In individual financial transactions the augmentation and return of value could, of course, be secured by both the conditions of the recipient and the law. Yet, a financial system constitutes a myriad of interrelated financial transactions, and neither the specific conditions of the recipients of value, nor the law could provide an adequate basis for regularity of value augmentation and return in the aggregate. For that it would be necessary to have appropriate social conditions applying to participants in finance, in addition to the specific conditions of individual recipients of value as well as the law.

The paradox of finance is that its institutions, markets and assets can secure the return of value in particular instances, but cannot guarantee the systematic augmentation and return of value in the aggregate. The components of finance do not produce monetary value but merely intervene in its advance and repayment. Thus, a prerequisite for a system of finance to emerge is that social relations must exist such that the deployment, expansion and accrual of monetary value across the economy could be taken for granted by participants in financial transactions. Only if such relations were already in place, would it be possible to form a financial system.

In short, a system of finance could emerge only if capitalist relations already permeated economic life. The components of finance would then have a social basis on which to become an integral whole – a system – mobilizing and advancing monetary value systematically. The actual form of the financial system would naturally vary according to particular historical conditions, but the system itself would be based on the social practice of regularly recouping value with increment. Under other social and historical conditions, financial practices would remain partial, fragmentary, and particular, even if they were complex and sophisticated.

---

3   A point made with particular force by Marx, *Capital*, vol. 3, ch. 36.

It is a theoretical point of paramount importance that appropriate relations for the emergence of a system of finance emerge only within the capitalist mode of production. Under capitalist social conditions – independent, competing capitalists who own the means of production and hire wage labour – the deployment and expansion of monetary value becomes a fixed social practice, providing the foundation for the emergence of a financial system. A financial system is a specifically capitalist phenomenon, although sophisticated financial practices can be observed in a wide variety of other social formations.[4]

Even assuming the existence of capitalist conditions, however, the emergence of a financial system continues to pose thorny theoretical problems, as is shown in the rest of this chapter. Two related points are worth making at the outset. First, theoretical analysis ought to establish the logical sequencing of economic relations that give to the financial system its characteristic outlook. Mobilizing and advancing monetary value results in a layering of financial relations with its own internal logic, thus structuring the financial system. In Marxist terminology, the financial system represents a dialectical unfolding of relations among industrial, commercial, and financial capitalists. Second, theoretical analysis ought to correspond broadly to the actual historical development of finance, if it is not to become ideally abstract. This is particularly important in view of the multiplicity of forms of the financial system, but also of the transformation of finance in the course of financialization.

Interest-bearing and loanable money capital
Some general definitions provide the point of departure for the theoretical analysis of the financial system.[5] Finance is a broad economic category that refers to the various methods through which capitalist enterprises obtain and deploy funds to support profit-making activities. Credit, on the other hand, is a narrower category that refers

---

4   This point often eludes historians of non-capitalist societies, who are enthralled by the complexity of ancient financial practices. It can also befuddle Marxists, such as Jairus Banaji, who appears to think that a financial system existed in antiquity. His views on ancient finance are part of his campaign against 'Weberianism' in the historiography of ancient economies in the course of which he also discovers 'free' labour in a variety of unlikely circumstances. As far as finance is concerned, the real problem in the historical literature is not 'Weberianism' but the invention of capitalism where none properly existed. This tendency would have been a more appropriate target for Banaji's critical efforts, if he were not prone to it himself. Jairus Banaji, *Agrarian Change in Late Antiquity: Gold, Labour, and Aristocratic Dominance*, Oxford: Oxford University Press, 2001.

5   The definitions and distinctions developed in this section draw heavily on Makoto Itoh and Costas Lapavitsas, *Political Economy of Money and Finance*, London: Macmillan, 1999, ch. 4; and Costas Lapavitsas, *Social Foundations of Markets, Money and Credit*, London: Routledge, 2003, ch. 4.

to the advance of value against a promise to repay later, plus increment. Finance is broader than credit not least because it includes relations of equity (or property) rather than borrowing and lending. Moreover, for Marxist political economy, as was seen in connection with Hilferding's work in Chapter 3, the distinction between trade (or commercial) and monetary (or banking) credit lies at the foundation of the financial system.

All credit has monetary foundations, but these differ between its trade and monetary forms. Trade credit is the advance of commodity output against a promise to pay later. In transactions of trade credit, money acts as measure of value (accounting unit of contracts) and as means of payment that eventually settles transactions; however, the original form of value advanced is commodities. Monetary credit, on the other hand, is the advance of money against a promise to pay later, plus interest. In transactions of monetary credit, money acts as measure of value and as means of payment, but it also is the original form of value advanced.

The focus of analysis in this chapter lies mostly on monetary credit, which is inextricably linked to interest-bearing or loanable money capital and provides the backbone of the financial system. The first step in establishing the theoretical content of monetary credit, therefore, is to consider more closely the relationship between borrowers and lenders.

The borrower–lender relationship in neoclassical theory

Mainstream economics focuses overwhelmingly on monetary credit and assigns a secondary role to trade credit; moreover, the mainstream treatment of borrowing and lending has traditionally focused on the institutions, laws and market practices of France.[6] However, during the last three decades, a change has taken place which has also affected financial policymaking. The advent of 'new financial economics' in the late 1970s – essentially a branch of microeconomics that relies on game theory – has entailed a highly abstract analysis of the relationship between borrowers and lenders.[7]

Simplifying ruthlessly, the new financial economics analyses the borrower–lend-

---

6   Sayers's classic book on banking, which has trained generations of economists across the world but is rarely read today, is typical of the traditional focus on institutions and practices. But even Gurley and Shaw, a post-war work that could have changed the direction of monetary and financial economics if it were not for the unfortunate rise of monetarism, is in a similar mould. R.S. Sayers, *Modern Banking*, Oxford: Oxford University Press, 1938; John Gurley and Edward Shaw, *Money in a Theory of Finance*, Washington, DC: Brookings Institute, 1960.

7   The relevant literature is very broad, although its innovative dynamism appears to have been exhausted by the early 2000s. For informative overviews see Xavier Freixas and Jean-Charles Rochet, *Microeconomics of Banking*, Cambridge, MA: MIT Press, 2008; and Franklin Allen and Anthony M. Santomero, 'The Theory of Financial Intermediation', *Journal of Banking and Finance* 21, 1998.

er relationship as the interaction between two individuals who approach the credit transaction from very different standpoints: the borrower holds a project and possesses specific knowledge of its details and possesses; the lender holds money but has no knowledge of the project. The asymmetry of information is problematic for the relationship between the holder of money (the principal) and the holder of the project (agent) since the latter can use specific knowledge about the project to gain an unfair advantage over, or even to defraud, the former.

Consequently the relationship between borrower and lender takes the contractual form of the lender advancing money to the borrower for a given period of time in exchange for a proportionately fixed share of the proceeds from the project (interest).[8] The lender must also practise information collection and monitoring of the borrower in order, first, to minimize the chances of the borrower undertaking fraudulent or careless action (moral hazard) and, second, to avoid attracting disproportionate numbers of poor quality borrowers (adverse selection). The outcome of moral hazard and adverse selection could be the rationing of credit actually provided by lenders, and hence the failure of credit markets to clear.[9]

In this light, banks and other financial institutions are providers of services that presumably improve the efficiency of the interaction between borrowers and lenders. It is evident that information asymmetry among borrowers and lenders reduces efficiency since it forces the lender to carry the costs of monitoring. Banks are institutions that specialize in collecting information and monitoring borrowers; these tasks can be undertaken cheaply due to the size of banks but also because of the peculiar nature of banks as businesses. Banks borrow short-term funds from many lenders (depositors) and make longer-term loans to many borrowers. The more they diversify their lending, the less the risk posed for ultimate lenders (depositors) by the actions of the borrowers. Thus, banks create liquidity by turning short-term deposits into long-term loans; they also gather information and manage the risks attached to lending.[10]

---

8   An elegant exposition of such analysis of financial contracting can be found in Robert M. Townsend, 'Optimal Contracts and Competitive Markets with Costly State Verification', *Journal of Economic Theory* 22, 1979.

9   See, for instance, Joseph Stiglitz and Andrew Weiss, 'Credit Rationing in Markets with Imperfect Information', *American Economic Review* 71:3, 1981, pp. 393–410; Nobuhiro Kiyotaki and John Moore, 'Credit Cycles', *Journal of Political Economy* 105:2, 1997.

10   Once again, the literature is very broad; see, very selectively, Hayne Leland and David H. Pyle, 'Informational Asymmetries, Financial Structure and Financial Intermediation', *The Journal of Finance* 32, 1977; John Bryant, 'A Model of Reserves, Bank Runs, and Deposit Insurance', *Journal of Banking and Finance* 4, 1980; Douglas Diamond and Philip Dybvig, 'Bank Runs, Deposit Insurance and Liquidity', *Journal of Political Economy* 91, 1983; Douglas Diamond, 'Financial Intermediation and Delegated Monitoring', *Review of Economic Studies* 51, 1984; John H. Boyd and Edward C. Prescott, 'Financial Intermediary-Coalitions', *Journal of Economic*

It is apparent that this is a highly abstract approach to the borrower–lender relationship which focuses heavily on the content of the interaction at the expense of its broader social and economic context. Access to information is an important aspect of the borrower–lender relationship, and there is little doubt that banking relies on systematic collection of information and management of risk. However, information is always context-specific. The methods and practices of information-gathering and assessment in the realm of finance reflect the social and economic character of borrowers and lenders. Furthermore, banks could practise information-gathering and risk-management in ways that could actually induce instability in the relationship between borrowers and lenders. The strength of Marxist political economy is that it acknowledges the information-related operations of financial institutions while bringing the social aspects of the borrower–lender relationship to the fore.

Borrowers, lenders, and 'monied' capitalists in Marxist political economy

Marxist theory of the borrower–lender relationship rests on a special form of capital: interest-bearing capital, or in less abstract form, loanable money capital. Similarly to neoclassical theory, Marx's analysis of the borrowing and lending of money begins at a highly abstract level.[11] Unlike neoclassical theory, however, the counterparties to the credit transaction are assumed to be capitalists and not merely individuals with different endowments and access to information. Immediately, therefore, the transaction has a specific social context: both parties are profit-seeking entities that deploy the cost-return calculus of the capitalist enterprise.

The assumption that both borrower and lender are capitalists does not preclude the possibility that in practice one or both of the counterparties are not capitalists, and might even be wage labourers, as indeed happens commonly under conditions of financialization. The point is, rather, that the content of the borrower–lender relationship would emerge most clearly if both parties were assumed to be capitalists. Once that content is established theoretically, other credit transactions which do not necessarily involve capitalists on both sides could also be analysed.

For Marx moreover, the moneylending transaction is inherently an act of exchange, a trade, occurring in the sphere of circulation.[12] Since it is an act of exchange, it must satisfy the characteristic *quid pro quo* of value transfer among the counterparties. The question then immediately rises: what is the traded commodity? Marx's answer is that it is interest-bearing capital: the lender advances a sum of money that is considered

---

Theory 38, 1986; Douglas Diamond and Raghuram Rajan, 'Liquidity Risk, Liquidity Creation, and Financial Fragility: A Theory of Banking', *Journal of Political Economy* 109:2, 2001; Franklin Allen and Anthony M. Santomero, 'What Do Financial Intermediaries Do?', *Journal of Banking and Finance* 25, 2001.

11   See Marx, *Capital*, vol. 3, ch. 21.

12   Ibid., pp. 462–3.

from the start to be capital; the borrower gives in exchange a promise to return the money after a fixed period of time, plus an increment.[13] Thus, from the lender's standpoint, the entire transaction has the characteristic reflux form that is appropriate to capital in general. Since both counterparties are capitalists, the presumption is that the borrower will use the borrowed money to generate value and surplus-value to meet the contractual promise. The increment paid to the lender is a share of the surplus value (profit) that the borrower is expected to generate – it is interest.

Interest-bearing capital captures the fundamental content of the borrower–lender relationship and represents the abstract kernel of moneylending. It is a form of capital that differs greatly from industrial and merchant capital, not least because it is itself traded as a commodity from its inception. Nonetheless, interest-bearing capital is a commodity *sui generis* since it is neither produced, nor does it have an obvious use value. Rather, it is a sum of money that is advanced for a definite period of time on condition of repayment. Hence its price is equally peculiar: it is interest, or a share of the profits that could in general be created by deploying the money borrowed.

Three points are particularly striking regarding Marx's theoretical analysis of interest-bearing capital. The first is that he placed tradability at the heart of the credit relationship: the act of credit is an act of exchange, even if it is highly peculiar as such. Trading is an inherent aspect of finance that reaches highly advanced forms as the financial system develops. This is a crucial aspect of financialization resulting in new forms of profit examined in Chapter 6.

Second, Marx implicitly assumed – similarly to contemporary mainstream theory of finance – that the relationship of borrower to lender occurs between the owner of money and the holder of a project. However, for Marx, both lender and borrower are characteristic capitalist types, and hence are subject to prior determinations that shape the act of lending. The project holder, in particular, is typically an industrial capitalist.[14] By this token, the transaction of monetary credit has an underlying productive purpose: it aims at commencing or expanding a circuit of industrial capital.

Third, for Marx interest is a share of the surplus value produced by the industrial capitalist that has deployed the borrowed capital.[15] Mainstream economics also defines

---

13   Ibid., pp. 464–5.

14   There are many scattered references to this effect in Marx's work, for instance, ibid., pp. 468–9.

15   Ibid., ch. 22. The Marxist tradition of the Uno School would be very sceptical about this argument. Makoto Itoh for instance, has claimed that the specific character of interest-bearing capital is based on merchant's capital and on the profit that the latter earns through trade (*The Basic Theory of Capitalism*, London: Macmillan, 1988, pp. 98–100). There is a degree of formal validity to this point, particularly as interest-bearing capital has historically predated industrial capital. However, there is also formal validity to the argument that the content of interest-bearing capital cannot be adequately defined without explicit reference to industrial capital, even if

interest as a share of the returns generated by the project of the borrower. For Marx, however, the owner of capital for loan is remunerated purely because of property rights over the capital lent. Interest is a return for ownership of money capital for loan, and there is no question of the lender playing a role in organizing, or managing the creation of surplus value.

The question that naturally arises at this point is: what kind of capitalist owns money capital available for loan and trades it for interest with industrial capitalists? In the part of his work that discusses the abstract core of the borrower–lender relationship, Marx suggested that the lender is a 'money' or 'monied' capitalist.[16] That is, the lender is an owner of money capital who does not wish to become directly involved in the grubby business of productive accumulation. The 'monied' capitalist has the right to receive interest – which is simply a part of the surplus value that is subsequently generated – because of ownership rights over of the capital lent. In effect, the monied capitalist is a rentier, though this word appears very rarely in Marx's writings.

To be more specific, for Marx, the act of lending implies the splitting of surplus value into interest and 'profit of enterprise'.[17] This quantitative division of surplus value corresponds to the qualitative distinction between, respectively, 'monied' capitalist and 'active' capitalist, or capital-as-property and capital-as-function. By this token, 'monied' capitalists form a distinct section of the capitalist class defined by owning interest-bearing capital and receiving interest income. It follows immediately that there is an inherent tension between 'monied' and 'functioning' capitalists: the more surplus value that accrues as interest to the former, the less that remains as 'profit of enterprise' for the latter.

The 'monied' capitalist is, by construction, remote from the process of production and accumulation. Consider, for instance, the characteristic formula that Marx proposes for interest-bearing capital.[18] The formula for the circuit of industrial capital is given by: $M - C - \ldots P \ldots - C' - M'$, where M is money capital invested, C is inputs purchased, P is productive capital set in motion, C' is finished output, and M' is sales revenue that incorporates surplus value. The motion of interest-bearing capital is superimposed upon the motion of industrial capital, resulting in a circuit of the form: $M - M - C - \ldots P \ldots C' - M' - M''$, where M is the interest-bearing capital initially advanced and M'' is the restored capital of the lender plus interest. From the perspective of the lender this complex motion can be simplified to the first and the last point, resulting in the 'superficial' form of $M - M''$ which leaves out the actual process of accumulation. For the 'monied' capitalist, money simply begets money.

---

the latter emerges later in the course of history. Marx had good dialectical reasons to assume that the borrower is an industrialist in the first instance.

16   Ibid., p. 475.

17   Ibid., ch. 23.

18   Ibid., p. 461.

The remoteness of the lender from the process of production could be interpreted as the lender's essential indifference toward the creation of value. Moreover, the inherent tension between 'monied' and 'functioning' capitalists over the division of surplus value could be interpreted as the predatory attitude of 'monied' capitalists toward accumulation. What matters to lenders is the return of capital plus interest – the intervening accumulation process is merely a detour. Thus, the negative features of the rentier are discernible in the 'monied' capitalist: distant from production, at loggerheads with the active capitalist, indifferent and even predatory toward accumulation.

Marx's theoretical emphasis on 'monied' capitalists reflects the influence of classical political economy and should be treated with caution.[19] Relative remoteness from productive activities and a potentially predatory outlook are important features of the lender, but the relationship of lender to borrower is considerably deeper, as is shown immediately below and in Chapter 6. The accrual of interest, furthermore, is hardly limited to a distinct section of the capitalist class that owns capital available for lending. In mature capitalism the typical lending agent is a financial institution that lends money capital collected across the capitalist class, and even across other classes. The concept of the 'monied' capitalist has limited explanatory power over the lending phenomena of financialized capitalism.

To be more specific, the lender is typically more knowledgeable of the project of the borrower than is implied by the analysis of the 'monied' capitalist. The lender must ensure the return of interest-bearing capital as M'', and although the contractual aspect of the lending relationship offers some legal guarantees, better assurance could only be provided by the borrower's ability to generate M'. Paradoxically enough, the lender is obliged to examine and monitor the business of the borrower precisely to remain remote from production and accumulation. For, if the borrower failed, the lender would be obliged to take over the borrower's project with the aim of recouping some of the capital advanced, thus becoming involved in the grubby business that the lender aimed to avoid in the first place. The requirement to monitor the borrower is even more pressing when the lender uses other people's money, as is the case for financial institutions; banks have entire departments devoted to the monitoring task.

Note that Hilferding was fully aware of the monitoring role of financial institutions in advanced capitalism, as was shown in Chapter 3. His concept of finance capital was based on the assumption that the lender actively participates in the business of the borrower, indeed to such an extent that banking and industrial capitals presumably become amalgamated. Finance capital rests on the implicit view that the relationship between lenders and borrowers cannot be summed up as relative indifference and tension of one toward the other. It was apparent to Hilferding that the lender of money

---

19   See Makoto Itoh, *The Basic Theory of Capitalism*, London: Macmillan, 1988. Costas Lapavitsas, 'Two Approaches to the Concept of Interest-Bearing Capital', *International Journal of Political Economy* 27:1, Spring 1997, pp. 85–106.

in mature capitalism is a far more complex creature than a mere 'monied' capitalist, or a 'parasitical' coupon clipper.

One last question to consider is: what is the use value of the thing traded among borrowers and lenders, and how does it relate to the rate of interest? For Marx, interest-bearing capital has a *sui generis* use value that corresponds to its *sui generis* character as a commodity.[20] Specifically, the money capital advanced by the lender gives to the borrower the ability to generate the average rate of profit. This ability constitutes the peculiar use value that the lender sells to the borrower for the – equally peculiar – price of the rate of interest. In other words, what is traded in the markets for credit is capital's general ability to produce surplus-value for given periods of time.[21]

Two further analytical points by Marx are pertinent in this connection. First, the price of this peculiar commodity bears no relation to the labour theory of value, and nor to the actual production of values and commodities. It is the outcome of a mere quantitative division of total profit that reflects the demand and supply of interest-bearing capital at a particular moment, and nothing else. In short, there is no such thing as 'natural' rate of interest.[22] No material, social or economic realities are captured by the rate of interest, other than the transient balance of demand and supply for interest-bearing capital.

Second, the rate of interest tends to be below the rate of profit, the latter normally acting as the upper boundary for the former.[23] This argument is characteristic of Marxist theory of finance, and sets it apart from neoclassical theory, though the absence of equalization is not fully explained by Marx. To an extent the excess of the rate of profit over the rate of interests reflects the difference between active and hoarded money

---

20 Marx, *Capital*, vol. 3, pp. 473–79.

21 The analysis of interest-bearing capital by Marx differs from that by Laurence Harris ('On Interest, Credit and Capital', *Economy and Society* 5:2, 1976, pp. 145–77), which was subsequently reworked in Ben Fine, 'Banking Capital and the Theory of Interest', *Science and Society* 49:4, 1985–86, pp. 387–413; and Ben Fine and Alfredo Saad-Filho, *Marx's Capital*, London: Pluto Press, 2004. For Harris, the nature of interest-bearing capital is determined largely by the use to which the borrower puts the borrowed funds; hence, interest-bearing capital emerges properly if the borrower is a capitalist who uses the loan to produce surplus-value, but not otherwise. For Marx, in contrast, the lender sells the use-value of 'being able to produce surplus-value' irrespective of the borrower's plans, expectations and actual operations. The real issue here is not the difference with Marx, which by itself means very little. It is, rather, that determining the character of interest-bearing capital along the lines proposed by Harris would lead the analysis of contemporary finance to a dead end. Much of present-day lending is for unproductive purposes, including mortgages; if interest-bearing capital does not directly relate to such lending, Marxist theory has little to say about contemporary finance.

22 Marx, *Capital*, vol. 3, p. 484.

23 Ibid., p. 482.

capital. It further reflects the inherent cyclical motion of capitalist economies that tends to keep the rate of profit above the rate of interest, except for periods of crisis when the relationship could be reversed.[24]

Marx's argument on the use value of interest-bearing capital and its importance for determining the rate of interest has to be approached with care. The notion that the ability to produce surplus-value is inherently contained in a sum of money (even if that is capital) is not immediately persuasive. The potential for surplus-value is also contained in the project that the borrower brings to the transaction; and that is without even mentioning the borrower's presumed role in mustering and supervising the accumulation process. Availability of money capital is a necessary but not sufficient element for the generation of surplus-value. Without the project and the active role of the borrower, the money capital of the lender would be a barren sum of money.

The point is important for the further analysis of the borrower–lender relation. Establishing the potential of the borrower to generate surplus value is precisely the reason why the lender has to gather information and subsequently to monitor the borrower. This is an integral part of credit transactions and characterises the operations of financial institutions. In normal commodity transactions, the buyer checks the quality of the use value of commodities, ensuring that value is borne adequately by the commodity traded.[25] In the case of interest-bearing capital, the buyer (borrower) need not check the quality of the use vale traded because money (as long as it is not fraudulent) possesses an undifferentiated ability to buy, which is all that is required by the borrower. However, the seller (lender) has to check the buyer's potential to generate surplus-value, if the money lent is not to be wasted. This is yet another aspect of the *sui generis* character of interest-bearing capital.

To recap, the use-value of interest-bearing capital is the ability to produce surplus value, which is a necessary but not sufficient condition for the borrower to generate surplus value. For surplus value to materialize, the borrower must also possess and supervise an appropriate project. It is not true that any sum of money possesses the

---

24   See Itoh and Lapavitsas, *Political Economy of Money and Finance*, pp. 69–73. Note that Marx's analysis of interest as the price of interest-bearing or loanable capital is very different from Knut Wicksell's analysis of loanable funds. First, unlike Wicksell, Marx did not connect price fluctuations to the rate of interest; second, by the same token, Marx did not accept the notion of a 'natural' rate of interest determined by the demand and supply of real capital from which the money rate of interest might diverge, thus inducing price changes. For Marx, interest is purely a monetary phenomenon with no 'real' substance. Above all, interest relates to a special type of capital – loanable capital – and not simply to liquidity, to credit, or even to capital in general. The inherent monetary dimension of interest results precisely because loanable capital is inherently monetary. See Knut Wicksell, 'The Influence of the Rate of Interest on Commodity Prices', in *Selected Papers on Economic Activity*, New York: Augustus M. Kelley Publishers, 1969.

25   Lapavitsas, *Social Foundations of Markets, Money and Credit*, ch. 2.

ability to generate surplus value in general, which is made available by the lender to the borrower, and for which the lender can demand a share of the putative surplus value.

Idle money and the practice of systematic lending

Marx's discussion of the borrower–lender relationship, however, contains yet another analytical strain that provides a far more nuanced view of the capitalist who possesses interest-bearing capital. This might be called the 'hoards' approach to monetary credit, which was briefly mentioned in connection with Hilferding's work. To be specific, Marx showed in Volume II of *Capital* that the circuit of industrial capital systematically releases money funds that lie temporarily idle as money hoards.[26] These funds provide the wherewithal for the regular formation of interest-bearing capital. From this perspective, the financial system is a set of social mechanisms that systematically convert temporarily idle funds into money capital available for lending.

This is a very different approach to assuming that interest-bearing capital belongs to a distinct, 'monied', fraction of the capitalist class. Far from being the exclusive property of a layer of rentiers, interest-bearing capital is in large measure the reallocated spare money capital of the capitalist class. By the same token, interest accrues across the capitalist class and does not constitute the revenue foundation of a separate social group – of the 'monied' capitalists.

The appropriate concept for analysis of the borrower–lender relationship within the 'hoards' approach is loanable money capital rather than interest-bearing capital. Indeed, loanable capital is the developed form of interest-bearing capital both in theory and in the actual operations of the capitalist economy. The term 'loanable capital' was proposed by Marx, although it was heavily deployed only in the later chapters of the third volume of *Capital* that deal with more concrete financial phenomena.[27] Loanable capital rests on the advanced functioning of the financial system, and thus corresponds to a lower level of theoretical abstraction than interest-bearing capital.

The 'hoards' approach places heavy emphasis on the active formation of loanable capital by the financial system as the latter collects idle funds across society. For this reason the typical form of loanable capital is that of financial assets – cash, deposits with financial institutions, and securities – which are promises to pay (liabilities) of financial institutions. Creating loanable capital involves mobilizing idle money funds generated within the circuits of industrial and commercial capital. It also involves mobilizing funds generated outside capitalist circuits, for instance, the private hoards

---

26   Marx, *Capital*, vol. 2, pp. 158–9 and 163–6. Hoard formation has been further analysed in Rudolf Hilferding, *Finance Capital*, London: Routledge & Kegan Paul, 1981, pp. 67–81; Makoto Itoh, *The Basic Theory of Capitalism*, London: Macmillan, 1988, pp. 259–60, 401; and more formally in Costas Lapavitsas, 'On Marx's Analysis of Money Hoarding in the Turnover of Capital', *Review of Political Economy* 12:2, 2000, pp. 219–35.

27   Marx, *Capital*, vol. 3, ch. 30–2.

formed out of personal income across social classes. The latter is a characteristic mode of creation of loanable capital in financialized capitalism, led by a host of institutional investors, such as pension funds, insurance companies and the like; it also provides a route to financial expropriation, as is shown in Chapter 6.

More complexly, the creation of loanable capital further involves the anticipation of the future accrual of idle funds to the financial system. A fundamental practice of financial institutions is actively to create their own liabilities after advancing their own credit in the expectation that there will be future accrual of idle funds as well as future accrual of returns, both of which would post-validate the creation of liabilities.[28] By advancing their own credit, financial institutions enlarge the circuits of industrial capital, thus indirectly expanding the potential sources of future idle funds. The financial system thus acts as lever for the formation of loanable capital but in a highly mediated and precarious way.

It is worth stressing that the operations of the financial system spontaneously lessen the importance of the 'productive' purpose of borrowing. In advanced financial systems, for instance, money is systematically lent by financial institutions for purposes of consumption, or to facilitate financial transactions by other institutions. It follows immediately that the actual returns to loanable capital in advanced financial systems do not necessarily originate in surplus value directly, or even at all. Note that the important aspect of the accrual of interest to the owner of loanable capital is that it occurs for reasons of capital-as-property. Interest takes the form of a reward for merely parting with the money lent regardless of the purpose of the loan. This appearance prevails even when lending is for productive purposes. Thus, it provides a formal basis for the payment of interest even when there is no productive purpose to the loan. The source of interest accruing to the owner of loanable capital does not necessarily have to be surplus value resulting from a capitalist project.

Note further that in developed financial systems the inherent tradability of interest-bearing or loanable capital is accentuated. An important reason for this is that the financial system extends the range of potential counterparties in financial transactions far beyond the immediate participants to the circuit of a particular industrial capital. Another reason is that the financial system increases the variety of tradable credit instruments, which no longer need to be directly linked to particular industrial sectors. The

---

28   Following Suzanne de Brunhoff, Martha Campbell states that bank credit pre-validates value realization. In addition to this important point, however, banks also anticipate the accrual of idle funds when making their own loans. This is a fundamental point about the operation of banks in a capitalist economy: banks first lend and subsequently seek deposits and reserves to back up their lending. See Suzanne de Brunhoff, *Marx on Money*, New York: Urizen Books, 1976, p. 46–7; Martha Campbell, 'The Credit System', in *The Culmination of Capital: Essays on Volume III of Marx's Capital*, ed. Martha Campbell and Geert Reuten, London: Palgrave, 2002, pp. 218–19.

financial system also homogenizes the types and methods of trading securities.[29] At the same time, the financial system intensifies the tendency to trade financial assets. Means of payment (liquidity) are required by financial institutions to settle obligations, particularly as institutions are actively issuing their own liabilities in advance of future returns. The financial system itself becomes a major source of demand for liquid funds at short notice, hence encouraging trade in financial assets.

Loanable money capital, like interest-bearing capital, is distant from production, and thus its functioning is only partially dependent on material factors – that is, on the world of use values. Marx demonstrated the importance of labour skills, technology, and the rate of turnover for the fundamental functioning of industrial and merchant's capital, including the determination of its profitability.[30] In sharp contrast, the functioning of loanable capital is strongly conditioned by the design of financial institutions, customary practice, legal framework, and even cultural and moral elements. These factors also shape the impact of material factors on the functioning of loanable capital. Thus, both the volume and the rate at which loanable capital is advanced depend on technology and labour skills; nonetheless, similar sums could be lent from the modest offices of a hedge fund in Mayfair as from the tower of a bank in Wall Street.

It follows that the enterprises specializing in handling and managing loanable capital could exhibit considerable variety in actual practice, even if they adopted similar organizational form. The institutional, legal, customary and cultural framework within which financial institutions operate stamps their practices across countries and areas.[31] For the same reason, the financial system necessarily exhibits significant differences in design and operation across countries, and even across areas within the same country. This is a commonly observed aspect of finance that is discussed in more depth in the rest of this book. The ineluctable variation among financial systems is important to analysing financialization.

In sum, the 'hoards' approach provides more analytical mileage than the 'monied' capitalist approach in analysis of contemporary finance. The borrower–lender relation can be more fruitfully considered in terms of two 'functioning' capitalists interacting to trade loanable money capital. The lender approaches the transaction as the owner of money capital that is of no immediate use to the operations of the circuit of capital for a specific period of time; the borrower seeks money capital to inject into an existing, or to start a new, circuit of capital. There is no need for prior (economic or social)

---

29 As noted by Hilferding, securities have a peculiar nature since they are qualitatively identical. Even when there are qualitative differences, they are all reduced to mere quantitative differences – those of the rate of return. Hilfdering, *Finance Capital*, p. 144.

30 Marx, *Capital*, vol. 3, ch. 2–5, 17, 18.

31 Mainstream theory appreciates this point even to the extent of turning legal practices into the principal means for differentiating among financial systems in different countries; see Rafael La Porta et al., 'Law and Finance', *Journal of Political Economy*, vol. 106, no. 6, 1998.

links between the two counterparties, and their relationship unfolds on the basis of the borrower returning the money to the lender, plus interest. Thus, the financial system emerges out of the unplanned interactions of 'functioning' capitalists, and provides order to the advance and return of loanable capital.

Finance and real accumulation: A two-way relationship

The preceding analysis of the borrower–lender relationship provides a point of departure for the theoretical examination of the structure of the financial system and its relationship to real accumulation. Analysis in the rest of this chapter has roots in Marx's discussion of finance in the 'chaotic' chapters of section five of the third volume of *Capital*. This part of Marx's work contains key insights into the structure of the financial system drawing on the institutional and historical specificities of the time.[32] Marx's views were the basis for Hilferding's theory of finance which is, in turn, the bedrock for the theoretical exposition of the financial system in the rest of this chapter.

Discussion of the financial system in the following sections also draws on Suzanne de Brunhoff's seminal *Marx on Money* and on Duncan Foley's sustained output, even if it does not openly acknowledge its debts at all times and nor does it agree with these two authors on all points.[33] It draws still more heavily on Japanese Marxism, especially the Uno tradition, though again it differs in important particulars. Unlike post-war Anglo-Saxon Marxism, Japanese Marxists have been fully aware of the classical Marxist debates on finance already since the early interwar years. Economic thought came to Japan mostly from Europe at the turn of the twentieth century, and perhaps the weightiest part of it was Marxism.[34] Hilferding's book has been used as a standard university economics textbook for decades during the post-war period; its influence on Japanese Marxism has been enormous.

Several insights regarding the structure of the financial system in the rest of this chapter originate in Kozo Uno's *Principles of Political Economy* (*Keizai Genron*). This is an extremely dense and far from limpid book, though an abridged version appeared in Japanese in 1964 and was translated in English in 1980. To appreciate Uno's approach to the relationship between theoretical and historical concepts in the context of finance

---

32 As is always the case with Marx, there is a hard theoretical kernel even to casual remarks about financial practices, or state policies.

33 See, in particular, Duncan Foley, 'The Value of Money, the Value of Labour Power and the Marxian Transformation Problem', *Review of Radical Political Economics* 14:2, 1982; Duncan Foley, *Money, Accumulation and Crisis*, London: Harwood Academic Publishers, 1986; Duncan Foley, *Understanding Capital*, Cambridge, MA: Harvard University Press, 1986.

34 For an accessible discussion of this issue see Tessa Morris-Suzuki, *A History of Japanese Economic Thought*, London: Routledge, 1991; for a more advanced analysis, see Andrew Barshay, *The Social Sciences in Modern Japan: The Marxian and Modernist Traditions*, Berkeley: University of California Press, 2004.

it is perhaps easier to use *Keizai Seisakuron*, an English translation of which has been produced by Tomohiko Sekine, available in mimeo as *The Types of Economic Policy Under Capitalism*. With regard to the contradictory role of credit in capitalist accumulation, in particular, there is much to be gained from Uno's *Kyoukouron*, which is not available in English and is sometimes referred to as *Theory of Crisis*, though it would be more accurately rendered as *Theory of Panic*.

The Uno School is, of course, a broad current containing several smaller eddies. Its best-known exponent in the West is Tomohiko Sekine, whose *Dialectic of Capital* is fundamental to appreciating Uno's method of analysis as well as the Unoist order of economic investigation rising from merchant's capital, to moneylending capital, to industrial capital; Sekine has also examined the relationship between commercial credit and banking credit. Equally known in the West is Makoto Itoh, who however holds a distinctive position within the Uno School, always willing to examine and incorporate fresh ideas from other traditions. Itoh has had a long-standing interest in money and finance, evidenced by his (jointly authored) first book, *The Basic Theory of Money and Credit* (*Kahei Sinyou no Kihon Riron*). His influence on the analysis of the structure of the financial system in the remainder of this chapter is apparent. Less known in the West but even more prominent in analysing the functioning of finance and the role of money in contemporary capitalism has been Shigekatsu Yamaguchi. His *Theory of the Structure of Finance* (*Kinyuu Kikou no Riron*) lays out the basic relations between commercial, banking and money market credit, while independently capturing the key insights of post-Keynesianism on credit money. The exposition below has also drawn on Yamaguchi's analysis.

Summarily put, in the rest of this section the 'hoards' approach of Marx is taken as point of departure for developing a theoretical view of the structure of finance as a system. The financial system comprises a set of social mechanisms that emanate from real accumulation, incorporate commercial credit, and mobilize idle funds that are transformed into loanable capital subsequently to be returned to accumulation. The financial system emerges out of capitalist accumulation but also shapes and directs the path of the latter. There is a two-way relationship between accumulation and finance. This approach is capable of casting theoretical light onto the financialization of contemporary capitalism.

Finance is not a parasitical entity but an integral element of the capitalist economy. Developed capitalism without a developed financial system would be unthinkable. The financial system offers key services to capitalist accumulation and improves the profitability of industrial and commercial enterprises. This is ultimately the reason why financial institutions are able to make profits on a sustained basis. Nonetheless, the relationship between the financial system and real accumulation is contradictory – finance can also be predatory and destructive of real accumulation. Specifying some of the conditions under which such phenomena could occur takes up much of the rest of this book.

The fundamental insight of the Uno tradition in this respect is that finance comprises an integral whole of relations ordered in interconnected layers emerging spontaneously out of real accumulation. This is a path-breaking contribution that could be simply summed up by representing the credit system in the form of a pyramid of credit relations.[35] The pyramid rises from the elemental relations of trade credit, to the more complex relations of monetary (banking) credit, to the still more complex relations of money market credit, and finally to relations of central bank credit. The capital (stock) market, on the other hand, exists alongside the pyramid of the credit system, but is connected to the latter through value flows and price determination. Credit system and stock market together comprise the financial system.

The importance of this conceptual representation of finance does not rest on the specific institutions and markets to which it refers, and not even on the notion of ordering credit relations in the form of a pyramid. Financialized capitalism, as is shown in chapters 7 and 8, has thrown out a variety of financial institutions and practices that do not immediately fit the schematic view of the pyramid including, for instance, banks lending to individuals and trading in derivatives markets. Moreover, the actual design of the financial system can vary among particular countries and could well diverge from the abstraction of the pyramid, reflecting historical, institutional and other developments.

The importance of the ordered representation of credit and finance derives, rather, from two deeper theoretical features. The first is that the financial system emerges endogenously from real accumulation: finance is a necessary outgrowth of accumulation rather than an arbitrary set of institutions and practices devised by an extra-economic authority. The endogenous emergence of the financial system, on the other hand, does not prevent it from being highly changeable as well as malleable. The second is that credit relations contain an internal necessary order. Credit in a capitalist economy comprises chains of interconnected promises to pay – rising from the simple to more complex – that mutually sustain each other, thus generating social trust and validity in the system of credit as a whole. For this reason credit can stretch accumulation, but it can also have a destructive effect, particularly if the chains of promises to pay are disrupted leading to collapse of social trust.

Trade and banking credit
Consider now the layered and ordered relations of the credit system more closely. The first layer (from below) of the credit pyramid is trade credit, emerging directly from real accumulation. This is an elementary form of credit that occurs spontaneously and necessarily among competing enterprises. Trade credit requires neither loanable capital, nor complex financial institutions to emerge since it is simply the advance of finished output against promises to pay among enterprises. The financial instruments

---

35   See Itoh and Lapavitsas, *Political Economy of Money and Finance*, ch. 4; see also Lapavitsas, *Social Foundations of Markets, Money and Credit*, ch. 4.

to which it gives birth can take several forms, including bills of exchange, and promissory notes. Trade credit provides the grounds on which other credit relations are able to develop and form the financial system.

Trade credit typically emerges within particular sectors of production in which enterprises are already related to each other through pre-existing practices of buying and selling, thus already possessing a basis for trust necessary for the advance of credit.[36] Trade credit improves the profitability of 'active' capitalists because it, first, accelerates the turnover of capital and, second, reduces reserves of money and inventories of finished output held by enterprises. A striking aspect of financialization is the relative decline of trade credit, shown in Chapter 8, perhaps indicating increasing reliance of enterprises on other forms of credit for the needs of circulation.

The second layer of the credit pyramid is monetary (or banking) credit, which rests partly on, and incorporates elements of, trade credit. This is credit associated with the most fundamental institutions of the credit system – banks – and entails the trading of loanable capital, in which banks specialize. The question that immediately arises is: what are banks and how do they emerge?

Briefly put, banks are capitalist enterprises that develop skills in buying financial assets (securities) by extending their own liabilities (promises to pay).[37] A bank's assets fundamentally comprise promises to pay that others have made. In the first instance, banks acquire financial assets that are spontaneously generated among enterprises through trade credit relations. To this purpose banks advance loanable capital that belongs either to themselves or to others. As banking develops, the range of financial assets acquired by banks expands enormously. In advanced capitalism bank assets are only very partially related to trade credit instruments and include government securities, private securities, loans of various descriptions, and so on.

The most striking aspect of banking as a capitalist activity is that a bank can acquire financial assets by simply relying on its own creditworthiness, rather than by advancing loanable capital. The purest form of banking credit is the advance of a bank's own promises to pay in anticipation of the future accrual of loanable capital to the bank, which would thus allow the bank to honour promises that it has already made. In short, the liabilities of a bank are often promises to pay made by the bank in anticipation of regularly receiving sufficient inflows of loanable capital. This is the basis on which banks begin to mobilize loanable capital across the capitalist class, rather than through simply waiting for loanable capital to arrive in the form of deposits, or otherwise.

Banks are able to operate in this ground-breaking way because they evolve out of what Marx called 'merchant's capital', and more specifically out of 'money-dealing capital'.[38] Merchant's capital exists in the sphere of circulation and specializes in the

---

36 Lapavitsas, *Social Foundations of Markets, Money and Credit*, ch. 4.

37 Ibid.

38—Marx, *Capital*, vol. 3, ch. 19.

operations of buying and selling; money-dealing capital is a part of merchant's capital focusing on aspects of circulation that are narrowly related to money, such as storing, safekepinging, transmitting, and changing money from one national denomination to another. Merchants and money-dealers are in pivot position among capitalists to undertake the business of banking. Since the assets of banks consist of promises to pay made by enterprises and others across economic sectors, banks need a broad range of information and knowledge about the creditworthiness of potential borrowers. Merchants and money-dealers naturally develop such knowledge and acquire the related skills to assess creditworthiness by regularly dealing with a broad range of unrelated capitalists.[39]

Two interrelated points merit further emphasis. The first is that the approach to banking summed up in this section has a direct correspondence to the historical debate on the emergence of banks typically referred to as the contrasting 'goldsmiths' and 'bills' approaches.[40] For the goldsmiths view, the historical roots of banks lie with goldsmiths who presumable began to accept deposits subsequently making advances to borrowers. Thus, banks are passive financial intermediaries collecting spare value and making it available to others. For the bills view, in contrast, the historical roots of banks are to be found with merchants who began to specialize in bill discounting. Thus, banks are active capitalists who seek to make loans by using both their capital and their credit; Marx's sympathies lay with the bills approach.[41]

To avoid confusion, however, it is necessary to consider in a little more detail Marx's view of the historical emergence of banks. There is no doubt that, for Marx, banking is an ancient form of capitalist economic activity.[42] However, banking in classical antiquity, or even in medieval Italy, hardly emerged on the basis of commercial bill discounting. On the other hand, banking in England in the early modern era certainly developed and grew on that basis.[43] This historical observation lies at the root of Marx's

---

39   Lapavitsas, *Social Foundations of Markets, Money and Credit*, ch. 4.

40   The debate is summarized by Schumpeter, who, however, breezily dismisses the 'bills' view. This is far from the only occasion on which Schumpeter's great book is misleading on the development of economic thought. Joseph A. Schumpeter, *History of Economic Analysis*, New York: Oxford University Press, 1954, pp. 729–790.

41   See, for instance, Marx, *Capital*, vol. 3, pp. 736–737.

42   Ibid., ch. 36.

43   Peter Spufford's historical work establishes this point clearly (*Money and Its Use in Mediaeval Europe*, Cambridge: Cambridge University Press, 1988; *Power and Profit: The Merchant in Medieval Europe*, New York: Thames & Hudson, 2002). But even the older historical literature on continental banking demonstrates the mercantile origins of banks as well as the close connection between banking practice and commerce; consider, for instance, Raymond De Roover on the Medici. Abbott Usher reveals that pure deposit banking was a historical dead-end, even

dialectical approach to banking capital. Even if banking is an ancient economic activity, the form which best allows for its analysis as a capitalist activity is not necessarily the most ancient. English banking is the reference point for analysis of banking because it captures its deeper content in advanced capitalism. From this perspective, the bills view is capable of casting light on banking in both advanced capitalist economies and pre-capitalist societies, even if it does not necessarily match the specific form of banking in previous historical periods. Conceptually and analytically, the bills view is capable of dominating the goldsmiths view of banking.

The second point is even more important as it relates directly to contemporary banking theory. The goldsmiths view lies at the foundations of the conventional fractional reserve approach to banking; it also provides underpinnings for contemporary microeconomics of banking which seeks to explain the emergence of banks in terms of information asymmetries between borrower and lender, as was seen in earlier sections of this chapter. Banks are treated as fundamentally passive financial intermediaries that acquire reserves by collecting loanable funds thus creating a basis on which to engage in lending. In contrast, the bills view is the foundation of the alternative and far more fruitful contemporary approach to banking that is associated with post-Keynesianism. In a nutshell, banks are active agents who first make loans and then seek to secure the reserves that will support the advances already made.[44]

The Marxist view of banking summed up in this section has considerable sympathy with the post-Keynesian approach. Banks do not passively intermediate the flows of loanable money capital. On the contrary, banks are active capitalist agents that specialize in acquiring financial assets, that is, in making loans of various types. Banks engage in lending by using loanable capital that they already hold – both their own and that of other people – but also by anticipating incoming flows of loanable capital that could support advances already made. By engaging in these practices banks help to stretch accumulation, and thus to generate the flows of loanable capital which they have already anticipated. This is ultimately the source of the mysterious power of banking in advanced capitalism.

Recapping, banks are capitalist enterprises that specialize in collecting and advancing loanable capital. Banks also undertake money-dealing operations, including foreign exchange transactions, management of deposits, transmission of money, the making of payments, and so on. Banks invest their own capital to support their activities, and aim at making competitive profits. The following section pays closer attention to bank

---

if that was not his intention. *The Early History of Deposit Banking in Mediterranean Europe*, Cambridge, MA: Harvard University Press, 1943; see also *The Origins of Banking: The Primitive Bank of Deposit*, 1200–1600, London: A&C Black, Ltd, 1934.

44 A forceful presentation of this approach was given in Basil J. Moore, *Horizontalists and Verticalists: The Macroeconomics of Credit Money*, Cambridge: Cambridge University Press, 1988.

profits since they are an integral element of financial profit the rise of which has been a striking feature of financialization.[45]

Bank profit, solvency and liquidity

Bank profit flows from a variety of sources, reflecting the mix of activities in which banking capital typically engages. It arises as the spread between the interest that banks earn on assets and that which they pay on liabilities. It arises also through money-dealing operations, which normally earn the average rate of profit since these activities are integral to the circuit of the total social capital. It arises, finally, from banks operating in financial markets and earning fees and commissions as well as obtaining capital gains. The relative weight of each source of profit differs according to a bank's specialization as well as the specific institutional and historical framework of banking in particular countries.

Bank profit does not arise from directly deploying the bank's own capital, and this constitutes a qualitative difference between banking and other forms of capital. Banks are enterprises that engage exclusively in the sphere of circulation and do not produce value. The profits of banks, consequently, do not reflect the mobilization of resources directly through the investment of bank capital.[46] Banks are intermediaries that sustain

---

45   In 'Banking Capital and the Theory of Interest', Fine presents banking capital as a combination of loanable and merchant's capital that varies according to historical and institutional circumstances. This is a mistaken approach that confuses the substance of bank lending (loanable capital) with what banks are (a form of capital evolving out of merchant's capital). The point is far from academic – for, if banks were themselves loanable capital, the rate of profit in banking would be determined differently from the rate of profit in other sectors; by this token, systematic differences would have to exist in the mobility of capital between the banking and the other sectors of the economy. For Fine, such differences arise from the actions of the banks themselves. The normal way for profit rates to be equalized is through bank lending which mediates the shifting of resources from low to high profitability sectors. However, for Fine, banks would be unlikely to lend to other banks, since that would undermine the lenders' own profitability; thus, in developed capitalist economies banks tend to avoid lending to other banks. This is manifestly fallacious – in practice banks customarily and regularly lend to other banks, and such lending is precisely the core of the money market. In developed capitalism banks *must* lend to other banks, if the credit system is to deliver its normal functions. Fine's error originates in treating banking capital as loanable capital rather than as a form of capital evolving out of merchant's capital.

46—The net profit of a bank arises only after costs of wages, salaries, equipment, rents, and so on, have been subtracted, but since the bank does not produce value, these costs are simple subtractions from revenue. In short, although bank costs represent a certain mobilization of resources, the profits generated do not directly result from the mobilization of these resources, as would be the case for the profits of industrial capitalists. This point is sometimes not appreciated in Marxist literature. Carlo Panico, for instance, partly in debate with Ben Fine, treats

their profit-making assets mostly through borrowing. They are highly leveraged enterprises that provide only a small proportion of own capital. Unlike industrial enterprises, the capital invested by banks only partially provides the resources required by banks (labour power, buildings, technical equipment and so on). Rather, bank capital is mostly required to guarantee bank solvency, and thus to secure the chains of credit pivoting on banks.

The defining aspect of banking is the acquisition of promises to pay (assets) made by others, which is financed by issuing the bank's own promises to pay (liabilities). Therefore, bank profitability depends on the validity of the promises made by others and acquired by the bank, as well as on the composition of the bank's assets and liabilities. Bank profit would be, for instance, directly affected if borrowers failed to pay, if fluctuations in interest rates altered the value of assets and liabilities, if interest rate spreads changed unpredictably, and so on. These risks force banks to collect information and monitor borrowers, to which purpose they develop skills and devote appropriate resources. Nonetheless, it is impossible entirely to eliminate losses since some borrowers will certainly fail as well as for other reasons. The primary purpose of bank capital is to cushion banks against such losses, ultimately ensuring solvency.

At the same time, the own capital of banks is important for purposes of liquidity. From the standpoint of Marxist political economy, the definition of liquidity is simple: the ease of converting a financial asset into the universal equivalent, the latter being the absolute form of liquidity. The fundamental banking practice of acquiring assets by issuing liabilities has direct implications for liquidity since bank liabilities tend to be shorter-term than assets. There is no mystery in this respect: banks seek to acquire promises to pay made by others in exchange for their own; hence, other things equal, they would be more likely to succeed if bank promises were shorter-term, thus entailing quicker return to the money form.[47] At the limit, a bank's promises to pay become credit money with absolute liquidity. They are deposits and banknotes payable on sight. 'Maturity transformation' is thus an integral aspect of capitalist banking; it is the 'banking' side of money creation by banks. Therefore, banks are in constant need of liquid assets to meet pressures generated by the holders of liabilities who are requesting payment.

The standard way for banks to deal with the demands of liquidity is to keep reserves of liquid assets, which are, however, costly since they tend to have a low return; banks can also obtain liquidity by selling assets, which is even more costly, particularly when liquidity has to be obtained urgently; banks, finally, can borrow liquidity in the open markets for loanable capital. The mix of methods actually deployed by banks is a matter of customary practice – partly reflected in law – but also resulting from the institu-

---

bank costs as a necessary input that must earn profits. This is an erroneous approach to the intermediary role of banks.

47   Lapavitsas, *Social Foundations of Markets, Money and Credit*, ch. 4.

tional and historical framework within which banks operate. Problematic access to liquidity by banks is a characteristic feature of capitalist crises, and the turmoil that began in 2007 is typical in this respect, as is shown in Chapter 9.

Regardless of the particular methods of obtaining liquidity, 'maturity transformation' implies that banks would necessarily fail if the holders of liabilities demanded payment *en masse*.[48] The only fail-safe way to deal with this danger would be for banks to keep reserves of liquidity that would fully match their liabilities. The implication would be apparent: the essential function of banks to advance loanable capital would be impaired, not least because banks would not be able to advance their own credit in expectation of future accrual of loanable capital to back the advance.[49]

Bank liquidity and bank solvency are thus related to each other: if the quality of a bank's assets declined, its solvency would come into question; the holders of bank liabilities would probably demand that the bank should honour its promises to pay. The solvency of the bank would be protected by its capital which could absorb losses generated by its assets; by this token, capital would also protect liquidity, since others would remain prepared to hold the bank's promises to pay. However, there is no theoretical basis on which to ascertain the level of capital that would provide adequate protection to banks at a given point in time. Both solvency and liquidity are empirical categories, resulting from historical experience and particular institutional structures.

Bank profits reflect the integral role of banks in a capitalist economy. For one thing, banking credit is highly fungible and could be made available to functioning capitalists with varying specializations across the economy. Consequently, banking credit allows functioning capitalists to accelerate turnover, to expand the scale of existing operations, and to develop new activities. Banks also mobilize the reserves of idle money generated by individual functioning capitalists, and therefore reduce the idle money held by capitalists in the aggregate. Finally, but no less vitally, banking credit mobilizes idle money capital and therefore facilitates the mobility of capital among sectors of the economy. Banking credit is a fundamental component of the equalization of the rate of profit in advanced capitalist economies.

Banks, moreover, regularly collect information across the economy in order to advance loans. They become the repository of economic and social knowledge in a capitalist economy, and typically possess an overall view of real accumulation, in contrast

---

48 Bank runs are fairly rare events in the history of mature capitalism, though the crisis of the 2000s has lent renewed relevance to this phenomenon. Mainstream theory is fully aware of the ineluctable risk of bank runs given the normal practices of commercial banking; see Douglas Diamond and Philip Dybvig, 'Bank Runs, Deposit Insurance and Liquidity', *Journal of Political Economy* 91, 1983.

49 The idea of 100% reserves for banks, or 'narrow banking', is associated with the Chicago tradition in economics. It represents the goldsmiths view of banking taken to an extreme limit; for a brief discussion see n. 33 in Chapter 10.

to the partial and fragmented view held by non-financial enterprises. The breadth of the information on which banking credit is necessarily based gives to it a more objective and social character than the inevitably parochial commercial credit. The credit relationship between two specific capitalists in a given line of business is inevitably more particular than the credit relationship between a capitalist and a bank operating across several lines of business; credit, and thus trust, attains a more social and less personal character when it is advanced by a bank.[50]

Yet, banking capital also undermines capitalist accumulation. Banks anticipate the future to make loans, but always on the basis of expected profits. Managing liquidity and solvency with an eye to ensuring profitability is the cause of inherent instability in banking. Capitalist crises typically involve banks, as is shown in the final section of this book in relation to the global crisis that broke out in 2007.

Money market and central bank credit

The third layer of the credit pyramid is money market credit. The term 'money market' typically captures a range of short-term wholesale markets for loanable capital. In this book the term is used in the narrower and stricter sense of the interbank market – of a wholesale credit market among banks. In practice the money market is far broader and contains wholesale credit trading among other financial institutions but also large industrial and other corporations.

In Marx's and Hilferding's writings, the money market is not specified as a distinct entity within the financial system, although it is present in analysis of particular financial events and phenomena. Both tended to treat it as yet another financial market, often indistinguishable from the capital market. In *Keizai Seisakuron*, Uno made a conceptual breakthrough in this respect by identifying the interbank market as a distinctive element of the credit system.[51] The interbank market is separate from the capital market, even though the latter belongs to the financial system in general.

The power of Uno's insight does not derive from his view that the object traded in the money market is 'money as funds' (*shikin*) while the object traded in the capital market is 'money as capital' (*shihon*). This distinction – which makes natural linguistic sense in Japanese – purports to capture the difference between a mere sum of money and a sum of money traded as capital. It is fundamental to Uno's 'doctrine of circulation' and forms part of his claim that the object generally traded between borrower and lender is a mere sum of money (*shikin*), while capital (*shihon*) is traded in the stock market. In effect it is a denial of Marx's claim that interest-bearing capital is a sum of money traded 'as capital'. For Uno, money 'as capital' is traded in the stock market.

Uno's argument regarding the nature of the traded object between borrower and lender faces a profound conceptual difficulty: if it is a mere sum of money, rather

---

50   Lapavitsas, *Social Foundations of Markets, Money and Credit*, ch. 4.

51   Kozo Uno, *Keizai Seisakuron*, Tokyo: Kobundo Shobo, 1936, part 3, ch. 1, section 2.

than capital, why does the lender have the right to demand (and obtain as a matter of course) its return plus interest? There is no solution for this problem in terms of Uno's distinction between *shikin* and *shihon*. On the other hand, if one were to adopt Marx's assumption that the traded object is money capital available for loan, the problem would largely disappear. For, the funds in both the money and the capital market would then constitute loanable money capital that naturally returns to its owner. In the rest of this analysis we will assume that the traded object in the money market is interest-bearing, or more accurately loanable, capital.

Uno's insight is nonetheless path-breaking because it brings to the fore the creation of the money market by financial institutions rather than by the ultimate owners and users of loanable capital.[52] Ultimately, the reason for the emergence of the money market is demand for liquidity due to the normal operations of banking, which leads banks to trade spare liquidity with each other. More specifically, supply of loanable capital in the money market emerges as banks find it expensive to hold spare liquidity; demand comes from banks seeking to borrow liquidity to fund assets. From this perspective, the money market is, at its core, an interbank market for reserves of liquidity.

Money market credit is a variant of banking (or monetary credit) but it typically occurs among financial institutions which already specialize in providing banking credit. Consequently, it represents a more developed form of banking credit compared to credit between banks and functioning capitalists. Creditworthiness in the money market is established among specialist lenders who hold assets spread across a range of economic sectors. Money market credit thus possesses a general and objective aspect – participants have to take a view of accumulation as a whole, rather than simply monitoring a particular circuit of capital in which the funds would be deployed. By this token, trust in the money market has social determinants, even if it relates to private transactions among bankers and other intermediaries.[53]

Broadly speaking, the money market is the site where loanable capital is traded in a society-wide manner rather than simply between individual borrowers and lenders. In the money market, loanable capital is a social entity traded among specialists who are indifferent to particular applications of borrowed funds. Credit transactions become impersonal acts among participants that are specialists in lending, even though they remain private acts between a lender and a borrower. In the money market, loanable capital truly emerges as a commodity *sui generis* commanding a price (rate of interest) that can act as general reference point for other credit transactions.

---

52 This point escapes the new financial economics which treats the emergence of financial institutions as the result of market failure – that is, of the inability to have equilibrating give-and-take between owners and users of funds. However, the money market is created by financial institutions for reasons associated with financial intermediation, not by the owners and final users of loanable capital.

53 Lapavitsas, *Social Foundations of Markets, Money and Credit*, ch. 4.

Money market credit is vital to capitalist accumulation because it increases the fungibility of loanable capital. A deep and wide money market is an integral requirement of an advanced credit system since it allows banks to deliver their own functions more effectively. If the money market malfunctioned, banks would face difficulties in obtaining liquidity and hence banking credit would also begin to malfunction. It is characteristic of capitalist crises to emerge first in the money market, subsequently becoming broader credit crises and perhaps developing into general economic crises.

The final layer of the credit pyramid is central bank credit. The nature and role of central banks has already been discussed in Chapter 4, suffice it here to state that central banking represents a peculiar mixture of public and private credit, while being the most social form of credit available in capitalist economies. The central bank emerges spontaneously and necessarily as the bank of banks: it is the dominant bank of the money market at which other money market banks keep reserves of liquidity.[54] Central banks offer services to accumulation by minimizing the liquidity reserves kept by the financial system as a whole, but also by allowing banks to manage liquidity more flexibly and efficiently.

Central bank credit is directed primarily at money market banks; it is a variant of banking credit deployed by the foremost specialists in trading loanable capital. Consequently, it is necessary for the central bank continually to examine the entire terrain of accumulation thus engaging in the required collection of information and monitoring of borrowers. Central bank credit, by the same token, is the highest grade of credit available in the capitalist economy. For this reason, the liabilities of the central bank tend to be the money used in large financial transactions even before becoming the fundamental form of credit money.

The pre-eminent and broadly social role of central bank credit in a capitalist economy is strengthened by two further factors. First, the central bank becomes the bank of the state and, second, it becomes the holder of the nation's reserves of world money. Both functions have proven of critical importance throughout the twentieth century, providing the basis for state intervention in finance. Financialization rests on the tight connection between the central bank and the state. The dependence of the central bank on the state derives, first, from the public securities held to support its liabilities, second, from the state officially declaring central bank liabilities to be legal tender and, third, from the state implicitly guaranteeing the solvency of the central bank. In financialized capitalism, central bank credit is, in effect, a variant of public credit, while central bank liabilities have acquired aspects of fiat money.

---

54   See Costas Lapavitsas, 'The Political Economy of Central Banks: Agents of Stability or Source of Instability?', *International Papers in Political Economy* 4:3, 1997, pp. 1–52; and Lapavitsas, *Social Foundations of Markets, Money and Credit*, ch. 4.

Capital markets, investment banks, institutional investors and the design of the financial system

In addition to the credit system, the financial system also comprises the capital (or stock) market. Relevant aspects of the capital market are discussed in more detail in Chapter 6; suffice it here to state that the term effectively refers to a range of securities markets in which loanable capital (and other idle money across society) is traded as both equity and debt. Equity poses complex theoretical problems through the form of joint-stock capital, and the consequent separation of ownership from control which characterises mature capitalism. Debt traded in capital markets, on the other hand, represents primarily longer-term bonds and similar instruments that allow lenders and borrowers to bypass lending by banks. The existence of capital markets, consequently, raises issues of mixing debt and equity to fund capitalist operations, a problem that characterises the modern joint-stock corporation.

Capital markets are frequently analysed as providing 'direct finance' to corporations, in contrast to 'indirect finance' provided by banks.[55] This is a powerful distinction, as is argued immediately below and in Chapter 6, but its importance should not be exaggerated. For one thing, capital markets also generate further financial intermediation. Thus, investment banks engage in a form of banking that is integrally related to capital markets in terms of fundamental activities and profit extracted. Moreover, mature capitalism is characterized by the rise of 'institutional investors' – pension funds, investment funds, and so on – that typically transact with investment banks. Capital markets are not necessarily, and nor even predominantly, places where owners meet eventual users of loanable funds. Both investment banks and institutional investors have been fundamental to financialization, and empirical aspects of their rise are examined in chapters 8 and 9. In the rest of this chapter consider some brief theoretical observations regarding these forms of financial intermediation in contrast to ordinary (commercial) banks.

Investment banking is fundamental to capital markets, indeed to several markets in which financial assets (securities) are traded, not least because investment banks are necessary to create such markets. In Chapter 1 it was briefly shown that investment banks are the cornerstone of the vast over-the-counter derivatives markets since they provide market-making services and organize the infrastructure of derivatives markets. For essentially similar reasons, investment banks are integral to capital and other securities markets.[56] Fundamental to investment banks is the separation of owner-

---

55 There is a wide literature on this issue, including among mainstream economists; see Franklin Allen and Douglas Gale, *Comparing Financial Systems*, Cambridge, MA: MIT Press, 2000; and Franklin Allen and Douglas Gale, 'Comparative Financial Systems: A Survey', Working Paper 01–15, Center for Financial Institutions, Wharton, 2001.

56 For a penetrating analysis of this topic, see Duncan Lindo, 'Political Economy of Financial Derivatives: The Role and Evolution of Banking', unpublished PhD dissertation, School of Oriental and African Studies, University of London, 2013.

ship from control, which characterises joint-stock corporations. The holders of equity (shareholders) resemble strongly the lenders of money, and receive profits as passive owners of capital. Equity and debt securities, therefore, are similar as traded instruments in capital markets, even if they differ inherently from each other since equity stands for outright property over capital.

Investment banking is, in the first instance, the practice of managing the issuing of securities by guaranteeing sale through the bank's own resources, subsequently breaking the total issue into saleable lots and finding buyers. The distinguishing feature of investment banks is thorough knowledge of potential counterparties based on information collected and relations maintained with potential buyers. Thus, investment banks are the denizens *par excellence* of capital markets. The main function of investment banks, however, is far broader than merely managing the initial issuing of securities. For, buying securities could be considered as equivalent to depositing money with a bank since securities buyers generally want to be able to convert newly acquired assets into money. Liquidity is a prime concern of participants in securities markets which means, above all, possessing the ability to sell. Investment banks provide the required liquidity by 'making markets' – by standing ready to buy and sell securities at constantly varying prices. Securities buyers can be assured that the return of their loanable capital (or plain idle money) to the money form would be possible as a matter of course. Investment banks strengthen the equity holder's essential similarity to the lender of money, while also reaffirming the debt holder's character as lender of money.

A fundamental difference between investment and ordinary (or commercial) banks, therefore, is that the former create liquidity by dictating the terms of trading of securities, while the latter create liquidity by transforming deposits into longer-term assets. The basis of liquidity creation is qualitatively different between the two since the former involves trading securities in open markets, while the latter entails issuing promises to pay by banks. For this reason, continuous trading is a necessary feature of securities markets, and investment banks must continually participate in securities trading.

Investment banks make securities markets by continually varying the rate of interest for traded securities, and thus the attached prices. The price differences that occur while buying and selling securities are a source of profit for issuers, holders and intermediating banks. The fundamental elements of profit extraction through the associated mechanisms are examined in detail in Chapter 6. Investment banks are able to extract profits essentially due to services provided, which include, above all, liquidity creation, but also information collection about counterparties, monitoring potential buyers, and handling the technical aspects of transactions. They are also able to extract profits by trading securities on own account, an aspect of investment banking that has been vital to financialization.

Institutional investors, on the other hand, are a very different kind of intermediary in securities markets. Individual holders of loanable capital or idle money face a pronounced asymmetry in trading with investment banks as market makers. Individuals typically do not have requisite skills to undertake monitoring, to collect information either about counterparties or the economy, and even simply to engage in the technicalities of transacting. They are in an inherently weaker position relative to banks and this can be a source of financial expropriation, discussed in Chapter 6. The asymmetry can be partly overcome through aggregation of the holders of loanable capital, or idle money. Institutional investors are essentially agents in securities markets that allow the owners of capital, or of money for loan, to transact on a less asymmetric basis with investment banks. They are able to hold a large and diversified portfolio of securities, against which they could borrow thus expanding their trading options; they could also employ specialists to engage in monitoring counterparties and markets.

Institutional investors are qualitatively different from banks in important respects, even though both collect idle funds available for lending. Above all, institutional investors do not anticipate future incoming flows of loanable capital, or idle money, by advancing their own credit to make loans; institutional investors typically collect idle funds, subsequently making them available to issuers of securities. For the same reason, the liabilities of institutional investors do not have to be short-term, much less payable on sight; in other words, the liabilities of institutional investors do not generally become money. Furthermore, the assets of institutional investors must be marketable to ensure the ready return of loanable capital collected. This is not the same concern as that of a bank attempting to ensure the repayment of a loan, which requires direct monitoring of the operations of the borrower from a bank. Institutional investors engage less in monitoring the issuers of securities, and more in ensuring the tradability of the securities held.

The final issue to note in this chapter is that the capital market is closely related to the pyramid of the credit system, even if the two stand at some distance from each other. More specifically, there are two types of organic link between the credit system and the capital market. First, both draw funds from a common pool of idle money generated in the course of capitalist accumulation but also more broadly across society. At the margin, the holder of idle money opts between making the funds available within the credit system, or in the capital market. Second, prices in the capital market are closely related to prices in the credit system. The rate of interest in the money market acts as the benchmark not only for all other rates of interest within the credit system, but also for returns in the capital market. Securities prices are closely related to the rate of interest, with profound implications for financial profit, as is shown in Chapter 6.

Ascertaining the balance between credit system and capital market within the financial system is a complex theoretical problem that underpins the traditional distinction among financial systems into, respectively, bank-based (or German–Japanese) and capital market–based (or Anglo-Saxon). There has been extensive debate regarding the significance of the two types of financial system in the course of capitalist development, particularly for late developing countries.[57] The presumed advantages of bank-based finance have to do with the long-term commitment between banks and enterprises which presumably results in investment performance that is more conducive to growth. Market-based finance, on the other hand, is characterized by short-term relationships between banks and enterprises; it could be argued, however, that it provides better assessment of the cost of capital and more flexibility in dealing with risk. The debate has evident significance for financialization, as was already mentioned in Chapter 2. Aspects of it are considered in the following chapters in connection with the transformation of finance in the US, Japan, Germany and the UK.

It should be stressed that the debate on the design of financial systems has very old antecedents. Elements of it can be found, for instance, in Steuart's *Inquiry into the Principles of Political Economy* which effectively advocated long-term credit banks funded through the mobilization of landed property. This was in contrast to the focus

---

57 The literature is very extensive indeed and in its recent form goes back to Alexander Gerschenkron, *Economic Backwardness in Historical Perspective*, Cambridge MA: Harvard University Press, 1962. The historical argument has been developed more fully in Rondo Cameron (ed.), *Banking in the Early Stages of Industrialisation*, New York: Oxford University Press, 1967. Further discussion can be found in Rondo Cameron and V.I. Bovykin (eds), *International Banking*, New York: Oxford University Press, 1991. The empirical work of Colin Mayer ('The Assessment: Financial Systems and Corporate Investment', *Oxford Review of Economic Policy* 3:4, 1987) has been of seminal importance to the theoretical discussion, as has that of Jenny Corbett and Tim Jenkinson ('How Is Investment Financed? A Study of Germany, Japan, the United Kingdom and the United States', *The Manchester School* 65, supplement, 1997). The political economy of bank–enterprise relations in Japan has been examined in Masahiko Aoki and Hugh Patrick (eds), *The Japanese Main Bank System*, New York: Oxford University Press, 1994; and Ronald Dore, *Stock Market Capitalism*, Oxford: Oxford University Press, 1998. German bank enterprise relations have been researched by John Cable ('Capital Market Information and Industrial Performance', *Economic Journal* 95:377, 1985); Jeremy Edwards and Sheilagh Ogilvie ('Universal Banks and German Industrialization', *Economic History Review* 49:3, 1996); Caroline Fohlin ('Relationship Banking, Liquidity, and Investment in the German Industrialization', *The Journal of Finance* 53:5, 1998); and Julian Franks, Colin Mayer, and Hannes Wagner ('The Origins of the German Corporation', Discussion Paper 65, SFB/TR15, Government and the Efficiency of Economic Systems, 2005). Support for market-based systems has frequently emanated from international organizations, where it has often appeared as an argument in favour of 'modern' finance – for instance, Asli Demirgüç-Kunt and Ross Levine, 'Stock Markets, Corporate Finance and Economic Growth', *The World Bank Economic Review* 10:2, 1996; Asli Demirgüç-Kunt and Ross Levine, 'Bank Based and Market Based Financial Systems', World Bank Policy Research Working Paper No. 2143, 1999; Ross Levine and Sara Zervos, 'Stock Market Development and Long-Run Growth', *The World Bank Economic Review* 10:2, 1996; Ross Levine and Sara Zervos, 'Stock Markets, Banks, and Economic Development', *American Economic Review* 88, 1998, pp. 537–88.

on commercial banks funded through deposits and other short-term funds in Smith's *Wealth of Nations*. By this token, support for bank-based systems has long retained an element of state direction of the economy, often with a socialist admixture.

In Marx's writings, the spontaneously arising form of the capitalist credit system has close affinities with market-based finance.[58] That is, the credit system comprises banks that lend essentially on a short-term basis by mobilizing idle money capital. Hilferding's innovative argument about the transformation of capitalism due to the emergence of finance capital can thus be understood in terms of the market-based financial system of competitive liberal capitalism spontaneously becoming the bank-based system of mature (and declining) capitalism. For Hilferding, banks dominate the financial system in mature capitalism, even though the capital market also grows as it supports finance capital. The future of capitalism for Hilferding lay in Germany, a late developer that relied on her banks, not England, a declining power in which banks kept their distance from corporations.

This is not how the design of financial systems has developed in the course of subsequent history, however. Financialization, in particular, can be considered as the ascendancy of Anglo-Saxon, market-based finance, though the empirical reality is far more nuanced, as is shown in Chapter 8. The complex empirical outcomes that have obtained in the course of the last three decades indicate that the character of the financial system cannot be captured fully by the distinction between bank-based and market-based systems. In practice, financial systems present considerable variety and cannot be neatly slotted in the two categories. After all, financial systems are sets of institutions and markets that specialize in mobilizing and trading loanable capital. Since loanable capital has a highly flexible form that depends on the performance of institutions and the nature of state intervention, the outlook of the financial system is also a matter of historical development and cannot be determined in the abstract.

---

58   Lapavitsas, *Social Foundations of Markets, Money and Credit.*

6. THE CONUNDRUM OF FINANCIAL PROFIT

Financial profit: Multiple forms underpinned by heterogeneous social relations

Rising financial profit is a characteristic feature of financialization, empirical evidence for which is provided in Chapter 8. Several theoretical approaches to financialization have interpreted rising financial profit as an indication of constrained profitability in the sphere of production and a corresponding escape of capital in the sphere of finance. Thus, in *The Long Twentieth Century*, Giovanni Arrighi has argued that financial expansions take place when capital switches 'from trade and production to financial speculation and intermediation' and profits increasingly come from 'financial deals'.[1] Greta Krippner, following Arrighi, has defined financialization as 'a pattern of accumulation in which profits accrue primarily through financial channels rather than through trade and commodity production'.[2]

The notion that financialization could be defined in such terms is problematic for reasons discussed in Chapter 2, but even if it was not, financial profit would continue to pose a major theoretical and conceptual conundrum. The nature of the conundrum was identified by Robert Pollin in debate with Arrighi. For Pollin, 'Arrighi never explicitly poses the most basic question about the, M $\rightarrow$ M' circuit, which is, where do the profits come from if not from the production and exchange of commodities?'[3] Pollin's remark succinctly captures the theoretical difficulty posed by rising theoretical profit: what is its economic source and thus its social content?

Pollin sketched an answer to this question by linking various forms of financial profit to flows of value. Thus, financial profit could come from: first, zero-sum redistribution within the capitalist class; second, distribution 'from workers and communities' in favour of the capitalist class; and third, surplus value, the increase of which might be facilitated by financial mechanisms. Pollin suggested that only the last source properly relates to Arrighi's analysis. Arrighi replied that Pollin's three possible sources of financial profit correspond to different stages of financial expansion, which is hardly an answer for the deeper issue raised by Pollin.[4]

Rising financial profit presents a thorny theoretical problem at the heart of finan-

---

1   Giovanni Arrighi, *The Long Twentieth Century*, London: Verso, 1994, pp. 221–9.

2   See Greta Krippner, 'The Financialization of the American Economy', *Socio-Economic Review* 3, 2005, p. 174. For related arguments by the *Monthly Review* current, see John Bellamy Foster, 'The Financialization of Capitalism', *Monthly Review* 58:11, 2007; and John Bellamy Foster and Fred Magdoff, *The Great Financial Crisis: Causes and Consequences*, New York: Monthly Review Press, 2009.

3   Robert Pollin, 'Contemporary Economic Stagnation in World Historical Perspective', *New Left Review* 219, 1996, p. 115.

4   Giovanni Arrighi, 'Financial Expansions in World Historical Perspective: A Reply to Robert Pollin', *New Left Review* 224, 1997.

cialization: what are the social and economic relations that correspond to its creation and accrual? Insight into the issue can be gained by considering some of the forms of financial profit. A tentative initial description would be that of monetary returns deriving, first, from money capital advanced on the basis of debt and, second, from money capital obtained as equity in capital markets; the former would be interest, the latter would be dividends. Even with this elementary description, however, complex conceptual questions immediately arise. Why would returns to tradable equity be considered a form of financial profit, when returns to other owned capital would be plain profit? This question has a direct social equivalent: how does a shareholder differ from the owner-operator of a capitalist enterprise? At a further remove, why is it legitimate to add up dividends and interest as forms of financial profit? This question also has an evident social equivalent: how does a plain lender to an enterprise differ from a shareholder?

If the description of financial profit moved beyond the simple sum of interest and dividends, even more severe conceptual difficulties would emerge. For, financial profit could also take the form of capital gains arising due to changes in the prices of financial assets which would accrue when sale actually took place; capital gains, moreover, could be obtained by holders of both equity and debt securities. What would be the source of financial profit accruing from trading financial assets that were often completely unrelated to production?

More complexly, a form of financial profit similar to capital gains could also accrue from the sale of assets that were not inherently financial but simply fell within the purview of the financial system. Most prominent among these assets would be housing, which has indeed become a source of financial gain and loss for broad layers across all social classes in financialized capitalism. Gains and losses from selling houses present one of the hardest conceptual problems relating to financial profit. Given that both seller and buyer could be wage workers, what would be the social source of financial profit from trading houses?

The last question also applies to a broad range of other transactions that could result in further forms of financial profit as individual workers and households have been drawn systematically into the financial system. Thus, financial profit could be earned by those who lend to workers as well as by those who handle workers' savings; financial profit could also be made by households that trade directly in securities markets. What would be the source of such profit, and what would be its significance in terms of social stratification?

This is hardly the end of the conceptual difficulties posed by the multiple forms of financial profit, however. For, in addition to profit received by the owners of debt, equity and other assets, there is also profit received by financial institutions. It is intuitive that financial profit earned by capitalist enterprises through commercial and other activities differs conceptually from financial profit accruing to those who simply own, or trade, financial assets. For one thing, and as was discussed in Chapter 4, financial institutions draw profits by handling money reserves and flows that are necessary for payments and purchases across the economy. These are money-dealing profits accruing for delivering functions integral to the circulation of commodities; therefore, they derive from the flow of surplus value and accrue at a rate equal to the average rate of profit.[5]

Financial institutions, nonetheless, are intermediaries that also earn returns in the form of interest spreads, fees and commissions. These are financial profits that derive from managing the flows of loanable capital (and spare money) of others. Financial institutions, moreover, could also generate proprietary profits by trading in financial markets on own account – by operating as holders of loanable capital. Not least in this connection are the bonuses and other forms of remuneration received by employees of financial institutions. These are typically excluded from the national data on the profits of financial institutions, often appearing as salaries and other types of personal income; nonetheless, they are in reality a form of financial profit with significant implications for the social structure of financialized capitalism.

In sum, financial profit could be described in terms of the formal function of the recipient. It could be profit accruing to a final lender, an equity holder, a trader in financial assets, a financial institution, or an employee of a financial institution. Financial profit could also be described in terms of the social character of the recipient. It could be profit accruing to a capitalist, a worker, a household belonging to a 'third' class, a financial institution, or even an employee of a financial institution. The multiplicity of functions and of social types among recipients corresponds to the variety of processes through which financial profit is generated. Several disparate returns comprise financial profit, broadly including interest, dividends, and capital gains.

The element that provides conceptual and practical unity to these returns is the financial character of the processes through which the returns are generated. The processes are financial because, at one remove, they are associated with the flows of loanable money capital and plain money in circulation. The relevant agents are capitalists but also other individual holders of money, including workers. At a further remove, the processes are financial because they are associated with the functioning of financial institutions which systematically transform idle money into loanable money capital.

In this light, the primary form of financial profit in analytical terms is that which accrues to the owners of loanable capital, or idle money. Broadly speaking, the receivers of this form of profit hold financial assets associated with either loans or equity. The primary form of financial profit, thus, includes returns from lending, returns from holding equity, and returns from trading financial assets. Financial profit, however, also has a secondary form: profit earned by financial institutions. The latter typically function as intermediaries in the flows of loanable capital, or plain money, of other people and are consequently remunerated out of returns emanating from these flows. Profits drawn by financial institutions do not present additional conceptual problems

---

5   Karl Marx, *Capital*, vol. 3, London: Penguin/NLR, 1981, ch. 19.

in terms of their sources: they are fractions of the flows of surplus value, personal income, or the stock of money capital (or plain money) belonging to others and accruing as recompense for services provided. The exception – which is important to financialization – refers to profit earned by financial institutions through independent trading of financial assets. But even this form of profit does not pose significant additional complexities since it could be treated analogously to financial profit accruing to the owners of loanable capital through trading in financial assets.

Financial profit is thus an envelope term covering several forms of financial return that arise in complex and variable ways. In the rest of this chapter the conceptual content of financial profit is examined by focusing on its primary forms: profit accruing to the owners of loanable capital (or idle money) from advancing loans, from holding equity, and from trading financial assets. Its secondary forms – profits accruing to financial institutions – are considered only in the light of the primary forms. By examining its primary forms, the specific character of financial profit relative to 'normal' capitalist profit can also be established, allowing for conclusions regarding the social structure of financialized capitalism. A necessary first step in this regard is to introduce the notion of 'profit from alienation or expropriation' – an important, though relatively ignored, part of classical and Marxist political economy.[6] Pollin's question to Arrighi could then begin to be answered.

Profit in Marx's economics

Marx's chief innovation in the field of political economy was his analysis of capitalist profit in chapters 7 to 9 of the first volume of *Capital*, even though his views on the issue have been far from generally accepted. Briefly put, for Marx, profit is the money form of surplus value generated in production. Wage workers receive the equivalent of the value of labour power as money wages, but are normally obliged to work for longer than the time-equivalent of the value received, thus creating additional, or surplus, value. This process is exploitation in production and constitutes the defining feature of capitalism.

Thus, profit in Marxist political economy is fundamentally treated as a flow of surplus value – and of net output – freshly created in the sphere of production. Surplus value attains a monetary form in the sphere of circulation through the sale of finished output, and accrues as the exclusive property of the capitalist who owns the capital advanced. Particular types of return emerge as the aggregate flow of surplus value is subsequently divided among various claimants in the sphere of circulation. Ground rent is the part accruing to landlords for having property in land; industrial profit and merchant's profit, on the other hand, are the parts accruing to capitalists for having

---

6   For further discussion of this issue see also Costas Lapavitsas and Iren Levina, 'Financial Profit: Profit from Production and Profit Upon Alienation', Discussion Paper No. 24, Research on Money and Finance, May 2011.

property in capital as well as for functioning in economic reproduction. Both industrial and merchants' profit are further subdivided into interest and profit of enterprise. Interest accrues to the owners of money capital available for lending, while profit of enterprise accrues to capitalists actively engaged in production or trade.

Marx's analysis of capitalist profit is rooted in extensive study of political economy, summed up in *The Theories of Surplus Value*, which is arguably the first systematic treatise on the history of economic thought. Marx's theory of profit relied heavily on David Ricardo, though Marx also diverged drastically from Ricardo on this issue. In *Principles of Political Economy and Taxation*, Ricardo postulated that profit is a newly produced flow of value (embodied labour) that accrues per period. Yet, profit is not a self-standing part of net output emerging due to a characteristic profit-generating process. Rather, it is the residual net output that accrues to capitalists once workers have claimed the share corresponding to wages, and landlords have claimed the share corresponding to ground rent.[7] For this reason, profit tends to fall as population grows and less fertile land is brought under the plough: rising wages and rent crush the residual net output accruing to capitalists. Marx, similarly to Ricardo, treated profit as part of the flow of net output accruing to capitalists. However, he rejected Ricardo's view that profit is a residual and put forth his theory of exploitation to explain the emergence of profit as the result of a characteristic capitalist process.

Equally important for our purposes is that Marx's theory of profit was also influenced by other strains of classical political economy which identified forms of profit unrelated to the newly produced flow of value. This strain of Marx's theory is vital to analysing financial profit. The key concept in this regard is 'profit upon alienation', originally formulated by Sir James Steuart, who had a strong impact on Marx's economics in general, and on Marx's theory of money and finance in particular. In his *Inquiry into the Principles of Political Economy*, Steuart claimed that the price of a commodity contains 'real value' and 'profit upon alienation'. The former is determined by three factors: the normal labour required for production, the cost of subsistence of workers, and the cost of materials; the latter is determined by any excess of price over 'real value', and constitutes the profit of the manufacturer.[8]

Steuart subsequently drew a distinction between 'positive profit' and 'relative profit'.[9] 'Positive profit' derives from the general 'augmentation' of value and output, and improves the 'public good'. 'Relative profit' derives from a 'vibration of the balance of

---

7   David Ricardo, *On the Principles of Political Economy and Taxation*, in *The Works and Correspondence of David Ricardo*, vol. 1, ed. Piero Sraffa and Maurice Dobb, Cambridge: Cambridge University Press, 1951, ch. 6; also pp. 48–51.

8   James Steuart, *An Inquiry into the Principles of Political Economy*, vol. 1, book 2, ch. 4, in *Works, Political, Metaphysical, and Chronological, of the Late Sir James Steuart*, London: Routledge, 1995.

9   Ibid., vol. 1, book 2, ch. 8.

wealth between parties' – from trade, and has nothing to do with the general increase in output. This is an important distinction, even though Steuart's terms in discussing it were, as ever, imprecise. On the one hand, profit could arise from the expansion of productive capacity – it could be an addition to previous output. On the other, profit could arise purely from a zero-sum trading game relative to output – it could simply represent the loss of another party in the sphere of circulation. For Steuart, 'profit upon alienation' belongs to the latter type, it constitutes 'relative profit'.

Steuart's analysis contains manifest error, as Marx pointed out in Part 1 of *Theories of Surplus Value*, since it identifies capitalist profit in general with 'profit upon alienation'.[10] That is, Steuart considered capitalist profit generally to emerge from a zero sum game in exchange. For Marx, in contrast, capitalist profit is already contained in 'real value', not least as part of the 'normal labour required for production'. Nonetheless, Marx was impressed by Steuart's argument that the profit of one party in circulation could be the loss of another. This would be a type of profit that differed qualitatively from the flow of surplus value created in production through the exploitation of workers.

Marx deployed Steuart's concept of 'profit upon alienation' (or 'upon expropriation') in his work, though not extensively, and often in analysis of financial transactions relating to the personal income of workers.[11] Marx considered such transactions to be, first, exploitative and, second, unrelated to surplus value. It cannot be overstressed that exploitation occurring in financial transactions is qualitatively distinct from exploitation in production. To be specific, exploitation in financial transactions amounts to a direct transfer of value from the income of workers to the lenders – that is, it stands for a re-division of money revenue streams, typically taking the form of interest. The social factors that account for such exploitation are related to the sphere of circulation, reflecting in particular the unequal position of workers and capitalists in financial transactions, as is discussed in more detail in the rest of this book. The more standard form of exploitation in production, on the other hand, amounts to creating a fresh flow of value out of unpaid labour, which accrues as the exclusive property of the capitalist who owns the finished output. Its social underpinnings lie in production – in the lack

---

10   Karl Marx, *Theories of Surplus Value*, part 1, London: Lawrence & Wishart, 1969, ch. 1.

11   The significance of 'profit upon alienation' to Marx's economics has generally escaped Anglo-Saxon Marxism in the post-war years, though the concept was certainly noticed by Roland L. Meek (*Studies in the Labor Theory of Value*, New York: Monthly Review Press, 1975, p. 286). More recently, Anwar Shaikh has implicitly used the notion since he has stressed the importance of value transfers in determining the variability of aggregate profits in the context of the transformation problem. See Anwar Shaikh, 'The Transformation from Marx to Sraffa: Prelude to a Critique of the Neo-Ricardians' in *Marx, Ricardo, Sraffa*, ed. Ernest Mandel, London: Verso, 1984, pp. 52–6. Shaikh has also explicitly related Marx's to Steuart's theory of profits in more recent but as yet unpublished work.

of property rights by workers over the means of production, as well as in the power that capitalists exercise over the production process.

Insight into the analytical content of the distinction between the two types of profit can be gleaned from various passages in the *Theories of Surplus Value*. The following statement by Marx in Part 3 of that book, for istance, referring to interest being potentially unrelated to surplus value merits extensive reference:[12]

> [Here] the fact is disregarded that interest may be a mere transfer and need not represent real surplus-value, as, for example, when money is lent to a "spendthrift", i.e. for consumption. The position may be similar when money is borrowed in order to make *payments*. In both cases it is loaned as money, not as capital, but it becomes *capital* to its owner through the mere act of lending it out … In this case interest, like profit upon expropriation, is a fact independent of capitalist production – the production of surplus value. It is in these two forms of money – money as means of purchase of commodities intended for consumption and as means of payment of debts – that interest, like profit upon expropriation constitutes a form which, although it is reproduced in capitalist production, is nevertheless independent of it and [represents] a form of interest which belongs to earlier modes of production.

It follows that profit 'upon expropriation' that arises from lending to workers represents a form of exploitation which is independent of surplus value. In the third volume of *Capital*, Marx also argued that lending to workers represents 'secondary exploitation', the latter including further exploitative processes that occur in circulation. Specifically, for Marx:[13]

> It is plain enough that the working class is swindled in that form too [the renting of housing], and to an enormous extent; but it is equally exploited by the petty trader who supplies the worker with the means of subsistence. This is a secondary exploitation, which proceeds along the original exploitation that takes place directly within the process of production itself.

The historical dimension of secondary exploitation was also posited by Marx in the *Grundrisse*, and it is again worth quoting at length:[14]

---

12   Karl Marx, *Theories of Surplus Value*, part 3, London: Lawrence & Wishart, 1972, p. 487, emphasis in the original.

13   Marx, *Capital*, vol. 3, p. 745.

14   Karl Marx, *Grundrisse*, London: Penguin/NLR, 1973, p. 853.

The relation in which on one side the worker still appears as independent, i.e. not as wage labourer, but on the other side his objective conditions already possess an independent existence alongside him, forming the property of a particular class of usurers, this relation necessarily develops in all modes of production resting more or less on exchange … Where this relation repeats itself within the bourgeois economy, it does so in the backward branches of industry, or in such branches as still struggle against their extinction and absorption into the modern mode of production. The most odious exploitation of labour takes place still takes place in them … What takes place is the exploitation by capital without the mode of production of capital. The rate of interest appears very high because it includes profit and even a part of wages. This form of usury, in which capital does not seize possession of production, hence is capital only formally, presupposes the pre-dominance of pre-bourgeois modes of production.

To recap, for Marx, the characteristic type of capitalist profit is that of a fresh flow of value generated in production through the exploitation of workers. However, there is also 'profit upon alienation or expropriation' resulting from zero-sum transactions that relate to money revenue or existing stocks of money, and accruing through commercial or financial transactions. Marx's (or, rather, Steuart's) insight is deployed throughout this book to analyse financial profit, particularly profit from lending to individuals and profit from trading financial assets. In sum, financial profit could result from subdividing the newly produced flow of surplus value per period, but it could also emerge from expropriating the income and the money stocks of others through the operations of the financial system. Furthermore, the two processes could be systematically linked, especially when it comes to trading financial assets, as is shown in the rest of Chapter 6.

Financial profit, in both its primary and secondary forms, is thus distinct from 'normal' capitalist profit deriving from surplus value generated in production. The latter is integral to the capitalist mode of production, capturing the fundamental class division between capitalists and workers that permeates the sphere of production. Surplus value is the specifically capitalist form of the 'augmentation' of value which Steuart considered to be the foundation of 'positive profit'. Financial profit, in contrast, contains elements of surplus value but is, by construction, a broader category of profit that also includes other forms of monetary increments. Indeed, financial profit resembles a primordial form of profit capturing purely the excess of money returned over money advanced.

The concept of 'profit upon alienation or expropriation' is vital to the analysis of financial profit earned from trading financial assets as well as from capital gains. It is also vital to analyse financial profit earned from mortgage and consumption loans to households, or from handling pension and other funds. These forms of financial profit could accrue directly to the holders of financial assets, or to financial institutions as fees, commissions and proprietary profits. They comprise the gist of the notion of 'financial expropriation', proposed elsewhere as an integral aspect of financialized capitalism.[15] At core this is an exploitative relationship representing the direct appropriation of personal money income, or of loanable capital and plain money that belongs to others. But it is different from exploitation at the point of production and rests on a zero sum game between the counterparties to financial transactions. More complexly, it could also be an intermediate step to appropriating a share of the flow of surplus value, as is shown below.

The social foundations of financial expropriation lie, in part, in the non-capitalist character of personal income. Workers and others enter financial transactions in order to obtain use-values, whether immediately in the form of wage goods or in the future through a pension. In contrast, financial institutions approach financial transactions in order to make profits. There are systematic differences in information, organization and social power between the two counterparties, which potentially allow financial institutions to exploit the holders of personal income. To be sure, it is also possible for individual workers to approach financial transactions from the perspective of making a profit, but this does not eliminate the systematic difference between individuals and financial institutions as counterparties to transactions.

The social foundations of financial expropriation lie, further, in the peculiar content of the act of trading loanable capital in financial markets. Transactions of loanable capital, as was argued in Chapter 5, involve the advance of value against future claims which continue to be traded. Profit emerges for counterparties in the first instance as a share of the loanable capital initially traded – that is, it derives from a zero-sum game. If the attached claims were validated out of future flows of value, however, the zero-sum game would become a preamble to drawing profits out of surplus value, or future income. If, on the other hand, the claims were not validated, profits from the initial trade would remain a share of someone else's loanable capital. The economic relations involved in this complex process are analysed in the rest of this chapter; suffice it here to state that they are integral to all financial trading.

In broad historical terms, financial expropriation represents a throw-back to ancient forms of capitalist profit-making that are independent of the generation of surplus value. Some of the conceptual issues involved in pre-capitalist profit making are further examined in the following section. In financialized capitalism, however, profit-making that is unrelated to surplus value no longer represents a survival of ancient pre-capitalist relations. On the contrary, it stands for the spreading of new and exploitative relations across society as financial markets grow and as individuals are

---

15 See Costas Lapavitsas, 'Financialised Capitalism: Crisis and Financial Expropriation', *Historical Materialism* 17:2, 2009, pp. 114–48. In earlier work this concept was called 'direct exploitation' to stress the analogy with 'secondary exploitation'. To avoid semantic debates with Marxists unfamiliar Marx's concept, however, the term was dropped in favour of 'financial expropriation'.

increasingly drawn into the formal financial system. Present-day extraction of financial profit reaffirms the relatively remote and predatory disposition of finance toward
accumulation in mature capitalism. In this respect, financial profit is reminiscent of
elemental money-making activities that go back at least to classical antiquity. Further
insight into financial profit can thus be gained by considering Aristotle and Demosthenes on profit making in classical Greece.

Pre-capitalist profit and financial profit

Aristotle wrote systematically about value and economic activity in *Politics*, although
he made only fleeting references to profit (*kerdos*). The fundamental distinction he
proposed was between *oikonomike* (obtaining goods by managing the household –
oikos) and *chrematistike* (obtaining goods by engaging in exchange).[16] *Chrematistike*
he further subdivided in two – that which allows for the acquisition of goods necessary
for self-sufficiency (*autarkeia*), and that which allows for the making of money through
obtaining goods.

Aristotle reserved a special term for the latter – *kapelike*, a word that typically
described petty trading and huckstering in the markets of Athens. The aim (*telos*) of the
first type of chrematistike is to obtain goods to use for the purpose for which they were
designed; hence, this form of chrematistike constitutes a path to acquiring 'true wealth'
(*alethinos ploutos*). In contrast, the aim of kapelike is to obtain goods only as a means
to acquiring money (*nomisma*). This is an unnatural activity as money was originally
meant simply to facilitate the acquisition of goods and is not a good in itself; it is also
an activity without end since more money is always better than less.[17]

For Aristotle, profit pertains to kapelike. As chrematistike develops, money arises to
facilitate the exchange of goods; the emergence of money in turn encourages and ena-

---

16   Aristotle, *Politics*, Cambridge, MA: Harvard University Press, 1932, pp. 38–50. In standard
treatments of the history of economic thought, Aristotle often appears as the progenitor of
economics, together with Xenophon and Plato. However, Moses Finley has argued powerfully
that Aristotle has no 'economic analysis' in the contemporary sense since he was not concerned
with price and based much of his argument on 'koinonia' – association or fellowship ('Aristotle
and Economic Analysis', *Past and Present* 47, May 1970). Indeed, Aristotle had no notion of
economic production, even though he discussed various aspects of agriculture and husbandry
as mechanisms of obtaining goods (*chremata*). The concept he generally deployed in connection
with obtaining goods was *ktetike* (acquiring, possessing). Hence arose – in his eyes – the generic
equivalence between agriculture and robbery (*lesteia*) as methods of obtaining goods without
exchange or trade, which is shocking to contemporary sensibilities.

17   These distinctions are discussed with exemplary perspicacity by Scott Meikle, who also
demonstrates the debt owed by Marx to Aristotle with regard to both exchange value and money. See Scott Meikle, 'Aristotle on Money', *Phronesis* 39:1, 1994; Scott Meikle, 'Aristotle on Business', *The Classical Quarterly*, New Series 46:1, 1996.W

bles the development of kapelike. Engaging in kapelike inevitably generates monetary returns, which are profit and indeed comprise the aim of kapelike. Aristotle was perfectly aware that profit could be generated by a range of commercial activities within kapelike. Initially profit might have been simply the result of buying and selling goods; however, through experience, the extraction of profit came to require more skill and involved more sophisticated commercial practices (*technikoteron*).[18] In all its forms, nonetheless, profit arising from kapelike does not constitute 'true wealth' since it results from trading goods and takes the form of money. Therefore, profit creates a frame of mind among participants in kapelike that is geared to expanding wealth without limit. This acquisitive outlook is conducive to living but not to the good life.

The acquisitive and even predatory aspect of profit making is most apparent in moneylending, a subdivision of kapelike for which Aristotle reserved the Athenian term for usury (*obolostatike*). The reason is that moneylending makes apparent an inherent aspect of kapelike – that profit is drawn not from wealth acquired naturally (*kata physin*) – which anyway happens only in oikonomike – but from wealth acquired from other people (*ap' allelon estin*). Interest is the augmentation of money by itself rather than through exchanging goods and is rightly called 'birth' (*tokos*) since money makes money; this is the most unnatural (*para physin*) manner of obtaining wealth.

The various money-making methods of kapelike were not directly discussed by Aristotle, even though he mentioned extant accounts of individual successes in profit making. But there is no doubt about their complexity. Thus, Aristotle made reference to Thales of Miletus who, after being mocked for his philosopher's poverty, sought to prove that philosophers could easily command the ways of chrematistike but chose not to do so (*ou tout' esti peri o spoudazousin*). In the midst of winter Thales predicted that there was going to be a bumper olive crop, raised money and pledged the functioning of all the oil presses of Miletus and Chios. Come the time, he made a large profit by renting the presses out at a price of his choosing. Cornering the market in this manner (*monopolian auto kataskeuazein*) was a recognized principle of money making in Aristotle's time. History does not tell us whether other impoverished Greek philosophers deployed their skills with similar success, but in the years of financialization plenty of economists have followed in the steps of Thales of Miletus with none of his disdain for the filthy business of money making.

The commercial and predatory character of profit, particularly in its financial form, is also apparent in the forensic speeches of Demosthenes, the richest literary source on moneylending and its associated practices in Greek antiquity. Most of the material refers to maritime (bottomry) loans which were the typical form of productive lending in the ancient Greek world.[19] Note, though, that '*Paragraphe pros Pantaineton*',

18   *Eita di' empeirias ede technikoteron, pothen kai pos metavallomenon pleiston poiesei kerdos'.* Aristotle, *Politics*, Cambridge, MA: Harvard University Press, 1932, p. 42

19   As Schaps states, however, there were several other forms of lending for profit-making

one of the most complex of Demosthenes's speeches, refers to loans to finance silver mining in Attica.[20] The institutional and legal framework of such lending is hard to ascertain not least because the difference between lender and owner is far from clear in the transactions debated.

It appears that the lending of money afforded property rights over the mine, even if the latter was merely collateral for the loan. The lender was able to transfer owner-ship of the mine to another lender via a separate transaction while the operator of the mine remained in place. The monetary return to the lender took the form of interest payments, or of rent that was equivalent to the putative interest payments. Thus, at least as far as can be inferred from this particular text, the economic forms of lending, buying, renting and their associated returns were inextricably bound up both in prac-tice and in law. Moneylending and profit making were prominent in Greek antiquity, but the characteristic economic categories did not emerge with clarity similar to that of capitalist society.

The overlapping of categories is a point of particular importance in analysis of bottomry loans. Note first that bottomry loans reached great complexity of form in the ancient Greek world. Thus, Demosthenes in *Pros tin Lakritou Paragraphen* leaves no doubt about the remarkable sophistication of counterparties with regard to risk premia.[21] The contract (*syggrafe*) stated that the borrowers would pay 22.5 percent interest to sail for trade to the west coast of the Black Sea (*ep' aristera*) and back to Athens, but 30 percent if the return journey started 'after the rising of Arcturus' (*met' Arktouron*) which meant likely stormy weather.[22] The contract further specified the stages of the journey, the loads to be carried at each stage, the commander of the boat, and the obligations of crew and borrower upon returning to Athens. Similarly complex are the transactions discussed in *Pros Formiona peri Daneiou*, which also makes clear that merchants could settle debts during the course of the journey by paying in the money of other cities, whose rate of exchange varied with place.[23] Above all, it was stated that the borrower could not use the goods purchased through a loan as collateral for a further loan. It appears that this practice was not unusual in Athens, certainly for cases that ended up in court.

Fraud was a feature of bottomry loans, as is trivially obvious for the speeches of

---

purposes in classical Athens. David Schaps, *The Invention of Coinage and the Monetization of Ancient Greece*, Ann Arbor: The University of Michigan Press, 2004, appendix 4. Note that lending to engage in profit making was certainly not the dominant form of lending.

20　References to Demosthenes are to the edition by Frederick A. Palley and John E. Sandys, *Select Private Orations of Demosthenes*, Cambridge: Cambridge University Press, 1874. For this speech see ibid., pp. 84–129.

21　Ibid., pp. 49–83.

22　Ibid., pp. 55–6.

23　Ibid., pp. 1–48.

Demosthenes, since they refer to court cases. The predatory and fraudulent aspect of such lending – and of the returns to which it gave rise – is most apparent in the contract clauses regarding repayment. The practices of the ancient Greek world in this respect were quite unusual by contemporary capitalist standards. Thus, the law specified that in the case of loss of ship, or of being obliged to throw the commodities overboard in a storm, the borrower had no further liability to the lender. This has been interpreted as a form of insurance, by Geoffrey de Ste. Croix, no less; but it was not insurance since no-one was subsequently indemnified for the loss of either ship or commodities, which was entirely borne by the parties involved.[24]

Releasing the borrower from liability in case of disaster signifies that bottomry loans in Greek antiquity had an inherent aspect of joint investment – the lender effectively becoming equity holder and taking losses. The advance of a bottomry loan was not necessarily matched by its return, although the lender earned a pre-determined interest rate rather than a variable share in the profits of the enterprise. Moreover, the advance was not made for a definite period of time, earning interest proportionately, but for the entire trip irrespective of duration.[25] The advance thus resembled joint investment although, again, the remuneration of the owner was as a pre-determined percentage of the money advanced (*tokos*) rather than as a proportion of the overall profit generated. Thus arose the opportunity for predatory and fraudulent action by the borrower who, however, would be personally liable for the lost property, if fraud was demonstrated. Chrematistike could be a dangerous pursuit, if the urge to make profit took the better of the judgement of the counterparties.[26]

In short, there were several types of profit making in classical Greece, some associated with straight lending, others with pure commercial transactions, others with

---

24 See Geoffrey de Ste. Croix, 'Ancient Greek and Roman Maritime Loans', in *Debits, Credits, Finance and Profits*, ed. Harold Edey and Basil Yamey, London: Sweet and Maxwell, 1974, pp. 41–3. De Ste. Croix was unduly impressed by the spreading of risk that bottomry loans meant for the ship's owner. But this was no more than joint investment, which inevitably spreads risk; there was no insurance, as is apparent from the damage to all involved in case of loss of ship, or of jettisoning of the cargo.

25 A point made by de Ste. Croix in his path-breaking essay (ibid., pp. 55–6).

26 Note that bankers, of whom there were several in classical Athens, were not the dominant lenders for bottomry. This issue has been part of the substantivist – formalist debate in classical history. Paul Millett, arguing for the former, implied that banker's were marginal, while Edward Cohen, arguing for the latter, claimed that bankers were significant. See Paul Millett, *Lending and Borrowing in Ancient Athens*, Cambridge: Cambridge University Press, 1991; and Edward E. Cohen, *Athenian Economy and Society*, Princeton: Princeton University Press, 1992, ch. 5. As C.M. Reed shows, however, the evidence indicates that bankers could have played, at most, a minor role in bottomry loans. The main lenders were not bankers. See C.M. Reed, *Maritime Traders in the Ancient Greek World*, Cambridge: Cambridge University Press, 2003, pp. 39–40.

arbitrage among foreign exchange rates and still others with rental income from slave-based mining. The similarities of form with contemporary financial profit are apparent, despite the passage of more than two millennia; ancient profit also had a predatory aspect, mixed with fraud and deception. On the other hand, there are equally apparent differences with contemporary financial profit. Returns from financial transactions, for instance, were mingled inextricably with returns from commerce and production. The rights of property and the rights of recompense for value advanced were not as clearly delineated as in mature capitalist society.

At least for Aristotle, finally, financial profit was unnatural and contributed nothing to genuine wealth, deriving purely from the wealth of others. In a capitalist economy, however, there is a rational foundation for the accrual of financial profit, even if that is only the provision of services boosting profitability across the economy. This is not to deny that, as Aristotle noted, financial profit could be a share of the wealth belonging to others. In the rest of this chapter financial profit is considered in further depth to establish the sources of the characteristic profit forms of financialization.

Financial profit from advancing loans: The importance of leverage (gearing)

The simplest primary form of financial profit is that earned by making loans: receiving interest, a process that has been discussed extensively in this and previous chapters. Purely in terms of its analytical content, such profit can be broadly divided into, first, interest earned from loans made among capitalists and, second, interest earned from loans made between capitalists and workers (or even a 'third' class). The former typically represents a share of surplus value, though it could also have aspects of financial expropriation, as is shown below for trading financial assets. The latter includes a share of personal income and is a characteristic outcome of financial expropriation.

Further analytical insight into financial profit could be gained by focusing more closely on interest as a share of surplus value paid for loans among capitalists. The complexity of the relationship between borrowing and lending capitalists would then emerge more fully, casting light onto the nature of financial profit. As was discussed in Chapter 5, there are two strains to Marx's work in this regard: the first assumes that the lender is a 'monied' capitalist who owns capital for lending; the second assumes that loanable money capital is created out of idle money generated by the circuit of capital. Both approaches assume that the borrower is a functioning capitalist (typically an industrialist) who obtains the capital necessary for the project in hand and proceeds to generate surplus value. The flow of surplus value is subsequently divided between interest accruing to the lender, and profit of enterprise accruing to the borrower. Interest thus corresponds to a quantitative division of total profit, which subsequently becomes a qualitative distinction between profit accruing purely due to ownership of loanable capital, and profit accruing as a result of functioning as a capitalist in the process of production.

Marx related this qualitative distinction to the putative division of the capitalist class into the 'monied' and the 'functioning' fractions that are presumably in opposition to each other over the division of total profit. As was discussed in Chapter 5, this is not a persuasive argument especially in conditions of financialized capitalism. Nevertheless, Marx's focus on the inherent opposition between interest and profit of enterprise could have fruitful implications in analysing the capitalist economy, provided that it was further developed. To be specific, the relationship between borrower and lender is not simply a zero sum game corresponding to a tug-of-war between the 'monied' and the 'functioning' fractions of the capitalist class. Borrowing has a complex effect on the profitability of the functioning capitalist and involves more than a straighforward opposition between borrower and lender.

A crucial factor in this regard is that the borrowing capitalist could also own some of the capital invested in the project, a possibility that is largely absent from Marx's analysis. If allowance was made for it, the opposition between profit of enterprise and interest would emerge in a different and more informative light. For, profit of enterprise and interest would then relate to each other through leverage, or gearing, a concept that is of paramount importance in mature capitalism. The nature of financial profit in contemporary capitalism would then acquire a different complexion. Consider the following simple presentation of the issue.

Following Marx in chapter twenty-one of the third volume of *Capital*, take an industrial capitalist with a project requiring capital, K, to generate the average rate of profit, r, and hence resulting in total profit, Π:

$$\text{(i)} \quad \Pi = rK$$

Marx mostly assumed that the industrialist borrows the entire capital invested. Consequently, total profit, Π, is split between the borrower, who retains profit of enterprise, E, and the lender, who receives interest, I. Thus:

$$\text{(ii)} \quad \Pi = E + I$$

Interest and profit of enterprise are inversely related, and that is the simplest way of capturing the opposition between borrower and lender. Marx further postulated that the rate of interest, i, tends to be below the rate of profit, r, as was discussed in Chapter 5. Given the assumption that the entire capital has been borrowed, the postulate is trivially true since by, construction, $i = I/K < r = \Pi/K$. The true significance of the postulate becomes clear only when it is assumed that the capital of the project is partly borrowed and partly owned by the functioning capitalist. Marx was aware of this possibility but did not fully discuss it. If the borrower already owned some capital, the opposition between interest and profit of enterprise would take a different aspect compared to the simple zero sum game implicit in $\Pi = E + I$.

Assume that the capital of the project is divided between a borrowed part, B, and a part owned by the functioning capitalist, S:

$$\text{(iii)} \quad K = B + S$$

The project is thus run with leverage B/S. The key point in this respect is that the level of leverage is not externally given (technologically or otherwise) but constitutes a decision variable of the functioning capitalist. There is, of course, a qualitative difference between deciding the level of leverage and deciding the precise mix of real resources to be mobilized by the enterprise. The latter is a material magnitude – workers, raw materials, machinery, plant, equipment – that corresponds to living standards, technology and the speed of capital turnover. It refers to use values which must be deployed in specific ways to generate the surplus value that the project is capable of producing. In contrast, the former is a financial magnitude referring to the balance sheet of the enterprise. And yet, as is shown below, leverage matters to the profitability of the project holder – finance affects the operations of productive capitalists.

Consider now the form taken by the return to the project once leverage is introduced. As before, $\Pi = rK$, since nothing would have changed in the operations of the enterprise other than its financing.[27] Also, $\Pi = E + I$. Total profit would be similarly divided between profit of enterprise and interest. Once again, the quantitative division of total profit would result in a rate of interest, that is, $i = I/B$, or $I = iB$. However, since some of the capital would now belong to the functioning capitalist, the profit of enterprise would be given explicitly by $e = E/S = (\Pi - I)/S$. Given that $\Pi = rK$ and $I = iB$, it follows immediately that:

$$\text{(iv)} \quad e = (r - i)B/S + r$$

This result states that the rate of profit of enterprise rises with leverage as long the rate of profit exceeds the rate of interest, $i < r$. Not only this, but leverage makes the rate of profit of enterprise higher than the average rate of profit. Algebraically this is trivially true since the functioning capitalist would add a further amount of surplus value (equal to $r - i$ per unit of S) to that already generated by S.

The implications for the general relationship between interest and profit of enterprise are far-reaching. At one remove, the opposition between the two remains present: for every level of Π, the higher is I, the lower would be E, and hence the lower would be the rate of profit of enterprise. At a further remove, however, the opposition is tempered because leverage gives a general boost to the rate of profit of enterprise. In sum, the borrower opposes the lender, since interest lowers the profit of enter-

---

27   It goes without saying that leverage expands the capital invested and thus makes it possible to adopt projects that would have been previously out of reach. In and of itself, however, this says nothing about profitability, and nor about the relationship between financial and non-financial profit. Indeed, it occludes the issue by simultaneously changing real and financial variables. The proper way to proceed analytically is to assume that the project has remained the same but its financing has changed.

prise; but the borrower also relies on the lender, since lending boosts the profit of enterprise.

On these grounds, treating borrowers and lenders as belonging to two opposing fractions of the capitalist class is a very partial representation of the fundamental relationship of lending, which could even prove misleading. Rather, borrowers and lenders ought to be treated as economic agents that develop contradictory relations stretching across the capitalist class. By the same token, the distinction between non-financial and financial profit does not represent a simple opposition, and certainly not a putative split, between active (functioning, borrowing) and passive (parasitical, lending) capitalists. Once leverage is taken into consideration, it becomes clear that access to loanable money capital could directly affect the profitability of the functioning capitalist. Financial profit is complexly, and contradictorily, related to profit drawn by active capitalists.

Two questions immediately arise at this point. First, does it follow that all functioning capitalists would engage in borrowing part of their capital? Second, does it also follow that functioning capitalists would continually increase leverage, thus raising the rate of profit of enterprise? Both questions are directly related to the Modigliani–Miller theorem, the cornerstone of mainstream theory of finance.[28] The theorem argues that, if capital markets are perfect and there are no transactions costs and taxes, the level of leverage of an enterprise is irrelevant to its stock market valuation and to the cost of financing its liabilities. What matters instead is the combination of real resources mobilized by the enterprise – labour power, raw materials, technology, and so on. By the same token, financial decisions are irrelevant to overall profitability, and can be disregarded by economic theory.

The Modigliani–Miller theorem reflects the extraordinary focus of mainstream economics on the substance of economic processes at the expense of form. In terms of substance the theorem is valid, and is reflected in the simple assumption underpinning the analytics above. Namely, the total profit generated by the enterprise would remain at $\Pi = rK$ irrespective of the financing mix that the functioning capitalist adopted. Total profit is dictated by real wages, technology (the organic composition of capital) and the turnover of capital; the mix of borrowed and own capital is irrelevant to the flow of surplus value. However, form is also of paramount importance to capitalist economic processes, as practising capitalists know all too well. It is intuitive that enterprises

---

28   Franco Modigliani and M.H. Miller, 'The Cost of Capital, Corporate Finance and the Theory of Investment', *American Economic Review* 48, 1958. The theorem assumes that the capital owned by the functioning capitalist could be freely traded – that is, it is tradable equity. This hardly applies to all owner-operated capitalist enterprises that also borrow. Nonetheless, the gist of the Modigliani–Miller argument has a bearing on the issues raised in this section, irrespective of the particulars of the proof. For a useful review of the significance of the theorem for the theory of finance see Milton Harris and Artur Raviv, 'The Theory of Optimal Capital Structure', *Journal of Finance* 48, 1991.

would not be indifferent to rising leverage, even if substantive activities (and therefore the ability to generate profit) had remained unchanged. Insight into this issue can be obtained through brief discussion of the difference between debt and own capital in the rest of this section as well as in the next section.

Briefly put, debt imposes a fixed, external obligation on the borrower: interest and principal have to be repaid in pre-determined amounts at fixed times, or bankruptcy would result. Indeed, capitalist crises are characterized by the inability of borrowers to settle existing debt obligations, often resulting in failure. Leverage, therefore, increases risk for functioning capitalists because, first, it makes the rate of profit of enterprise more variable and, second, it raises the danger of bankruptcy. From the perspective of the functioning capitalist, the higher the level of leverage for any given size of capital, the greater the risk posed by unforeseen fluctuations in output and profitability. The beneficial effect of rising leverage on the profit of enterprise is tempered by rising risk.[29]

Yet, there is no a priori optimal level of leverage that could be determined by analysing the material conditions of production – wages, technology and turnover of capital. Functioning capitalists must base their leverage decisions on the levels of leverage normally prevailing in their sectors, subsequently deciding on what is appropriate for their own enterprises. The empirical regularities of leverage reflect the characteristics of each sector – preponderance of fixed over circulating capital, rapidity of turnover of capital, institutional practices of sale and purchase, access to telecommunications, but also plain custom and tradition. Needless to say leverage would also vary according to the phase of the economic cycle.

The level of leverage is thus a financial decision that directly affects profitability but also the survival of functioning capitalists. It is a decision that relates to the balance sheet rather than the material reality of production or circulation, but it could still affect the profitability and the development of an enterprise. In this regard, leverage is an instance of the capitalist form of organization impinging directly upon the performance of production and circulation. The financial profit drawn from the flow of surplus value as the borrower pays the lender has a complex and contradictory relationship to the non-financial profit remaining to the functioning capitalist. However, in advanced capitalism, even the profit remaining after the lenders have been paid off could also acquire a financial character. Thus, further to explore the social content of financial profit, the following section turns to the holding of equity.

Financial profit from holding equity: Shareholders compared to lenders of money

Equity and the profit to which it gives rise are inextricably bound with the operations of the capital market. The latter covers a range of open financial markets that deal in

---

29   This is well appreciated by mainstream economics; see, for instance, Joseph Stiglitz, 'More Instruments and Broader Goals: Moving Toward the Post Washington Consensus', WIDER Annual Lecture, Helsinki, 7 January 1998.

loanable capital but also in plain sums of idle money mobilized on the basis of both equity and debt, as was discussed in Chapter 5. Returns to traded equity (shares) are distinct from returns to traded debt (bonds, typically long-term). Strictly speaking, the return to debt is interest whose conceptual content has already been analysed. In contrast, the return to equity is dividends, which correspond to different underlying relations and pose new conceptual problems. Moreover, the holders of both bonds and shares could also earn further returns by simply trading both bonds and shares in the capital market. This form of financial profit and the underlying similarity between shares and bonds are considered in the next section.

The equity market corresponds to joint-stock capital – to the leading form of organization of capital (productive, merchant and banking) in mature capitalism. The joint-stock corporation is a long-standing historical form of large capitalist enterprises, but has become dominant only since the emergence of monopoly capitalism in the late nineteenth century. The period of financialization has been stamped by the supremacy of the joint-stock corporation, and the global economy is dominated by large multi-national enterprises.

The joint-stock organization of the capitalist enterprise derives from two sources, both of which have a long historical pedigree.[30] The first is the legal and institutional formalization of the principle of partnership in providing capital. This principle characterized merchant capital 'companies' already at the dawn of commercial capitalism. In advanced capitalism it has become associated with the legal principle of limited liability that restricts the exposure of the property of the capitalist to the project in hand. Accordingly, joint-stock enterprises function on the basis of pro-rata ownership of both the corporation and its profits, backed by limited liability. Shares are titles of ownership that confer rights to a part of profits and could be traded in stock markets. Ownership of capital becomes impersonal, delimited from other personal property, and easily transferable.

The second source is the adoption by capitalist enterprises of elements of corporatist organization of labour. Corporatist organization has also had a long historical

---

30 The brief analysis of joint-stock capital in this section draws primarily on Uno's outstanding exposition, which was in turn heavily based on Hilferding (Kozo Uno, *Keizai Seisakuron*, Tokyo: Kobundo Shobo, 1936, part 3, section 2). The capital market for Uno is where trading occurs of 'capital-as-value', that is, of capital as a profit-producing entity as opposed to capital as a set of value-containing commodities. Hence prices in the capital market result from capitalization – that is, they have an element of fictitiousness. These are certainly proper grounds on which to assess contemporary theories of finance, including the Modigliani–Miller theorem. However, the further distinction that Uno draws – that trading in the money market involves plain sums of money rather than capital – is problematic, as was argued in Chapter 5. Further analysis of joint-stock capital can also be found in Makoto Itoh and Costas Lapavitsas, *Political Economy of Money and Finance*, London: Macmillan, 1999, ch. 5.

pedigree and can be found in pre-capitalist economies, for instance, among the craft guilds of medieval cities. Joint-stock corporations are hierarchical and bureaucratic organizations that frequently fix the career patterns of employees. In this regard they have little in common with the perception of the capitalist enterprise that still populates economic ideology, namely of a flexible entity run by an innovative and thrusting owner. Joint-stock capital typically is a multi-layered bureaucratic entity whose performance depends on strategic insight as well as on the efficient operation of its internal structure. The methods of internal organization, with their corresponding rules of bureaucracy and hierarchy, often reflect the specific historical and institutional context of different countries. This is one of the reasons for differential performance among various forms of capitalism discussed in Chapter 2.

For the purpose of analysing the conceptual content of financial profit, the most prominent feature of joint-stock capital is the separation of ownership from control. This is a direct result of enterprise organization that relies on pro-rata, tradable, limited liability ownership combined with a corporatist internal bureaucracy. Marxist economics was quick to notice the separation of ownership from control, as was already discussed in Chapter 3 in connection with Hilferding, whose insights are further discussed below. Note that, for Marx, the separation of ownership from control allows capital to emerge as a social entity in itself without the irrelevant complications brought by the preferences and initiatives of individual owners.[31] The impersonal and self-driven nature of capitalist accumulation is thus brought to the fore.

It took longer for mainstream economics to appreciate the importance of separating ownership from control, though in recent years the separation has become a standard feature of microeconomic analysis under the guise of the opposition between principal (owner) and agent (manager).[32] The essential notion behind this literature is simple: the agent has considerable independence of decision-making and could therefore pursue interests that are different from those of the principal. Agent independence could ostensibly result in actions that are inconsistent with profit maximization, hence creating inefficiency. This view lies at the heart of the ideology of 'shareholder value'

---

31 Marx, *Capital*, vol. 3, ch. 27. Marx went too far when he claimed that joint-stock capital represents 'the abolition of capital as private property within the confines of the capitalist mode of production itself' (p. 567).

32 The mainstream literature on ownership and control and its implications for the organization of capitalist enterprises goes back at least to the inter-war years with Adolph Berle and Gardiner Means (*The Modern Corporation and Private Property*, New York: Macmillan, 1932) who generally overemphasized the role of the law in altering property relations and thus separating owners from managers. Albert Hirschman's post-war work on 'voice' and 'exit' as characteristic features of shareholder behaviour offers greater analytical range (*Exit, Voice, and Loyalty: Responses to Decline in Firms, Organizations, and States*, Cambridge, MA: Harvard University Press, 1970).

which has characterized the rise of financialization. Summarily put, economic efficiency requires that the interest of principals should be paramount in the running of joint-stock enterprises, which means that enterprises ought to guide activities with an eye to the value of shares in the stock market. The threat of takeover is a disciplining mechanism on managers, forcing the latter to pay attention to the rate of return on the capital invested. This is evidently an appropriate ideological shroud for the financialization of non-financial enterprises.[33]

The principal–agent framework is a narrow way to approach the internal organization of joint-stock capital and the social content of the relations involved. Two points are worth making, which also facilitate the analysis of financial profit arising from holding equity, both of which derive from Uno's analysis of the joint-stock corporation in *Keizai Seisakuron*. First, principals are far from equal since pro-rata ownership means that those who hold more shares also have more influence over the internal organization and the operations of joint-stock enterprises. Large shareholders are qualitatively distinct from the small buyers who acquire shares by deploying saving out of personal income. Joint-stock capital does not eliminate the hierarchical and socially divisive role of property in capital, even if it turns the latter into an impersonal and limited relationship.

Second, the divide between managers and large shareholders is not nearly as absolute as the principal–agent framework implies; on the contrary, managers often are substantial shareholders. Furthermore, under conditions of financialized capitalism, managers but also other elements of the bureaucratic structure of large corporations – particularly of large financial corporations – are often remunerated through stock options, shares, and other forms of financial assets. Profits accrue to those who control joint-stock capital separately and independently of their pro-rata investment in the enterprise. In this respect, the ideology of 'shareholder value' could rebound in favour of managers and large owners of stock.

For the purposes of this chapter, therefore, shareholders can be thought of as economic agents committing money capital, or plain idle money, to acquire property rights over the enterprise, and thus over future flows of surplus value. Dividends are a share of surplus value accruing due to property rights over the enterprise. The money capital committed by shareholders could be loanable capital mobilized through the financial system; but shareholders differ from lenders insofar as they commit potential loanable capital, or idle money, indefinitely rather than for given period of time. The payment of returns, moreover, is not predetermined in terms of either time or magnitude.[34] By the same token, the obligation of the enterprise to make payments out of

---

33 The original insight in this field, within a principal - agent framework, comes from Michael C. Jensen and William H. Meckling, 'Theory of the Firm: Managerial Behavior, Agency Costs and Ownership Structure', *Journal of Financial Economics* 3:4, 1976.

34 These are general categorizations to facilitate analysis. There are several types of equity

profits to shareholders allows for an element of discretion compared to the obligation to make payments to lenders, which is an external requirement and typically assumes precedence over payments to shareholders.

Despite these well-known formal differences between equity and debt, there are also strong similarities between shareholders and lenders. For one thing, the returns to both arise out of the flow of surplus value, even if the right to receive a fraction of surplus value has a different content for shareholders compared to lenders. Above all, the money committed by both to the enterprise comes essentially from the social pool of loanable capital and idle money. Furthermore, even though the shareholder does not have the formal right to receive the principal back at some predetermined point in time, in practice the money could be recouped through the sale of shares in the stock market. Investment banks are fundamental to this process, as was shown in Chapter 5. In short, for equity investment, both the fluidity and the tendency of loanable capital to return to its owner re-emerge through the opportunity to sell shares in the capital market.

Shareholders can, thus, be thought of as owners of capital who share key characteristics with the lenders of money. They are not formally charged with managing the capitalist enterprise, even though in practice managers often are substantial shareholders. Equity purchases are an investment of loanable or idle money that commands a return but does not require active involvement in the running of the enterprise. Similarly to lenders, shareholders could potentially secure the return of the capital invested through the resale of equity. The similarity between lender and shareholder implies that, if the lender was thought of as a rentier, the shareholder could also be treated in the same way. There is heuristic value this notion, provided that shareholders were not mistakenly identified with a rentier fraction of the capitalist class.

Finally, the underlying similarity between lender and shareholder is also implicit in the structural connection between the credit system and the capital market. For the purpose of ascertaining the content of financial profit, the most important link between the two components relates to forming prices in the capital market. Put simply, share prices pivot on the rate of interest determined in the money market. The return earned by shareholders has a financial character, first, because it is generated through transactions in the stock market and, second, because it is partly based on the rate of interest. Consider now the character of financial profit made through trading financial assets, particularly equity, which includes capital gains.

Financial profit from trading financial assets
Financial profit derived from trading financial assets is by far the most complex form of financial profit for a variety of reasons, and not least because it requires analysis of cap-

---

and even more types of debt, and the terrain between the two is rather grey. This is further confirmation of the underlying similarity of the two types of financial asset, despite differences.

ital gains. Profit from trading financial assets it often considered speculative and deriving from a zero sum game between buyer and seller. Hilferding for instance, related gains from trading to speculation and zero sum transactions, as did Keynes who more generally associated capital markets with speculation.[35] In recent heterodox literature there have been several references to the speculative aspect of gains from trading.[36] However, speculation is a notoriously difficult concept to define with precision, and it cannot provide an adequate point of departure for the analysis of financial profit resulting from trading financial assets. There is a systemic role for financial markets in advanced capitalist economies and, without denying the existence of speculation, there must also be a systemic point of departure to analyse financial profit from trading financial assets. This could only be the fundamental relations of loanable capital.[37]

Trading in financial assets constitutes transactions in which, typically, the seller receives money, while the buyer receives a claim on future income denominated in money. Each transaction is ostensibly an exchange of equivalents, and therefore it does not immediately follow that the profit of the seller would be a loss to the buyer. It is shown below that profit from trading financial assets accrues through a complex and mediated process that could indeed be a zero sum game, but it could also include appropriation of a share of surplus value, or of personal income. Profit from trading financial assets has a strong dimension of 'profit upon alienation or expropriation' while remaining associated with the fresh flows of surplus value.

Analytical focus in this section will be on equity because it presents more complex conceptual problems the answers to which could also apply to profit from trading in debt instruments. The first step is to consider more closely the prices of shares, which are pure market prices that are not directly related to value generated in production. Share prices are monetary sums advanced against the right to receive an indeterminate share of the flow of future surplus value from a project. The fundamental insight in this respect is that the price of shares results from discounting expected future dividends.[38]

---

35   See Rudolf Hilferding, *Finance Capital*, London: Routledge & Kegan Paul, 1981, ch. 8.1; and John Maynard Keynes, *The General Theory of Employment, Interest and Money*, London: Macmillan, 1973, ch. 12.

36   Özgür Orhangazi has, for instance, added 'speculative profits' to Robert Pollin's three sources of financial profit. See Özgür Orhangazi, *Financialization and the US Economy*, Northampton: Edward Elgar, 2007, pp. 47–8; and Robert Pollin, 'Contemporary Economic Stagnation in World Historical Perspective', *New Left Review* 219, 1996. Wray has also noted the significance of speculation in financial markets. See L. Randall Wray, 'Minsky's Money Manager Capitalism and the Global Financial Crisis', Working Paper 661, Levy Economics Institute of Bard College, 2011, p. 11.

37   Note that, from a Marxist standpoint, Chesnais has also been critical of 'singling out "speculation" instead of providing a proper analysis of money-capital'. See François Chesnais, 'The Economic Foundations of Contemporary Imperialism', *Historical Materialism* 15:3, 2007, p. 133.

38   Marx, *Capital*, vol. 3, pp. 597–8. See also Costas Lapavitsas, *Social Foundations of Markets,*

Discounting future streams of income is a fundamental practice of financial markets in determining prices. The underlying logic of discounting derives from the quantitative division of the flow of surplus value into interest and profit of enterprise, which subsequently acquires qualitative characteristics. Any regular income accruing to capitalists could appear as the receipt of interest on some imputed capital. Consequently, the form of interest is capable of generating a range of peculiar prices and profits that characterise the financial system. It could, for instance, make profit of enterprise appear to be a return paid for a capital that has been fictitiously lent by the owner to himself or herself. It could even make wages appear as interest-like return on the fictitious (human) capital of the worker.

Marx called the imputed capital 'illusory' and 'fictitious', terms that have several meanings, some of which will be further developed below.[39] Simply put, however, the meaning is apparent: the price of a share is fictitious capital in the sense that, for the owner, it represents value that does not exist but is the monetary equivalent of future dividends. If the share was sold, fictitious would become actual capital accruing to the seller. However, the share price would continue to fluctuate depending on the discounting of still future dividends, and independently of the capital paid at the point of purchase. For its new holder, there would be another fictitious capital attached to the share.

Dividends apart, it follows that financial profit generated in capital markets derives from the relation between the fictitious capital attached to a share, and the actual capital realized at the point of sale in capital markets. The buyer of a share could make profits by subsequently selling at a higher price – that is, by making capital gains; by the same token, there could be capital losses. The thorniest issues with regard to financial profit relate to capital gains. What is the source of value out of which capital gains materialize? How could a sum of fictitious capital generate profits for those who trade financial assets? Are there regularities in the determination of capital gains?

Note that, in essence, the issue of capital gains is not qualitatively different for debt instruments, since the price of the latter could similarly fluctuate subsequent to purchase. Note also that the issue of capital gains can cast light on the profits of financial institutions operating in capital markets. Intermediaries in financial markets are remunerated out of the prices of financial assets, that is, out of the money capital used to pay for assets. Profits, whether in the form of fees and commissions or of own trading, ultimately arise out of value committed to buying financial assets.

Marx opened a theoretical path to analysing financial profit associated with financial asset prices by pointing out the fictitious character of financial prices, but his argument was only the first step. Hilferding made a more important contribution than Marx in this respect, though he fell some way short of analysing financial profit in

---

Money and Credit, London: Routledge, 2003, ch. 2, for further analysis of the qualitative difference between financial prices and the prices of produced commodities, including the role of custom, institutions and rumours in determining the former.

39   Marx, *Capital*, vol. 3, p. 595.

general. Hilferding, as was discussed in Chapter 3, put forth the theoretical innovation of founder's (or promoter's) profit (*Gründergewinn*). The natural point of departure for analysis of capital gains, and thus of financial profit from trading financial assets, is Hilferding's notion of founder's profit.

For ease of exposition take again the enterprise of 6.3, but assume that its own capital, S, now comprises exclusively shares sold in capital markets. The profit of enterprise, E, accrues as dividends, D, to the shareholders.[40] The share price, S, would be related to future dividends, D, through a process of discounting. The issue then becomes: what would be the rate of discount? Answering this question depends on the analysis of shareholders relative to lenders and to traditional owner-operators, summed up in the previous section. The benchmark rate of discount for dividends would be the rate of interest, i, determined in the money market, but it would also include a risk premium.[41] The latter would depend on the sector in which the enterprise operated as well as on the particular characteristics of the enterprise itself – past history, internal organization, strategic plans, quality of management, structure of balance sheet, and so on.

Broadly speaking, the divergence of the rate of discount from the rate of interest would reflect the difference between shareholder and lender as economic agents. Both advance money capital from the common pool of loanable capital and idle money, but the basis of the advance is distinct and reflected in the rates of return. The lower bound of the shareholder's rate of discount, therefore, would be the rate of interest. The upper bound for both the rate of discount and for the rate of interest, on the other hand, would be the average rate of profit – the real rate of return generated through mobilization of resources by the enterprise. That would reflect the difference between shareholder and lender compared to the owner-operator of the entire enterprise.

In short, the rate of discount, d, would lie in the range:[42]

$$i \leq d \leq r$$

---

40   Strictly speaking this is not necessarily true since profit of enterprise is merely the part of profit that is not paid as interest. The managers of the joint stock enterprise actually decide how much of the after-interest profit to distribute as dividends and how much to distribute in other forms, including as salaries and other types of remuneration of the bureaucracy employed by the enterprise. But for the purpose of analysing financial profit, little is lost by assuming that the entire after-interest profit is distributed as dividends.

41   Hilferding, *Finance Capital*, ch. 7.

42   These are boundaries that hold generally and in the normal operation of capital markets. Nothing prevents the rate of discount from breaching the boundaries in exceptional circumstances. In a crash characterized by forced sales of shares, for instance, the rate of discount would exceed the normal rate of profit, resulting in a collapse of share prices. However, the analysis of financial profit has to start with normal operations in order to be able to analyse extraordinary occurrences.

In this light, and assuming for simplicity that the enterprise had an infinite life, the share price would be:

$$S = D/d$$

Hilferding's 'founder's profit' is now easy to formalize. To keep analysis simple, ignore the risk premium and assume that the rate of discount is equal to the lower bound – to the rate of interest. Thus, share prices would be given by $S = D/i$. If, for further simplicity, it was also assumed that the enterprise had no debt (leverage was zero), then $D = rK$, or $K = D/r$. Since $i \leq r$, it would follow immediately that $S \geq K$. The difference $(S - K)$ would constitute 'founder's profit'. Hilferding's economic reasoning behind 'founder's profit' becomes apparent through these simple formulations. If an enterprise was floated on the stock market, an actual capital equal to K would be required in order to generate future, average profits; but the shares issued would represent a larger fictitious capital, S, reflecting the rate of discount relevant to prospective shareholders. When the shares would be bought, the difference $(S - K)$ would accrue partly to the founder and partly to the intermediaries that facilitated the process of share issue.

Founder's profit is thus an original form of financial profit deriving from trading financial assets. In Hilferding's formulation, it corresponds to the profits from what would today be called initial public offerings – that is, the original floatation of a private enterprise in the capital market. Furthermore, according to Hilferding, the source of founder's profit is the future profit of enterprise which accrues in a lump sum to the founder, or to the financial institution that has acted as promoter of the floatation.[43] This is potentially an important insight for analysis of capital gains, but needs further elaboration than Hilferding afforded to it.

Consider what would happen if the shares continued to be traded in the capital market giving rise to further financial profits (or losses). To pursue the analysis assume that the price of the shares rises – that there are capital gains – and a further two transactions take place following floatation. The path of the financial asset could be simply depicted through a time-line. Thus, the enterprise is floated at t_0 with capital actually invested equal to K and financed through the sale of shares at total price S_0. The shares are then resold at t_1 for S_1 and again at t_2 for S_2, after which they are held indefinitely. All in all, there is one initial seller, one final buyer and two other buyers who subsequently turn into sellers. Assuming that the shares are traded under normal conditions (there are no forced sales) it holds that $S_0 < S_1 < S_2$ – that is, capital gains are realized in both transactions.

---

43   Ibid., p. 129.

$$t_0 \qquad\qquad t_1 \qquad\qquad t_2$$

Floated (sold) for S_0 Sold for S_1 Sold for S_2 and held

On this basis, the following separate sums of realized financial profit emerge for the three sellers during the life of the asset:

$\Phi\Pi_0 = S_0 - K$, founder's profit accruing to the founder at t_0.

$\Phi\Pi_1 = S_1 - S_0$, capital gains accruing to seller 1 at t_1.

$\Phi\Pi_2 = S_2 - S_1$, capital gains accruing to seller 2 at t_2.

Total financial profit throughout the life of the financial assets evidently comes to:

$$\text{(v)} \qquad \Sigma\, \Phi\Pi = S_2 - K$$

That is, total financial profit (capital gains) is given by the money capital committed by the last buyer minus the investment costs of the project. By substituting for S_2 and K, total financial profit could also be written as:

$$\text{(vi)} \quad \Sigma\, \Phi\Pi = D/d_2 - D/r = [(r - d_2)/rd_2]D$$

Total realized financial profit is thus the difference between discounting expected dividends, on the one hand, by the discount rate of the last buyer and, on the other, by the average rate of profit.

This simple presentation immediately demonstrates several key aspects of financial profit from trading financial assets. The sum total of financial profit originates, in the first instance, in the loanable capital (or idle money) advanced by the final buyer, net of the initial actual investment. Each intermediate seller draws financial profit out of the loanable capital of the next buyer, while the final buyer finances the entire series of transactions resulting in financial profit. There is no qualitative difference in this respect between Hilferding's founder's profit and capital gains in general. Founder's profit is a narrower concept, a particular instance of capital gains accruing to the founder from the loanable capital of the first buyer.

But loanable capital is not the deeper source of financial profit. Assuming that all share buyers are equally informed about future dividends, each successive buyer finances the financial profit of the seller, given that share prices rise. The rise in share prices could arise for a variety of reasons, including falls in the rate of interest in the money market, or from applying lower risk premia. The precise reasons are unimportant to the issue addressed here, and could include speculative and psychological factors since share prices are not directly related to value generated in production. What matters is that the final buyer advances S_2 in order to obtain dividends D ad infinitum, carrying an implicit rate of return (discount), d_2, which is evidently lower than the average rate of profit, r.

The final buyer thus obtains rights to the entire flow of surplus value from the project but at a greater expense than each previous owner of shares. In effect, the loanable capital advanced by the final buyer acts as a down payment for all future profits, and a part of it is divided among intermediate sellers as capital gains. This part is recouped by the final buyer out of surplus value equal to $[(r - d_2)/rd_2]D$, which is thus the ultimate source of capital gains. All intermediate instances of capital gains amount to the same process: loanable capital is advanced as down payment for future surplus value and is recouped (plus increment) from the loanable capital of the next buyer. Capital gains in the pure case of capitalists trading equity with each other – and all dividends being paid as expected – ultimately amount to a re-division of surplus value among counterparties.

In this light, the source of financial profit from trading shares can be posited in two ways. In direct and immediate terms, such financial profit arises from the loanable capital of the buyer, and in particular from the loanable capital of the final buyer who subsequently holds the shares. In indirect and mediated terms, however, it arises out of future profits – from the surplus value generated by the enterprise.[44] At the limit, if the rate of discount of the final buyer became equal to the rate of interest, i, financial profit would obviously be made equal to what Marx called the 'profit of enterprise' at t_2.

Contrary to Hilferding's claims, however, founder's profit is not the future profit of enterprise accruing to founder or promoter, and nor is it a remuneration for original 'entrepreneurial' spirit.[45] Indeed, unlike the quantitative division of surplus value into interest and profit of enterprise, capital gains (of which founder's profit is a partial example) represent no formal division of surplus value at all. Rather, the final buyer acquires the rights to the entire future flow of surplus value. The preceding transactions are merely down payments made by others out of their own loanable capital in the expectation of earning future surplus value. The risk of recouping the advance is shifted onto the next buyer, and eventually onto the final buyer, who holds the property rights over the entire flow of surplus value. There is no quantitative division of surplus value in this chain which could give rise to a qualitative division among capitalists.

---

44   The same holds for the profits of financial intermediaries. Fees and commissions charged by investment banks and other intermediaries are obviously part of the effective price of the security. They are paid in the first instance out of the loanable capital of the buyer, but are ultimately recouped out of surplus value.

45   Itoh has also criticized Hilferding's treatment of founder's profit as future surplus value accruing as a lump sum. For Itoh, founder's profit should be understood as a redistribution of the money capital of the buyer. This is certainly true, as the analysis in this section has shown, but the connection between founder's profit and surplus value is still not negated. The point is that profit from trading financial assets represents a share of loanable capital as well as a share of surplus value, the two aspects relating to each other in a structured and mediated way. See Makoto Itoh, *The Basic Theory of Capitalism*, London: Macmillan, 1988, p. 287.

It is apparent that the basic features of this analysis could also apply to other financial assets, including instruments of debt. The borrowing of an enterprise could be assumed to comprise bonds, that is, securities traded in the capital market. The price of bonds, B, similarly to that of shares, would be fictitious capital equal to the discounted value of future interest payments. The rate of discount would be the rate of interest in the money market, plus a risk premium. Capital gains would arise if the market rate of interest declined, or the risk premium fell. Again, the immediate source of capital gains would be the loanable capital of the next buyer, but the ultimate source would be the part of surplus value accruing as interest. In this case the quantitative division of surplus value would retain its qualitative aspect: bond buyers would remain lenders. Consequently, enterprise obligations toward bondholders would normally have priority over obligations to shareholders, including at bankruptcy. But the essential similarity between trading shares and bonds would still be evident as far as financial profit is concerned.

Difficult conceptual problems arise, however, when the traded financial assets are not the liabilities of an enterprise – be they shares or bonds – but of other economic entities, including individual workers. State instruments of indebtedness are a case in point. State bonds – the bedrock of financial markets – are promises to pay interest out of future tax revenues. It follows that interest paid by the state comprises surplus value collected through tax mechanisms. However, interest could also be a part of the money revenue of all social classes collected through the same mechanisms. Taxes paid by workers typically reflect transfers of surplus value to the state in the form of wages. Nonetheless, the value of labour power has a social and historical component that is flexible. In principle taxes could also squeeze real wages, thus shifting parts of the money revenue of workers onto the state.

In that context, financial profits made through state bonds would ultimately represent claims on future tax revenue, thus on surplus value and other money revenue collected by the state. The lenders would hold claims against the whole of society and would be remunerated out of the money revenue of society, but the repayment funds would be collected by the state. Control over the state mechanisms that determine and collect taxes would have decisive implications for the incidence of debt payments by the state on different classes. Unlike lending to particular enterprises, furthermore, the risk premium attached would tend to be low, reflecting the social character of the creditworthiness of the state. On the other hand, fluctuations of state indebtedness would also typically affect the rate of interest and could induce capital gains for bondholders. A rapid switch to a low-interest rate regime, in particular, could be the cause of sudden escalation of financial profits, and thus of enrichment of state bondholders out of the money income of society as a whole.

Even more difficult problems, finally, would emerge for profits relating to financial securities that were the liabilities of workers. These evidently refer to financial expropriation, and have been prominent in the course financialization. Derivatives that are ultimately based on worker debts, for instance, have proliferated in recent decades, and were of critical importance to the bubble and bust of the 2000s. These derivatives could be thought of as synthetic bonds, that is, securities promising to pay the holder a return (interest) out of a variety of payments made by workers which are pooled and then divided. The payments made by workers would be for debts relating primarily to the wage basket, including housing and various consumer debts. In effect, the holder of the derivative security would have a claim on the many and varied interest payments made by workers and others who incur personal debt.

What would be the nature of financial profit deriving from trade in such securities? The easiest way to answer this question would be to take the case of mortgage loans, though the results would also hold for other consumer debts. Assume that workers' mortgages were pooled together and bonds were issued giving a right to a fraction of the pooled interest payments. The price of a derivative security (bond) would represent fictitious capital, and it would result essentially from a process of discounting expected payments. The effective price of the security, incidentally, would also include the fees and commissions charged by the financial institutions involved in issuing the derivative bond. In the first instance, both the profits of sellers and the remuneration of intermediaries would come out of the loanable capital (or idle money) of the buyer of the security. In this regard the process would be similar to issuing a regular bond or share, including the payments to intermediaries.

But what would be the ultimate source of financial profit in this case? The final buyer would have financed all intermediate financial profits in the hope of recouping the costs out of the rights acquired on pooled payments. Thus the ultimate source of financial profits would be mortgage interest payments. Despite the complexity of securitization and the variety of fees and commissions attached, all financial profits would eventually come out of mortgage interest payments (or similar securitized consumer debt). Intermediate financial profits, meanwhile, would derive from down payments on the future mortgage payments made out of each buyer's loanable capital.

There is, thus, an evident difference between pooled mortgage instruments and other financial instruments issued by enterprises. Workers borrow in order to buy houses by mortgaging a part of future wages covering housing needs – they do not mortgage surplus value. Workers receive from lenders a lump sum which represents the discounted value of the housing part of future wages, but treated as fictitious capital. Workers then proceed to repay this debt plus interest through the regular sale of labour power.

In short, the money revenue of workers is transformed into loanable capital at a stroke, allowing financial intermediaries to absorb parts of it as financial profit by trading securities that are based on future wage payments. The path is thus opened for financial institutions to bring to bear predatory practices reflecting the systemic difference in power and outlook between financial institutions and workers. Financial profits could be extracted throughout the lifetime of the security, ultimately deriving from future wage payments. Similar considerations would hold for other consumer borrowing. This is a key aspect of financial expropriation, a form of 'profit upon alienation or expropriation' that is characteristic of financialization.

To recap, financial profit arising from trading financial assets can be theoretically approached on two levels. Immediately and directly it arises out of the loanable capital of each buyer of the financial asset; but in mediated and indirect terms financial profit arises out of the flows of surplus value as well as out of the flows of personal and other revenue. For financial assets issued by capitalist enterprises, financial profit originates in the flows of future surplus value. For financial assets issued by the state, financial profit originates in surplus value but also in the money revenue of all classes, collected through tax. For financial assets that are ultimately liabilities of workers and other households, financial profit originates in the money revenue of workers and others. Financial profit made from trading financial assets, consequently, spans the spheres of production and circulation, allowing for profit to be generated out of the processes of circulation. This is a distinguishing feature of financialized capitalism.

Needless to say, the price of financial assets can also decline. For our purposes, the reasons for such price falls do not matter – whether they are due to interest rate increases, sudden adjustments of risk premia, or even panic sales. The point is that, if prices fell, the financial profits made by the last seller would come entirely out of the loanable capital (or idle money) of the last buyer. This would be a zero sum game, a pure redistribution of loanable capital (and idle money) among different sections of economy and society.

This is far from a rare event in financial markets. Stock market bubbles, for instance, typically attract small shareholders who are caught in the euphoria of the boom and buy financial assets on exaggerated expectations of future returns. When the crash comes, they register net losses, which correspond to profits made by previous sellers of financial assets (and by the same token of the financial institutions which mediated the transactions). Such events could represent great transfers of value from one section of society to another, in the first instance, of loanable capital but, at a further remove, of future flows of value and surplus value.

Part 3 EMPIRICAL AND HISTORICAL FEATURES OF FINANCIALIZATION

7. THE CONTEXT OF FINANCIALIZED ACCUMULATION

Analysing financialization in historical terms

Financialization is the outcome of historical processes that have taken place across the world since the 1970s; it represents a period change of the capitalist mode of production entailing a systemic transformation of mature economies with extensive implications for developing economies, and should properly be examined in these terms. Finance has become ascendant in domestic accumulation, thus setting afresh both the terms of profit extraction and the relations of hierarchy among countries.

Several of the theoretical approaches discussed in Chapter 2 share the view – implicitly or explicitly – that financialization reflects a transformation of the capitalist mode of production. Period analysis, however, has particular requirements and poses characteristic difficulties. It cannot be a mere elaboration of historical events, and nor of patterns of social change, since it would then become either history or a concrete study of particular social formations. Equally, it cannot be an abstract discussion of the evolving relations of capitalist accumulation, since it would then lose much of the specificity characteristic of historical periods of development. Of necessity period analysis must occupy a middle ground, departing from theoretical concerns while systematically integrating historical phenomena in a theoretically informed way.

Period analysis in classical Marxist theory took shape in the early twentieth century in connection with the analysis of imperialism, summed up in chapters 2 and 3.[1] Lenin's analysis, in particular, was explicitly a theory of the succession of historical periods in the development of capitalism – laissez-faire, monopoly, and imperialist capitalism. His theory of imperialism was grounded on the fundamental tendencies of capitalist accumulation, while simultaneously incorporating prominent historical developments. Lenin, drawing on Hilferding, related imperialism to the rise of monopoly, the emergence of finance capital, and the export of capital from the metropolis to

---

1   The literature on the periodization of capitalism in recent decades has been dominated by the concepts of Fordism and post-Fordism proposed by the French Regulation School, but no prevalent view has emerged among Marxists, or radicals more generally. For an excellent collection of contemporary views see Robert Albritton et al. (eds), *Phases of Capitalist Development: Booms, Crisis and Globalizations*, New York: Palgrave, 2001.

the periphery resulting in inherently exploitative relationships among countries in the world market.[2]

In this light, the theoretical analysis proposed in Chapter 2 has sought the roots of financialization in the molecular processes of capitalist accumulation, namely in the altered conduct of enterprises, banks and workers. Fundamental to the structural transformation represented by financialization have been the financial operations of monopoly capitals (joint-stock multinational enterprises). Contemporary monopoly capitals rely on retained profits to finance investment; insofar as they require external finance they are capable of raising funds in open markets, thus also acquiring financial skills. Hilferding's assertion that in the course of capitalist development monopoly capitals rely increasingly on banks to fund fixed investment, hence giving rise to finance capital, does not hold in contemporary conditions.

Fundamental to financialization has also been the altered conduct of banks, including mediating and transacting in open markets as well as lending to, and handling the financial assets of, individuals. Perhaps most striking, however, has been the altered conduct of individuals – and households in general – who have been drawn into the realm of formal finance for purposes of both borrowing and lending. It is equally important to note that, given the transformation of domestic accumulation in mature capitalist countries, financialization has entailed new relations in the world market. Specifically, international financialization has taken a subordinate form in several developing countries, pivoting on the role of world money and involving the export of capital. Even so, financialization has been accompanied neither by extensive trade barriers, nor by formal empire.

However, a theoretical approach to financialization as period change in the development of capitalism must be examined and established empirically, if it is to carry

---

2   Note that Uno has proposed a historical periodization of capitalism that draws on Hilferding and Lenin but is also highly distinctive. Namely, Uno has suggested that capitalism has gone through the stages of mercantilism, liberalism and imperialism, which have been dominated by, respectively, mercantile, industrial and finance capital. Each stage has been characterized by a different set of relations between capital and the state, resulting in different economic policies. Uno was fully aware of Hilferding's excessive focus on Austrian/German economic phenomena, and consequently suggested that finance capital took different forms in the US and the UK compared to Germany. Nonetheless, for Uno, the driving force of the 'imperialist' stage was still the huge size of fixed investment which led non-industrial enterprises to rely on banks. Uno's periodization of capitalism was part of his general theoretical approach to political economy splitting the analysis of capitalism into pure theory, stages theory and concrete empirical study; the pure theory of capitalism reflects the period of liberalism. Based on this fundamental analysis, Sekine has argued that contemporary society has even moved beyond capitalism. See Kozo Uno, *Keizai Seisakuron*, Tokyo: Kobundo Shobo, 1936; Thomas Sekine, *The Dialectic of Capital*, Tokyo: Toshindo, 1986.

weight. The guide on this score is Lenin's work which was thoroughly based on empirical data matching his approach to dialectical materialism. For Lenin, the unfolding of analysis in social science should not be based exclusively on the internal logic of theoretical concepts but should acknowledge empirical developments; otherwise thought runs the risk of disappearing in the magnificence of its own constructions.[3]

Furthermore, a theoretical approach to financialization must be explicitly cognisant of the development of institutions, political struggles, legal systems, ideologies, and even cultural attitudes during the relevant period. Trotsky, in a short article written as a critique of Kondratiev's theory of long-term cycles of capitalist development, offered an exemplary Marxist perspective on the interaction between economic and non-economic forces as capitalist development passes through different historical phases.[4] For Trotsky, capitalist accumulation always occurs within a 'channel' shaped by 'external' conditions that are institutional, political, legal, ideological, cultural, and so on. These 'external' conditions are vital to determining the long-term – 'basic' – path of capitalist accumulation. Political economy must explicitly specify the 'external' conditions, if it is to grasp the direction and changes of accumulation, particularly in the context of crisis and historical period change. This insight is crucial to the analysis of financialization.

Chapters 7, 8 and 9 examine the 'basic' path of accumulation in the US, Japan, Germany and the UK by considering empirical regularities in the conduct of non-financial enterprises, banks and households. Several historical trends are integral to the 'basic' path of accumulation in these mature capitalist countries, including technologies, patterns of work, domestic and international specialization, and even changes in household life. After examining the 'basic' path of accumulation, it will become obvious that the form of financialization varies greatly. There is nothing surprising in this result: financialization is an outcome of historical changes and must therefore reflect the specific 'channel' of accumulation within which it occurs. Thus, chapters 7, 8 and 9 also discuss the 'channel' of accumulation in the US, Japan, Germany and the UK by briefly considering institutional, legal, and even ideological developments, particularly those relating to state intervention in the economy.

To be more specific, in historical terms financialization emerged in the 1970s at the end of a period of exceptional growth and rising incomes following the Second World War. The long post-war boom differed from the period of imperialism that led to the First World War and which came to an end with the Second World War. Formal empires were abolished, mass production and mass consumption dominated the domestic economy, aggregate demand was managed, capital exports were limited, controls prevailed over finance domestically and internationally and, above all, world money was again attached to gold through the Bretton Woods Agreement. During

---

3   A point made by Lenin indirectly but forcefully in his marginalia to Bukharin's *The Economics of the Transformation Period*.

4   Leon Trotsky, 'The Curve of Capitalist Development', *Fourth International* 2:4, 1941.

the long boom, growth in mature capitalist countries was generally strong, and real incomes for workers and others followed an upward path.

The period of financialization, in contrast, has been marked by uncertain and generally weak growth in mature capitalist countries punctuated by repeated economic crises, none as severe as that commencing in 2007. The material basis of accumulation has been shaped by profound technical change in information processing and telecommunications. The institutional, legal, political and ideological framework, on the other hand, has been largely determined by neoliberal policies that have replaced the Keynesianism of the years following the war. Neoliberalism has provided the ideology of the period of financialization, the umbrella under which the ascendancy of finance could take place. Financialization has drawn on the systematic deregulation of labour markets and of the financial system, both of which were purposely implemented by the state. Financialization would have been unthinkable without the systematic intervention of the state in the economy, which has gained effectiveness due to the state's command over domestic money operated via the central bank.

Accordingly, the next section of this chapter sketches the path of accumulation in mature countries by considering three trends. The first is the decline in the rate of growth of GDP in mature countries, which has also been strongly cyclical. Capitalist accumulation has generally lacked dynamism and resulted in repeated crises during the period of financialization. The second is the weakness of productivity growth signifying persistent difficulties in opening fresh fields of capitalist investment that could have led to sustained GDP growth and rising incomes. The third is the retreat of labour in the face of capital, partly due to technological and regulatory change, and partly due to the pressure of higher unemployment. The retreat of labour has meant that the balance of income distribution has shifted in favour of capital in the course of financialization. On this basis, the 'channel' of accumulation and the role of state intervention in the financialization of mature capitalist economies are discussed in more detail on pages 190–9. The focus is on central banks, which have emerged as the pre-eminent public institution of economic policy in financialized capitalism.

The path of accumulation in the course of financialization: Characteristic trends

Empirical analysis in this section, as in much of this book, refers to the four leading mature capitalist countries of the period of financialization: the US, Japan, Germany, and the UK.[5] Figure 1 gives a general indication of the relative weight of capitalist

---

5   Any choice of countries would inevitably have been arbitrary. However, the four countries actually selected offer several advantages. The US, Japan and Germany are the largest mature capitalist economies; even if the magnitude of Chinese GDP exceeded that of Japan and Germany by the end of the 2000s, China had not yet become a developed capitalist economy. France could have easily been included in the group, but the added complexity would not have substantially improved the content of the analysis. Finally, the financial systems of the four

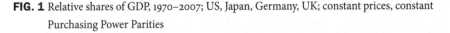

FIG. 1 Relative shares of GDP, 1970–2007; US, Japan, Germany, UK; constant prices, constant Purchasing Power Parities

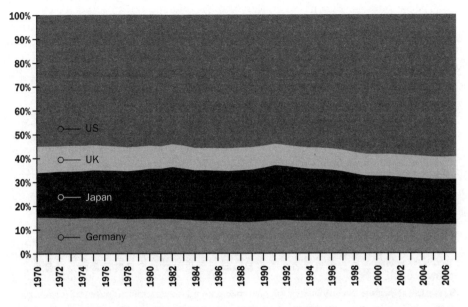

Source: Calculations by author based on OECD database. GDP data are OECD estimates for Germany in 1970–90, Japan 1970–93 and UK 1970–79.

accumulation in each country by comparing shares in the aggregate GDP of the group during the period of financialization.

There have been no major changes in relative rankings: the US has remained dominant and even increased its lead compared to the rest since the early 1990s; Japan, on the other hand, has gone into relative decline during the same period; Germany, whose economy is significantly smaller than both the US and Japan, has also been in gentle relative decline since the early 1970s; the UK has lagged behind Germany throughout the period.

The challenge to the position of the US as the major site of accumulation in the world has not come from within this group, but from the unexpected quarters of China. Had China been included in the figures, its share in 2007 would have been similar to Japan's, even though it would have been negligible in 1970. The emergence of dynamic capitalism in China is important to shaping the parameters of financialization globally, but it has not driven the ascendancy of finance and the associated transformation of mature countries. It would have been deeply misleading to include China in

---

selected countries can be naturally split into bank-based versus market-based, offering further insight into financialization.

FIG. 2 Real GDP annual growth rates, 1971–2007; US, Japan, Germany, UK

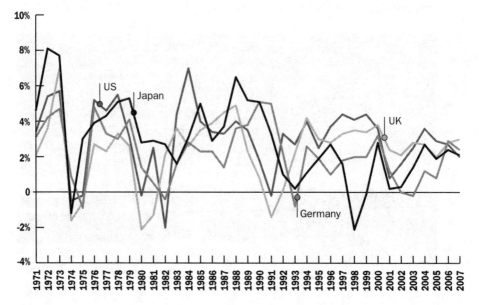

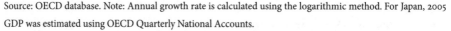

Source: OECD database. Note: Annual growth rate is calculated using the logarithmic method. For Japan, 2005 GDP was estimated using OECD Quarterly National Accounts.

the empirical analysis of the trends of financialization during the last four decades. The importance of China to financialization is mostly associated with the role of the dollar as world money and the accumulation of reserves of world money by the Chinese state, discussed in Chapter 8.

Lower GDP growth, repeated crises, higher unemployment, changing labour force
Initial evidence on the path of accumulation during the period of financialization is given by annual growth rates of real GDP, shown in figure 2.

The growth patterns of the four economies have been broadly synchronic, probably reflecting close links of trade and capital flows. A closer look indicates that the rates of growth have converged onto a lower average during the period; this is preliminary evidence of a relative loss of dynamism by accumulation in the course of financialization. Moreover, the period has been characterized by cyclical behaviour with four clear dips: the crisis of 1973–75, the crisis of 1980–82, the crisis of 1990–92, and the crisis of 2000–2002. The years following 2007 represent another major crisis that is not shown in figure 2 but is discussed at length in Chapter 9 as a structural crisis of financialization. It should be stressed, nevertheless, that significant differences in growth performance have remained among the four countries. Accumulation has continued to reflect the specific features of each country, as is clearly demonstrated by Japan, the only one of the four to have gone through a major crisis in the second half of the 1990s.

FIG. 3 Unemployment rates, US, Japan, Germany, UK

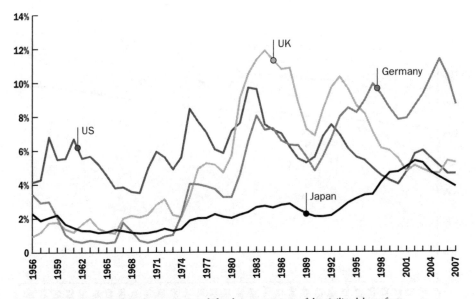

Source: OECD database. Unemployment rate is defined as a percentage of the civilian labour force.

The specificity of accumulation and the importance of particular institutional features in each country for the pace and pattern of accumulation have emerged vividly in the course of the crisis of 2007.

In sum, financialization has been marked by a gradual decline in the pace of accumulation punctuated by repeated crises in all four countries. The counterpart to this growth performance has been an upward shift in the rate of unemployment. Abstracting from cyclical fluctuations, figure 3 indicates that unemployment has generally edged upwards in the 1990s and 2000s compared to the 1970s.

The causes of weakening growth performance, repeated crises and higher unemployment in the course of financialization are neither immediately obvious, nor simple to establish. One factor that could have lent such a shape to the 'basic' path of accumulation in the four countries is the long-term change in the composition of both output and the labour force. Simply put, the service sector, which was already prominent, has become still more important across the four economies.

Figure 4 shows a steady rise of employment in the service sector as a proportion of the total labour force. The trend dates at least to the 1950s and hence it is not specific to financialization; however, the data leaves little doubt that financialized capitalism is primarily and increasingly a service economy. Figure 4 also indicates that both Germany and Japan have retained a more significant proportion of non-service-sector employment, corresponding to greater residual relative strength in the secondary (mostly industrial) sector. This is an early sign that the long-standing distinction

FIG. 4 Employment in services as proportion of labour force, US, Japan, Germany, UK

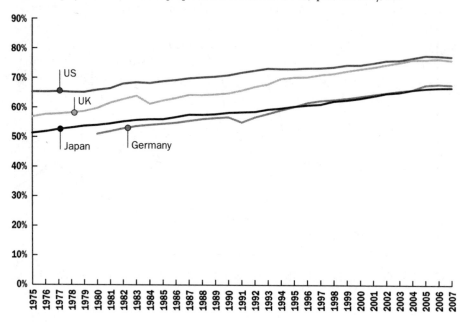

Source: OECD database. Note: Data are available for Germany since 1980.

between Anglo-American and German–Japanese capitalism has not disappeared in the course of financialization.

Two further aspects of the transformation of the labour force in the course of financialization have to be mentioned alongside the changing composition in favour of services. The first is the systematic deregulation of labour markets since the 1970s and the growth of casual and female labour.[6] The second is the wholesale transformation

---

6 The literature on women's participation and the spread of part-time work is large and many-sided. For the worsening of conditions as full-time work has declined and women's participation has become more pronounced, see Jill Rubery, 'Part-Time Work: A Threat to Labour Standards', in *Part-Time Prospects: An International Comparison of Part-Time Work in Europe, North America and the Pacific Rim*, ed. J. O'Reilly and C. Fagan, New York: Routledge, 1998; and Jill Rubery, Mark Smith, and Colette Fagan, 'National Working-Time Regimes and Equal Opportunities', *Feminist Economics* 4:1, 1998, pp. 71–101. For analysis of intensified exploitative conditions as these trends have prevailed, see Rosemary Crompton and Fiona Harris, 'Explaining Women's Employment Patterns', *British Journal of Sociology* 49:1, 1998, pp. 118–36. Irene Bruegel and Diane Perrons also confirm the worsening of employment conditions for women as more flexible employment has prevailed, in 'Deregulation and Women's Employment: The Diverse Experiences of Women in Britain', *Feminist Economics* 4:1, 1998, pp. 71–101. Susan Him-

of technology particularly with the introduction of artificial intelligence and rapid telecommunications; the impact on work practices has been strong and led to the prevalence of new skills in the labour process.[7] Furthermore, information technology has brought work into private time and encouraged a reversal to piece work and putting out practices. There are appears to have been a rebalancing of paid and unpaid labour in favour of the latter in the years of financialization.[8] In standard Marxist terms, finan-

---

melweit, on the other hand, has examined more closely the balance between paid and unpaid work as women's employment has increased ('The Discovery of "Unpaid Work"', *Feminist Economics* 1:2, 1995). For a global perspective on the interaction between part-time employment and women's entry into the labour force, see Guy Standing, 'Global Feminization Through Flexible Labor', *World Development* 17:7, 1989; and Guy Standing, 'Global Feminization Through Flexible Labor: A Theme Revisited', *World Development* 27:3, 1999.

7   There is sizeable mainstream literature arguing that new technology has altered the nature of work by adding intangible organizational assets to the production process; see Erik Brynjolfsson and Lorin Hitt, 'Beyond Computation', *Journal of Economic Perspectives* 14:4, 2000; Brynjolfsson and Hitt, 'Computing Productivity', MIT-Sloan Working Paper 4210–01, 2003; Brynjolfsson, Hitt, and Shinkyu Yang, 'Intangible Assets', *Brookings Papers on Economic Activity: Macroeconomics*, vol. 1, 2002; Timothy Bresnahan, Brynjolfsson, and Hitt, 'Information Technology, Workplace Organization, and the Demand for Skilled Labor: Firm-Level Evidence', *Quarterly Journal of Economics* 117:1, 2002; Marshall Van Alstyne and Brynjolfsson, 'Global Village or Cyber-Balkans', *Management Science*, 2004. Others have examined the change in the skill composition implied by new technologies, including in banking; see David Autor, Frank Levy, and Richard Murnane, 'The Skill Content of Recent Technological Innovation', *Quarterly Journal of Economics*, 118:4, 2003. There is an evident overlap with the parallel, and even earlier, debate on the impact of new technology on productivity growth, summed up below; see, for instance, Paul A. David, 'The Dynamo and the Computer', *American Economic Review* 80:2, 1990; Timothy Bresnahan and Manuel Trajtenberg, 'General Purpose Technologies: "Engines of Growth?"', NBER Working Paper No. 4148, 1992; and Roy Radner, 'The Organization of Decentralized Information Processing', *Econometrica* 61:5, 1993.

8   Within the Marxist tradition, labour process theory – going back at least to Harry Braverman (*Labor and Monopoly Capital*, New York: Monthly Review Press, 1974) – has examined the balance between labour and capital at the workplace to establish changing patterns of exploitation and loss of skill for labour. Already in the late 1970s it was shown that the introduction of new technology led to loss of skills for labour but also to a new balance of power at the shopfloor as labour resisted and devised new methods of confronting management. See Richard Edwards, *Contested Terrain: The Transformation of the Workplace in the Twentieth Century*, New York: Basic Books, 1979; and Michael Burawoy, *Manufacturing Consent: Changes in the Labor Process Under Capitalism*, Chicago: University of Chicago Press, 1979. Nonetheless, Juliet Schor estimated that during the preceding two decades working hours had increased by the equivalent of a month per year in the US. See Juliet Schor, *The Overworked American: The Unexpected Decline of Leisure*, New York: Basic Books, 1992.

FIG. 5 Labour productivity (GDP/hour worked, levels), US, Japan, Germany, UK

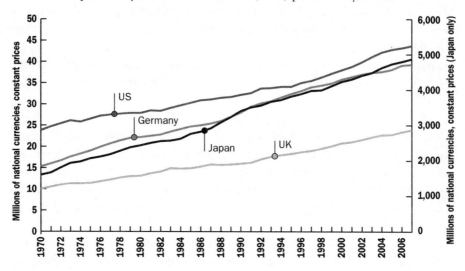

Source: OECD database. Note: For Germany, estimates of GDP per hour worked prior to 1991 are based on data for West Germany.

cialization has probably been accompanied by the intensification of labour as well as by the extension of unpaid labour. Intensification resulting from new technology was probably an important reason for dissatisfaction with work in developed countries, together with loss of discretion over work choices.[9]

Weak productivity growth

However, the transformation of the labour force and the adoption of new technologies in mature countries have not led to sustained and rapid increases in the productivity of labour. This is one of the most prominent aspects of financialization as a historical period in the development of capitalism. Consider, first, the evolution of the levels of labour productivity, shown in figure 5. The US has remained ahead of the others, while Germany and Japan have gradually closed much of the gap; the UK has lagged persistently behind. There has been steady growth of productivity in all four countries, but this is hardly the most important feature of productivity performance during the period.

---

9 Francis Green, *Demanding Work: The Paradox of Job Quality in the Affluent Economy*, Princeton: Princeton University Press, 2006; Francis Green and Nicholas Tsitsianis, 'Can the Changing Nature of Jobs Account for National Trends in Job Satisfaction?', Studies in Economics no. 0406, Department of Economics, University of Kent, 2004; and Francis Green and Nicholas Tsitsianis, 'An Investigation of National Trends in Job Satisfaction', *British Journal of Industrial Relations* 43:3, 2005.

FIG. 6 Labour productivity (GDP/hour worked, annual growth rates)

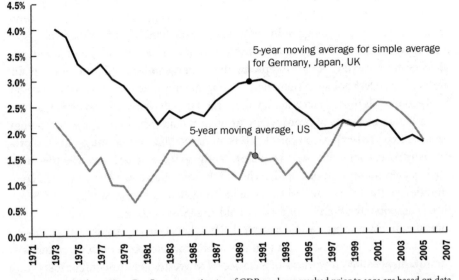

Source: OECD database. Note: For Germany, estimates of GDP per hour worked prior to 1991 are based on data for West Germany.

If the rate of growth of labour productivity is considered, the underlying problem becomes apparent. Figure 6 shows five year moving averages for productivity growth in the four countries; a simple average was generated for Japan, Germany, and the UK, while the US has been kept separate. The reason is the unusual performance of the US in productivity growth, which has significant implications for financialization. Thus, labour productivity growth in the US has drifted sideways for most of this period, with the exception of a bulge that emerged in the mid-1990s and began to peter out in the early 2000s. The bulge was due to particular US developments that are discussed below. Germany, Japan and the UK, on the other hand, have been steadily converging to the historically lower levels of productivity growth of the US.[10] Taken as a whole, the four leading countries of financialization present a picture of weak productivity growth despite the introduction of new technology, the transformation of the labour force and the wholesale restructuring of their economies.

The growth of labour productivity is a factor of decisive importance in characterising historic periods of capitalist development. Marx considered labour productivity to be a fundamental factor in determining the production of surplus value (profit), and

---

10 This statement refers more accurately to Japan and Germany which have had high rates of growth of productivity historically, rather than to the UK which has generally been a laggard. But the gist of the argument is not affected by the inclusion of the UK with the other two.

thus shaping capitalist competition and the rate of profit.[11] If the length of the working day is prescribed by institutional practices and by the balance of class struggle (including the legal system) and if nominal wages are given, capitalists could improve competitiveness either by raising productivity, or by intensifying labour. Of the two, raising productivity is by far the more sustainable option over the medium and long term. The long-term method for raising productivity, on the other hand, is to develop and introduce new technology systematically. Consequently, Marx was the first among the great economists to study technical change and the evolution of technology in depth.[12]

Sustained increases of productivity through the introduction of new technology could be expected to have powerful effects on profitability, other things equal. If productivity rose, competitiveness would evidently be increased because the (per unit) value of commodity output would decline. If the lowering of value spread to the commodities entering the wage basket, it would follow that real wages would also fall over time; consequently, the rate of profit would rise. Sustained, long-term productivity increases, in other words, would alter the balance between wages and profits in favour of the latter. The beneficial impact on profitability would occur even if productivity improvements allowed workers to have access to greater volumes of (cheaper) wage goods.

Rising profitability would have important implications for future growth since a larger share of output would accrue in the form of profit. From the perspective of classical political economy and Marxism, however, the beneficial impact of rising productivity on growth must not be understood in terms of the motivation, or the calculations, of the individual capitalist. The boost to growth would not result from, say, capitalists opting to increase investment in the expectation of higher profits as productivity rose. For Marx – and Ricardo – the point rather was that, if a greater share of output accrued to the capitalist class in the form of profit, there would be greater command over resources necessary to support investment plans. The field of investment for capitalists would expand, allowing for reproduction on an expanded scale, boosting accumulation and spurring the rate of growth, other things equal. The actual effect on growth would clearly depend on a host of other factors, including the availability of wage labour and the expansion of aggregate demand.[13]

---

11 See, for instance, Marx, *Capital*, vol. 1, pp. 647–8 and 752–3.

12 Consider, for instance, the remarkable Chapter 15 on 'Machinery and Large Scale Industry' (ibid., pp. 492–639).

13 For a classic analysis of this point, see Maurice Dobb, *Studies in the Development of Capitalism*, London: Routledge and Kegan Paul, 1946, pp. 285–300. Shaikh has stressed that in Marx's reproduction schemata the maximum rate of growth is the rate of profit since maximum sustainable growth occurs when all profits are reinvested. On this basis Shaikh has proposed the 'throughput ratio', that is, the ratio of the actual growth rate to the maximum growth rate as an indicator of the degree to which the growth potential of an economy is realized. See Anwar

Technological innovation and novel methods of labour organization capable of raising productivity have characterized periods of dynamic growth in the history of capitalism. The introduction of new techniques of steel and chemical production, for instance, was important to productivity gains that sustained the period of growth beginning in the 1890s and lasting until the outbreak of the First World War. New methods of mass production, new raw materials and generalized electrification were instrumental to productivity gains in the course of the long boom after the Second World War. In contrast, the new technologies and changes in labour organization in the years of financialization have not resulted in sustained productivity growth in mature countries. The weakness of productivity growth underscores the relatively poor results of GDP growth during the period, shown in figure 2.

Looking more closely at figure 6, from the middle of the 1970s to the middle of the 1990s, productivity growth was broadly flat or declining, including in the US, the leading country in introducing the new technologies of the era.[14] Robert Solow observed that 'You can see the computer age everywhere but in the productivity statistics', and his quip became the 'Solow Paradox' characteristic of the new era.[15] After 1995, however, significant technological improvements in the microprocessor industry and faster productivity growth in general seemed to materialize for the US economy. A debate took place within mainstream economics in the second half of the 1990s regarding the validity of the upsurge. One side claimed that the upsurge represented an eventual breakthrough in productivity gains caused by the spread of new technologies; another argued that the upsurge was due mostly to rapid growth in the IT industry and

---

Shaikh, 'Explaining Inflation and Unemployment: An Alternative to Neoliberal Economic Theory' in *Contemporary Economic Theory*, ed. Andriana Vlachou, London: Macmillan, 1999.

14 The measurement of productivity is a conceptual minefield, particularly in services. For Marxist theory, productivity is measured primarily in physical output per worker, but could also be measured as physical inputs per worker, since labour transforms inputs into output. There are insuperable problems in aggregating disparate use values, which are well appreciated by mainstream economic theory; for discussion, see Zvi Griliches, 'Productivity, R&D, and the Data Constraint', *American Economic Review* 84:1, 1994. Note that the US uses hedonic indexes to deflate price series, unlike European countries, and this could create complications when the output of new technology is considered; see Jack Triplett, 'High-Tech Industry Productivity and Hedonic Price Indices', *OECD Proceedings*, 1996. There is an intractable problem here posed by new technology: if, say, it is considered that computer 'output' has risen because computers have become more powerful and have more functions (reflected in hedonic indices) then it follows that wholesale and retail output would also be considered to have risen. But then the output of the service sector would appear to have increased even if retailers have continued to do exactly what they have always done – selling a given number of boxes of computers per period.

15 Robert Solow, 'We'd Better Watch Out', review of *Manufacturing Matters*, by Stephen S. Cohen and John Zysman, *New York Times*, 12 July 1987.

reflected events within that sector rather than the general dynamism of productivity growth.[16]

By the early 2000s it had become widely accepted that a structural break had taken place in the US around 1995, and productivity growth had shifted toward the higher levels of the 1950s and 1960s. The spur was apparently driven by extremely fast productivity growth in the microprocessor industry that had caused a drastic decline in new technology prices by the mid-1990s, thus boosting investment in information technology in the second half of the 1990s. Economists claimed that rising investment in information technology had at last led to significant productivity gains in sectors that produced and used information technology. Even more strongly, it was claimed that the services sector had also begun to respond to new technologies by raising productivity substantially, mostly in wholesale, retail and financial trading (though not in banking). Presumably the productivity transformation was broadly based, and a cure had been found for 'Baumol's disease', that is, for the tendency of the service sector to register weak productivity growth.[17]

Mainstream studies of productivity growth typically comprise macro-level, econometrics papers, engaging in growth-accounting.[18] Arguments are usually based on total factor productivity (TFP) – on the econometric residual of growth accounting, which is a vastly different concept to labour productivity. TFP is deeply problematic as an explanation of macro-level movements in productivity not least because it is a residual and therefore by definition 'unexplained'. However, there have also been micro-level (firm level) studies, mostly in the US, which have broadly argued that productivity growth did indeed assume a rising path in the late 1990s. The usual explanation was that computers have favoured the employment of highly skilled university graduates as well as improving organization practices within companies. For some of these studies, computers even appeared to produce an 'intangible capital' that was perhaps related to some 'intangible output', such as better service and more varied choice. The revolution in technology and productivity in

---

16   Leading representatives of the former were Stephen Oliner, Daniel Sichel, Dale Jorgenson, Kevin Stiroh, Mun S. Ho, and William Nordhaus; on the opposite side stood mostly Robert J. Gordon; see also Ian Dew-Becker and Robert J. Gordon, 'Where Did the Productivity Growth Go? Inflation Dynamics and the Distribution of Income', NBER Working Paper No. 11842, 2005.

17   Jack Triplett and Barry Bosworth, 'Productivity in the Services Sector', *Brookings Economics Papers*, January 2000; Jack Triplett and Barry Bosworth, 'What's New About the New Economy? IT, Economic Growth and Productivity', *International Productivity Monitor*, vol. 2, 2001, pp. 19–30.

18   See, for instance, John Fernhald and Shanthi Ramnath, 'The Acceleration in US Total Factor Productivity After 1995: The Role of Information Technology', *Economic Perspectives* 28:1, First Quarter 2004, pp. 52–67; or Peter B. Meyer and Michael J. Harper, 'Preliminary Estimates of Multifactor Productivity Growth', *Monthly Labour Review* 125:6, June 2005.

the US in the late 1990s appeared to have had some truly extraordinary outcomes.[19]

Even at the peak of the 'productivity miracle' period, however, it was clear that the putative success of new technology was confined to the US. This outcome baffled mainstream theorists given that information technology had spread along similar lines to Europe, where productivity growth had not shown any signs of improving. The most awkward case was Britain, which registered substantial information technology investment in the late 1990s as well as fostering deregulation of labour markets for years, only to witness poor productivity growth.[20] Perhaps US enterprises had found some mysterious way of extracting higher productivity growth out of the same technology. What was less emphasized in those debates was that productivity growth in manufacturing *per se* had not shown much upward dynamism even in the US, once the sector of information technology was excluded.

By the end of the 2000s and after the crisis of 2007 had fully emerged, it transpired that there had not been much of a 'productivity miracle' in the US, or anywhere else. The strong productivity gains of the late 1990s were associated with the investment boom in new technology that partly led to the stock market bubble of 1999–2000. In the second half of the 2000s productivity growth in the US and in the other three countries showed no exceptional vitality. Whatever gains have been registered in the latter half of the 2000s appear to have been related to reductions in employment and other 'efficiency' measures, rather than to technological progress. Financialization has reverted to type with weak productivity growth; perhaps 'Baumol's disease' has not been cured after all.[21]

---

19   Some even claimed that the rising stock market in the US in the late 1990s had somehow captured a mysterious e-capital while producing enormously inflated valuations of the new technology sector (Hall 2001, 2002). The ensuing crash of 2000–2001 put things in a rather different perspective.

20   Susanto Basu, John Fernald, and Matthew Shapiro, 'Productivity Growth in the 1990s: Techology, Utilization, or Adjustment', *Carnegie-Rochester Conference Series on Public Policy* 55, 2001, pp. 117–65; Susanto Basu, John Fernald, Nicholas Oulton, and Sylaja Srinivasan, 'The Case of the Missing Productivity Growth', Working Paper 2003–08, Federal Reserve Bank of Chicago, 2003; Mary O'Mahony and Bart van Ark (eds), *EU Productivity and Competitiveness: An Industry Perspective*, Luxemburg: Office for Official Publications of the European Communities, 2003; Robert J. Gordon, 'Why Was Europe Left at the Station when America's Productivity Locomotive Departed?', NBER Working Paper No. 10661, 2004; Nick Bloom, Raffaella Sadun, and John van Reenen, 'It Ain't What You Do It's The Way That You Do I.T.', Centre for Economic Performance, London School of Economics, 2005.

21   Once the 2000s had got fully under way, both sides to the debate effectively agreed that there had been no productivity miracle; see Dale Jorgenson, Mun S. Ho, and Kevin Stiroh, 'Projecting Productivity Growth: Lessons from the US Growth Resurgence', *Federal Reserve Bank of Atlanta Economic Review*, 2002; Robert J. Gordon, 'Revisiting the US Productivity Growth over the Past

Rising inequality

During the period of financialization there have also been severe distributional changes which have varied significantly among mature countries. In general, inequality has increased but there have also been differences among countries depending on the composition of the labour force, work practices, and patterns of productivity growth as well as the concentration of wealth, the operation of the tax system and the broader political and institutional framework of each country. Inequality appears to have grown most strongly in Anglo-Saxon countries – precisely where financialization has been at its most forceful.

There has been extensive empirical work on the personal distribution of income, generating time series data on income distribution mostly in developed countries; the focus of attention has been on top incomes, both earned (wages and salaries) and unearned (capital assets).[22] In the interwar years the income share of the richest lay-

---

Century with a View of the Future', NBER Working Paper No. 15834, March 2010; Robert J. Gordon, 'The Evolution of Okun's Law and of Cyclical Productivity Fluctuations in the United States and in the EU-15', June 2011; see also Lawrence Mishel and Kar-Fai Gee, 'Why Aren't Workers Benefiting from Labour Productivity Growth in the United States?', *International Productivity Monitor* 23, Spring 2012. So powerful has been the reversal of outlook that Gordon has claimed that the US is set for a long period of low growth, or indeed that the historical experience of sustained long-term growth might be over ('Is U.S. Economic Growth Over? Faltering Innovation Confronts the Six Headwinds', NBER Working Paper No. 18315, 2012). For Gordon, the new technologies presumably have a weaker impact on productivity compared to 'one off' changes in the nineteenth century, such as urbanization and running water. This pessimistic argument takes materialism to crude extremes. The impact of new technologies on productivity also depends on the social conditions within which technologies are deployed, and these have been unfortunately shaped by the ascendancy of finance.

22   See, selectively, Thomas Piketty and Emmanuel Saez, 'Income Inequality in the United States, 1913–1998.' *Quarterly Journal of Economics* 118:1, 2003, pp. 1–39; Thomas Piketty and Emmanuel Saez, 'The Evolution of Top Incomes: A Historical and International Perspective.' *American Economic Review* 96:2, 2006, pp. 200–5; Thomas Piketty, 'Income Inequality in France, 1901–1998.' *Journal of Political Economy* 111:5, 2003, pp. 1004–42; Thomas Piketty, 'Top Incomes over the Twentieth Century: A Summary of Main Findings', in *Top Incomes over the Twentieth Century: A Contrast between Continental European and English-Speaking Countries*, ed. A.B. Atkinson and Thomas Piketty, Oxford: Oxford University Press, 2007, pp. 1–17; Emmanuel Saez, 'Income and Wealth Concentration in a Historical and International Perspective', in *Public Policy and the Income Distribution*, ed. Alan Auerbach, David Card, and John M. Quigley, NY: Russell Sage Foundation, 2006, pp. 221–58; Facundo Alvaredo and Emmanuel Saez, 'Income and Wealth Concentration in Spain from a Historical and Fiscal Perspective', *Journal of the European Economic Association* 7:5, 2009, pp. 1140–67; Anthony Atkinson, Thomas Piketty, and Emmanuel Saez, 'Top Incomes in the Long Run of History', *Journal of Economic Literature* 49:1, 2011, pp. 3–71.

ers of the population dropped dramatically and remained low until the 1970s. High taxation on capital income and real estate were important factors in preventing the income share of the rich from rising. Since the 1970s, however, the rich have reasserted themselves with a vengeance, particularly in the Anglo-Saxon world, and less in Germany and Japan.

There has been a pronounced rise of income inequality in the US, facilitated by the laxer tax regime for the rich characteristic of the ascendancy of neoliberalism. It is striking that the reassertion of income inequality has taken place through earned income (wages and salaries) often taking the form of stock options and other financial returns. Financial profit appears to have been a major lever for the enrichment of the top layers of the income distribution, but without a return to the coupon-clipping rentiers of the first decades of the twentieth century. The income share of the top 1 percent of the distribution in the US and the UK rose dramatically after the 1980s, approximating the levels of the 1920s and 1930s. If capital gains (one of the main forms of financial profit) were also included in the statistics, it is probable that the income share of the top 1 percent in the US would have reached unprecedented levels.

These results on the personal distribution of income contradict Kuznets's law of inequality in the course of capitalist development, which is still the fundamental empirical treatment of this issue.[23] Kuznets expected inequality to rise in the early stages of industrialization as incomes attached to capitalist production rose faster than agricultural incomes; however, as capitalism matured, inequality would recede. It appears that Kuznets's law has been reversed in the course of financialization, as neoliberalism has dominated the ideological sphere: a U-shaped path for inequality has emerged in the course of the twentieth century.[24]

The rise in personal income inequality has been related to the financial practices of large non-financial enterprises, particularly their increased involvement in open financial markets and accretion of financial skills. The ideology for such practices has been provided by 'shareholder value', briefly discussed in chapters 2 and 6. The impact of shareholder value on income distribution appears to have been substantial, bearing in mind the characteristic tendency of managers to be remunerated through

---

23   Simon Kuznets, 'Economic Growth and Income Inequality', *American Economic Review* 45:1, 1955.

24   Branko Milanovic has produced innovative work that assesses global inequality by measuring within-country as well as across-country inequality. The top 10 percent of the income distribution in a poor developing country, after all, might have a lower average income than the bottom 10 percent of a rich developed country. It appears that the years of financialization have witnessed a sharpening of global inequality, although the trends can vary. See Milanovic, *Worlds Apart: Measuring International and Global Inequality*, Princeton University Press, 2005; and Milanovic 'Global Income Inequality: What Is It and Why It Matters?', DESA Working Paper No. 26, 2006.

financial means. Stock options tend to acquire a higher value when share prices rise, thus encouraging managers to deliver short-term boosts to share prices. Policies could include repurchasing own shares as well as granting higher dividends. On this basis, it appears that financialization has had a deleterious effect on the performance of non-financial enterprises, particularly on productive investment.

Lazonick, who has been a leading researcher in this field, has provided empirical estimates for such management practices in some of the largest US enterprises during the years of financialization.[25] The value of stock repurchases increased dramatically in the course of the bubble of the 2000s, partly due to rising share prices, but mostly due to a sustained increase of actual repurchases by enterprises. The ratio of repurchases to the net income of these enterprises has increased dramatically during the bubble, as has also the value of dividends. In short, financial techniques and skills have been deployed by large non-financial enterprises to bring about a transfer of value via the stock market, a part of which has ended up with managers. Financialization of non-financial enterprises has thus affected income distribution in the US.

The rise in inequality in the personal distribution of income, however, is too broad and general a trend to be explained purely in terms of financial expropriation and other forms of financial profit making. The sphere of distribution is, after all, dependent on the spheres of production and circulation; the phenomena of distribution are related to underlying trends in the organizational and technological restructuring of both production and circulation. Mainstream economics is aware of this connection as is shown by the debates on inequality. The prevalent approach has been to relate rising inequality to the changing composition and skills of the labour force. Since rising inequality in the era of financialization has been primarily related to income rather than wealth, it could be claimed that inequality has been skill-based, reflecting the underlying changes in the forces of production.

Thus, in the 1980s and 1990s it was argued that the transformation of production and circulation favoured skill-intensive sectors, resulting in a 'skill premium' that exacerbated inequality compared to less skilled workers. Skill-biased technological progress has been considered the main cause of rising inequality.[26] However, the effect of skill-bias, even if it existed, would depend on the response of the supply of skilled workers, and hence of the education and training systems. Thus, it has been argued that the rapid technological change of the 1980s and 1990s in the fields of information technology and telecommunications has surpassed the ability of the

---

25 William Lazonick, 'The Fragility of the US Economy: The Financialized Corporation and the Disappearing Middle Class', in *The Third Globalization*, ed. Dan Breznitz and John Zysman, Oxford: Oxford University Press, 2013.

26 Edward Anderson, 'Openness and Inequality in Developing Countries: A Review of Theory and Recent Evidence', *World Development* 33:7, 2005; Ann Harrison, John McLaren, and Margaret McMillan, 'Recent Perspectives on Trade and Inequality', *Annual Review of Economics* 3, 2011.

education system to respond, thus raising the remuneration of skilled labour and intensifying unemployment.[27]

Yet, the transformation of the labour force and the associated patterns of inequality have produced much more complex phenomena as financialization has deepened. The pattern that has emerged in mature countries in the 2000s is not that of simple opposition between, on the one hand, high-skilled and well-paid and, on the other, low-skilled and badly paid workers. As financialization has advanced, the result has been to weaken the position of the middle of the income range. The upper and lower deciles of the income distribution, at least in the US, have done relatively better than the middle deciles. It appears that remuneration has behaved better among highly skilled and low-skilled workers, than among workers with moderate skills.[28] The factors contributing to these trends are very complex and there is no easy way to connect them purely to technical change, such as the introduction of new technology.[29] The broader aspects of the balance between capital and labour at the workplace must also be taken into account, as should the political and institutional framework of income distribution in the years of financialization.

Finally, a still broader perspective on the rise of inequality could be obtained from evidence on the functional distribution of income between capital and labour. Financialization of mature countries has been characterized by a uniform worsening of the position of labour relative to capital throughout this period. Consider figures 7 to 10 summing up the relative position of capital and labour in the US, Japan, Germany and the UK. Each figure shows, first, the share of wages in annual national income, second, the real GDP per hour worked and, third, the real wage per hour worked. The three variables are not directly related to each other and care is necessary when drawing conclusions. Nonetheless, the figures still convey the evolution of productivity, real wages and the division of national income among capital and labour in each of the four countries.

Labour has lost income share in all four countries in the course of financialization.

---

27   David Card and Thomas Lemieux, 'Can Falling Supply Explain the Rising Return to College for Younger Men? A Cohort-Based Analysis', *Quarterly Journal of Economics* 116:2, 2001; Claudia Goldin and Lawrence F. Katz, *The Race Between Education and Technology*, Cambridge, MA: Belknap Press of Harvard University Press, 2008.

28   This is often called 'polarization'; see David Autor, Lawrence Katz, and Melissa Kearney, 'The Polarization of the US Labor Market', *American Economic Review* 96:2, 2006; and Daron Acemoglu and David Autor, 'What Does Human Capital Do? A Review of Goldin and Katz's *The Race Between Education and Technology*', NBER Working Paper No. 17820, February 2012.

29   This is what Autor and Dorn attempt to do by claiming that computers have destroyed jobs of middle skill and pushed workers toward lower-paid jobs; David Autor and David Dorn, 'The Growth of Low Skill Service Jobs and the Polarization of the US Labor Market', Cambridge, MA: MIT Department of Economics, 2012. However, the impact of computers on skills (and productivity) is far from clear, as was argued in the previous section.

FIG. 7 Labour income share, GDP/hour worked, real wages/hour worked, US

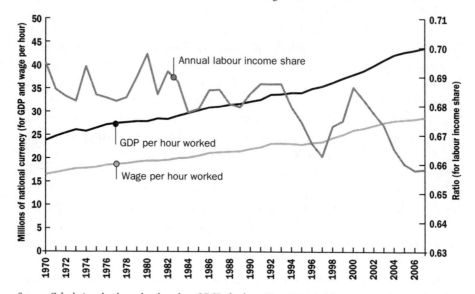

Source: Calculations by the author based on OECD database. Note: Data on labour income share are based on estimates for Germany in 1970–90, Japan in 1970–95, UK in 1970–79 and US in 1970–86.

FIG. 8 Labour income share, GDP/hour worked, real wages/hour worked, Japan

Source: Calculations by the author based on OECD database. Note: Data on labour income share are based on estimates for Germany in 1970–90, Japan in 1970–95, UK in 1970–79, US in 1970–86.

FIG. 9 Labour income share, GDP/hour worked, real wages/hour worked, Germany

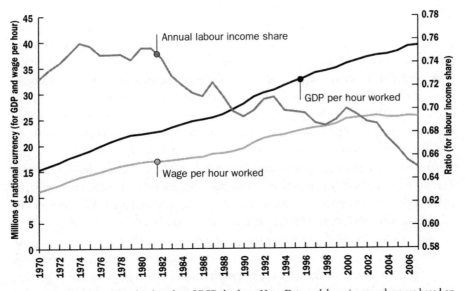

Source: Calculations by the author based on OECD database. Note: Data on labour income share are based on estimates for Germany in 1970–90, Japan in 1970–95, UK in 1970–79 and US in 1970–86.

FIG. 10 Labour income share, GDP/hour worked, real wages/hour worked, UK

Source: Calculations by the author based on OECD database. Note: Data on labour income share are based on estimates for Germany in 1970–90, Japan in 1970–95, UK in 1970–79 and US in 1970–86

The steepest decline in the share of labour has occurred in Japan, followed by Germany: it appears that maintaining manufacturing strength has been at the cost of shifting the distribution of national income in favour of profits. Decline in the share of labour has also occurred in the US and the UK, with a strongly cyclical aspect. However, some of the losses of labour in the UK appear to have been reversed in the 2000s. During the same period productivity measured by real GDP per hour worked has continued to rise steadily in all four countries. Nonetheless, real wages per hour worked have shown a much less steep rise – the gap between the two lines becoming progressively wider, especially in Japan and Germany. The divergence between the two curves is a further indication of the worsening position of labour in the course of financialization.

The rise of income inequality and the retreat of labour during the last three to four decades are highly complex phenomena. They are related to the change in the composition of the labour force in favour of services, to the altered skills required by the jobs newly created, and to the general transformation of the labour force; they are also related to the downward pressure on real wages throughout this period, associated with labour market deregulation and changing institutional practices at work. The rise in unemployment, shown in figure 3, has acted as a disciplining force on employed workers during the period of financialization. The domination of neoliberal ideology in policymaking, finally, has also contributed to the retreat of labour during the period.

The disciplining of labour by resurgent capital is also apparent in figure 11 showing the annual growth rate of labour compensation per unit of labour input. There has been sustained decline in the growth rate of labour compensation and a reduction of the amplitude of its cyclical variations throughout the decades of financialization. From the early 1980s onwards, capital appears to have had the advantage against labour in all four countries.

The distributional content of financialization as a period change of mature capitalism can now be simply summed up: capital has managed to appropriate the bulk of output increases from rising productivity, even if the latter has not grown with much dynamism. During this period, the top layers of the income distribution have enormously increased their command over aggregate income, while the middle of the distribution has suffered losses. Several mechanisms have allowed capital and the rich to appropriate an increasing share of the social wealth in the course of financialization, often varying in each country, but frequently relying on financial processes.

Remuneration through financial assets but still taking the form of wages has marked the rising incomes of the rich. Financial profit has been an important lever for the rise in inequality in the years of financialization, and the framework for its extraction is examined in further detail in chapters 8 and 9. The remaining sections of this chapter consider the 'channel' of accumulation by discussing the role of the state in facilitating the growth of financial profit in the years of financialization.

FIG. 11 Growth rate of labour compensation, US, Japan, Germany, UK

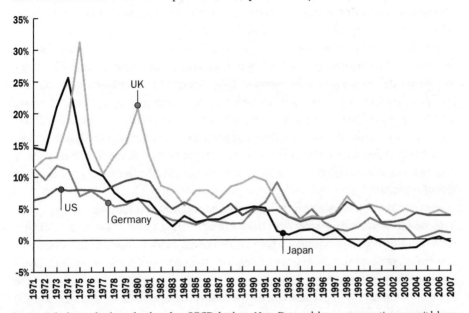

Source: Calculations by the author based on OECD database. Note: Data on labour compensation per unit labour input are based on estimates for Germany in 1971–90, Japan in 1971–95 and UK in 1971–79. Growth rates are calculated by the logarithmic method.

The state shapes the 'channel' of financialized accumulation

Fundamental features of state intervention in finance

The 'channel' within which financialized accumulation has flowed has been shaped in large measure by the state, even though the dominant ideology of the period has been neoliberalism. Unfortunately, classical Marxist debates at the turn of the twentieth century are of limited help regarding the role of the state in shaping the context of accumulation. Hilferding did propose the notion of 'organized capitalism' subsequent to writing *Finance Capital*, but he assumed that even 'organized capitalism' had emerged spontaneously, deriving from interactions among large monopolies. In effect, Hilferding downplayed the essentially autonomous character of state intervention in the capitalist economy. More innovative was Bukharin's *Imperialism and World Economy* treating 'state capitalism' as an integral whole of large monopoly capitals, banks and the state competing in national blocs across the world market. Nonetheless, Bukharin's disposition toward abstract generalization as well as his misleading view of capitalist competition in the world market occurring among national blocs weakened the impact of his theory.

In the years following the Second World War, Marxist political economy has devoted considerable attention to the economic role of the state in mature capitalism, typically stressing the importance of state ownership of means of production, including public utilities. Fundamental in this respect has been the rise of Keynesianism, including the strengthening of the welfare state and managing aggregate demand through fiscal and monetary policy. Still, Marxist theoretical discussions of these issues never achieved the clarity and persuasiveness of the classical debates on imperialism.

The period of financialization, on the other hand, has been accompanied by the ascendancy of neoliberalism which has generally treated state intervention in the economy with extreme suspicion, or even outright hostility.[30] Deregulation, privatization and liberalization have been bywords for neoliberal ideology, implying that the state tends to have a deleterious influence on capitalist accumulation. However, state intervention in the economy has far from disappeared in the course of the last four decades. As far as financialization is concerned, suffice it to say that the transformation of mature economies would have been inconceivable without the facilitating and enabling role of the state.

Intervention by the state in the course of financialization has been multifaceted, including in the labour market, and has naturally varied among particular countries reflecting historical specificities. There are, however, three features of the state's role that represent profound change associated with financialization and merit special reference. All three indicate that the state has actively and independently shaped the channel of financialized accumulation. The first is considered in further detail in the rest of this chapter, the remaining two are discussed in chapters 8 and 9.

First, the state has made financialization possible through command over state-backed central bank money. The evolution of the form of money has led to the domination of domestic circulation by valueless credit-money that is ultimately exchangeable only into central bank-generated legal tender. Domestic money has come to depend entirely on socially constructed trust buttressed by the institutional mechanisms of the credit system. At the heart of financial ascendancy lies absolute state monopoly over the final means of payment – a direct negation of neoliberal thinking as far as money is concerned.

State control over valueless legal tender means that the central bank can function

---

30   For a succinct presentation of the rise and content of neoliberalism as ideology and framework for economic policy, see Andrew Glyn, *Capitalism Unleashed*, Oxford: Oxford University Press, 2006. Heterodox thinking has been highly critical of the economic, social and political implications of neoliberalism, rightly treating it as the ideological shroud for resurgence of capital against labour; useful collections of essays are Alfredo Saad-Filho and Deborah Johnston (eds), *Neoliberalism: A Critical Reader,* London: Pluto Press, 2005; and Saad-Filho, Elmer Altvater, and Gregroy Albo, 'Neoliberalism and the Left: A Symposium', in *Socialist Register 2008,* ed. Leo Panitch and Colin Leys, London: Merlin Press, 2007. Note that Gérard Duménil and Dominique Lévy consider neoliberalism to be a period of capitalist development; see 'Costs and Benefits of Neoliberalism: A class Analysis', *Review of International Political Economy* 8:4, 2001; *Capital Resurgent,* Cambridge, MA: Harvard University Press, 2004; and *The Crisis of Neoliberalism,* Cambridge, MA: Harvard University Press, 2011.

as the ultimate support of the financial system in terms of liquidity. The ability of the central bank to provide generally acceptable liquidity derives, in large part, from substantial holdings of state securities to back its own liabilities as well as from having an implicit state guarantee of its solvency. State securities, furthermore, are the bedrock of liquidity in the money market since they presumably carry a low risk of default. In the absence of state-issued instruments of debt, money markets would have had less depth and liquidity as well as lacking a benchmark for interest rates. The dominant role of the central bank in the money market, including its ability to influence interest rates, relies on the presence of the state.

Second, the state has enabled the global spread of financialization through command over world money. Classical Marxism has typically associated imperialism with the export of capital from developed to developing countries, which creates a hierarchy of imperial power, allows for the extraction of surplus from the periphery, and sustains territorial empires. In the years of financialization there have been no territorial empires, and capital exports have occurred mostly among developed countries, even if there have been substantial flows to developing countries since the 1990s. One of the most striking features of financialization – discussed in Chapter 8 – is that, on a net basis, capital flows have reversed direction: capital has been exported by developing to developed countries. The reverse flow of capital is inextricably linked to the role of the US dollar as world money. The US dollar has provided new mechanisms and pathways for the projection of imperial power, thus generating flows of capital that resemble a form of tribute paid by developing to developed countries for the use of world money. It is worth stressing that the net export of capital from developing to developed countries has resulted from financial interactions among states rather than from the investment decisions of private agents.

Third, and related to the previous two, the state has smoothed the path of financialization by altering the regulatory and supervisory framework of finance. The impact of institutional and legal measures is disproportionately large on the operations of finance, as was discussed in Chapter 5. Financialization has been directly facilitated by the deregulation of the domestic financial sphere in terms of interest rates but also in terms of the activities and practices of financial institutions. Even more decisively, financialization has been facilitated by the lifting of international monetary and financial controls. Exchange rates among key countries have become flexible since the final collapse of the Bretton Woods Agreement in 1973, and cross-border capital flows have been progressively deregulated. These forms of state intervention – both of which have again been associated with the international role of money – have encouraged the spread of financialization in ways discussed in chapters 8, 9 and 10.

Central banking as a lever of financialization: Independent central banks and inflation targeting
The importance of central banks in advanced capitalism derives, first and foremost, from control over legal tender. The ascendancy of central banks in the years of financialization

has been ultimately linked to the search for a new framework of monetary operations in the 1990s and 2000s. The years that immediately followed the collapse of the Bretton Woods Agreement in 1971–73 were marked by rapid price inflation, indicating problematic management of valueless money as well as the malfunctioning of money as unit of account. Inflation constitutes a risk for loanable capital since it lowers the relative value of the capital advanced. The ascendancy of finance would have been undermined, if relations of credit were systematically disrupted by losses to lenders due to high inflation. Therefore, the initial response of monetary authorities in the US and elsewhere was to attempt to control inflation by instigating large and sustained increases in the rate of interest in the late 1970s and early 1980s, thus pushing economies into recession.[31]

Even more important, however, were changes in the theory and practice of central banking that gradually emerged in response to the malfunctioning of money as unit of account. Two approaches to central banking have dominated monetary policy since the early 1990s: central bank independence and inflation targeting. They have jointly dictated the functioning of central banks in developed and developing countries, thus shaping the course of financialization. For a lengthy period in the 1990s and 2000s the inflation performance of developed countries improved significantly. The lowering of inflation was deemed a great success of monetary policy – the 'Great Moderation' – and was attributed by mainstream theorists to the new orthodoxy of central bank independence and inflation targeting.[32] The crisis of 2007 put an end to this illusion, showing that money and finance continue to have a strongly disruptive role in contemporary capitalism.

The theoretical rationale for central bank independence is plain. First, it is postulated that an equilibrium natural output exists from which current output diverges only temporarily. If, for instance, current inflation was above expected inflation, there would be a temporary drop in real wages and thus a rise of current above natural output. But when expectations adjusted ('rationally') to current inflation, the divergence would disappear.

---

31   The so-called 'Volcker shock' in the US in 1979 is often considered a seminal event in the ascendancy of finance; for discussion see Eric Helleiner, *States and the Re-emergence of Global Finance*, Ithaca, NY: Cornell University Press, 1994, pp. 115–22 and 131–40. See also Susan Strange, 'Still an Extraordinary Power', in *The Political Economy of International and Domestic Monetary Relations*, ed. Raymond Lombra and Willard Witte, Ames: Iowa State University Press, 1982; and Susan Strange, 'Finance, Information and Power', *Review of International Studies* 16:3, 1990, pp. 259–74. Volcker's determination to defend US financial interests is summed up in Neikirk (1987) but also in Paul Volcker, 'The Role of Private Capital in the World Economy', in *Private Enterprise and the New Economic Challenge*, ed. Stephen Guisinger, Indianapolis: Bobbs-Merrill, 1979; and Paul Volcker and Toyoo Gyohten, *Changing Fortunes*, New York: Times Books, 1992.

32—For a concise summary of the putative success of policy in the 1990s and 2000s see one of the main exponents of the 'Great Moderation': Ben Bernanke, 'The Great Moderation', remarks at the meeting of the Eastern Economic Association, Washington, DC, 20 February 2004, at federalreserve.gov.

Second, it is assumed that current inflation depends on the rate of growth of the money supply, that is, the quantity theory of money is valid. Third, it is further assumed that macroeconomic policy is fundamentally a choice between, on the one hand, the level of current inflation and, on the other, the difference between current and desired output.[33]

The policy problem, and hence the mismanagement of money as a unit of account in the 1970s but also more generally, is assumed to originate in the preferences of policymakers, namely the predilection of elected politicians for higher current inflation. Characteristic to elected politician preferences is 'time or dynamic inconsistency', that is, plain dishonesty. They have an in-built incentive to cheat on inflation policy since they could reap short-term benefits from temporarily rising output by purposely accelerating inflation. Policymakers could resort to this approach, if fiscal policy had exhausted its potential to expand output and employment. Alternatively, they could encourage current inflation simply to curry favour with the electorate.

The cure for the disturbance of the measuring function of money caused by unreliable politicians would be a conservative central bank. It is typically assumed that a central bank would be more strongly averse to inflation than an elected government. Therefore, if monetary policy was exclusively assigned to a central bank that was kept independent of political interference, there would be fewer instances of purposeful acceleration of inflation temporarily to boost output. Moreover, the central bank could gain credibility by persevering in its commitment to keep inflation low, thus encouraging the inflation expectations of economic agents to adjust accordingly. The measuring function of money would be protected and, presumably, gains would ensue for economy and society.

The theoretical rationale for inflation targeting is also straightforward and closely related to independent central banking. The policy draws partly on the quantity theory of money and partly on the notion that there is a temporary trade-off between current inflation and current output. It is also assumed that there is a 'natural' rate of unem-

33   The literature on this topic is extensive. Very selectively, see Finn E. Kydland and Edward C. Prescott, 'Rules Rather than Discretion: The Inconsistency of Optimal Plans', *Journal of Political Economy* 85:3, 1977; Robert Barro and David Gordon, 'A Positive Theory of Monetary Policy in a Natural-Rate Model', *Journal of Political Economy* 91:4, 1983; Barro and Gordon, 'Rules, Discretion and Reputation in a Model of Monetary Policy', *Journal of Monetary Economics* 12:1, 1983; Alberto Alesina and Guido Tabellini, 'Rules and Discretion with Non-coordinated Monetary Policies', *Economic Enquiry* 25:4, 1987; Kenneth Rogoff, 'The Optimal Degree of Commitment to an Intermediate Monetary Target', *Quarterly Journal of Economics* 100:4, 1985; Rogoff, 'Reputational Constraints on Monetary Policy', *Carnegie-Rochester Conference Series on Public Policy* 26, Spring 1987. For a critique see Bennett T. McCallum, 'Two Fallacies Concerning Central Bank Independence', *American Economic Review* 85:2, May 1995; and McCallum, 'Crucial Issues Concerning Central Bank Independence', *Journal of Monetary Economics* 39:1, 1997. From a political economy perspective, see Costas Lapavitsas, 'The Political Economy of Central Banks: Agents of Stability or Source of Instability?', *International Papers in Political Economy* 4:3, 1997, pp. 1–52.

ployment consistent with stable inflation; attempts to lower unemployment below the natural rate would simply result in higher inflation. To be more specific, monetary policy by an independent central bank ought to take into account, first, the expectations of inflation among capitalists and workers, and, second, the 'output gap'. The latter can be thought of as the difference between the actual and the natural rate of unemployment. The most influential policy prescription for central bank policy in this respect is the Taylor Rule, which prevailed in the US for nearly two decades.[34]

The Taylor Rule is based on the assumption that monetary expansion would lower the real rate of interest, stimulate economic activity, and thus reduce the output gap; monetary contraction would have the opposite result. The real rate of interest is given by the nominal rate minus the expected inflation rate. Consequently, the central bank should set an inflation target and should then manipulate the nominal rate of interest in the hope of influencing inflation expectations. By so doing it would affect aggregate demand, eliminating the difference between the actual rate and the target rate of inflation over a period of time. The measuring function of credit money would again be protected.

Two issues immediately stand out with regard to this approach to central banking that has stamped financialization. The first is that there is little evidence of a stable trade-off between inflation and unemployment.[35] For much of the post-war period, rising unemployment levels in developed countries have been associated with falling growth rates of output; there is no clear evidence that the price level is driven by monetary fac-

---

34   John B. Taylor, 'Discretion Versus Policy Rules in Practice', *Carnegie-Rochester Conference Series on Public Policy* 39:1, 1993; see also Dale Henderson and Warwick McKibbin, 'A Comparison of Some Basic Monetary Policy Regimes for Open Economies', *Carnegie-Rochester Conference Series on Public Policy* 39:1, 1993.

35   The empirical literature on the Taylor rule is extensive although, after the crisis of 2007, it has become hopelessly dated. For work broadly supporting the rule see Ben Bernanke et al., *Inflation Targeting: Lessons from the International Experience*, Princeton University Press, 1999; Manfred J.M. Neumann and Jürgen von Hagen, 'Does Inflation Targeting Matter?', *Federal Reserve Bank of St. Louis Review* 84:4, July/August 2002; for differing critical perspectives see Philip Arestis and Malcolm Sawyer, 'Inflation Targeting: A Critical Appraisal', Working Paper no. 388, The Levy Economics Institute, 2003; Lars Svensson, 'What Is Wrong with Taylor Rules? Using Judgement in Monetary Policy Through Targeting Rules', *Journal of Economic Literature* 41:2, 2003; and Thomas I. Palley, 'A Post-Keynesian Framework for Monetary Policy', March 2003. For broader ranging work that even challenges the existence of a non-accelerating inflation rate of unemployment, see Robert J. Gordon, 'The Time-Varying NAIRU and its Implications for Economic Policy', *Journal of Economic Perspectives* 11:1, 1997; Sawyer (1997); Atish Ghosh and Steven Phillips, 'Warning: Inflation May be Harmful to Your Growth', *IMF Staff Papers* 45:4, 1998; Peter Van Els et al., 'Monetary Policy Transmission in the Euro Area', Working Paper no. 94, European Central Bank, 2001; Philip Arestis and Malcolm Sawyer, 'Can Monetary Policy Affect the Real Economy?', Working Paper no. 355, The Levy Economics Institute, 2002.

tors. Contemporary money malfunctioned as measure of value for much of the 1970s, but it is misleading to explain this phenomenon as simply the result of lax monetary policy and excessive creation of money. Rather, the malfunctioning of money is partly due to the complex processes linking real accumulation to the monetary circulation, as was discussed in Chapter 4. Inflation is also the outcome of poor performance by capitalist accumulation, rather than being simply the result of faulty monetary processes.

Second, the underlying assumption of inflation targeting was that the achievement of price stability would also result in overall financial stability. This view was put across by Anna Schwartz and was adopted generally for much of the period of Great Moderation.[36] For Schwartz, financial instability arises primarily from unexpected changes in the rate of inflation. If the central bank focused on keeping inflation low, it would thereby reduce the risk of lending booms (induced by high inflation) and recessions (induced by unexpected deflation or disinflation). The "Schwartz Hypothesis" has been tested by mainstream economists, who duly found a positive association between price instability and financial instability.[37]

However, it was also observed that financial asset price bubbles tended to occur as central banks applied the policy of inflation targeting.[38] Consequently, arguments in favour of central bank pragmatism began to emerge in the 2000s emphasizing 'flexible inflation targeting' that also took into account financial asset prices. Nonetheless, the core of the inflation targeting approach remained intact, and no concrete steps were taken by central banks to prevent the huge bubble of 2001–2007 in the US and elsewhere. The ensuing crisis has left the policy of inflation targeting in tatters since it has become apparent that exclusive focus on price stability has actually exacerbated the risk of financial collapse. The certainties of the Great Moderation have vanished.

Once it became clear that inflation targeting had failed, a debate emerged on the future role of central banks.[39] The crisis has required urgent intervention by central

---

36   See Anna Schwartz, 'Financial Stability and the Safety Net', in *Restructuring Banking and Financial Services in America*, ed. William S. Haraf and Rose Marie Kushmeider, Washington, DC: American Enterprise Institute For Public Policy and Research, 1988; and Anna Schwartz, 'Why Financial Stability Depends on Price Stability', in *Money, Prices and the Real Economy*, ed. Geoffrey Wood, Northampton: Edward Elgar, 1998. See also Ben Bernanke and Mark Gertler, 'Monetary Policy and Asset Price Volatility', *Economic Review* 4, 1999.

37   Michael Bordo and David Wheelock, 'Price Stability and Financial Stability: The Historical Record', *The Federal Reserve Bank of St. Louis Review* 80:4, 1998, pp. 41–62. Michael Bordo, Michael J. Dueker, and David Wheelock, 'Aggregate Price Shocks and Financial Instability: A Historical Analysis', Working Paper 2000–005B, Federal Reserve Bank of St. Louis, 2000.

38   See, for instance, Robert McGee, 'What Should a Central Bank Do?', Department of Economics, Florida State University, 2000; and Charles Bean, 'Asset Prices, Financial Imbalances and Monetary Policy: Are Inflation Targets Enough?', *Revue d'Economie Politique* 110:6, 2003.

39   Some economists advocated strengthening the traditional role of lender of last resort (De

banks, thus resulting in an even stronger role for central banking within financialized capitalism. The reason is apparent: central banks have retained control over legal tender, particularly through commercial bank reserves. The ability of the US and the UK central banks to confront the worst of the crisis of 2007 has relied on the enormous expansion of bank reserves, as was briefly shown in Chapter 4 and will be discussed in more detail in chapters 8 and 9. Re-strengthened intervention, however, has compromised the so-called independence of central banks, since it has often been undertaken under direct pressure from elected governments, as is shown in connection with the eurozone crisis in Chapter 9. There is little doubt that central banks have been pivotal to state intervention under conditions of financialized capitalism.

Last but not least, the importance of central banks in shaping the context of financialized accumulation has also been demonstrated with regard to the evolving form of money. When the rise of e-money proper but also of access e-money assumed significant proportions in the late 1990s, a question emerged among mainstream economists whether the position of the central bank would be threatened. In particular, if significant volumes of e-money were created outside normal credit channels, concern was raised that central banks might become less able to undertake monetary policy and influence the rate of interest.

The debate that ensued has cast light on the deeper relationship between contemporary money and the central bank under conditions of financialization.[40] It was

---

Grauwe, 2007, pp. 159–61). Others have proposed complementing it with market making of last resort, which effectively means that the central bank should step in as last resort buyer for untradeable securities (Buiter and Sibert, 2007).

40   Concern about the impact of e-money on central banks was first voiced by the Bank for International Settlements ('Implications for Central Banks of the Development of Electronic Money', October 1996). The baton was taken up by Mervyn King in a few pregnant remarks ('Challenges for Monetary Policy: New and Old', in *New Challenges for Monetary Policy*, Federal Reserve Bank of Kansas City, 1999). Benjamin Friedman then speculated that, if e-money spread generally, the central bank might become unable to adopt effective monetary policy ('The Future of Monetary Policy', *International Finance* 2:3, 1999). Friedman subsequently reiterated the view that e-money might make the central bank incapable of influencing the interest rates that mattered in the economy ('Decoupling at the Margin', *International Finance* 2:3, 2000). Others asserted that this was unlikely; see, for instance, C.A.E. Goodhart, 'Can Central Banking Survive the IT Revolution?', *International Finance* 3:2, 2000; Woodford (2000); and McCallum (2000). The matter was pursued further by Woodford (2001, 2003) within a very influential theoretical framework relying on Wicksell's concept of the natural rate of interest and seeking to determine the price level independently of the quantity of money. Buiter (2005) rejected the idea that technological change might make monetary policy irrelevant, but was equally dismissive of Woodford's framework. For Benjamin Cohen, on the other hand, e-money might weaken central banks by enhancing international competition among currencies ('Electronic Money: New Day or False Dawn?', *Review of Interna-*

eventually, and rightly, recognized that e-money does not pose a major threat to the central bank's absolute dominance over the monetary sphere, even though e-money is a novel form of money unrelated to the advance of credit. At the very least, competitively issued e-money proper would still require a common unit of account to standardize commodity prices and monetary contracts. The same unit of account would probably act as the instrument for the mutual clearance of privately issued liabilities of e-money proper. In developed capitalist economies the most plausible unit of account for these purposes would be legal tender instituted by the state.

Consequently, the issuers of e-money would still need to keep reserves of legal tender to support their e-money liabilities, and these would be provided competitively by a central bank-like institution through an open market. In effect, the channels of monetary policy would be gradually re-instituted as this process unfolded. And even if this outcome did not come to pass, it would always be open to the central bank to issue its own e-money while requiring that other issuers of e-money kept central bank e-money as reserves. Again, the central bank's ability to determine monetary policy and influence the rate of interest would be re-established. Since a mechanism of this kind has been historically constructed for credit money through the institution of state-backed central money, there is no reason why it could not also be constructed for e-money.[41] Central banks would remain the pivotal institutions of the monetary and credit domain in mature, financialized capitalism.

---

tional Political Economy 8:2, Summer 2001). The issue inevitably attracted the interest of Austrian neoclassicals who have long been critical of central bank monopoly over money. Otmar Issing noted the obvious affinities between the spread of e-money and the Austrian views on money and the economy ('Hayek, Currency Competition and European Monetary Union', 27 May 1999; 'New Technologies in Payments: A Challenge to Monetary Policy', June 2000). Others, more closely associated with Austrian economics, have explored further the possibility that the role of the central bank might be diminishing due to competitive, private issue of e-money, thus weakening the monopoly of the state over the issue of money; see, selectively, James A. Dorn (ed.), The Future of Money in the Information Age, Washington, DC: Cato Institute, 1996; Michael Latzer and Stefan Schmitz, Carl Menger and the Evolution of Payments Systems, Cheltenham: Edward Elgar, 2002; Randall S. Kroszner, 'Currency Competition in the Digital Age', in Evolution and Procedures in Central Banking, ed. David Altig and Bruce D. Smith, Cambridge: Cambridge University Press, 2003, pp. 275–305; Stefan W. Schmitz and Geoffrey Wood (eds), Institutional Change in the Payments System and Monetary Policy, London: Routledge, 2006.

41   Friedman has exaggerated the possible impact of continuous technological innovation, which could presumably lead to ever newer issuers of e-money proper, thus forcing the central bank into a race that it cannot win. However, the same possibility also exists with credit money, but in practice it has not come to pass. Friedman, 'The Future of Monetary Policy' and 'Decoupling at the Margin'.

8. UNDERLYING TENDENCIES AND VARIABLE FORMS: MATURE AND SUBORDINATE FINANCIALIZATION

Empirical analysis of financialization in this chapter is undertaken on three levels. First, financialization is gauged in the aggregate with the aim of identifying its general form and features. To this purpose a conceptual framework is developed drawing on the distinction between real and financial accumulation within Marxist political economy. By deploying this framework financialization can be compared across the four reference countries: the US, Japan, Germany, and the UK. Comparison reveals systematic differences in the form of financialization, partly reflecting the traditional contrast between market-based finance, characteristic of the US and the UK, versus bank-based finance characteristic of Japan and Germany.

Second, the fundamental tendencies of financialization are investigated by examining the conduct of non-financial enterprises, banks and households. Once again, significant differences emerge among the four countries broadly consistent with the differences in the aggregate form of financialization. There has been financialization across the group, but its economic and social forms differ significantly among individual countries.

Third, financialization is examined in the context of developing countries identifying substantial differences with developed countries in both content and form. To be more specific, financialization in developing countries is heavily associated with the operations of world money and the resulting accumulation of foreign exchange reserves; it is further associated with the entry of foreign banks. For these reasons, financialization has taken a subordinate character in developing compared to developed countries.

The empirical analysis of financialization on these three levels presents complex conceptual difficulties. It is intuitive, for instance, to seek evidence of the ascendancy of finance in the activities of financial enterprises and the financial sector in general. However, the financial system is an intermediary entity that does not produce value, and therefore there is no obvious way of capturing either its magnitude or its specific gravity relative to accumulation as a whole. Furthermore, a broad range of financial activities bear only a partial connection to the operations of financial enterprises, including financial operations that are undertaken by non-financial enterprises in open markets. Establishing the footprint of contemporary finance, therefore, must take into account the operations of both financial and non-financial entities in the economy.

Moreover, there are substantial data problems, particularly when comparisons are attempted across countries. The evidence adduced in this chapter has been drawn mostly from flow of funds statistics composed either by national income statistics agencies, or by central banks, and referring to a range of financial assets. Yet, there are major difficulties in aggregating and comparing financial assets across national accounts. Methods of data collection and reporting differ widely, and there are gaps and variations in the time periods for which data is available, as is made clear in the

Appendix to this chapter. Data difficulties greatly compound the conceptual problems of measuring financial activities and call for additional caution in interpreting the figures. The empirical material presented below is more important for the trends it indicates rather than for the absolute size of the financial magnitudes to which it refers.

Distinguishing between real and financial accumulation

The financial system serves a variety of purposes in capitalist accumulation, both monetary and financial, as was discussed in Chapter 5.[1] Monetary services include creation of credit money, safekeeping of money hoards, transferring sums of money across the economy, facilitating foreign exchange transactions, and so on. Financial services include primarily the mobilization of loanable capital across the economy and its subsequent advance through loans. Financial services further include collecting spare money funds across society as well as trading loanable capital in open markets.

To deliver these services financial institutions have to gather information and assess risks across the economy. The financial system, consequently, acts as the nerves and brains of the capitalist economy; it is the social entity that turns the marshalling of spare resources by society into an integral whole, although on the basis of private property and profit making. Monetary and financial services are closely interwoven, above all, through the creation of credit money by financial institutions. Debates on financialization often overlook the monetary operations of the financial system, despite the pivotal importance of the latter in contemporary capitalism, particularly in relation to world money.

The first step in gauging the relative importance of the financial system is to distinguish between real and financial accumulation. This distinction originates with Marx who argued that 'money' capital available for lending possesses a separate form of accumulation compared to capital employed in production.[2] From this perspective, financialization could be conceptualized as a change in the balance between real and financial accumulation; specifically, financialization represents the asymmetric growth of financial compared to real accumulation during the last four decades. Deploying this idea empirically could shed light on the content of financialization, but it is first necessary to consider in further depth the relationship between the two types of accumulation.

Real accumulation involves industrial and merchant's capital and occurs across both production and circulation. The concrete forms it takes include the expansion and development of the means of production, the increase of the labour force, the

---

1 A succinct summary from a mainstream perspective of the services provided by the financial system to capitalist accumulation has been given by Ross Levine, 'Financial Development and Economic Growth', *Journal of Economic Literature* 35:2, 1997.

2 See, for instance, Marx, *Capital*, vol. 3, pp. 599 and 607. Needless to say, the two forms of accumulation take place concurrently and conjointly.

growth of physical output, the improvement of the means of communication, and so on. Real accumulation also relates to the sphere of distribution, since it leads to the division of output between wages and profit. The characteristic feature of real accumulation is the creation of surplus value in production, which accrues as money profit through the sale of output, and is subsequently re-invested. The outward signs of real accumulation, therefore, include growth of output (value and use value) increase of the labour force, enlargement of capital invested, and so on. National income statistics are a ready-made source of empirical analysis for these phenomena, despite inevitable conceptual problems.[3]

Financial accumulation, in contrast, occurs primarily in the sphere of circulation and at a distance from the sphere of production; it also encroaches on the sphere of distribution mostly through the formation of financial profit, as was discussed in Chapter 6. Financial accumulation fundamentally involves mobilizing, trading, and advancing loanable capital, that is, processes which are often undertaken by intermediary financial institutions. Unlike real accumulation, financial accumulation does not produce measurable final output (value and use value). Although labour is employed and work effort is expended in undertaking financial transactions, there is no direct relationship between the expenditure of financial labour and the magnitude of financial accumulation. Similarly the capital invested in setting up financial intermediaries does not reflect the magnitude of financial accumulation since this capital is only indirectly related to mobilizing, trading and advancing loanable capital. The concrete form taken by financial accumulation is the piling up of claims on others, that is, the amassing of financial assets which have their own (fictitious) prices.

A distinctive feature of financial compared to real accumulation is that it relates primarily to flows rather than stocks. To be specific, financial accumulation refers to the enlargement of the flows of loanable capital, in contrast to real accumulation which refers to the growth of the stock of industrial and merchant's capital. Thus, financial accumulation is not accumulation in the normal sense of an underlying magnitude becoming augmented. Nonetheless, it takes the outward form of normal accumulation since it results in piled up claims on others – in amassed financial assets. The conceptu-

---

3 At the root of the difficulty of using national income statistics to capture real accumulation lies the category of value – what value is and how it is created. For Marxist political economy value is abstract labour expended in the sphere of production, a notion that hardly corresponds to 'value creation' in national income statistics. The category of 'services', which is paramount to measuring financialization, creates particularly intractable problems as certain types of 'service' could be categorized as social consumption rather than production – for instance, some of the services provided by state administrators; see Anwar Shaikh and E. Tonak, *Measuring the Wealth of Nations: The Political Economy of National Accounts*, Cambridge: Cambridge University Press, 1994. Nonetheless, national income statistics remain a reasonable first port of call for the purpose of gauging real accumulation.

al difficulty of gauging financial accumulation and its balance with real accumulation originates precisely in this characteristic feature of the former.

The analysis of financial accumulation could be developed further by examining more closely the flows of loanable capital. Specifically, there are flows generated as loanable capital is released from, or returned to, real accumulation in the form of, respectively, idle money capital of industrialists, or fresh loans made to industrialists; but there are also flows generated as loanable capital is traded independently of real accumulation, and often at some distance from the latter. Taken together over a period of time, the two types of flow naturally determine a stock of loanable capital standing aside the process of real accumulation. However, the expansion of the stock of loanable capital is an incidental outcome rather the motive force of financial accumulation; it is a by-product, a residual, of the expansion of the flows of loanable capital.

This point is vital to establishing the conceptual and empirical difference between real and financial accumulation. The aim of real accumulation is to augment the stock of capital engaged in producing value and surplus value. In contrast, financial accumulation contains no corresponding drive to expand the stock of loanable capital engaged in financial transactions during any period of time, even though financial transactions are motivated by profit. The owners of loanable capital as well as the financial institutions that handle its flows have a limited capacity to augment its magnitude through their own actions. For, as was discussed in Chapter 5, the forces that enlarge loanable capital are located primarily within real accumulation and, in the first instance, take the form of tendencies to hoard money. Financial accumulation, consequently, does not correspond to the self-driven augmentation of a well-defined stock of capital. It refers to the expansion of the flows of loanable capital, even though it implicitly determines a stock of loanable capital engaged in financial transactions at any time.

In this light, the balance between financial and real accumulation is shaped by the characteristic difference between the two forms of accumulation. As was argued in Chapter 5, the operations of finance depend on the historical, institutional, legal, customary and even cultural framework within which industrial and merchant's capital interact with loanable capital. Consequently, the relationship between real and financial accumulation has a historically contingent character. Real accumulation requires a complex financial system, and hence necessarily entails the emergence of financial accumulation; however, the outlook and the conduct of the financial system vary according to specific and historical factors. A given state of real accumulation in terms of growth rates, employment, profitability, and so on, could correspond to greatly differing states of financial accumulation. Since historical, institutional, political, and even cultural factors play a decisive role in the relationship between the two, there can be no ideally optimal balance between real and financial accumulation.

Financial accumulation in the aggregate

Given the nature of financial accumulation, there is no obvious way empirically to gauge its magnitude, and nor to establish its balance with real accumulation. However, an outline of financial accumulation as an aggregate phenomenon could be obtained through indicators based on flow of funds data, thus affording insight into financialization. The same indicators could also begin to establish variations in the ascendancy of finance among the core countries of financialization. To be specific, four indicators are deployed in this section to capture financial accumulation in the aggregate: first, relative size of stocks of financial assets, second, value added by the financial sector, third, employment by the financial sector, and fourth, financial profits by financial institutions. Based on this aggregate picture, the underlying tendencies of financialization – namely the conduct of non-financial enterprises, banks, and households – are discussed on pages 217, 45.

Stocks of financial assets

The flows of loanable capital, irrespective of whether they have a direct connection with real accumulation or they occur at some distance from the latter, leave a visible trail of financial asset stocks. The nominal values of financial assets indicate neither the magnitude nor the formal availability of loanable capital, for reasons discussed in Chapter 6 and elsewhere in this book. Nonetheless, they constitute evidence of flows of loanable capital that have already occurred: they are the outward signs of financial accumulation. Moreover, financial asset values also represent potential claims by holders over future flows of loanable capital.

Financial assets can be created through a variety of disparate processes, for instance, by obtaining a bank deposit, by advancing a loan, by issuing a bond in financial markets, and so on. Furthermore, financial markets are capable of 'churning' loanable capital, that is, generating flows of loanable capital unrelated to real accumulation and sustained through pure buying and selling of financial assets. There can thus be trails of financial assets that have no corresponding link with real accumulation. Above all, financial asset prices incorporate a fictitious element – discussed in Chapter 6 – and hence systematically over- or under-estimate the corresponding flows of loanable capital.[4]

With these provisos in mind, a first approximation of the trajectory of financial accumulation is given by the sum total of financial assets as well as by its allocation among different sectors of the economy. The simplest aggregate indicator of the rise of finance is the ratio of total financial assets relative to gross domestic product (at current prices).[5] The ratio is calculated below for the US, Japan, Germany and the

---

4   The disparity between financial asset prices and the value of the underlying loanable capital flows is most apparent in the markets for financial derivatives, discussed in Chapter 1. These markets have produced gigantic nominal values that bear no clear relationship to underlying flows of loanable capital, not to mention real accumulation.

5   Ratios of 'financial deepening' are commonly deployed in mainstream economics, including with reference to developing countries. An early approach was to use money supply aggregates (M2) relative to GDP; see Raymond Goldsmith, *Financial Structure and Development*, New Haven Yale University Press, 1969. More recently, use of liquid liabilities of banks and non-bank interme-

FIG. 1 Total financial assets (excluding rest of the world) as percentage of GDP; US, Japan, Germany, UK

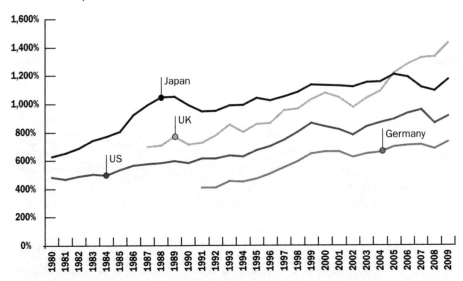

Source: Flow of Funds, NIPA, Table 1.1.5 (US); ONS, Financial Statistics Consistent, Tables 12.1, UK Output, Income and Expenditure, Table C.1 (UK); Deutsche Bundesbank, Financial Accounts; Statistisches Bundesamt Deutschlands (Germany); Bank of Japan, Flow of Funds; Cabinet Office, Government of Japan, National Accounts (Japan). Data for the US are truncated; however, the ratio has fluctuated around an average of 470 percent in 1959–79, without an upward trend.

UK, indicating extraordinary growth but also pronounced variation of finance across the four countries.

Specifically, figure 1 traces this ratio for the four countries during the last three decades (financial asset data excluding the rest of the world). What matters is the trend rather than the comparative position of each country; in the US, for instance, there is a large 'shadow' financial sector, briefly discussed below and in other parts of this book, which does not appear in flow of funds data; in Japan, on the other hand, there is prominent

---

diaries relative to GDP can be found in Robert G. King and Ross Levine, 'Finance and Growth: Schumpeter Might be Right', *Quarterly Journal of Economics* 153, 1993; as well as Ross Levine, Norman Loyaza, and Thorsten Beck, 'Financial Intermediation and Growth: Causality and Causes', *Journal of Monetary Economics* 46, 2000. For use of claims by financial intermediaries on the private sector relative to GDP, see Michael W. Klein and Giovanni Olivei, 'Capital Account Liberalization, Financial Depth, and Economic Growth', *Journal of International Money and Finance* 27:6, October 2008. All these measures focus on financial intermediaries; for the purposes of gauging financialization as a whole, however, it is better to use total financial assets relative to GDP.

FIG. 2 Total financial assets (including rest of the world) as percentage of GDP; US, Japan, Germany, UK

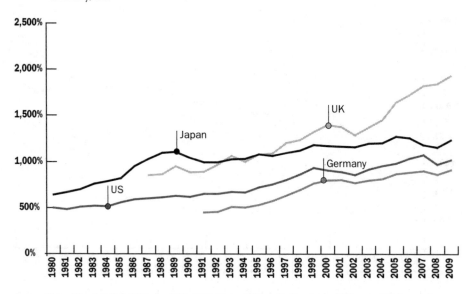

Source: Flow of Funds, NIPA, Table 1.1.5 (US); ONS, Financial Statistics Consistent, Tables 12.1, UK Output, Income and Expenditure, Table C.1 (UK); Deutsche Bundesbank, Financial Accounts; Statistisches Bundesamt Deutschlands (Germany); Bank of Japan, Flow of Funds; Cabinet Office, Government of Japan, National Accounts (Japan).

cross-share-holding among enterprises and financial institutions which is characteristic of the bank-based nature of the country's financial system. Nonetheless, the ratio remains informative about the path of financial development for the US and Japan as well as for Germany and the UK. Thus, the figure shows that there has been sustained rise of finance along broadly similar lines, given that the ratio has roughly doubled in all four countries over the period for which data is available. The figure also captures key financial events of the last three decades, including the Japanese stock market and real estate bubble of the late 1980s, the more general stock market bubble at the end of the 1990s, and the extraordinary British and US real estate bubble of the 2000s.

If the rest of the world was included in financial assets, affording a first glimpse of the international aspect of financialization, things would not change dramatically, except for the position of the UK. Figure 2 indicates that Britain has the strongest global financial interests relative to real accumulation among the four countries. This is a reflection of the historical evolution of British capitalism and of the continuing international role of the City of London.

Both figures further show that, despite the similarity of trends, there has been no uniformity in the rise of finance. Financial accumulation has exhibited significant differences among mature capitalist countries, which are important to analysing financialization, including the crisis of 2007. The surge of Japanese financial accumulation in the 1980s, for instance, has remained a rather isolated event. Financial accumulation in the UK and the US grew strongly in the 2000s, but its dynamism has been less pronounced in Germany and Japan.

These differences reflect the variable relationship between finance and real accumulation in line with historical, institutional, customary, and other contingent factors in each country. They also reflect variations in the performance, composition and direction of real accumulation itself. A long-standing way of capturing these complex interactions has been to distinguish between, on the one hand, Anglo-Saxon capital market–based capitalism and, on the other, German–Japanese bank-based capitalism, briefly discussed in Chapter 2. In the former, real is connected to financial accumulation primarily through arm's-length interactions in financial markets; in the latter, the two are connected primarily through relational interactions occurring via financial intermediaries.

It would seem reasonable to assume that financialization has been stronger in the countries of Anglo-Saxon market-based finance. However, figures 1 and 2 do not show that that the expansion of Anglo-Saxon finance has consistently surpassed that of German–Japanese finance during the last three decades. On the contrary, amassing financial assets has been notable in Japan, including during the huge bubble of the late 1980s; the US has exhibited more modest outcomes, though the absence of the 'shadow' banking sector significantly distorts the picture; German financial accumulation, meanwhile, has systematically lagged behind the rest. It would be more accurate to say, therefore, that there has been sustained rise of finance across all four countries. The trajectory of financial ascendancy, moreover, does not necessarily match preconceived ideas about the behaviour of different financial systems. The financial sector has grown across mature capitalist countries, although national specificities have far from disappeared. Nonetheless, the growth of finance in the 2000s has been stronger in the Anglo-Saxon systems, with attendant changes in instruments and practices. This dimension of financialization has been pivotal to the vast crisis of 2007 and is examined in more detail in Chapter 9.

Unexpected variation in the growth of finance emerges even more clearly when the sum total of financial assets is split between the holdings of the financial and the non-financial sector, both normalized for GDP. The former could be taken as rough proxy for the activities of financial institutions – banks, savings institutions, pension funds, insurance companies, and so on; the latter as proxy for the financial activities of non-financial enterprises and individuals (households). Some insight could thus be obtained into the distinction drawn in Chapter 6 between financial transactions directly associated with financial institutions and financial transactions undertaken by non-financial agents.[6]

---

6   The correspondence is very imperfect and conclusions have to be drawn carefully. Financial assets held by households, for instance, are typically mediated by financial institutions, and generate profits for the latter. Even so, there are considerable differences among the four countries regarding the financial flows associated with the financial and the non-financial sectors. Crude as they might be, the ratios proposed here can still highlight these differences.

FIG. 3 Financial assets held by the financial sector as percentage of GDP; US, Japan, Germany, UK

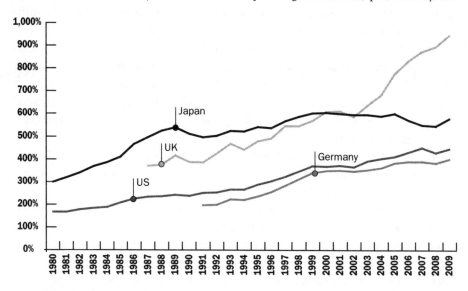

Source: Flow of Funds, NIPA, Table 1.1.5 (US); ONS, Financial Statistics Consistent, Tables 12.1, UK Output, Income and Expenditure, Table C.1 (UK); Deutsche Bundesbank, Financial Accounts; Statistisches Bundesamt Deutschlands (Germany); Bank of Japan, Flow of Funds; Cabinet Office, Government of Japan, National Accounts (Japan).

Figure 3 shows the financial asset holdings of the financial sector in the four countries; the following three aspects stand out. First, the UK financial sector has been on a rapid upward trend since the early 1990s, sharply accelerating in the 2000s. Purely in terms of the relative size of the financial sector, the UK is the most heavily financialized of the four countries. A profound asymmetry appears to have emerged between the UK financial and productive sectors in recent years, again reflecting the pivotal place of the City of London in global financial flows and thus its extraordinary role within the UK economy. Second, the Japanese financial sector has been in persistent stagnation since the early 1990s, even declining in relative size in the 2000s. Financialization is present in Japan, but the financial sector has been decisively weakened by the bubble of the late 1980s. Third, the US financial sector, while the largest in the world and on a clear upward trend throughout this period, has lagged behind the UK in relative terms, if 'shadow banking' is excluded.

The rise of 'shadow banking' has been an important aspect of financialization, particularly in the US. 'Shadow banking' essentially refers to the emergence of financial institutions that do not accept deposits in the normal manner of commercial banks but finance themselves typically through issuing liabilities in the money market. The lending process also involves securitization and the commercial trading of loans. Strong growth of 'shadow banking' in the US has been a characteristic feature of the 2000s contributing to the bubble and subsequent crash, as is shown in more detail in Chapter 9. Suffice it here to say 'shadow banking' reached a comparable size to regular commercial banking in the US toward the end of the 2000s. The relative decline of commercial banks has been perceived by mainstream economists as marginalization, or 'disintermediation', often in conjunction with the rise of direct finance through open markets. But commercial banks have also transformed themselves, while 'shadow' financial institutions are often dependent on banks for funding. Commercial banks have remained the pivotal institution of the financial system even in the US, as has become apparent in the gigantic crisis that broke out in 2007.[7]

Pursuing the analysis of financial asset stocks further, figure 4 turns to financial assets held by the non-financial sector – mostly households and non-financial enterprises.

Figure 4 indicates, once again, that finance has strongly penetrated the non-financial sector, but considerable care is needed when drawing general conclusions. First, there has been a clear upward trend across the four countries, signalling increasing penetration of the non-financial sector by financial relations. Second, both the Japanese bubble of the late 1980s and the wider stock market bubble of the late 1990s were driven by the acquisition of financial assets by the non-financial sector. This is far from unusual for stock market bubbles, which typically involve late purchases of financial assets by small investors that eventually result in capital losses. Third, in sharp contrast, the bubble of the 2000s in the US and the UK was not accompanied by significant increases in the holdings of financial assets by households and enterprises. The nature of that bubble was quite different from the Japanese bubble of the 1980s and relied on the accumulation of debt by the non-financial sector (primarily households) which subsequently led to the amassing of financial assets by financial institutions. Fourth, the penetration of the non-financial sector by financial relations, once again, does not match the *a priori* expectation that market-based finance has

---

7 For analysis of disintermediation and continuing concern about the role of banks see Mark Gertler and John H. Boyd, 'U.S. Commercial Banking: Trends, Cycles and Policy', in *NBER Macroeconomics Annual*, ed. O. Blanchard and S. Fischer, Cambridge, MA: MIT Press, 1993; and E. Gerald Corrigan, 'Are Banks Special? – A Revisitation', *The Region*, The Federal Reserve Bank of Minneapolis, March 2000. The role of shadow banking in the crisis of 2007 is discussed in Chapter 9. For analytical and descriptive accounts of shadow banking, including the institutional patterns of lending, see Tobias Adrian and Hyon Song Shin, 'The Shadow Banking System: Implications for Financial Regulation', *Banque de France Financial Stability Review* 13, 2009; Tobias Adrian and Hyon Song Shin, 'The Changing Nature of Financial Intermediation and the Financial Crisis of 2007–09', *Annual Review of Economics* 2, 2010; Zoltan Pozsar et al., 'Shadow Banking', Staff Report 458, Federal Reserve Bank of New York, July 2010, rev. February 2012; and Tobias Adrian and Adam Ashcraft, *Shadow Banking Regulation*, Staff Report No. 559, Federal Reserve Bank of New York, 2012.

FIG. 4 Financial assets held by the non-financial sector as percentage of GDP; US, Japan, Germany, UK

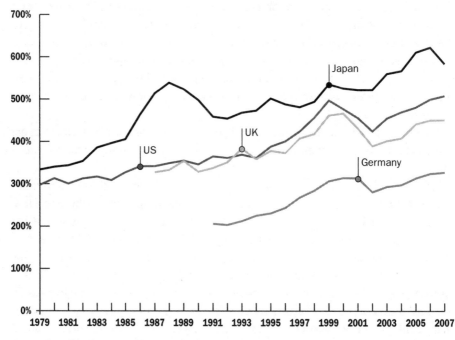

Source: Flow of Funds, NIPA, Table 1.1.5 (US); ONS, Financial Statistics Consistent, Tables 12.1, UK Output, Income and Expenditure, Table C.1 (UK); Deutsche Bundesbank, Financial Accounts; Statistisches Bundesamt Deutschlands (Germany); Bank of Japan, Flow of Funds; Cabinet Office, Government of Japan, National Accounts (Japan).

been preponderant in the decades of financialization: the leading country in this respect has been Japan, while the UK has lagged consistently behind.

Value added

The character of aggregate financial accumulation can be further established by examining national data on value added. The ground here is particularly treacherous since value added essentially refers to the value of output minus the value of inputs (intermediate consumption) thus capturing the fresh value contributed by particular sectors; the sum total of value added across sectors is equivalent to GDP (adjusted for taxes and subsidies). The conceptual problems posed by finance with regard to value added are immediately apparent, since the financial sector is an intermediary entity that does not produce value. Nevertheless, in practice, national statistical agencies include the financial sector in the calculation of GDP. The net receipts of interest by financial institutions plus fees and commissions are typically counted as a measure of the 'output' of financial services.

Consequently, officially published data on value added could be used to obtain some

FIG. 5 Value added in FIRE as percentage of total value added (current prices); US, Japan, Germany, UK

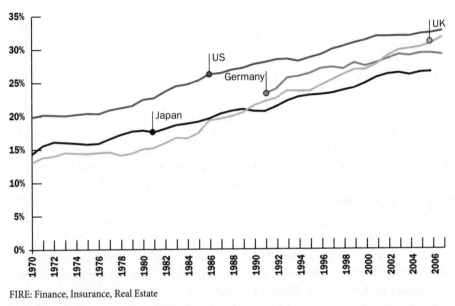

FIRE: Finance, Insurance, Real Estate

Source: Author calculations, OECD database

(highly imperfect) insight into the value appropriated by the financial sector relative to the annual total of value added. This proportion would convey the relative weight of the financial sector in the national economy, particularly its evolution over time. The indicator has solely heuristic value, since the concept of value added, properly speaking, does not apply to finance. A further complication in this respect is that national income statistics often include the financial sector into the considerably broader category of Finance, Insurance, and Real Estate (FIRE). The data used in figure 5 refer to the trajectory of value added by FIRE rather than by the financial sector narrowly defined.

There is a clear upward trend in all four countries, but the rise of the financial sector also exhibits considerable variation. It is instructive to note the different ranking of the four countries regarding financial value added compared to financial asset holdings: the US leads in value added, while Japan comes last. In other words, gross holdings of financial assets offer no guide to the appropriation of value by the financial sector. However, the most remarkable evidence refers to the UK where, from a relatively low base, the share of value added by FIRE has risen much faster than for the other three, approaching US levels by the mid-2000s. The acceleration of the UK began in the mid-1980s indicating rapid financialization for more than two decades.

Together, these last two chapter sections offer evidence that finance has become a more significant sector of activity in all four countries. There is also greater penetration of the non-financial sector by financial relations, while the value appropriated by the financial sector as gross revenue has generally increased. This evidence – taken togeth-er with the analysis in Chapter 7 – indicates that the balance between real and financial accumulation has moved in favour of the latter, at least for the countries at the core of the global economy. However, it would be incorrect to conclude that all economic magnitudes associated with finance have been on a rising trend during this period. In the area of employment things look different, and this is a point of considerable importance for the analysis of financialization.

Employment in the financial sector

National statistical data on aggregate employment by the financial sector in the four countries are problematic for much of the post-1973–74 period because employment in the financial sector has been included with business services, insurance, retail and real estate. In recent years, however, data has been made available which focuses more closely on the financial sector and, above all, on financial intermediation (though the starting point of the change is different for each country). Thus, figure 6 shows employ-ment in financial intermediation as a percentage of total employment.

The countries of market-based finance, US and UK, have higher levels of financial employment than the countries of bank-based finance, Japan and Germany. Howev-er, the most striking aspect of figure 6 is that employment levels have been low and stable across the four countries: the proportion of the labour force employed in finan-cial intermediation has been flat (or even gently declining) as the financial sector has surged ahead. If employment in financial intermediation (mostly banking) was taken as a proxy for aggregate financial employment, it would appear that financialization has not brought a sustained increase in the proportion of the labour employed in the realm of finance.[8]

The reasons for stagnant employment in financial intermediation are not imme-diately clear, and are probably related to the transformation of banking discussed in subsequent sections of this chapter. Suffice it to note that banks have been deep-ly restructured during the last three decades, altering the mix of labour skills and technologies deployed. Automation has transformed the work of traditional bank tellers, while information technology has changed the nature of back-office work. Banks have also rebalanced the network of branches and ATMs in favour of the latter. Finally, banks have been under competitive pressure to reduce employment altogether, as has been apparent in Japan since the end of the bubble of the 1980s.[9]

---

8   Greta Krippner has shown that the financialization of the US economy has not generated a commensurate increase in employment in the financial sector. Greta Krippner, 'The Financial-ization of the American Economy', *Socio-Economic Review* 3, 2005.

9   For further analysis of these issues, see Costas Lapavitsas and Paulo Dos Santos, 'Globaliza-tion and Contemporary Banking: On the Impact of New Technology', *Contributions to Political Economy* 27, 2008, pp. 31–56.

FIG. 6 Employment in financial intermediation as percentage of total employment; US, Japan, Germany, UK

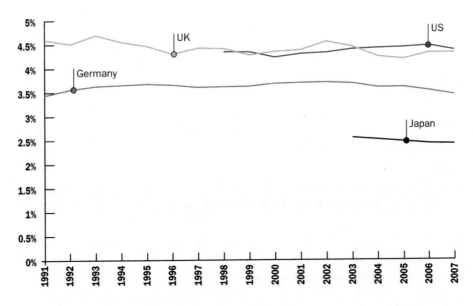

Source: Author calculations, OECD database and OECD Stat. Extract.

Note: There are structural breaks in the data due to redefinition of employment in finance. Generally the sector has been reclassified from the broad 'financing, insurance, business services, and real estate' to the much narrower 'financial intermediation'.

The strong growth of banking in the 1990s and 2000s has been achieved with a relatively stable input of labour.

Financial profit

The relatively small proportion of the labour force employed by banks brings into sharp relief the final piece of evidence regarding the changing balance between real and financial accumulation. Financial profits have become a large and rising part of total profits in the course of financialization.

The clearest and most easily accessible data on this issue is provided by the US national income and product accounts (NIPA); using NIPA data, figure 7 traces the movement of US financial profit as proportion of total profit. Financial profit here refers to pre-tax profits of finance, insurance, bank and other holding companies; calculations include inventory valuation adjustment and capital consumption adjustment. The results partly reflect the method of calculation, but the overall trend and fluctuations of financial profits would remain substantially the same, if other calculation methods were used.

There has been a generally upward trend in the proportion of financial profits

FIG. 7 Financial profit as proportion of total profit; US

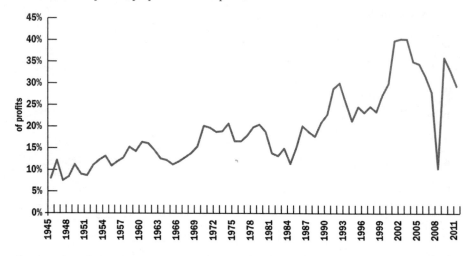

Source: Author calculations based on NIPA, Table 6.16. 'Financial' consists of finance, insurance, bank and other holding companies. Domestic profit includes Inventory Valuation Adjustment and Capital Consumption Adjustment. Both financial and domestic profit are pre-tax.

throughout the post-war period in the US, but also three distinct phases. First, sustained growth in financial profits took place from 1945 to the early 1970s, the years of the long post-war boom during which finance was heavily controlled. Second, a period of stagnation – and even gentle decline – prevailed from the early 1970s to the early 1980s. Third, from the early 1980s to the present, the trend has become notably steeper, financial profits reaching the extraordinary proportion of 45 percent of total profits in the early 2000s. Fourth, the behaviour of financial profits has been cyclical throughout the post-war period, but the cycles have become more pronounced since the early 1980s. By far the most violent fluctuation has occurred in the course of the crisis of the 2000s for reasons discussed in Chapter 9.

Comparable data is not available for the remaining countries in the sample. However, for the UK and Japan it is possible to use national income statistics to cast some light on financial profits as proportion of total profits. Financial and non-financial profits could be approximated through the gross disposable income of, respectively, financial and non-financial enterprises to which would be added (respectively) taxes on income and wealth.[10] The sums, crude as they might be, could offer a glimpse of the behaviour of financial profits in both the UK and Japan during the last two to three decades.

For the UK relevant data is available for a much shorter period of time than for

---

10   UK gross disposable income is available net of current taxes and hence an adjustment has had to be made to allow for broad comparability with US pre-tax profits.

FIG. 8 Pre-tax profits of financial corporations as proportion of total domestic pre-tax profits and of GDP (market prices); UK

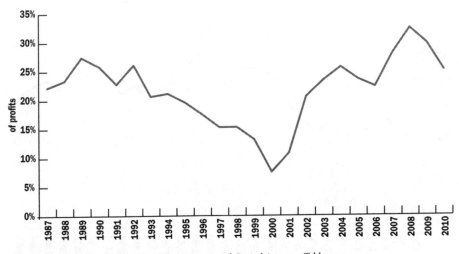

Source: Author calculations based on ONS, Income and Capital Account, Tables 14.2–14.4.

Note: The sum of gross disposable income and taxes on income is used as proxy for the pre-tax profits of financial corporations. Domestic sectors include financial corporations, public corporations, and non-financial private corporations.

the US, starting only in the late 1980s.[11] Figure 8 shows a mild upward trend for UK financial profits, but the cyclical aspect is more pronounced. Similarly to the behaviour of financial profits in the US during the same period, following an increase in the late 1980s and early 1990s, UK financial profits declined steadily as proportion of total profits until the early 2000s. In the course of the 2000s, however, financial profits rose rapidly, ending the period at a significantly higher level.

Japan presents a similar but also different picture.[12] Figure 9 shows that financial profits rose rapidly during the bubble of the 1980s but then entered a period of stagnation, and even gentle decline, though still at a generally higher level. There has also been a cyclical aspect to Japanese financial profits, but it has been milder compared to the US and the UK.

The trajectory of financial profits is perhaps the most striking aspect of financialization, and a strong sign of changing balance between real and financial accumulation. Figures 7, 8 and 9 broadly confirm that financialization has been associated with rising

11 UK national accounts include financial corporations, public corporations, and non-financial private corporations. The sum of their pre-tax profits is taken as total domestic profit.

12 Japanese national accounts provide data on financial and non-financial corporations. The sum of their pre-tax profits is taken as total domestic profit.

FIG. 9 Pre-tax profits of financial corporations as proportion of total pre-tax domestic profits and of GDP; Japan

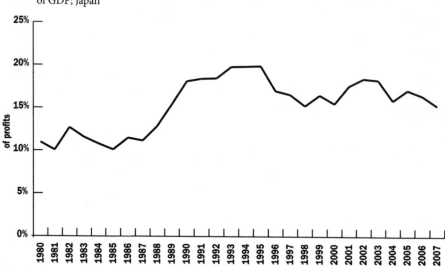

Source: Author calculations based on Cabinet Office (Government of Japan) Annual Report on National Accounts of 2009.

Note: The sum of gross disposable income and current taxes of financial and non-financial corporations is used as proxy for total pre-tax domestic profits.

financial profit compared to profit from real accumulation. Put differently, the weight of profits generated in circulation appears to have increased compared to profits generated in production. Note that the figures underestimate aggregate financial profits since they do not include profits accruing to individuals and enterprises from holding financial assets. Furthermore, the figures do not include financial profits accruing to functionaries of finance in the form of bonuses and salaries.

Summing up, the evidence presented in this section indicates that in mature capitalist countries financial accumulation has been generally on the ascendant, though with considerable variations. The flows of loanable capital and the magnitude of financial revenue relative to GDP point to a cumulatively greater weight of finance in the economy. Above all, financial profits have become a larger part of total profits, even though employment in the financial sector has been relatively stagnant. Given that finance is an intermediary activity that does not generate value and surplus value, the source of financial profit lies in profits and incomes created in other parts of the economy. Thus, even at this highly aggregate level, it would appear that financial expropriation, or 'profit upon alienation and expropriation', has become significant in the course of financialization. This issue is considered in more depth in the following section in conjunction with the core relations of financialization.

Core relations of financialization in mature countries

The ascendancy of financial accumulation is an aggregate reflection of financialization but does not by itself reveal much about the defining tendencies of the latter. Financialization in developed capitalist countries, as has been stated in several places in this book, relates to fundamental changes in the conduct of non-financial enterprises, banks, and individuals (or households). This section, consequently, turns to the economic and social relations constituting the core of what might be called mature financialization. It is shown that industrial and financial capitals have altered their operations, in part aiming at financial profit and thereby re-strengthening the ancient predatory tendencies of finance. New social layers have been created, receiving finance-related income and bearing only a passing resemblance to the rentiers of old. In these respects, financialization represents a systemic transformation of mature capitalism.

Financialization of non-financial enterprises

The core relations of financialization are rooted in the financial operations of non-financial capital. Nonetheless, financialization represents neither the escape of productive capital into the realm of finance in search of higher profits, nor the turn of productive capital toward financial activities at the expense of productive investment. It stands, rather, for a transformation of the mix of financial and non-financial activities that are integral to the circuit of productive capital. This transformation has implications for the financing of investment, the pursuit of financial profit, the internal organization of non-financial enterprises, and the tendency to crisis, broadly considered in the remaining chapters of this book.

It cannot be over-emphasized that both monetary and financial operations are integral to the circuit of productive capital. Such operations include committing money capital to the initial investment, receiving commercial credit to buy inputs, advancing commercial credit to sell output, borrowing loanable capital to expand or maintain circuit flows, handling receipts, payments and hoards of money, lending temporarily idle money capital to others and, far from least, receiving the money value of output with sufficient regularity to prevent the circuit from stopping. Productive capital is constantly active in the realm of finance, and systematically combines monetary and financial with productive and commercial operations. Money and finance are present at the inception of the circuit of productive capital and remain intertwined with its operations.

The financialization of productive capital represents a transformation of financial activities as well as a change in the balance between financial and non-financial activities that are integral to the circuit. Non-financial capital (industrial and merchant's) has altered the financing of its core activities, acquired further financial skills and accordingly rebalanced its profit-making operations. To establish the financialization of non-financial enterprises, therefore, theoretical analysis must take as point of departure the financial operations intrinsic to the circuit of productive capital. The analysis of the financial system in Chapter 5 is of critical importance in this regard since both the pyramid of credit relations and the associated terrain of stock market operations were shown to be rooted in the processes of real accumulation. The financial requirements and operations of productive capital lie at the foundation of the financial system, even if the latter retains its relative autonomy and some of its institutions have an ancient provenance.

Mainstream economics proposes the so-called 'pecking order' theory to capture the financial activities of non-financial enterprises – a sequential order of financing that is determined by cost and ease of access on the basis of information asymmetry between managers and holders of funds.[13] Firms normally prefer to finance investment through retained profits, but new and rapidly growing firms often need external finance. The forms of external finance depend on risk, costs and availability over time; a common preference ordering would be trade credit, commercial paper, bank loans, bonds, convertible bonds and equity. Equity comes last because it signals the belief of managers that the corporation is overvalued. The 'pecking order' theory is typically contrasted to the 'trade off' theory, which essentially argues that enterprises decide on the level of leverage by balancing the tax benefits against the costs of bankruptcy from holding debt. The 'trade-off' theory can be given a dynamic aspect by considering the interaction of financing and investment practices, also taking into account taxes, financial distress costs and equity floatation costs, to adjust a target level of leverage.[14] The empirical record for the US, at least, offers some support for the 'pecking order' theory but results are far from decisive; in practice, leverage for large US enterprises is not as high as the theory would predict and firms hold too much equity.[15]

From the perspective of Marxist political economy, both theories are 'too abstract' at the outset, thus falsely opposing each other. There cannot be a general theory of the financing decisions of the capitalist enterprise because of the nature of credit and loanable capital, discussed in Chapter 5. In practice capitalist enterprises order their financing options and choose among equity and debt based on contingent factors. A striking feature of finance for large enterprises for most of the twentieth century, nonetheless, has been the dominant role of retained profits. On this issue political economy can shed fresh light.

---

13   Stewart C. Myers, 'The Capital Structure Puzzle', *Journal of Finance* 39:3, 1984; Stewart C. Myers and Nicholas S. Majluf, 'Corporate Financing and Investment Decisions When Firms Have Information That Investors Do Not Have', *Journal of Financial Economics* 13:2, 1984. See also Stewart C. Myers, 'Capital Structure', *Journal of Economic Perspectives* 15:2, 2001.

14   See, for instance, Mark T. Leary and Michael R. Roberts, 'Do Firms Rebalance Their Capital Structures?', *Journal of Finance* 60:6, December 2005, pp. 2575–619.

15   Eugene Fama and Kenneth French, 'Testing Trade-Off and Pecking Order Predictions About Dividends and Debt', *Review of Financial Studies* 15:1, 2002. See also Murray Frank and Vidhan Goyal, 'Tradeoff and Pecking Order Theories of Debt', in *The Handbook of Empirical Corporate Finance*, ed. B. Espen Ecko, Amsterdam: Elsevier, 2008.

The most fundamental financial operations of productive capital are, first, to commit money capital of sufficient size to commence the circuit and, second, to ensure the regular return of money capital to maintain the continuity of turnover. Productive capital is self-financing in the fundamental sense of supporting its own circuit primarily out of sales revenue, a condition that depends on adequate demand for its output. The replacement of cost and the outlay of fresh investment by productive capital in principle rely on recouping costs from sales as well as on retaining profits over time. The financing of productive capital, therefore, has an 'internal' character that becomes dominant as monopolistic tendencies prevail in mature capitalism.[16]

The engagement of productive capital in 'external' financial relations, on the other hand, first arises with commercial credit. The latter emerges spontaneously among industrial and commercial capitals and becomes inextricably linked with banking credit, as was shown in Chapter 5. Commercial credit is the training ground for the acquisition of financial skills by productive capital, partly in trading relations among buyers and sellers, partly in connection with banks. Borrowing loanable money capital from, and making idle money capital available to, banks are financial practices of industrial capital undertaken against the background of commercial credit. For productive capital, accessing loanable money capital in open markets, whether in the form of debt or equity, requires significant familiarity with banking credit as well as considerable financial skill. This is typically an activity of larger units of capital, the monopolies of Marxist theory.

Financialization of productive capital in this context is a change in the composition of 'external' finance: funds obtained in open markets gain in importance relative to funds obtained from banks. The skills and activities of productive capital change accordingly. However, changes in the composition of 'external' finance always occur against a shifting balance between 'internal' and 'external' finance. This balance depends on the technological aspects of production, the rapidity of turnover, the extent of monopolization, the institutional organization of markets, and a host of other historically specific factors. Analysis of the financialization of productive capital, consequently, must commence with examining the balance of 'internal' relative to 'external' finance.

Hilferding claimed that, as the scale of production grew larger, the balance between 'internal' and 'external' finance moves inexorably in favour of the latter, and banks come to dominate 'external' finance. The first part of Hilferding's syllogism is incorrect; the second is specific to his time and does not fit contemporary evidence. Indeed, there can be no a priori theoretical formulation of either the balance between 'internal' and 'external' finance, or of the composition of 'external' finance. They are both historically contingent, reflecting the specific features of industrial and financial capital in par-

---

16 This is the substance of the objection rightly raised by Sweezy to Hilferding's analysis of the financing of investment by monopoly capital.

ticular periods and instances, and ought to be analysed in these terms. Nonetheless, Hilferding made a decisive contribution by stressing the impact that 'external' finance has on the operations of the capital that already supplies 'internal' finance. The internal organization and the conduct of productive capital are influenced by the debt and equity characteristic of the money capital that commences and sustains the productive circuit. This is an important aspect of financialization that is further considered below.

Note that, for the purposes of establishing the underlying relations of financialization, it is not necessary to examine in further detail the forces that determine the balance between 'internal' and 'external' finance for productive capital. It is likely, for instance, that new information and telecommunications technologies during the last three decades have altered the investment requirements of productive capital while also speeding turnover and thus strengthening the role of 'internal' finance. It is also likely that the ascendancy of large monopoly capitals has further accentuated the significance of retained profits for investment. However, for the analysis of financialization it suffices simply to establish the actual path of 'internal' relative to 'external' finance. This is an adequate basis on which to examine the changing composition of 'external' finance, which lies at the core of financialization.

Empirical analysis of the financialization of non-financial enterprises in this section thus proceeds in two stages. The first considers the trajectory of 'internal' relative to 'external' finance in funding aggregate investment during the last four decades. Data is deployed on a net basis, that is, after balancing out the sources and uses of funds by non-financial enterprises as a whole. There is an obvious risk in this approach: the cancelling out of the financial activities of non-financial enterprises on both sides of the balance sheet. Nonetheless, the results can still cast a revealing light on the funding practices of the productive sector in the four countries. The second stage then turns to the composition of 'external' finance, and considers the balance between 'trade credit', 'banking' and 'market' sources of funds. Analysis focuses on the relative size but also on the mix of financial assets and liabilities of non-financial enterprises. The calculations are undertaken without netting out and thus offer an additional and corrective light to the first stage.

Data is again drawn from flow of funds accounts of the four countries, thus presenting significant problems, two of which stand out and merit reference in advance. First, and by far the most severe, the data does not differentiate between large monopolistic enterprises and other non-financial enterprises. Since the analytical argument in this book is that the tendency to financialization holds primarily for large enterprises in mature countries, it would be necessary to interpret the results with caution. Second, the data on financial assets and liabilities for non-financial enterprises in the US contains an enormous 'Net Worth' category, typically exceeding 50 percent of aggregate liabilities. It is not clear how the category has been constructed, making it difficult to analyse the composition of the financial liabilities of US enterprises.

The first stage examines the financing of aggregate investment by deploying a framework originally developed by Jenny Corbett and Tim Jenkinson.[17] The framework – which has been adapted for use in this chapter in ways discussed in detail in the Appendix to this chapter – establishes the financing of investment by netting out sources from uses of funds. Investment is thus shown to be financed by retained earnings ('internal') as well as a variety of other methods, including loans, securities, and so on ('external'). To fit the analytical concerns of this book, 'external' finance has been grouped into 'market' and 'bank' along lines again explained in the Appendix. The results for trade finance have not been presented in the diagrams below because their magnitude was not large enough to merit inclusion, and they would have complicated the presentation needlessly.

Thus, figure 10 for the US shows that throughout the entire period following the Second World War 'internal' finance has been dominant in financing investment. The dominance has been near absolute in the years of financialization as 'internal' finance has typically accounted for the whole of investment; and even substantially more, once the crisis of 2007 had burst out, as US corporations have been holding much larger funds than they invest. 'External' finance for US enterprises, on the other hand, has been far less important and more strongly cyclical throughout this period. It is notable that 'bank' and 'market' finance have frequently moved in opposite directions, and strongly so in the 2000s. If 'external' funding is added up, as in figure 11, it becomes clear that its relative weight has declined in the US since the end of the 1970s. In sum, financialization in the US has been a period of heavy reliance of non-financial enterprises on retained earnings and of declining reliance on 'external' finance.

Similar results hold for the UK, shown in figure 12. The financing of investment on a net basis throughout the years of financialization has relied overwhelmingly on retained earnings; in the 2000s, in particular, UK non-financial enterprises have held substantially greater funds than they have invested. 'External' finance has been strongly cyclical, while 'bank' and 'market' finance have often moved in opposite directions. Finally, the declining importance of 'external' finance in the years of financialization is also apparent in figure 13 that adds up 'bank' and 'market' funding.

Equally striking are the figures for Germany, although the data does not allow for the funding of investment to be estimated for a length of time comparable to the US and even to the UK. Nonetheless, it is clear from figure 14 that retained earnings have

---

17   See Jenny Corbett and Tim Jenkinson, 'The Financing of Industry, 1970–1989: An International Comparison', *Journal of the Japanese and International Economies* 10:1, 1996. There has been criticism of the framework, not least for its reliance on net rather than gross funding; see, for instance, Andreas Hackethal and Reinhard Schmidt, 'Financing Patterns: Measurement Concepts and Empirical Results', Working Paper Series: Finance and Accounting, No. 125, Goethe University Frankfurt, January 2004. For our purposes, the framework is very useful, particularly as the financial activities of non-financial enterprises on a gross basis are also considered in the latter part of this section.

FIG. 10 Net sources of finance as percentage of capital expenditures; US

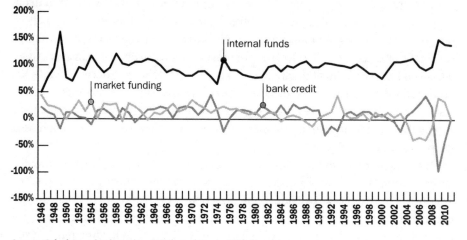

Source: Calculations by the author, US Flow of Funds, Table F.102

FIG. 11 Total net external funding as percentage of capital expenditures; US

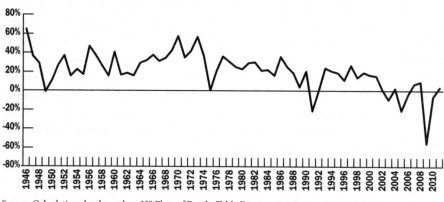

Source: Calculations by the author, US Flow of Funds, Table F.102

Note: Total net external funding is calculated as a sum of net bank and net market funding.

been the dominant form of funding and their significance has steadily increased in the 2000s. German non-financial enterprises are not different to US and UK enterprises in this respect, despite the bank-based character of the German financial system. Note that 'external' finance has also behaved in a broadly cyclical manner, while 'bank' and 'market' funding have generally moved in opposite directions. Finally, figure 15 shows that total 'external' finance of investment has declined in importance similarly to the US and the UK.

The most striking results, however, are those for Japan, a historic cradle of bank-based finance and a country in which non-financial enterprises have traditionally

FIG. 12 Net sources of finance as percentage of gross capital formation; UK

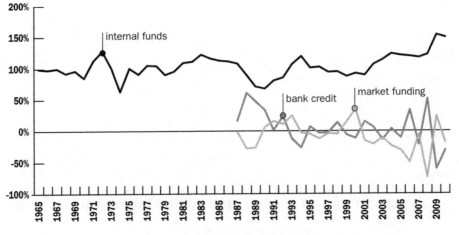

Source: Calculations by the author, ONS, Financial Statistics, Tables 11.1D and 14.3C

FIG. 13 Total net external funding as percentage of gross capital formation; UK

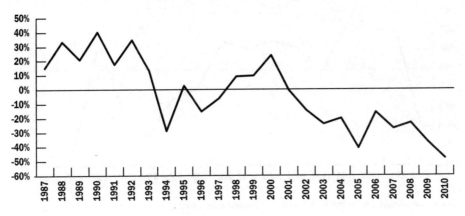

Source: Calculations by the author, ONS, Financial Statistics, Tables 11.1D and 14.3C

Note: Total net external funding is calculated as the sum of net bank and net market funding.

relied on bank loans to finance investment. The data for Japan presents particularly intractable problems, explained in the Appendix, and as a result the figures should be treated with considerable caution. What matters are the trends and not the absolute levels estimated. Thus, figure 16 shows that 'internal' funds began to rise in importance in the early 1990s and after the burst of the Japanese bubble of the 1980s. The ascendancy of retained profits in the following two decades has been astounding, with Japanese non-financial enterprises holding substantial volumes of liquid funds by 2010. Bank credit and market funding have declined steadily in importance, while fluctuating in

FIG. 14 Net sources of funds as percentage of gross capital formation; Germany

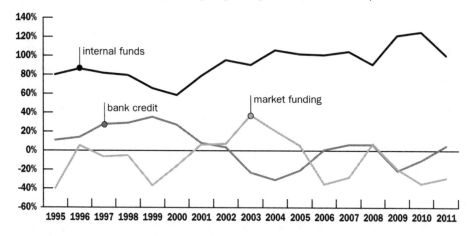

Source: Calculations by the author, Eurostat, Annual Sector Accounts

FIG. 15 Total net external funding as percentage of gross capital formation; Germany

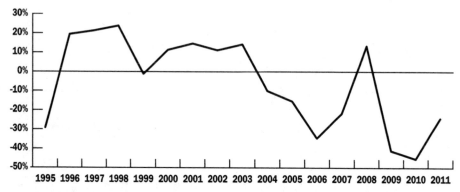

Source: Calculations by the author, Eurostat, Annual Sector Accounts

Note: Total net external funding is calculated as the sum of net bank and net market funding.

opposite directions. The decline of 'external' finance is also apparent in figure 17. There is little doubt that Japanese non-financial corporations have become far less dependent on bank (and other external) finance than at any time in the post-war period.

In sum the first stage of the empirical investigation of non-financial enterprises has established their rising independence from 'external' finance across the four countries. Productive capital in the leading countries of both bank-based and market-based finance relies increasingly on retained earnings to finance investment on a net basis. Financialization is characterized by a widening space between non-financial enterprises and banks. In this fundamental sense financialization is present across mature

FIG. 16 Net sources of finance as percentage of capital expenditures; Japan

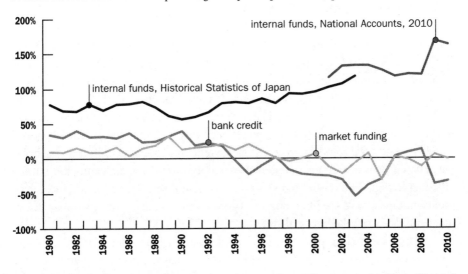

Source: Calculations by the author, Bank of Japan, Flow of Funds; Cabinet Office, Government of Japan, Historical Statistics of Japan, Tables 3-29-b and 3-30-a (1980–2003); Cabinet Office, National Accounts, 2010, Flow, Tables 2.2, 3.1 (2001–2010).

FIG. 17 Total net external funding as percentage of gross capital formation; Japan

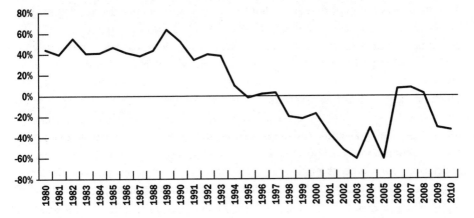

Source: Calculations by the author, Bank of Japan, Flow of Funds; Cabinet Office, Government of Japan, Historical Statistics of Japan, Table 3-30-a (1980–2000); Cabinet Office, National Accounts, 2010, Flow, Table 3.1 (2001–2010).

capitalist countries irrespective of the historic characterization of financial systems. At the same time, non-financial enterprises have acquired skills and capabilities that allow for closer engagement with the operations of the financial system. In this regard, there are significant differences among the leading capitalist countries, as is shown below.

The second stage of the empirical examination of non-financial enterprises turns to the composition of 'external finance' by considering gross uses and sources of funds. The aim is to capture the changing involvement of non-financial enterprises with the financial sector on both sides of the balance sheet, showing non-financial enterprises as both borrowers (recipients) and lenders (suppliers) of finance. A further aim is to demonstrate the changing composition of 'external' activities, again on both sides of the balance sheet, establishing the content of financialization more fully.

Consider first the composition of financial assets held by non-financial corporations, shown for each of the four countries in figures 18, 19, 20, and 21. The categories chosen to reflect the composition are, first, currency and deposits indicating the holding of liquidity by non-financial enterprises; second, securities, indicating the lending of loanable capital but also cross-share-holdings; and third, trade credit, indicating provision of a type of credit among enterprises which retains a substantial degree of independence from the financial system.

It is necessary to interpret these figures with caution, particularly for the US where the trends are distorted by the vast entry of 'Other', as has already been mentioned. The most striking feature has been the steady decline of trade credit supplied by non-financial corporations in the US, Japan and the UK, while trade credit has risen in Germany. It appears that non-financial enterprises have become more directly dependent on the financial system for the needs of capital circulation, except in Germany. Equally striking, but not surprising, has been the inverse relationship between money and securities held by non-financial corporations in all four countries. There are no strong trends: non-financial corporations tend to alter the composition of financial assets according to general economic conditions and the fluctuations of the rate of interest.

Important in this respect have been mergers and acquisitions (M&A) by non-financial enterprises particularly in Anglo-Saxon financial systems during the last several decades. M&A is a key lever of the centralization of capital and is therefore implicit to the funding activities of monopolistic enterprises, though its extent obviously depends on the overall character of the financial system. M&A activity also offers opportunities to extract financial profit and could therefore warp the internal functioning of monopolies. This is a regular theme in heterodox literature on finance, typically also stressing the deleterious effect of stock market involvement for investment by non-financial enterprises, and thus directly related to the debate on 'shareholder value'.[18] For the approach

---

18   For a historical analysis of the US merger movement at the turn of the nineteenth century, see Naomi Lamoreaux, 'The Great Merger Movement in American Business, 1895–1904', Cambridge: Cambridge University Press, 1985. For critical analysis of the effects of mergers on the power of managers and the rise of financial imperatives among US corporations see William Lazonick, 'Financial Commitment and Economic Performance', *Business and Economic History*, Second Series 17, 1988; and William Lazonick, 'Controlling the Market for Corporate Control', *Industrial and Corporate Change* 1:3, 1992.

FIG. 18 Composition of total financial assets of non-financial corporations, 1975–2008; US

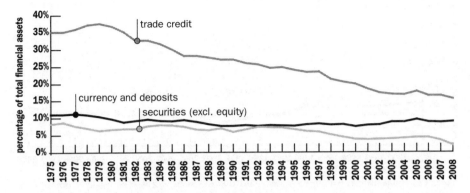

Source: Calculations by the author based on data from US Flow of Funds. Securities (excl. equity) are defined as a sum of credit market instruments, mutual fund shares, and repo. By contrast to other countries, equity is not included in securities.

FIG. 19 Composition of total financial assets of non-financial corporations, 1978–2008; Japan

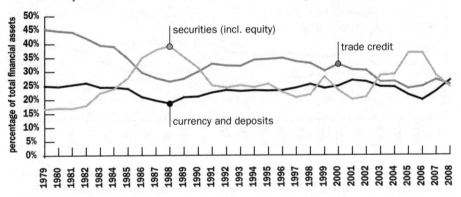

Source: Calculations by the author based on data from Bank of Japan. Securities (incl. equity) is defined as the sum of 'securities other than shares' and 'shares and other equity'.

to financialization adopted in this book, however, changes in the mix of financial assets and liabilities of non-financial enterprises – including independent transactions in the stock market – have an indirect and mediated relationship with investment decisions. There is little doubt that the internal organization of monopoly capital is altered when stock market M&A becomes an important part of its activities, but the causal link with investment is far from obvious. This is not to deny the empirical fact of weak investment in mature capitalist countries, which is further discussed in Chapter 9.

On the other side of the aggregate balance sheet, the composition of the financial liabilities of non-financial corporations are shown in figures 22, 23, 24 and 25 for each

FIG. 20 Composition of total financial assets of non-financial corporations, 1991–2008; Germany

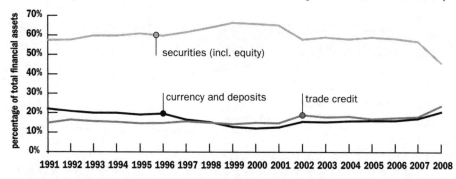

Source: Calculations by the author based on data from the Bundesbank. Securities (incl. equity) is defined as the sum of money market paper, bonds, shares, other equity, mutual funds shares. 'Other claims' is used as a proxy for trade credit.

FIG. 21 Composition of total financial assets of non-financial corporations, 1987–2008; UK

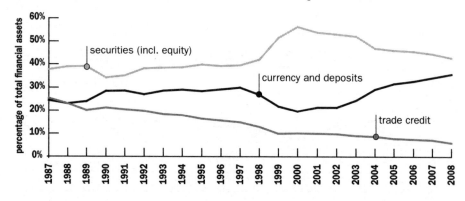

Source: Calculations by the author based on data from ONS. Securities (incl. equity) is defined as a sum of 'securities other than shares' and 'shares and other equity'. 'Other accounts receivable/payable' is used as a proxy for trade credit.

of the four countries. The categories chosen to capture the composition are, first, securities other than shares; second, total equity; third, total loans; and fourth, trade credit. The first two can be thought of as market funding that includes commercial paper, bonds, shares and other securities issued in open markets; the third indicates provision of funding from banks; the fourth offers evidence of credit funding that is generated spontaneously among enterprises.

It is apparent that trade credit as a source of funding has been in steady decline in the US, Japan and the UK, although data is not available for Germany. The decline is consistent with the evidence on trade credit from the asset side, and again points to a greater direct involvement by non-financial enterprises in the activities of the financial system to obtain liquidity for purposes of circulation. Bank loans, on the other hand,

FIG. 22 Composition of non-farm non-financial corporations' liabilities, 1975–2009; US

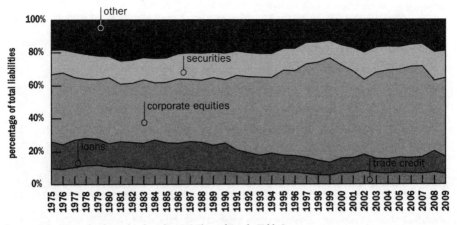

Source: Calculations by the author based on US Flow of Funds, Table L.102

FIG. 23 Composition of non-financial corporations' liabilities, 1979–2009; Japan

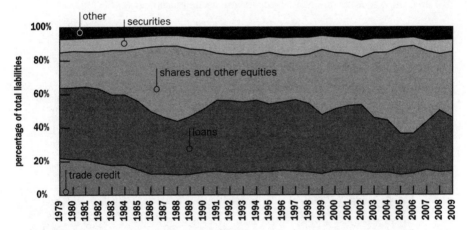

Source: Calculations by the author based on Bank of Japan, Flow of Funds. 'Other' includes deposits money, accounts payable, other external claims and debts, and others. 'Securities' are securities other than shares and financial derivatives.

have declined steadily as a proportion of liabilities in the US, and even more prominently in Japan and Germany. Needless to say, Japanese and German corporations continue to carry a greater proportion of bank debt than US corporations, reflecting the bank-based character of German–Japanese finance.

The UK, finally, has exhibited unusual behaviour in the 2000s as bank borrowing by enterprises appears to have grown strongly. This aspect of the UK is discussed further below; note, however, that the rise in bank borrowing by UK corporations has been heav-

FIG. 24 Composition of non-financial corporations' liabilities, 1991–2008; Germany

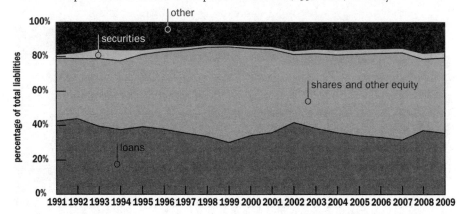

Source: Calculations by the author based on Deutsche Bundesbank, Financial Accounts. 'Securities' are the sum of money-market paper and bonds, 'other' is the sum of claims from company pension commitments and other liabilities.

FIG. 25 Composition of non-financial corporations liabilities, 1987–2008; UK

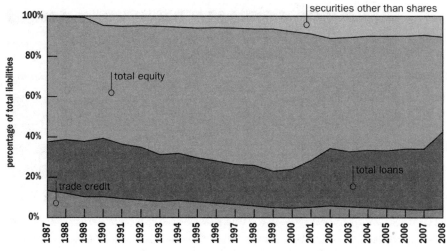

Source: Calculations by the author based on ONS, Financial Statistics Consistent, Table 12.1B

ily due to foreign banks. Market funding, finally, shows a steady increase in the US, Japan and Germany, but declines in the UK in the 2000s, in line with the rise in bank funding.

Summing up, the evidence from both the asset and the liability side of the balance sheet of the non-financial corporate sector indicates that financialization has occurred in all four countries. To be specific, non-financial enterprises exhibit more reliance on securities markets and less reliance on banks for funding; they also exhibit weaker spontaneous generation of trade credit. On this basis, the financialization of non-financial corporations means that they have become more closely integrated with the financial system, while becoming more distant from banks. Productive capital is financializing, but there is no return of finance capital.

Transformation of banks

The financialization of non-financial enterprises has had significant implications for banks, the transformation of which has been a key feature of the period. Consider the expansion of the banking sector indicated by the financial assets of commercial banks with respect to, first, GDP, second, the financial assets of the entire financial sector, third, total domestic financial assets and, fourth, total financial assets including the rest of the world, shown in figures 26, 27, 28 and 29 for each of the four countries.

There has been strong growth of commercial banks relative to GDP across all four countries. Even in Japan, where banks have gone through prolonged stagnation following the bubble of the 1980s, banks were substantially larger relative to the rest of the economy by the late 2000s. However, striking differences also exist among the four countries – banks have become proportionately larger in the UK compared to Japan, to Germany and even to the US.[19] Note also that, for the US and Japan, the weight of commercial bank assets relative to domestic financial assets is similar to that relative to financial assets held by the rest of the world; however, for Germany and the UK, the former is significantly higher than the latter. It appears that economic agents in Germany and the UK have been more heavily involved in international financial transactions than in the US and Japan.

The ratio of bank assets to the total assets of the financial sector merits closer attention. The ratio has declined in the US and Germany, although it has remained stable in Japan and even risen gently in the UK. The remarkable aspect of figures 26 to 29 in this respect is the reassertion of commercial banking in the 2000s: the ratio has stopped declining and even risen in all four countries. In the course of the enormous bubble of the 2000s, commercial banks have reaffirmed their key position in mature financial systems. The reassertion of commercial banks has occurred in part through acquiring functions associated with mediating transactions in open financial markets. Commercial banks have remained the hub of the financial system, although their activities have changed substantially to include open market mediation and lending to individuals. The accompanying transformation has had profound implications for the internal functioning of banks as well as for their ability effectively to mediate the flows of loanable capital. In particular, the internal reorganization of banks and the introduction of new technology appear to have affected the ability of banks to appropriate and assess information about borrowers, an issue that is further discussed in the next chapter.

These developments are important to analysing further the variations in the ascendancy of banks among the four countries. Consider figures 30, 31, 32, and 33,

---

19   Although the existence of the 'shadow' banking sector in the US distorts the picture.

FIG. 26 Commercial bank assets as a share of financial sector financial assets, of total economy financial assets and of GDP, 1959–2009; US

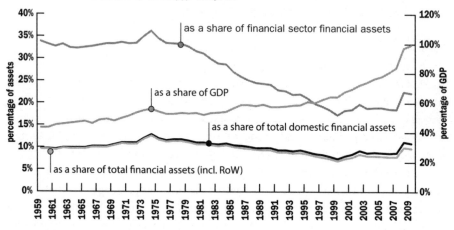

Source: Calculations by the author based on data from US Flow of Funds, NIPA, Table 1.1.5.

FIG. 27 Commercial bank assets as a share of financial sector financial assets, of total economy financial assets and of GDP, 1979–2009; Japan

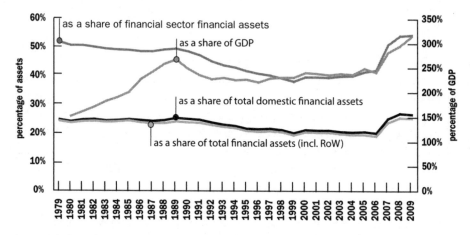

Source: Calculations by the author based on data from Bank of Japan, Flow of Funds; Cabinet Office, Government of Japan, National Accounts.

which show the composition of bank assets in each country. The categories chosen to reflect the composition are, first, lending to non-financial enterprises, second, lending to households for mortgages, consumption and other purposes, and third, lending to other banks or financial institutions. Data availability does not allow for these indexes to be calculated in the same way for all four countries, or even at all. Considerable

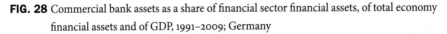

FIG. 28 Commercial bank assets as a share of financial sector financial assets, of total economy financial assets and of GDP, 1991–2009; Germany

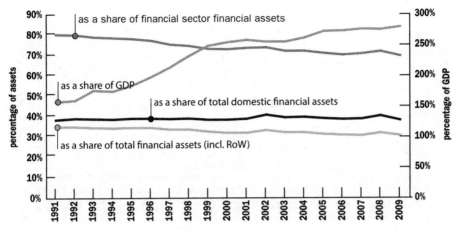

Source: Calculations by the author based on data from Deutsche Bundesbank, Financial accounts; Statistisches Bundesamt Deutschlands. Financial sector consists of MFI, insurance corporations, and other financial institutions.

FIG. 29 Commercial bank assets as a share of financial sector financial assets, of total economy financial assets and of GDP, 1987–2009; UK

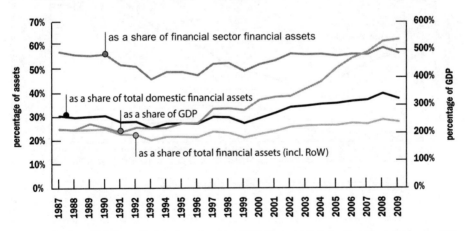

Source: Calculations by the author based on data from ONS, Financial Statistics Consistent, Tables 12.1, UK Output, Income and Expenditure, Table C.1.

caution is therefore necessary in interpreting the results.

Several distinctive features of bank conduct during the period of financialization are immediately apparent. First, lending to non-financial enterprises has declined in all four countries, particularly since the early 1990s, as financialization reached full

FIG. 30 Composition of commercial bank assets, 1950–2009; US

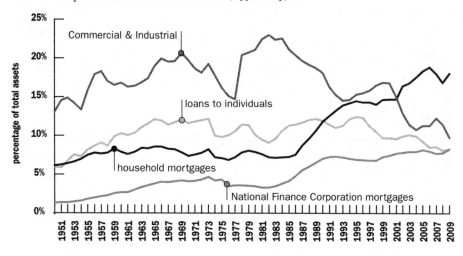

Source: Calculations by the author based on data from FDIC Historical Statistics on Banking, Tables CB09, CB11, CB12.

FIG. 31 Composition of bank assets, 1979–2009; Japan

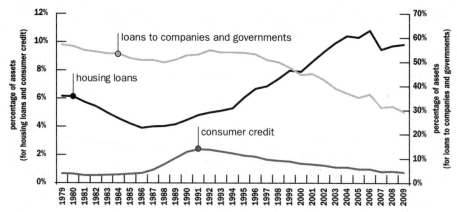

Source: Calculations by the author based on Bank of Japan, Flow of Funds.

swing. The relative detachment of banks from productive accumulation in the course of financialization, discussed in previous chapters, is broadly reflected in the figures. Second, lending to households for mortgages has risen strongly in the US and Japan; it has remained flat in Germany; and it appears to have fallen proportionately in the UK (mortgage loans are by far the largest part of bank loans to UK households). The relative decline of household lending by banks in the UK probably reflects the rising proportion of lending to non-residents by UK banks (not shown in the figure). It is also notable that lending to individuals for consumption purposes is a relatively minor

FIG. 32 Composition of domestic bank lending as a share of total bank assets, 1981–2010; Germany

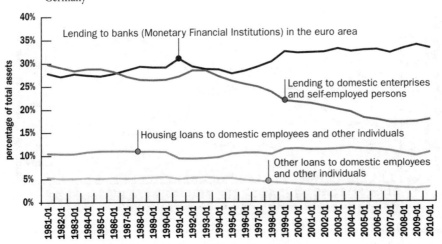

Source: Calculations by the author based on data from Deutsche Bundesbank.

FIG. 33 Composition of MFI loans as a share of MFI assets, June 1990–March 2010; UK

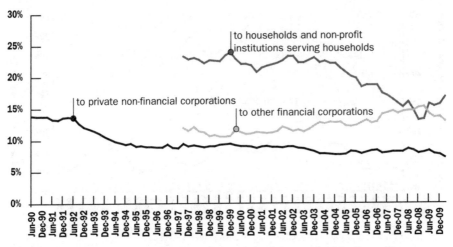

Source: Calculations by the author, Bank of England, Monetary and Financial Statistics, B2.1 and B2.1.1

Note: MFI stands for Monetary Financial Institutions

aspect of bank lending across the four countries, though significant volumes of consumer loans are almost certainly included in mortgage loans; third, lending by banks to other banks has risen significantly in the UK and Germany, but the data does not allow for this ratio to be calculated in the US and Japan. The turn of banks to mediating in open markets is clear at least for the UK and Germany.

FIG. 34 Composition of commercial bank liabilities and equity capital, 1970–2009; US

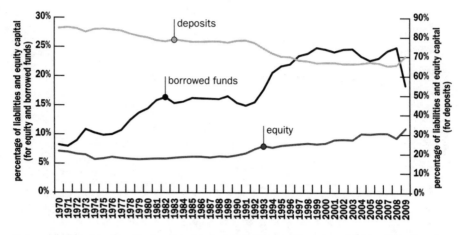

Source: Calculations by the author based on data from FDIC Historical Statistics on Banking, Table CB14. Borrowed funds include borrowed funds proper, subordinated notes, and other liabilities.

FIG. 35 Composition of bank liabilities, 1979–2009; Japan

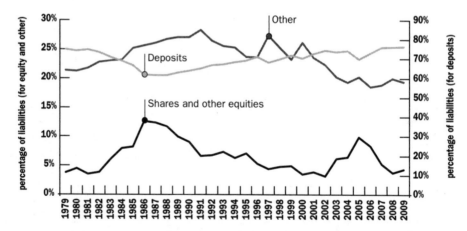

Source: Calculations by the author based on Bank of Japan, Flow of Funds.

In sum, the figures confirm the ascendancy of commercial banks as well as their gradual detachment from productive accumulation in the course of financialization. There also appears to be a general tendency for banks to turn toward lending to households; lending to households has been mostly for mortgages rather than for consumption. Finally, although the data generally makes it difficult to ascertain the extent of lending among banks, there is evidence of its rise consistent with the turn of banks toward transactions in open financial markets.

FIG. 36 Composition of bank liabilities, 1980–2010; Germany

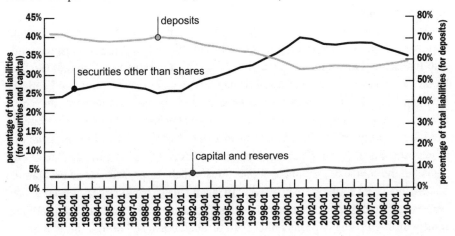

Source: Calculations by the author based on data from Deutsche Bundesbank.

FIG. 37 Composition of commercial bank liabilities as a share of total financial liabilities, 1987–2008; UK

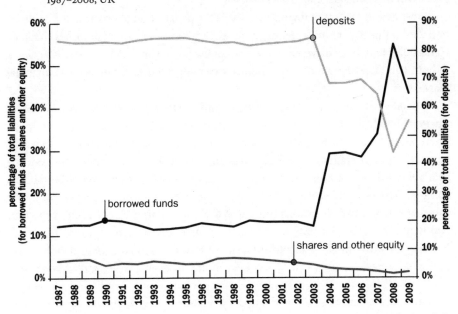

Source: Calculations by the author based on ONS, UK Economic Accounts, Table A58. Borrowed funds include securities other than shares, loans, and other accounts receivable/payable.

The last aspect of banking to consider in this connection is the composition of bank liabilities, shown in figures 34, 35, 36, and 37. The categories chosen to capture the composition are, first, deposits, second, securities and other borrowed funds, third, equity and capital.

There is significant variation in the funding of commercial banks among the four countries. Thus, US banks have increased their reliance on borrowed funds while also increasing bank capital; meanwhile, deposits have steadily declined. German banks have an even stronger and still rising reliance on borrowed funds, and deposits have similarly declined. It appears that both US and German commercial banks have adopted similar funding practices. UK banks have behaved along the same lines in the 2000s, heavily increasing the significance of borrowed funds, while reducing that of deposits. Equally remarkable for UK banks, however, has been the decline in own capital in the course of the bubble of the 2000s, which temporarily raised profitability but eventually left banks extremely weak. In Japan, finally, banks appear indeed to have behaved differently from the other countries. Japanese banks have financed activities mostly through rising deposits rather than through borrowed funds. This is yet more evidence that Japanese banks have been cautious in turning toward mediation in open markets, probably as a result of the protracted crisis of Japanese banking following the bubble of the 1980s.

Financialization of households and individuals

The most striking aspect of financialization is the penetration of financial transactions into the circuits of personal revenue, as has already been mentioned in earlier chapters. Households have been driven into the arms of the formal financial system with respect to both liabilities and assets. The implications are profound for banks and financial markets.

Consider, first, the side of financial liabilities. Households have amassed heavy financial liabilities in the course of financialization, reflecting rising indebtedness. There are several causes of this development which only partially relate to weakly increasing (or stagnant) real incomes among workers and others. Indeed, the available evidence reveals a nuanced and complex process of household financialization. Figures 38 to 41 disaggregate household indebtedness by splitting it into mortgage debt, unsecured consumer debt and other liabilities for each of the four countries. By far the largest component of indebtedness is mortgage debt, which has also grown strongly (except for Germany); unsecured consumer debt has also generally increased, but it is far from a dominant, or even a large, part of household liabilities.[20] The bulk of household indebtedness in the period of financialization in mature countries has been for mortgage purposes. To be sure, mortgage borrowing probably conceals some consumption loans that have been obtained against

---

20 This point holds for mature capitalist countries. In middle-income countries financialization of households appears to have followed a different path, including rapid growth of consumer borrowing, as is shown in the following section.

FIG. 38 Composition of household liabilities as a share of GDP, 1945–2009; US

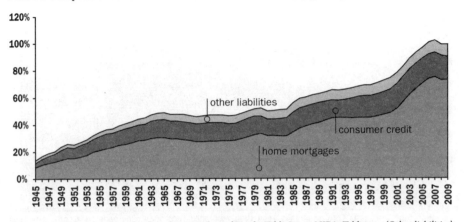

Source: Calculations by the author based on US Flow of Funds, Table L.100; NIPA, Table 1.1.5. 'Other liabilities' are calculated as a residual – the difference between total household liabilities and mortgages and consumer debt.

FIG. 39 Composition of household liabilities as a share of GDP, 1987–2009; UK

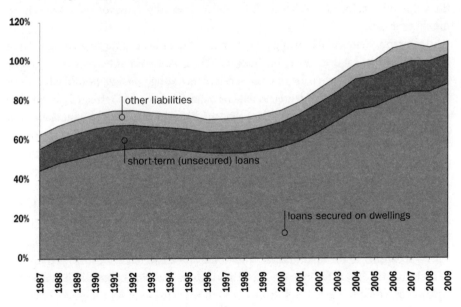

Source: Calculations by the author based on ONS, UK Economic Accounts, Table A64, UK Output, Income and Expenditure, Table C.1. 'Loans' include loans issued by both UK and rest of the world MFIs. 'Other liabilities' are calculated as a residual.

FIG. 40 Composition of household liabilities as a share of GDP, 1991–2009; Germany

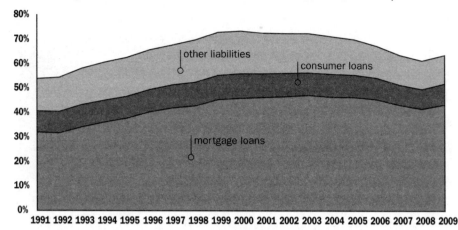

Source: Calculations by the author based on Deutsche Bundesbank, Financial accounts, and Statistisches Bundesamt Deutschlands. 'Other liabilities' are calculated as a residual.

the value of housing; nonetheless, housing remains the cause of most household indebtedness.[21]

The preponderance of housing points to a key factor behind the financialization of households in recent decades: rising household indebtedness has been associated with changes in the social provision of basic services including housing, health, education, transport and so on. To the degree to which social provision has retreated, or failed to expand, private provision has taken its place, mediated by finance. The financialization of personal revenue, in this light, is the process through which the financial sector has mediated the private provision of goods and services to households.[22] Attached to this process has been financial expropriation – the transfer of personal income directly to the profits of the financial institutions that have played this mediating role.

The evidence shows that financialization of households has meant, above all, heavy reliance on private providers of finance – banks, or institutions associated with banks – to obtain housing. For this reason, financialization of households and individuals has varied according to the institutional, traditional and customary housing mechanisms of each country. Japan, for instance, has had a gigantic housing bubble in the 1980s, the collapse of which has acted as a deterrent to the expansion of housing debt in recent years. Germany, on the other hand, has relied more heavily on rented accommoda-

---

21 Note that the category of 'Other' in Japan probably includes business loans taken as household loans.

22 This point has been more fully discussed in Costas Lapavitsas, 'Financialised Capitalism: Crisis and Financial Expropriation', *Historical Materialism* 17:2, 2009.

FIG. 41 Composition of household liabilities as a share of GDP, 1980–2009; Japan

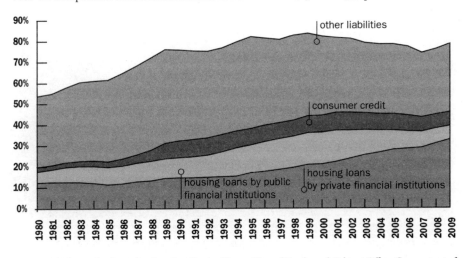

Source: Calculations by the author based on Bank of Japan, Flow of Funds, and Cabinet Office, Government of Japan, National Accounts. 'Other liabilities' are calculated as a residual.

tion than the other countries. Thus, there has been no housing bubble in Germany (and Japan) in the 2000s and by this token household indebtedness has been much lower relative to the US and the UK. Indeed, figures 38 to 41 show that in recent years household indebtedness has declined in Japan and Germany compared to the US and the UK. This difference has played a vital role in the unfolding of the global crisis after 2007, as is shown in Chapter 9.

However, financialization of households does not relate only – or even mostly – to household liabilities, and therefore to household borrowing. Households have also become heavily involved in the formal financial system to manage saving out of personal income. Important to this process have, once again, been changes in the social provision of basic services, above all, pensions. A vital part of financialization has been increasing private provision of pensions which has directed a part of personal income toward financial assets held privately.[23]

---

23 The gradual withdrawal of public provision of pensions and the substitution of private mechanisms typically associated with the stock market are well attested in both critical and mainstream literature. The rise of pension funds as powerful institutional investors in financialized capitalism is an integral part of this trend. For analysis of the changing pensions mechanisms, see Richard Minns, 'The Political Economy of Pensions', *New Political Economy* 1:3, 1996; and Robin Blackburn, *Banking on Death, or Investing in Life*, London: Verso, 2002. Blackburn has outlined the risks and losses from these changes for pensions holders in the UK ('How to Rescue a Failing Pension Regime', *New Political Economy* 9:4, 2004; *Age Shock*, London: Verso,

FIG. 42 Composition of household financial assets as a share of GDP, 1945–2009; US

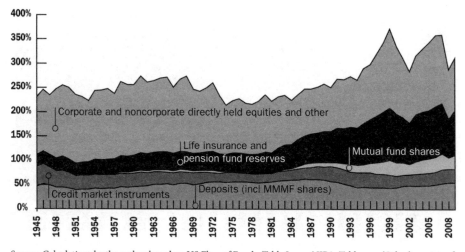

Source: Calculations by the author based on US Flow of Funds, Table L.100; NIPA, Table 1.1.5. 'Other' consists of security credit and miscellaneous assets.

Note: MMMF stands for Money Market Mutual Funds.

Private financial institutions have also participated in this aspect of financialization transforming pension savings into loanable capital, thus extracting financial profit and adding a further dimension to financial expropriation. Once again, patterns have varied from country to country according to historical, political, customary, and even cultural factors of pension provision. Figures 42 to 45 indicate some of the key differences by showing the composition of financial assets held by households in the four countries. Five categories have been deployed, according to data availability in each country: corporate shares and equity, insurance and pension funds, mutual funds, credit market instruments, and bank deposits.

Bank deposits have been a more significant part of household assets in Japan and Germany compared to the US and the UK. The US has also been quite exceptional with regard to the holding of equity by households – there is no comparison with the other three. The unusual position of the US in this respect reflects its historical trajectory, including the ideological strength of ownership of equity capital. The most

---

2007). Paul Langley has associated the emergence of the new pensions regime with financialization ('In the Eye of the "Perfect Storm"', *New Political Economy* 9:4, 2004). Adam Dixon has focused on the rise of pension funds as a structural change of European capitalism ('The Rise of Pension Fund Capitalism in Europe', *New Political Economy* 13:3, 2008). Others, however, have looked at these changes from a more sympathetic perspective; see, for instance, Neil Gilbert, *Transformation of the Welfare State*, Oxford: Oxford University Press, 2002.

FIG. 43 Composition of household financial assets as a share of GDP, 1987–2009; UK

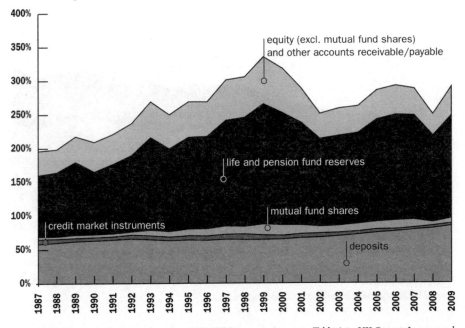

Source: Calculations by the author based on ONS, UK Economic Accounts, Table A64, UK Output, Income and Expenditure, Table C.1. 'Credit market instruments' consist of securities other than shares (mostly government bonds) and loans.

striking feature of household financial assets in all four countries, however, has been the strong and rising holdings of insurance and pension fund claims. This has been a characteristic part of the financialization of household income, providing a foundation for the expanded operations of non-bank financial intermediaries in financial markets. Household assets have been a source of financial profit both in terms of fees earned by the institutions involved but also in terms of capital gains and transactions in financial assets for both intermediaries and final holders.

Recapping, the two last sections have shown that both the ascendancy of financial accumulation and the rising weight of financial profit are commonly observed features of the US, Japan, Germany and the UK. Similarly present are the underlying tendencies of financialization: first, increasing involvement of non-financial corporations in financial transactions, but relatively independently of banks; second, a turn of banks toward financial transactions in open markets as well as with households; third, increasing involvement of households in formal finance, with regard to both liabilities and assets. The evidence has also revealed considerable variation of financialization reflecting the specificity of institutional and historical development of each country. Furthermore, the old distinction between bank-based and market-based finance has not disappeared; rather, it has assumed new characteristics,

FIG. 44 Composition of household financial assets as a share of GDP, 1991–2009; Germany

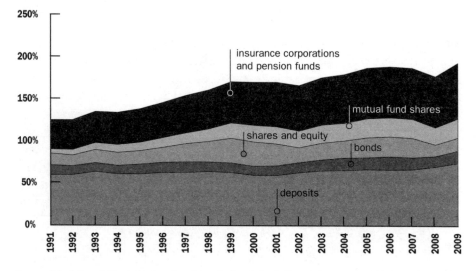

Source: Calculations by the author based on Deutsche Bundesbank, Financial accounts, and Statistisches Bundesamt Deutschlands. Deposits are both domestic and abroad.

FIG. 45 Composition of household financial assets as a share of GDP, 1980–2009; Japan

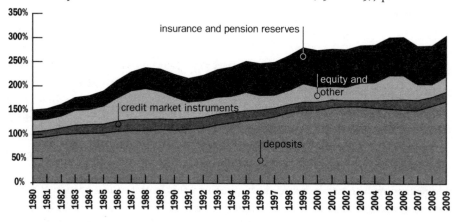

Source: Calculations by the author based on Bank of Japan, Flow of Funds, and Cabinet Office, Government of Japan, National Accounts. 'Credit market instruments' are the sum of loans, securities other than shares, and financial derivatives.

such as more limited financialization of households in countries with bank-based financial systems.

In view of the general but variable character of financialization in mature countries, the next section considers empirical evidence on financialization in developing countries.

Subordinate financialization in developing countries[24]

Financialization has been a process occurring primarily among advanced countries. However, there has also been financialization in developing countries, entailing structural transformation of domestic financial systems but also of the interaction between domestic economy and global finance. Financialization in developing countries has specific features reflecting the dominant role of developed countries in the world market. There has been no return to formal imperialism but financialization in developing countries has had a subordinate character deriving from the hierarchical and exploitative nature of interactions in the world market.

The beginnings of financialization in developing countries can be found in the wave of financial liberalization of the 1970s, which removed price and quantity controls in domestic financial systems. The results in terms of investment, efficiency and growth have been mediocre, but financial liberalization in developing countries has gradually accrued several other features, including introduction of stock markets; by the late 1980s it had morphed into an integrated development strategy, the Washington Consensus. Guided and enforced by the World Bank and the IMF, the Washington Consensus forced changes in domestic finance in developing countries generally favouring a shift away from bank-based, relational, government-controlled structures toward market-based, arm's-length, private institutions and mechanisms.[25] Financialization of developing countries began to take shape on this basis in the late 1990s and the 2000s.

A fundamental component of the Washington Consensus has been the opening of domestic economies to international capital flows, typically on the grounds that capital would flow from rich to poor countries, thus promoting development. Indeed,

---

24   The term 'subordinate financialization' was originally suggested by Jeff Powell.

25   The term 'Washington Consensus' was coined by John Williamson; see Williamson, 'What Washington Means by Policy Reform', in *Latin American Readjustment: How Much has Happened?*, ed. John Williamson, Washington: Institute for International Economics, 1990; John Williamson, 'The Washington Consensus Revisited', in *Economic and Social Development into the XXI Century*, ed. Louis Emmerij, Washington: Inter-American Development Bank, 1997. Joseph Stiglitz has put forth a sustained critique of the Washington Consensus in an effort to develop a Post-Washington Consensus drawing on the notion of market failure typically through information asymmetries; Joseph Stiglitz, 'More Instruments and Broader Goals: Moving Toward the Post Washington Consensus', 7 January 1998; Joseph Stiglitz, 'Whither Reform? Ten Years Of The Transition', World Bank, Annual Bank Conference On Development Economics, 28–30 April 1999. For analysis of both the Washington and the Post-Washington Consensus from a Marxist and heterodox standpoint, see Ben Fine, Costas Lapavitsas, and Jonathan Pincus (eds), *Development Policy in the Twenty-first Century: Beyond the Post-Washington Consensus*, London: Routledge, 2001; and Costas Lapavitsas and Makoto Noguchi (eds), *Beyond Market-Driven Development: Drawing on the Experience of Asia and Latin America*, London: Routledge, 2005.

the mode of integration of developing countries in the world market has been transformed since the 1990s. Although the bulk of foreign direct investment (FDI) has taken place among developed countries, there has also been sustained export of capital from developed to developing countries in the form of FDI as well as in the form of bank and portfolio flows. It is also notable that, as dynamic capitalist accumulation has emerged in several developing countries, including China, there have also been sizeable flows of FDI among developing countries.[26]

However, as developing countries have participated more closely in world capital flows, extraordinary patterns have emerged. Capital flows have become strongly negative for developing countries on a net basis, that is, capital has flown from poor to rich countries. This has been a striking feature of international financialization, marking a profound difference with the period of imperialism. The reverse flow of capital has not originated in actions taken by capitalist enterprises and other private agents but in actions by public agents in both developed and developing countries. The phenomenon of reverse capital flows is associated with the contemporary role of world money which has affected the hierarchy among capitalist countries in the world market as well as lending a subordinate character to financialization in developing countries.

The Washington Consensus has, furthermore, encouraged entry of foreign banks into developing countries. The rationale has typically been that foreign banks would improve efficiency while helping to meet domestic credit shortages. In practice, entry by foreign banks into developing countries since the 1990s has had unexpected results including the redirection of bank lending toward personal income. Foreign bank entry has been a factor leading to subordinate financialization.

In the following section subordinate financialization is considered primarily in connection with capital flows and foreign bank entry. The reversal of capital flows has entailed significant costs for developing countries, resembling the imposition of an informal tribute paid by developing to developed countries, above all, to the US. The reversal of capital flows has also contributed to strong growth of domestic financial markets, particularly for middle-income countries, thus further catalysing domestic financialization. Foreign bank entry, on the other hand, has also promoted domestic financialization encouraging phenomena reminiscent of the transformation of finance in developed countries.

Reversal of net capital flows

Fundamental to subordinate financialization have been the flows of both international capital and international trade, particularly after the Asian crisis of 1997–98. Figure 46 sums up net global flows of value between developed and developing countries. Stand-

---

26   For the factors accounting for the growth of FDI, bank and portfolio flows between developed and developing as well as among developing countries, see the world investment reports by UNCTAD for the years 1999, 2002, 2003, 2005, and 2006.

FIG. 46 Net global capital flows, emerging and developing countries, $bn

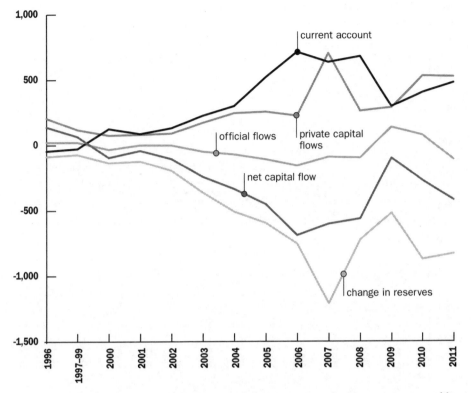

Source: World Economic Outlook, IMF, 2009. Net capital flows comprise net direct investment, net portfolio investment, and other long- and short-term net investment flows, including official and private.

ard categories are deployed, following IMF methodology; flows are defined as private, official, current account, and reserve, the sum of which results in an overall net flow.

A remarkable aspect of global flows has been the growing divergence between private and official flows after 2002. The Asian crisis of 1997–98 led to a collapse of private flows, but during 2002–2007 there was a strong recovery. During the same period, however, net official flows became negative, partly because aid flows remained weak, but mostly because developing countries repaid official debts, especially debts to international organizations that had been accumulated at the end of the 1990s. The expansion of capital flows in the 2000s ended in collapse, similarly to the late 1990s, but the outcomes of the ensuing crisis have been quite different.

Figure 47 affords further insight into private capital flows by showing their composition. Once again, standard IMF categories are deployed: foreign direct investment, portfolio, and 'other' flows – the last indicating mostly short-term bank lending.

FDI has been by far the most vigorous component of private flows in the 2000s, expanding even after the Asian crisis. The balance of productive capacity across the

FIG. 47 Private capital flows, emerging and developing countries, $bn

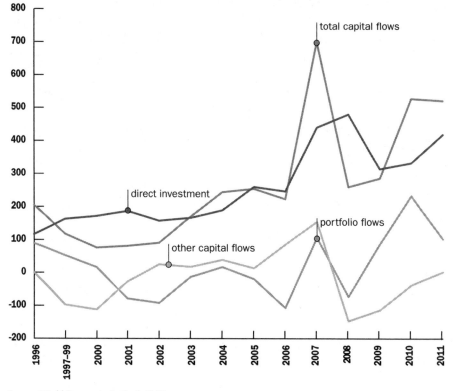

Source: World Economic Outlook, IMF, 2009

world has changed significantly as domestic capitalist accumulation has continued to expand in several developing countries.[27] Portfolio flows, on the other hand, have been weak and fluctuating throughout the period, but have rebounded strongly after the crisis of the 2000s as loanable capital in mature countries has sought profits in developing countries. 'Other' flows have remained weak until 2005, subsequently recovering strongly, even though far from uniformly across developing countries, as is shown below. However, 'other' flows declined severely once the crisis of the 2000s had burst out. The expansion of short-term flows has proven precarious, and was sharply reversed once financial turmoil had engulfed banks.

Figure 46 further shows that, during this period, substantial current account surpluses

---

27   Considerable care is needed in interpreting FDI. A significant proportion is in practice investment by financial institutions of developed countries in the financial systems of developing countries. Furthermore, portfolio investment is technically classified as FDI if it involves purchasing more than 10% of an enterprise listed in the stock market.

have emerged among developing countries. Underlying this phenomenon has been the closer integration of developing countries into the world market as policies of trade liberalization have been generally adopted after the 1980s. Increasing integration has held even for low-income countries in Africa and Asia, judging by exports relative to GDP.[28]

The trajectory of the current account in the 2000s has varied significantly among developing countries in line with trade specialization and other historically specific factors. However, two broad groups of developing countries stand out. The first comprises countries that have gained share in international manufacturing, most prominently China, and thus earned substantial surpluses from exports to developed countries, including consumer goods to the US and Western Europe. The second comprises commodities exporters, above all, oil exporters, including Russia and the Gulf countries, but also exporters of industrial metals. Rising commodity prices around the middle of the decade resulted in substantial trade surpluses for exporters, though less for agricultural raw materials.

By far the most striking aspect of figure 46, however, has been the growth of reserve holdings by developing countries. Accumulation of reserves is ultimately the reason why the net global flow of capital has been reversed leading to capital flowing from poor to rich countries. Reserve accumulation and the net outflow of capital from poor to rich countries became smaller during and after the crisis of 2007–2009 as current account surpluses declined in the global recession of 2008–2009, but the underlying trend has again manifested itself after 2009. This is a remarkable feature of subordinate financialization that runs counter to the precepts of the Washington Consensus regarding capital flows – that capital would flow from rich to poor countries.[29]

Table 1 gives further detail on reserve accumulation by developing countries. China has dominated reserve holdings, possessing more than a third of total reserves, on account of its persistent current account surpluses; significant other holders have included oil exporters. The most remarkable holder of reserves, however, is Sub-Saharan Africa, whose holdings have increased dramatically during the period. As subordinate financialization has spread, even impoverished Africa has contributed to the net flow of capital from poor to rich countries.

---

28   Massoud Karshenas, 'The Impact of the Global Financial and Economic Crisis on LDC Economies', United Nations Office of the High Representative for the Least Developed Countries, Landlocked Developed Countries and Small Island Developing States, 2009.

29   Hence it has been the cause of some bafflement among mainstream economists; see Eswar Prasad, Rajan Raghuram and Arvind Subramanian, 'Foreign Capital and Economic Growth', *Brookings Papers on Economic Activity* 38, 2007, pp. 153–230. Note that the actual out-turn of capital flows has been far more problematic than the issue that troubled Robert Lucas – namely the lack of sustained flow of capital from rich to poor; see Robert E. Lucas, 'Why Doesn't Capital Flow from Rich to Poor Countries?', *American Economic Review* 80:2, 1990. In the 2000s there has been a large flow of capital from poor to rich.

TABLE 1 Reserves of emerging and developing countries, US $bn

	China	India	Russia	Brazil	Mexico	Sub-Saharan Africa	Central and Eastern Europe
2001	216.3	46.4	33.1	35.6	44.8	35.5	72.8
2002	292.00	68.2	44.6	37.5	50.6	35.9	89.2
2003	409.2	99.5	73.8	48.9	59.00	39.8	110.6
2004	615.5	127.2	121.5	52.5	64.1	62.2	129.2
2005	822.5	132.5	176.5	53.3	74.1	82.9	157.9
2006	1069.5	171.3	296.2	85.2	76.3	115.8	196.3
2007	1531.3	267.6	466.7	179.5	87.1	146.3	248.9
2008	2134.5	271.7	421.3	192.9	94.6	163.5	258.6
2009	2847.3	258.7	416.7	239.1	90.9	155.1	287.6
2010	3253.6	267.8	443.6	288.6	113.6	157.9	324.4
2011	3181.1	262.9	454.0	352.0	142.5	180.1	339.1

Source: World Economic Outlook, IMF, 2009

There are several reasons why developing countries have accumulated reserves in the 2000s. The shock of the reversal of private capital flows in 1997–98 has encouraged a policy of so-called 'self-insurance'. This is an unfortunate euphemism for the policy of keeping expensive reserves imposed on developing countries by the functioning of the dollar as world money. Developing countries were left to fend for themselves in an environment of re-strengthened private flows in the 2000s, and hence attempted to reduce exposure to short–term and portfolio flows. Along similar lines, developing countries have increased reserves to protect themselves from the potentially disastrous implications of sudden private capital flow reversals.[30] 'Self-insurance' has been actively enforced by the World Bank and the IMF monitoring the levels of reserves relative to exports and to domestic monetary growth of even the poorest developing countries. Three rules have been used in practice to set the level of reserves; first, that the ratio of reserves to imports should be sufficient to confront an unexpected deterioration of the balance of trade; second, that the ratio of reserves to short–term external debt should be enough to cover all short term external debt due for a period ahead, typically twelve months (the Greenspan–Guidotti rule); third, that the ratio of reserves to the money

30　Alan Greenspan, 'Currency Reserves and Debt', Remarks Before the World Bank Confer-ence on Recent Trends in Reserves Management, Washington, DC, 29 April 1999. Matthieu Bussiere and Christian Mulder, 'External Vulnerability in Emerging Market Economies: How High Liquidity Can Offset Weak Fundamentals and the Effects of Contagion', IMF Working Paper WP/99/88, International Monetary Fund, July 1999.

supply should be sufficient to deal with a sudden capital outflow (typically reserves should correspond to 20 percent of M2).

Reserve accumulation has also resulted from exchange rate policies adopted by developing countries.[31] On the one hand, developing countries with current account surpluses have attempted to prevent exchange rates from rising. On the other, policies of inflation targeting have often been forced on developing countries as part of the Washington Consensus. Inflation targeting has meant that exchange rates were pegged relative to the dollar or other major currencies to control imported inflation; to be able to defend the peg, developing countries have had to accumulate reserves. By the same token, developing countries have adopted high domestic interest rates, thus even resulting in rising exchange rates during this period. The latter have encouraged forms of 'carry trade', that is, domestic residents borrowing abroad in order to invest in financial assets in developing countries.[32] As borrowing abroad rose, so did the pressure to hold reserves. The end result has been that developing countries have exported capital to the developed core of the world market. This is perhaps the most remarkable aspect of subordinate financialization and closely connected to the role of the dollar as world money.

World money forces subordinate financialization

The precise composition of international reserves is not publicly available, but there is little doubt that the bulk comprises US dollars. The policy of reserve accumulation has thus amounted to developing countries storing dollars in order to be able to participate in international trade and to confront financial flows in the world market. In terms of the Marxist theory of money discussed in Chapter 4, reserve accumulation is intensified hoarding of the dollar as world money. The extent of such hoarding by developing countries is unprecedented, in view especially of the US dollar being nothing more that

---

31   This is misleadingly called a 'mercantilist' practice in Michael P. Dooley, David Folkerts-Landau, and Peter Garber, 'An Essay on the Revived Bretton Woods System', NBER Working Paper No. 9971, 2003. There is nothing mercantilist about the policy of hoarding reserves as protection against the vagaries of the world market, particularly since developing countries have been encouraged to integrate their economies further in the world market. Reserve accumulation is a practice foisted upon developing countries by the logic of international markets, not by some outdated doctrine. In any case, Aizenman and Lee find that the 'precautionary' motive dominates the 'mercantilist' motive in holding international reserves. See Joshua Aizenman and Jaewoo Lee, 'International Reserves: Precautionary Versus Mercantilist Views: Hypothesis and Evidence', *Open Economies Review* 18, 2007; Joshua Aizenman and Jaewoo Lee, 'International Reserves: Precautionary Versus Mercantilist Views: Theory and Evidence', IMF Working Paper WP/05/198, October 2005.

32   Juan Pablo Painceira, 'Developing Countries in the Era of Financialisation: From Deficit Accumulation to Reserve Accumulation', RMF Discussion Papers 4, February 2009.

state-backed central money resting on US government securities. In effect, developing countries have been accumulating vast hoards of a form of money that rests solely on the promise of the US government to pay an (intrinsically valueless) dollar for every nominal dollar of its debt.

For this reason, the safest way for developing countries to accumulate dollars has been to purchase US public debt. The expansion of reserves by developing countries during the 2000s has thus meant that official institutions, primarily central banks, have held a growing share of US public securities. More specifically, an increasing proportion of US Treasury securities have been held abroad in the 2000s, including long-term securities issued by the Government Sponsored Agencies that are the backbone of the US housing market.[33] The capital flows associated with reserve holdings, consequently, have emerged from transactions among states, or public agents, not among private capitalists. These flows have also had a direct connection to the US housing bubble, discussed in Chapter 9.

Increasing hoards of quasi-world-money by developing countries, therefore, represent a form of official lending by developing countries to the US state undertaken with funds that could have been potentially invested domestically to support development. Consequently, international capital flows and reserves of world money have created a source of gain for the US economy under conditions of financialized capitalism. Developing countries have been implicitly subsidizing the hegemonic power in the world market purely to gain access to the dominant form of (valueless) world money.[34]

The cost of the subsidy for developing countries has been gauged through a variety of methods.[35] One way has been to focus on countries that have received significant inflows of private short-term capital and have thus been obliged to keep sizeable reserves in order to offset the risk of sudden reversal of flows. This group of developing countries has effectively received significant borrowing from abroad – incurred by private enterprises – and proceeded to 'insure' the private debts by advancing official loans to the US. The private borrowing, however, would have typically occurred at commercial rates of interest, while the 'insurance' earned much lower official US interest rates. In a pioneering study, Dani Rodrik has estimated the social cost of such an 'insurance' policy at perhaps 1 percent of developing country GDP.[36]

---

33   Ibid.

34   Japan has also been providing a vast subsidy to the US on a similar basis and for far longer, but the relationship between the two mature countries has little bearing on subordinate financialization.

35   Even without counting the risk of capital losses, if the dollar were to depreciate significantly in the future.

36   Dani Rodrik, 'The Social Cost of Foreign Exchange Reserves', NBER Working Paper No. 11952, January 2006. An alternative calculation of the cost has been proposed by Yılmaz Akyüz using the difference between borrowing rates and the annual carry costs of reserves, while also

Note that the beneficiaries of this informal tribute paid by the global poor to the US have included not only the US public sector but also capitalists in developing countries. Private enterprises and others in developing countries have been able to borrow abroad at rates that were typically lower than domestic rates, while indirectly 'insuring' the debt by imposing the costs on society as a whole. Moreover, private borrowers have also used the funds to invest in domestic financial assets in a form of 'carry trade' that has allowed for the direct appropriation by private borrowers of the benefits of interest rate spreads. Reserve accumulation has thus induced internal differentiation in developing countries.

A further way of gauging the cost of reserves for countries that run significant current account surpluses, or for poor countries in receipt of foreign aid, has been to focus on the impact on monetary policy.[37] Acquisition of reserves by central banks has typically been sterilized to prevent the growth of domestic money that could have jeopardized inflation targets. But the liabilities that central banks have issued to undertake sterilization have typically borne domestic interest rates. Domestic rates have tended to be significantly higher than interest rates on the foreign public assets also acquired by central banks, partly due to inflation targeting. The spread between domestic and foreign rates is a cost imposed on the central bank and thus carried by society as a whole. The main beneficiary has naturally been the US, since it has been able to continue borrowing at low rates. However, there have also been significant domestic implications for the financial systems of developing countries.

One of the most important domestic implications for developing countries has been increased issuing of public securities. Domestic bond markets have grown strongly across a range of developing countries since the middle of the 1990s, mostly in Asia which holds by far the largest foreign exchange reserves, but also in Latin America and elsewhere. The growth of domestic financial markets has represented increased financial deepening in developing countries and has promoted subordinate financialization. The availability of liquid domestic public securities has facilitated further financial transactions while also allowing for the emergence of new financial institutions in developing countries. Above all, expanded liquidity has made it possible for domestic banks to turn toward

---

referring to the distinction between borrowed and earned reserves ('Managing Financial Instability in Emerging Markets: a Keynesian Perspective', *METU Studies in Development*, 35:1, 2008). The same distinction has been deployed by Jacques Polak and Peter Clark in their calculation of the cost ('Reducing the Costs of Holding Reserves', *The New Public Finance*, ed. Inge Kaul and Pedro Conceição, Oxford: Oxford University Press, 2006).

37   See, for instance, J. Onno de Beaufort Wijnholds and Lars Søndergaard, 'Reserve Accumulation: Objective or By-Product?', European Central Bank, Occasional Paper Series, No 73, 2007; Joshua Aizenman and Reuven Glick, 'Sterilization, Monetary Policy, and Global Financial Integration', NBER Working Paper No. 13902, 2008; and Joshua Aizenman and Reuven Glick, 'Pegged Exchange Rate Regimes: A Trap?', *Journal of Money, Credit and Banking* 40:4, 2008.

open financial markets as well as toward transactions involving domestic households.[38] Characteristic forms of financialization have begun to emerge in developing countries, further accelerated by the entry of foreign banks in the 1990s and 2000s.

Foreign bank entry during the last two decades has placed significant proportions of total banking assets under foreign ownership in middle-income developing countries. However, there has also been sustained foreign bank entry even in low-income regions, including in Africa where foreign ownership has come to dominate banking assets in a host of countries.[39] The entry of foreign banks has inevitably had complex outcomes for growth as well as for the performance of the domestic financial sector. Mainstream economists have often advocated foreign bank entry on the grounds that foreign banks have superior efficiency and would therefore improve the performance of domestic financial systems as well as ameliorating persistent credit shortages for small and medium enterprises.[40] But even the mainstream has had doubts on whether the skills of foreign banks in assessing 'hard' information would be appropriate for developing countries in which lending has traditionally tended to rely on 'soft' information.[41]

A notable outcome of foreign bank entry has been the growth of banking operations aiming at personal and household income, particularly in middle-income countries in the 2000s. Foreign banks have expanded provision of mortgage and credit-card

---

38   For analysis of the characteristic instances of Brazil and South Korea, see Juan Pablo Painceira, 'Central Banking in Middle Income Countries in the Course of Financialisation: A Study with Special Reference to Brazil and Korea', unpublished PhD thesis, University of London, 2011.

39   Massoud Karshenas, 'The Impact of the Global Financial and Economic Crisis on LDC Economies', United Nations Office of the High Representative for the Least Developed Countries, Landlocked Developed Countries and Small Island Developing States, 2009.

40   The literature on this topic is extensive. For arguments in favour of foreign bank entry in terms of the putative benefits for domestic financial systems, including the operations of central banks, see Ross Levine, 'Financial Development and Economic Growth', *Journal of Economic Literature* 35:2, 1997; Michael Gavin and Ricardo Hausmann, 'Securing Stability and Growth in a Shock-Prone Region', in *Securing Stability and Growth in Latin America*, ed. Ricardo Hausmann and Helmut Reisen, Paris: Organisation for Economic Co-operation and Development, 1996; Stijn Claessens and Tom Glaessner, 'The Internationalization of Financial Services in Asia', World Bank Policy Research Working Paper 1911, 1998; Stijns Claessens, Asli Demirgüç-Kunt, and Harry Huizinga, 'How Does Foreign Bank Entry Affect Domestic Banking Markets?', *Journal of Banking and Finance* 25, 2001; and George Clarke et al., 'Foreign Bank Entry: Experience, Implications for Developing Economies and Agenda for Further Research' *The World Bank Research Observer* 18:1, 2003. For an excellent critical discussion, see Paulo Dos Santos, 'Foreign Capital and Familial Control in Philippine Banking', unpublished PhD thesis, University of London, 2007.

41   Thierry Tressel, Enrica Detragiache, and Poonam Gupta, 'Foreign Banks in Poor Countries: Theory and Evidence' IMF Working Paper No. 06/18, International Monetary Fund, 2006.

lending as well as related financial services. Furthermore, domestic banks have also been attracted to the field, thus accelerating the financialization of personal income. The result has been sustained growth of personal indebtedness in a host of developing countries, including among the poor.[42]

Summing up, the 2000s have been a period of accelerated integration of developing countries into the processes of world trade and finance – with significant variations – which has lent an international as well as a domestic aspect to subordinate financialization. In the 2000s there has been strong growth of FDI and significant short-term lending, but weak portfolio flows from developed to developing countries. At the same time, developing countries have registered large current account surpluses through rising commodity prices and manufacturing exports. Above all, there has been enormous accumulation of foreign exchange reserves by developing countries. The result has been the emergence of negative net capital flows: poor countries have financed a select few among the rich countries, mostly the US.

Holding enormous hoards of dollars as world money has been an integral part of subordinate financialization. The costs to developing countries have been substantial, gauged either as the spread between domestic and foreign interest rates or as the cost of sterilization by central banks. Developing countries have been paying an implicit tribute to developed countries, mostly to the US, the hegemonic issuer of the dollar. Reserve accumulation has contributed to the growth of domestic financial markets, thus also boosting domestic financialization. Sustained foreign bank entry into developing countries has exacerbated subordinate financialization by encouraging a shift of banking practices toward open financial markets and personal income as source of financial profits. Domestic financial expropriation appears to have taken root in several developing countries in the 2000s, resulting in rising individual indebtedness.

---

42   For a detailed discussion of such processes occurring in Turkey, see Nuray Ergüneş, 'Global Integration of the Turkish Economy in the Era of Financialisation', RMF Discussion Paper 7, 2009; also published in Lapavitsas (ed.), *Financialisation in Crisis*. A meticulous study of household lending by banks to workers in developing countries has been undertaken using Turkish data in Elif Karacimen, 'Political Economy of Consumer Debt in Developing Countries: Evidence from Turkey', unpublished PhD thesis, University of London, 2013.

APPENDIX

THE FINANCING OF AGGREGATE INVESTMENT: METHODOLOGY

Data sources

US	Federal Reserve System, *Flow of Funds*, Table F.102
UK	Office for National Statistics, *Financial Statistics*, Tables 11.1D and 14.3C
Germany	Eurostat, *Annual Sector Accounts*
Japan	Bank of Japan, *Flow of Funds*; Cabinet Office, Government of Japan, *Historical Statistics of Japan*, Tables 3-29-b and 3-30-a (1980–2003); Cabinet Office, Government of Japan, *National Accounts, 2010*, Flow, Tables 2.2, 3.1 (2001–2010)

The main identity:

Gross capital formation =

= internal funding + net external funding =

= internal funding + (net bank credit + net market funding + net other external funding)

1. US

Internal funds = gross saving including foreign earnings retained abroad less net capital transfers paid.

Net external sources for each type of finance are calculated as the difference between the corresponding liabilities and assets.

	Liabilities	Assets
Bank credit	Depository institution loans n.e.c., other loans and advances, mortgages	Checkable deposits and currency, total time and savings deposits, private foreign deposits
Market funding	Net new equity issues, commercial paper, municipal securities, corporate bonds	Money market fund shares, security RPs, commercial paper, Treasury securities, agency- and GSE-backed securities, municipal securities, mortgages, mutual fund shares
Trade credit	Trade payables	Trade receivables, consumer credit
Other	Miscellaneous liabilities, taxes payable	Miscellaneous assets

Statistical discrepancy is calculated as a sum of all net sources of finance as percentage of capital expenditures less 100 percent.

2. UK

Internal funds = gross saving.
Net external sources for each type of finance are calculated as the difference between the corresponding liabilities and assets.

	Liabilities	Assets
Bank credit	Short-term loans, long-term loans secured on dwellings, finance leasing	Currency and deposits
Market funding	Securities other than shares, shares and other equity	Securities other than shares, shares and other equity
Other	Direct investment loans (outward and inward), other loans by UK residents, other loans by the rest of the world, other accounts receivable/payable	Direct investment loans (outward and inward), finance leasing, long term loans by UK residents, prepayments of insurance premiums etc., other accounts receivable/payable

Statistical discrepancy is calculated as the sum of all net sources of finance as percentage of gross capital formation less 100 percent. Gross capital formation is the sum of gross fixed capital formation, changes in inventories, and acquisitions less disposals of valuables.

3. GERMANY

Data for non-financial corporations are consolidated.
Internal funds = gross saving.
Net external sources for each type of finance are calculated as the difference between the corresponding liabilities and assets.

	Liabilities	Assets
Bank credit	Short- and long-term loans	Currency and deposits
Market funding	Securities other than shares (short- and long-term), shares and other equity (excluding mutual funds shares)	Securities other than shares (short- and long-term), financial derivatives, shares and other equity (excluding mutual funds shares), mutual funds shares
Other	Net equity of households in life insurance reserves and in pension funds reserves, other accounts receivable/payable	Short- and long-term loans, prepayments of insurance premiums and reserves for outstanding claims, other accounts receivable/payable

Statistical discrepancy is calculated as the sum of all net sources of finance as percentage of gross capital formation less 100 percent. Gross capital formation is the sum of gross fixed capital formation, changes in inventories, and acquisitions less disposals of valuables.

4. JAPAN

Data are on a fiscal year basis. Non-financial corporations comprise private and public non-financial corporations.

Gross capital formation is calculated as the sum of gross fixed capital formation and changes in inventories.

Internal funds = gross saving.

Net external sources for each type of finance are calculated as the difference between the corresponding liabilities and assets.

	Liabilities	Assets
Bank credit	loans by private financial institutions, loans by public financial institutions, deposits money	currency and deposits, deposits with the Fiscal Loan Fund, deposits money
Market funding	repurchase agreements and securities lending transactions, securities other than shares, shares and other equities, financial derivatives	repurchase agreements and securities lending transactions, securities other than shares, shares and other equities, financial derivatives
Other	loans by the non-financial sector, instalment credit (not included in consumer credit), trade credits and foreign trade credits, accounts receivable/payable, other external claims and debts, others	call loans and money, loans by the non-financial sector, instalment credit (not included in consumer credit), trade credits and foreign trade credits, accounts receivable/payable, outward direct investment, outward investment in securities, other external claims and debts, others

Statistical discrepancy is calculated as the sum of all net sources of finance as percentage of gross capital formation less 100 percent.

National accounts for Japan contain data on financial transactions – namely, acquisition of financial assets and liabilities. These data are available in capital finance accounts published by the Cabinet Office, Government of Japan, in *Historical Statistics of Japan* (Table 3-30-a). Using the same data source for external finance as for gross saving and gross capital formation would have had the benefit of assuring compatibility between the measures of internal funds and investment, on the one hand, and external funding, on the other hand. There is nevertheless a drawback: the capital finance accounts do not provide sufficient detail to decompose external funds into bank credit and market funding. In particular, on the liability side, Table 3-30-a contains data on total loans of the non-financial corporations. Total loans would be, however, a poor proxy for bank credit proper. In addition to credit from financial institutions, total loans also include loans by the non-financial sector, instalment credit, and repurchase agreements and securities lending transactions. According to the Flow of Funds data available from the Bank of Japan that decompose borrowing into sub-categories, in 1980–2010 loans by private financial institutions and loans by public financial institutions averaged 78 percent of total borrowing by the non-financial corporations. The standard deviation of this ratio over the given time period, however, amounted to 64 percentage points, indicating a high variability of the share of bank credit in total loans. For this reason, to calculate net bank credit, net market funding, and net other external sources of finance as percentage of gross capital formation, Flow of Funds data were used, available through the Bank of Japan, instead of the capital finance accounts provided in Table 3-30-a of the *Historical Statistics of Japan*.

9. TENDING TO CRISIS: GIGANTIC TURMOIL BREAKS OUT IN 2007

Financialization has emerged out of the major economic disturbances of the 1970s signalling the end of the long post-war boom for mature capitalist countries. It has been marked by crises, often pivoting on the financial sector, none of which has been as profound as the global economic turmoil that began in August 2007. This particular crisis emerged in the US financial sector following the burst of the bubble of 2001–2007 that took place mostly in the housing market. A characteristic feature of the bubble was the prominent financialization of personal income, particularly through mortgage lending to US workers, even to the poorest among them.

The bubble had a modest impact on productive accumulation in the US and other mature countries, but the financial shock from its burst induced a global recession in 2008–2009, through both financial and trade mechanisms. The recessionary effect varied greatly across the world, and it took more than a year before its worst consequences emerged in Europe. The eurozone crisis, commencing in full earnest in 2010, ushered in a new phase of the global tumult revealing a further proneness of financialization toward instability, associated in particular with the role of world money.

The gigantic turmoil of the 2000s is a crisis of financialization that has brought to the fore several characteristic aspects of the period. For one thing, it has put in sharp perspective the transformation of banks, including lending to households and trading loanable capital in open markets. Banks have faced intractable problems of liquidity and solvency, while households and states have been weighed down with debts; indebtedness, on the other hand, has been less severe for industrial and commercial enterprises. The crisis has also cast light on the pivotal role of the state in sustaining financialization in mature countries. Central bank intervention has repeatedly rescued banks while ameliorating the impact of crisis on real accumulation.

Above all, the protracted and continually evolving nature of the turmoil has indicated that the proneness of financialized capitalism toward crisis is deeply embedded and will not be easily countermanded. The rise of finance and the penetration of economic life by financial practices have exacerbated the inherent propensity of capitalist accumulation toward instability and crisis. This chapter examines the crisis of the 2000s to draw broader conclusions about the causes and mechanisms of instability in financialized capitalism. The analysis also lays the ground for a general discussion of state intervention in financialized economies in Chapter 10. The first step in this respect is briefly to consider Marx's discussion of finance as a factor of capitalist crises.

Marx on finance and crises

Marx did not develop a coherent theory of crisis, although he offered a wealth of insights on the causes of crises, not all of which were entirely consistent with each other. For Marx, capitalist crises occur necessarily within capitalist accumulation, reflecting the fundamental contradictions between use-value and value in production, but also the lack of conscious organization of the capitalist economy. In turn, crises function as opportunities to restructure capitalist production thus making possible renewed bouts of accumulation.

Capitalist economic reproduction is organized through autonomous market interactions which give rise to price changes inducing corresponding flows of commodities and money. These flows enable the production of surplus value, and allow for the reproduction of the economy as a whole. The causes of crisis typically emanate from the sphere of production. However the immediate form of crisis is that of markets failing to clear because prices, money and commodities stop relating to each other as 'normal'. On one side, commodities (including labour) lie unsold, while on the other money lies idle – reproduction is disturbed as the relationship between prices, commodities and money breaks down.[1] In more conventional terms, unemployment emerges, there is excess supply of commodities, and liquidity is hoarded. At the same time, crises are a violent way of restoring the 'normal' interaction among prices, money and commodities. The sphere of production is restructured, the extraction of surplus value is placed on a new footing, and reproduction overcomes the disturbance.

Marxist theorists generally acknowledge the existence of an integral commercial – or market – dimension to capitalist crises; typically, however, market disequilibria are ascribed to the underlying processes of capitalist production. It is widely accepted in Marxist economics that crises occur because of contradictory tendencies of accumulation in the sphere of production which result in markets being thrown out of equilibrium. It is similarly accepted that crises are the lever through which the capitalist economy overcomes the disturbance, allowing accumulation to proceed anew until the contradictions of production reignite a crisis. In the wake of Marx's own writings, nonetheless, several Marxist theories have emerged contesting the specific causes of crisis within capitalist production.[2]

---

1   See, for instance, Karl Marx, *Grundrisse*, London: Penguin/NLR, 1973, pp. 410–20.

2   There is an inherent tension within Marxist theories of crisis which has been discussed by Richard Day in an excellent book that is unfortunately little read today (*The Crisis and the 'Crash'*, London: NLB, 1981). As Day argues, Marx's own analysis tends to be about cyclical crises, but subsequent Marxist writing has focused on secular crises. Thus, the classical Marxist debates on imperialism, and the subsequent Soviet debates, were largely about secular, long-term phenomena. Day's point is important and broadly holds for several of the Marxist theories of crisis and financialization considered in Chapter 2. Note, however, that both the form and the content of capitalist crisis have changed since the time of Marx's writings as monopolization has proceeded and state intervention has become vital to the capitalist economy. The short, sharp episodes of crisis that Marx witnessed in the middle of the nineteenth century have given way to periods of protracted turmoil of accumulation. The crisis of the 2000s has already lasted for five years and could well continue for longer. Thus, the shift of analysis toward a long-term outlook reflects reality and is not merely a theoretical quirk.

The well-known approaches of overaccumulation, disproportionality among the sectors of the economy, and underconsumption can find support in Marx's own work, though certainly not to the same extent.[3] Overaccumulation theories, in particular, have been the dominant approach during the last four decades. The cause of crisis is taken to be a fall of the rate of profit, resulting from the tendency of the organic composition of capital to rise as capitalists introduce labour-saving technologies.[4] Broadly speaking, crises occur because the accumulation of industrial capital is predicated on continuous introduction of new technology, thus altering the relationship between capital and labour, raising the organic composition of capital, and leading to a fall in the rate of profit.[5] The disturbance of profitability is manifested as the inability of enterprises to sell output, which entails collapsing markets, decline in production, bankruptcies, and rising unemployment. The resulting crisis opens a period of restructuring of capital that could potentially restore profitability, thus preparing the terrain for renewed accumulation.

On the other hand, there are also Marxist theories of crisis, such as disproportionality and underconsumption, which draw on 'realization' problems. Deficient 'realization' essentially amounts to aggregate demand falling short of aggregate supply, output remaining unsold, and thus leading to a fall in the rate of profit. 'Realization' problems can occur because of disproportions between the departments of capitalist production – Department I producing means of production and Department II producing means of consumption – a reflection of the unplanned and anarchical character of capitalism; the classic exposition of this view can be found in Tugan-Baranovsky's

---

3   For further discussion of this point see Makoto Itoh and Costas Lapavitsas, *Political Economy of Money and Finance*, London: Macmillan, 1999, ch. 6.

4   This approach has underpinned the influential Anglo-Saxon strain on Marxist theories of crisis after the 1970s. Elements of it can be found in Maurice Dobb, *Political Economy and Capitalism*, London: Routledge and Kegan Paul, 1937; and Maurice Dobb, *Theories of Value and Distribution*, Cambridge: Cambridge University Press, 1973; but even more significantly in Henryk Grossman, *Law of the Accumulation and Breakdown of the Capitalist System*, Leipzig: Hirschfeld, 1929; and Paul Mattick, *Economic Crisis and Crisis Theories*, Armonk, NY: M.E. Sharpe, 1981.

5   Several aspects of this approach were considered in Chapter 2 in connection with theories of financialization. Anwar Shaikh is perhaps the most prominent exponent of the view that crises are due to tendencies in production leading to a fall in the rate of profit. See Shaikh, 'Political Economy and Capitalism: Notes on Dobb's Theory of Crisis', *Cambridge Journal of Economics* 2:2, 1978; 'An Introduction to the History of Crisis Theories', in *US Capitalism in Crisis*, New York: Monthly Review Press, 1978; 'The Falling Rate of Profit and the Economic Crisis in the US', in *The Imperiled Economy*, New York: Union of Radical Political Economics, 1987; 'The Falling Rate of Profit and Long Waves in Accumulation', in *New Findings in Long Wave Research*, London: Macmillan, 1992; and 'Explaining the Global Economic Crisis', *Historical Materialism* 5, Winter 1999.

Les Crises industrielles en Angleterre. Disproportionality theory was influential at the time of classical Marxist debates on imperialism, but has largely fallen by the wayside in recent decades. 'Realization' problems can further occur because of the restricted consumption of the working class which results in a deficiency of aggregate demand. The tradition of 'underconsumption' is closely associated with Luxemburg's *The Accumulation of Capital* but also includes Baran and Sweezy's *Monopoly Capital* in the post-war era. The influence of underconsumption theory is limited at present, though the current has been instrumental to developing the concept of financialization, as was shown in Chapter 2.

This chapter does not intend to review Marx's insights on crisis, much less to examine subsequent debates on crisis theory among Marxists. Its objective is to discuss crises of financialized capitalism, thus suffice it in the next section to focus on Marx's analysis of the relation between the financial system and economic crisis. On this basis, an analytical approach to the turmoil of the 2000s could be developed in the latter parts of the chapter. To this purpose consider, first, the place of money and finance in Marx's discussion of crises and, second, the historical and institutional background against which Marx developed his views on crises.

Marx's analysis of money and finance as integral aspects of capitalist crisis

For Marx, capitalist crises have integral monetary and financial aspects, even if their causes lie within the sphere of production. Monetary and financial aspects were fundamental to Marx's analysis of the violent and sudden fluctuations characteristic of crises. After all, it is extremely difficult to capture in theory the violent shifts that mark capitalist crises without referring to the drying up of credit, or to the need to settle past obligations. Typical factors that induce a sudden worsening of economic activity in a capitalist economy are the fixed period of repayment embedded in credit relations and the ineluctable nature of debt settlement. Consequently, Marx devoted substantial effort to the study of the credit aspects of crisis, as is apparent in part five of the third volume of *Capital*.[6]

Unfortunately the monetary and financial elements of Marx's analysis of crises have been rather marginal to Anglo-Saxon Marxist debates on crisis since the 1970s. The tradition of the Uno School – and of Japanese Marxism in general – is very different in this regard, paying systematic attention to the monetary and financial aspects of capitalist crises. Drawing on the work of the Uno current and simplifying greatly it is

---

6   Recent research has begun to establish the meticulous attention with which Marx followed the financial and credit disturbances of his time. For instance, on Marx's notes regarding the great financial crisis that commenced in 1866 and brought the collapse of Overend, Gurney and Co., see João Antonio de Paula et al., 'Marx in 1869: Notebook B113, The Economist and The Money Market Review', Discussion Paper No. 417, Cedeplar, Universidade Federal de Minas Gerais, 2011.

possible to piece together a coherent account of Marx's analysis of the monetary and financial aspects of the capitalist crises of his time.[7]

The starting point of Marx's analysis is trade credit, which is assumed to expand in the course of a boom, creating large volumes of bills of exchange and thereby stretching production and trade.[8] As the boom unfolds, however, banking credit enters strongly into play: banks discount bills of exchange, thus supplying loanable money capital that covers the needs of capitalists for liquid funds. At the later stages of the boom, financial speculation begins to occur on a large scale mostly by creating bills of exchange purely to be discounted by banks. Such bills are often tenuously related, or even completely unrelated to productive activity. The overextension of credit (both trade and banking) contributes to overaccumulation and overproduction, resulting in inventory accumulation and excess supply in commodity markets. Given the difficulty of sales, the expansion begins to unravel and a commercial crisis emerges.

For Marx, the appearance of commercial crisis has a decisive impact on the overextended mechanisms of credit.[9] Inability to sell finished output implies inability to honour maturing bills of exchange on the part of borrowing capitalists. Consequently banks begin to accumulate non-performing assets. As the quality of bank assets falls and the creditworthiness of borrowers declines, banks become reluctant to lend. The restriction of banking credit occurs at a moment when liquid money capital is heavily demanded by functioning capitalists pressed by the difficulty of selling. Gradually banks become reluctant to lend even to each other, with the result that the money market becomes extremely tight and interest rates rise rapidly. That is, an absolute shortage of liquidity begins to emerge.

Faced with a liquidity shortage, capitalists no longer demand money capital to sustain or expand the circuit of productive capital. Rather, they are under pressure to obtain plain money to settle bills and other loans that fall due. Maturing loans would have been incurred during the upswing in the expectation that liquidity would be easily available at the time of settlement from banks, or elsewhere. But the destruction of confidence among banks implies that fresh funds are not forthcoming; the banks (and other participants in the money market) prefer to hoard money. In a liquidity crisis, cash becomes king and promises to pay among private capitalists are devalued. In a remarkable turn of phrase, Marx claimed that in a capitalist crisis there is 'a sudden transformation of the credit system into monetary system'.[10]

---

7   For further discussion of this issue, see Itoh and Lapavitsas, *Political Economy of Money and Finance*, ch. 6. Note that the Uno current typically stresses shortages in the supply of labour (in effect, labour supply bottlenecks) as the main factor inducing the turn of economic activity toward crisis (see for instance, Uno, 1936). However, it is not necessary to accept this particular aspect of the Uno tradition to acknowledge the power of its analysis of money and credit in the course of crisis.

8   See, for instance, Karl Marx, *Capital*, vol. 3, London: Penguin/NLR, 1981, pp. 619–25.

9   Ibid., pp. 674–9; see also the whole of Chapter 34 in ibid.

10 Karl Marx, *A Contribution to the Critique of Political Economy*, Moscow: Progress, 1970, p. 146.

The collapse of private credit leads to higher interest rates and catalyses the industrial aspect of crisis as enterprises go bankrupt, plants are closed and workers are made redundant. Recession thus emerges opening the gates for the restructuring of capital that would subsequently allow for a repetition of boom and bust. The sharp phase of the crisis (the crisis proper) has often already passed by the time recession truly sets in, since the crisis is mostly driven by the inability to obtain liquidity to honour maturing trade debt. After all, the time period of trade debt is typically fixed by customary practice (three months, six months, rarely more than a year) and thus the sharp phase of the crisis would inevitably come to an end as maturity arrived for the bulk of existing obligations. When the economy is in recession, the credit system is both unable and reluctant to generate fresh credit, while industrial and commercial capitals would not seek credit for expansion. For Marx, in short, recessions tend to be periods of weak credit activity and of falling interest rates compared to the heights of the crisis.[11]

Note that in several parts of his discussion of crisis, Marx suggested that the output which capitalists find difficult to sell often comprises exports, while the bills falling due are drawn on importers abroad.[12] The ensuing collapse of credit is thus associated with balance of trade deficits and enforced international flows of loanable money capital, inevitably impacting on exchange rates. Moreover, the preceding boom might also have witnessed rapidly expanding stock market activity. Speculation could have taken place with new industrial projects being floated, often bearing little relation to the underlying processes of value creation. The history of stock markets is replete with destructive flights of investor fancy, from tulips, to the colonization of the Mississipi, to building the railways. The bursting of a stock market bubble would lessen the ability to raise equity capital, thus exacerbating the recession.

Recapping, for Marx, money and finance are integral parts of capitalist crises manifested through the interaction of trade, banking, and money market credit. Crises have monetary and financial dimensions that emerge necessarily from capitalist accumulation. Finance sustains the overaccumulation of capital, and ushers in recession through wholesale destruction of credit and absolute shortages of money. Equivalently, the overaccumulation of capital is necessarily expressed through, and mediated by, monetary and credit mechanisms. The monetary and financial crises that are an integral part of industrial and commercial crises have been called 'type 1' crises.[13]

However, it is implicit in Marx's analysis that, in an economic system of producing, exchanging, and distributing commodities which is permeated by money and credit,

---

11   Marx, *Capital*, vol. 3, p. 622.

12   See, for instance, ibid., pp. 622–3; see also Costas Lapavitsas, 'The Classical Adjustment Mechanism of International Balances: Marx's Critique', *Contributions to Political Economy* 15:1, 1996, pp. 63–79.

13   Itoh and Lapavitsas, *Political Economy of Money and Finance*, p. 124.

crises could also emerge entirely due to the malfunctioning of monetary and credit mechanisms. If money hoards were not present when required; if money flows did not materialize at the requisite levels; if trade and banking credit were not articulated with each other at the required volume, time and place; if, above all, repayment of credit obligations did not occur with the forecast regularity, trade and production would inevitably suffer negative repercussions. For Marxist economic theory, the realm of money and finance contains its own mechanisms sustaining and expanding accumulation, but which could also disrupt accumulation. The monetary and financial crises precipitated by the malfunctioning of monetary and financial mechanisms have been called 'type 2' crises.[14]

Both types of monetary and financial crisis are characteristic of financialized capitalism, in view especially of the penetration of production and circulation by finance. Finance intervenes actively in the organization of financialized accumulation and affects the conduct of non-financial enterprises, banks and households. Consequently, finance tends to shape the crises emanating from accumulation as well as contributing autonomously to the emergence of crises. The crises of financialization have an irreducible financial aspect.

Marx's analysis of the monetary and financial aspects of capitalist crises was historically specific, drawing on the institutional framework of the British financial system in the mid-nineteenth century. Moreover, Marx relied heavily on the classic British monetary debates of the time. Analysis of crises in the period of financialization ought similarly to take into account the institutional and historical framework of financialization in addition to the relevant theoretical debates. It is instructive in this respect briefly to review the institutional and intellectual background against which Marx developed his analysis of money and finance.

Institutional and intellectual context of Marx's analysis of money and finance

Marx's analysis of money and finance was decisively influenced by the debates on monetary policy in Britain in the 1830s, 1840s, and 1850s. At that time well-developed monetary and credit institutions were already active within and among capitalist countries. Britain led the way with a complex credit system that had come into being during the first half of the century. The main instrument of credit was the bill of exchange issued among trading enterprises and subsequently discounted by banks, a feature that is strongly reflected in Marx's analytical work. Country banks engaged in bill discounting through which they transferred capital surpluses from agricultural to industrial areas. These banks had the right to issue their own banknotes usually with a local circulation.[15]

---

14 Ibid.

15 Analysis of institutions and theories in this section draws heavily on Itoh and Lapavitsas, *Political Economy of Money and Finance*, ch. 1–3.

Bills were traded in the London market, in which a variety of other financial enterprises, such as bill brokers, also operated. Banks in London did not have the right to issue their own banknotes, but several had become joint stock enterprises already by the 1840s. The dominant bank in London – by far – was the Bank of England, operating as a semi-public institution, with exclusive rights to issue banknotes that were also the money used among banks for their own transactions, primarily in clearing obligations. The stock market, finally, played a significant role in financing large projects, such as the railways, but did not weigh heavily on the operations of textile and metal enterprises that were the mainstay of British industrial might.

Money in circulation was primarily credit money – banknotes as well as deposits – created by private banks typically in discount of trade credit instruments. Gold also circulated widely alongside credit money, for instance, in personal income spending. The most prominent use of gold, however, was in international transactions, in which it acted as world money settling obligations and deficits among nations. The Bank of England hoarded gold for both international and domestic reasons, keeping a close eye on the fluctuations of its reserves. Once again, these stylized facts of British finance can be easily found in Marx's analysis of crises. During those decades, finally, the City of London had not yet reached the dominant global position which it enjoyed at the end of the nineteenth century. Britain did not yet function fully as the financier of world trade through bills drawn on London. By the same token, though loanable capital was traded internationally, there was no proper world market for short-term funds with a corresponding interest rate.

From the 1820s onwards a succession of economic crises hit Britain, and by extension the world market – in 1825, 1836, 1847, 1856, and 1866 – providing the template against which Marx developed his analysis of crisis. These were industrial and commercial crises, but with clear monetary and credit aspects. Thus, in the boom years that preceded each crisis, prices climbed higher, credit was easily available to industry, and interest rates rose steadily. Crisis manifested itself as sudden scarcity of credit and a rush to hold money. Interest rates rose to usurious heights and money was hoarded leading to bankruptcies. Meanwhile, the balance of trade went into deficit, exchange rates fell, and gold drained abroad. The sharp phase of the crisis lasted for a few months, after which credit creation remained stagnant and interest rates were low.

Two schools of economic thought contested the explanation of these phenomena, and left their stamp on monetary theory. The first was the Currency School, the forerunner of modern Monetarism.[16] Currency School writers accounted for monetary

---

16 It is difficult to find concise and appropriate references for the views of the Currency School. Perhaps the most pertinent is Robert Torrens, *The Principles and Practical Operation of Sir Robert Peel's Act of 1844 Explained and Defended*, 2nd ed., London: Longman, Brown, Green, Longmans and Roberts, 1857.

instability on the basis of the quantity theory of money.[17] Briefly put, the Currency School claimed that crises were due to the Bank of England overissuing its banknotes, leading to a drop in the exchange value of money and a concomitant fall in exchange rates. Given this putative cause of crisis, the cure would be to manage the supply of money in line with the fluctuations in exchange rates.

Following the advice of the Currency School, the British government introduced the Bank Act of 1844, which forced the Bank of England to regulate the quantity of its banknotes according to its reserves of gold, presumably reflecting the behaviour of exchange rates. The Act of 1844 is a landmark in the history of state intervention in the capitalist economy. It is the first instance of monetary policy that was explicitly based on theoretical analysis which, moreover, failed in its stated purpose and was suspended in subsequent crises.

The opponents of the Currency School were the Banking School, who rejected the quantity theory of money, arguing that prices determine the quantity of money in circulation and not the other way round.[18] Moreover, for the Banking School, credit money is created as a liability of financial institutions, hence it is issued according to demand for credit and drains away as existing loans are repaid. The views of the Banking School have broad affinities with contemporary post-Keynesian analysis of the endogenous money supply.[19] Banking School writers decried the Bank Act of 1844 as a measure that was likely to fail, and even to exacerbate crises. However, they had no clearly defined alternative monetary policies to offer.

Marx's writings on the monetary and financial aspects of capitalist crises – produced mostly in the 1850s and 1860s – make sense only against this background. Similarly to the Banking School, Marx rejected the quantity theory of money, both in *A Contribution to the Critique of Political Economy* and in *Capital*; for Marx, the aggregate quantity of money is determined by the aggregate price of output.[20] Marx arrived at the opposite monetary view to Ricardo, despite relying on the labour theory of value to determine commodity prices. Marx's rejection of the quantity theory is ultimately related to his analysis of the functions of money in capitalist circulation. The price of individual commodities results from money functioning as measure of value, thus

---

17 The Quantity Theory had already been put across with great clarity in David Ricardo, *The High Price of Bullion*, in *The Works and Correspondence of David Ricardo*, vol. 3, ed. Piero Sraffa and Maurice Dobb, Cambridge: Cambridge University Press, 1951.

18 Best summed up in Thomas Tooke, *An Inquiry into the Currency Principle*, London: LSE Reprint Series, 1959; and John Fullarton, *On the Regulation of Currencies*, London: John Murray, 1845.

19 See, for instance, Basil J. Moore, *Horizontalists and Verticalists: The Macroeconomics of Credit Money*, Cambridge: Cambridge University Press, 1988.

20 For further analysis of this point, see Costas Lapavitsas, 'The Banking School and the Monetary Thought of Karl Marx', *Cambridge Journal of Economics* 18:5, 1994, pp. 447–61.

rendering commodity value into price. Commodities are then circulated by money functioning as means of exchange.

In a little more detail, Marx argued – similarly to Ricardo – that the quantity of money necessary in circulation per period is determined by the aggregate value of commodities, the value of money, and the velocity of money.[21] Departing from this point, Ricardo's analysis subsequently considered money primarily as measure of value and means of exchange, thus adopting the quantity theory of money. In contrast, Marx stressed the function of money as money, particularly hoarding, and was thus able to reject the quantity theory. Following the Banking School, Marx argued that hoarding regulates the quantity of money in circulation, and hence money conforms to prices, rather than the other way round. Critics of the quantity theory have echoed this argument in subsequent decades, for instance, Keynes in discussion of liquidity preference.[22]

This is not to say, however, that for Marx the quantity theory is never valid. As was shown in Chapter 4, development of the form of money leads to emergence of fiat replacements (symbols) of commodity money created by the state. Unlike commodity money, valueless fiat money is not well suited to hoarding, and hence tends to remain in circulation. Consequently, if the quantity of fiat money increased without limit, the exchange value of money would collapse, and the result would be price inflation. This is a pure and simple form of the quantity theory of money that was propounded by Marx in *the Contribution*.[23] It applies primarily to fiat money, under very specific circumstances, and is not a general theory of money and the price level.

The narrowness of the quantity theory is apparent in the case of credit money, which is the dominant money of advanced capitalism. Credit money – rooted in money's function as means of payment – is created according to the demand for loans, and returns to its issuer as assets mature. Thus, credit money systematically drains away from the sphere of circulation due to its characteristic circular path. The Banking School called this property of credit money 'the law of reflux', one implication of which is that credit money is not normally subject to the quantity theory.[24] If prices tended to rise, as was typically the case in the run-up to periodic crises, the reason probably was altered conditions in the production and trading of commodities, rather than monetary malfunctioning. Marx was sympathetic to the

---

21 For a simple presentation see Costas Lapavitsas, 'The Theory of Credit Money: A Structural Analysis', *Science and Society* 55:3, 1991, pp. 291–322.

22 See, for instance, John Maynard Keynes, *The General Theory of Employment, Interest and Money*, London: Macmillan, 1973, p. 174.

23 For instance, Karl Marx, *A Contribution to the Critique of Political Economy*, Moscow: Progress, 1970, pp. 118–19.

24 This was one of the main claims made in John Fullarton, *On the Regulation of Currencies*, London: John Murray, 1845.

Banking School's law of reflux and – ever the scholar of monetary theory – attributed its discovery to Sir James Steuart.[25] Once again, there are affinities between Marx's analysis of credit money and contemporary post-Keynesian theories of the endogenous supply of credit money.

Finally, Marx dismissed the Act of 1844, partly drawing on his analysis of credit, but partly for deeper reasons. Unlike the Banking School, Marx treated periodic crises as a result of the pathology of capitalist production, not of commodity circulation and money. Monetary phenomena are integral but secondary aspects of crises, much as monetary circulation is an integral but secondary phenomenon of the capitalist economy. The primary aspect of capitalist accumulation is production of commodities and value, and this is typically where the root of crises is to be found. By the same token, it is ultimately pointless to attempt to deal with crises through monetary measures. That is not to say, however, that fallacious theory could not lead to problematic state intervention that would exacerbate crises, as happened for the Act of 1844.

The institutional framework of both the monetary and the financial sphere in advanced capitalist countries has been deeply transformed in the years following Marx's death. Change was already apparent at the end of the nineteenth century when the emergence of the City of London as the centre of global trade and finance allowed the Bank of England to operate monetary policy through the rate of interest. The rate of interest as a lever of intervention in the monetary sphere was absent in the debates on the Act of 1844. Its absence is also apparent in Marx's discussion of the monetary and financial phenomena of crisis. Manipulating the rate of interest has been pivotal to both monetary policy and the management of money since the end of the nineteenth century.

Conditions throughout the twentieth century have changed much further, needless to say. The monetary and financial framework of financialized capitalism has little in common with the time that Marx developed his ideas on crises. Not least, the link between gold and money in circulation was finally severed in 1971–73 with the collapse of the Bretton Woods Agreement, lending a highly distinctive and historically specific character to state intervention in the realm of finance. This is a point of considerable importance for analysis of the crisis of the 2000s.

Both the form and the content of capitalist crises have changed dramatically in the twentieth century. For one thing, the rise of monopoly capital has added much complexity to the links between trade credit, banking credit and the money market. The institutional make up of the financial system of mature capitalism is also very different from the framework that confronted Marx. To be more specific, bill markets have shrunk, private and public bond markets have grown, the money market comprises giant monopoly banks dominated by a public central bank, and the stock market has

---

25　See, for instance, Marx, *A Contribution to the Critique of Political Economy*, p. 102; and Karl Marx, *Capital*, vol. 1, London: Penguin/NLR, 1976, p. 210.

become vital to the formation of monopoly capitals through mergers and acquisitions. These financial changes have been associated with the underlying transformation in real accumulation. They reflect the shift from a relatively simple economy based on textiles produced mostly by owner capitalists, such as Britain was in the mid-nineteenth century, to complex economies in which huge monopoly capitals dominate several sectors of production, such as the US, Japan, Germany and the UK have become in the early twenty first century.

Given the underlying transformations, the overaccumulation of capital in mature capitalism produces very different financial phenomena to those of Marx's time. Gone is the inability of productive capitalists to honour bills of exchange; gone is also the corresponding impact on relatively small banks specializing in the discount of bills. Overaccumulation now entails vast monetary and financial phenomena, including stock market booms and busts, expanded bank lending that leads to mass insolvency, and state manipulation of interest rates in the money market. Crises, moreover, have lost what appeared to be clockwork regularity in nineteenth-century Britain. They could even become long-drawn affairs, capable of miring capitalist accumulation in stagnation. Even more complexly, in financialized capitalism, crises could result from the malfunctioning of the financial system, without having a substantial impact on real accumulation. They could be usefully described as 'type 2' crises.

In this light, the great crisis that broke out in 2007 stands out in several respects. It is a systemic crisis that reflects the advancing penetration of financial relations into the operations of enterprises and households, in part due to the transformation of banks. Financialization has led to the gradual expansion of the realm of finance, allowing financial activities to influence real accumulation directly. The interpenetration of financial and real accumulation has accorded to financial operations in mature capitalist countries a gravity which they did not previously possess. This is ultimately why the crisis of the 2000s has proven so complex and long-lasting, as is shown in the rest of this chapter.

A vast bubble, primarily in the US: 2001–2007

The crisis of the 2000s emerged on the wake of the bubble of 2001–2007 which took place primarily in the US real estate market. The causes of the bubble of 2001–2007 can be found in the aftermath of the earlier bubble of 1999–2000 which occurred mostly in the US stock market and was associated with the 'new technology' and the 'new millennium'. When the bubble of 1999–2000 burst, the US Federal Reserve drastically loosened monetary policy. Official interest rates were kept at close to 1 percent during 2002–2003, promoting extraordinary activity in the US housing market. Moreover, private US banks took advantage of low interest rates to engage in financial innovation – above all, in securitization – thus feeding financial expansion.

The real estate bubble in the US effectively came to an end in 2006 but booming conditions in the financial markets lasted until the summer of 2007. The bubble kept getting bigger after 2004, despite US interest rates beginning to rise, as the US received

TABLE 1 US mortgage loans, 2001–2006, $bn

Year	2001	2002	2003	2004	2005	2006
Total Originations	2215	2885	3945	2920	3120	2980
Subprime	160	200	310	530	625	600
Subprime Securitized	96	122	203	401	508	483

Source: Mortgage Bankers Association; Mortgage Origination Estimates, updated 24 March 2008

capital inflows from developing countries expanding dollar reserves. During the same period heavy buying and selling also took place in the housing market in the UK and elsewhere.[26]

Table 1 shows the path of the US housing market as bank lending and financial innovation came fully on stream inducing bubble conditions. Mortgage origination expanded rapidly as interest rates declined after 2001, but the pace of expansion in the prime mortgage market weakened after 2003, leading to a decline in total originations. At that time the volume of subprime mortgages began to rise thus sustaining

---

26 By the middle of the 2000s mainstream economics had become aware of the extraordinary conditions in financial markets but there was no agreement on an appropriate policy response. Note that Karl Case and Robert Shiller realized that bubble conditions were in place already by the early 2000s, but expected the situation to stabilize ('Is There a Bubble in the Housing Market?', *Brookings Papers on Economic Activity* 2, 2003). At the BIS, however, William White argued that central bank should 'lean against the wind' by raising interest rates when bubbles threatened, even if price stability and growth targets were not compromised ('Procyclicality in the Financial System', BIS Working Paper No. 193, 2006; 'Is Price Stability Enough?', BIS Working Paper No. 205, 2006). In contrast, Ben Bernanke, who became the head of the US Federal Reserve, argued that credit and asset bubbles should be allowed to follow their course, the authorities intervening aggressively only after the bubble would have burst ('The Global Saving Glut and the U.S. Current Account Deficit', 10 March 2005; 'The Subprime Mortgage Market', 17 May 2007). The response of economists following the burst of the bubble was similarly weak, typically offering bland technical advice, such as improving information flows and extending regulation across financial institutions; for instance, see Randall Dodd, 'Subprime: Tentacles of a Crisis', *Finance and Development*, December 2007. Immediately after the financial meltdown, heterodox economics had its moment in the sun as several economists and others claimed that the crisis was a 'Minsky moment'; see Charles Whalen, 'The U.S. Credit Crunch of 2007: A Minsky Moment', Levy Economics Institute Public Policy Brief No. 92, 2007; L. Randall Wray, 'Lessons from the Subprime Meltdown', Levy Economics InstituteWorking Paper No. 552, 2007; Wray, 'Financial Markets Meltdown: What Can We Learn from Minsky?', Levy Economics Institute Public Policy Brief No. 94, April 2008. By early 2009, however, normal service had resumed and systemic explanations of the crisis were gradually marginalized.

total mortgage originations; rapid subprime mortgage growth was possible because 80 percent of such mortgages became securitized by 2006.

Thus, aggressive household financialization took place in the subprime sector of the US housing market in the early 2000s, thereby sustaining growth of aggregate mortgage lending. Subprime borrowers – that is, borrowers of low creditworthiness – came from the previously excluded, poorer sections of the US working class, often black or Latino women. They were frequently offered adjustable rate mortgages, typically with an initially low rate of interest that was subsequently adjusted upwards. In the popular discourse of the time this trend appeared as the 'democratization' of finance and the reversal of the 'red-lining' of the poor by banks in previous decades.[27] The final outcome was disastrous for the poor but also for the US housing market and for economies across the world.

Other forms of financialization of household income also expanded in the US on the back of the housing boom: 'equity extraction' was a significant feature of the period, shown in table 2. As house prices rose, homeowners re-mortgaged and used the proceeds for consumption and other purposes.

TABLE 2 US mortgage refinance, 2000–2007

Year	2000	2001	2002	2003	2004	2005	2006	2007
Originations ($tr)	1.1	2.2	2.9	3.8	2.8	3.0	2.7	2.3
Refinance (%)	20.5	57.2	61.6	66.4	52.8	52.0	48.6	49.8

Source: Mortgage Bankers Association; Mortgage Origination Estimates, updated 24 March 2008.

Intensified 'equity extraction' was accompanied by a collapse of personal saving in the US, as is shown in table 3. Decline in personal saving has characterized financialization in several countries, for instance, in the weakest countries of the eurozone, discussed in subsequent sections of this chapter. The sharp decline in US personal saving, however, is a remarkable development for a mature capitalist country, indicating underlying weakness of real accumulation as well as changes in the relationship between real wages and consumption.[28]

---

27   For a critical analysis of the entry of private finance in previously 'redlined' areas of the housing market in the US, see Gary Dymski, 'Racial Exclusion and the Political Economy of the Sub-Prime Crisis', *Historical Materialism* 17:2, 2009. Earlier change in legislation but also the burgeoning ideology of 'home ownership' contributed to attracting poorer workers and others into the mortgage market.

28   Empirically establishing the path of saving in the US is far from straightforward, not least as there are several measures of saving that could be deployed. For our purposes suffice it to rely on personal saving figures from Federal Reserve flow of funds data.

TABLE 3 Personal saving, US, 2000–2007

Year	2000	2001	2002	2003	2004	2005	2006	2007
Saving ($bn)	168.5	132.3	184.7	174.9	181.7	44.6	38.8	42.7
Saving as % of disposable income	2.3	1.8	2.4	2.1	2.1	0.5	0.4	0.4

Source: Federal Reserve Bank, Flow of Funds, various

In addition to cheap credit from the Federal Reserve, the US bubble was sustained by reverse capital flows from developing countries. The fundamental causes of the reverse flows were discussed in Chapter 8 in connection with the hoarding of world money by developing countries. The poor of the world became net suppliers of capital to the US, keeping loanable capital abundant in the US markets during 2005–2006 as the Federal Reserve tightened credit and raised interest rates.

During the period of the bubble, consumption did not exhibit particularly strong growth. There is no evidence of over-consumption in the four key countries of financialization, indeed figure 1 shows that consumption as proportion of GDP remained stagnant during the bubble, or even declined in the UK and Germany. Consumption levels, on the other hand, have remained relatively high in the UK and especially in the US. Worker access to consumer goods improved due to imports from rapidly industrializing developing countries. Higher productivity growth in several developing countries – primarily in China – allowed workers in mature capitalist countries to maintain consumption at high levels despite generally low productivity growth.[29]

During the period of bubble, furthermore, there was no investment boom, thus no prima facie evidence of overaccumulation in any of the four countries, particularly in the US, as is shown in figure 2. This is in sharp contrast to the Japanese bubble of the late 1980s, which was similarly based on real estate but was accompanied by a significant expansion of domestic investment.[30] By the same token, the crisis of 2007 has not been associated with over-expansion of enterprise debt. The figure also shows the simultaneous collapse of investment in all four countries in 2008–2009, and its weak recovery in the period that followed. These fundamental features of the current crisis make it different to the classical capitalist crises discussed by Marx.

---

29   A point succinctly made by Mary Amiti and Kevin J. Stiroh, 'Is the United States Losing its Productivity Advantage?', *Current Issues in Economics and Finance* 13:8, 2007.

30   The differences between the US bubble of the 2000s and the Japanese bubble of the 1980s are summed up by Itoh, who also pointed out that the crisis of 2007 was unlikely to lead to a repetition of the 1930s mostly because of the exceptional presence of the state in contemporary capitalism. Makoto Itoh, 'The Historical Significance of the Social Costs of the Subprime Crisis: Drawing on the Japanese Experience', in *Financialisation in Crisis*, ed. Costas Lapavitsas, Leiden: Brill, 2012

FIG. 1 Consumption as percentage of GDP; US, Japan, Germany, UK

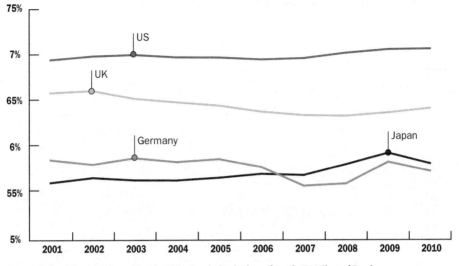

Source: Federal Reserve Flow of Funds, ONS, Bundesbank Flow of Funds, BoJ Flow of Funds

FIG. 2 Investment as percentage of GDP; US, Japan, Germany, UK

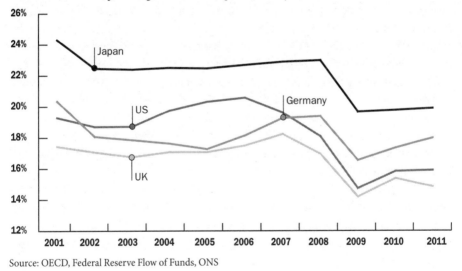

Source: OECD, Federal Reserve Flow of Funds, ONS

On the other hand, the indebtedness of households and non-profit institutions, shown in figure 3, increased greatly in the US and the UK, although during the same period it declined in Germany and Japan. The underlying differences in financialization among the four countries thus became apparent in the course of the bubble, particularly as there was no housing bubble in Japan and Germany. Household and

FIG. 3 Household and non-profit institution debt as percentage of gross disposable income, 2001–2007; US, Japan, Germany, UK

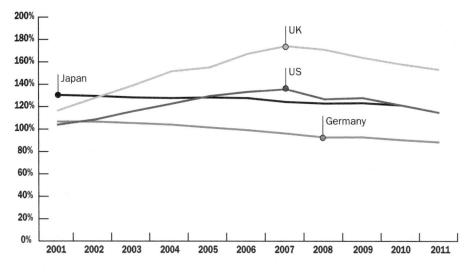

Source: Federal Reserve Flow of Funds, ONS, Bundesbank Flow of Funds, BoJ Flow of Funds

non-profit institution indebtedness in both the US and the UK declined significantly once the crisis set in.

In view of real wages in the US remaining essentially stagnant for a long period, the tremendous expansion of household debt rested on very slender foundations. Thus, when interest rates started to climb in 2004–2005, households began to face increasing difficulties in servicing housing debt. By 2006 the US housing bubble was over and the conditions were ready for the enormous crisis that followed. It is remarkable – and a true reflection of the content of financialization – that the historic crisis that commenced in 2007 was triggered by the poorest layers of the US working class defaulting on mortgage debt.

Figure 4, showing bank assets relative to GDP, indicates that in the course of the bubble, banks and the financial system in general grew rapidly in the UK and significantly in Japan; there was much less rapid growth in Germany. The figures for the US are partially misleading in this respect because there has been a large increase of 'shadow banking' including institutions engaging in mortgage and other activities, which does not appear in the commercial bank data, as was noted in Chapter 7. Nonetheless, they still make it apparent that there has been significant variation in financialization.

The expansion of banking in the US and the UK has reflected the underlying transformation of banks in the course of financialization, discussed in Chapter 8. Specifically, in the course of the bubble commercial banks have relied heavily on obtaining liquidity from the money market to transform customer-specific loans (mortgages) into tradable securities. On this basis, banks were able to 'churn' their own capital by

FIG. 4 Bank assets as percentage of GDP; US, Japan, Germany, UK

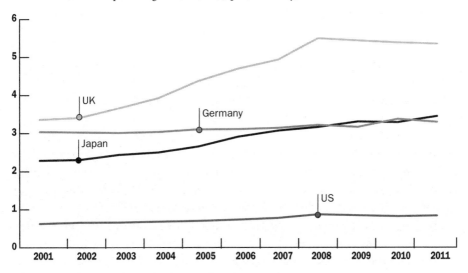

Source: Federal Reserve Flow of Funds, ONS, Bundesbank Flow of Funds, BoJ Flow of Funds

expanding off-balance-sheet activities, thus raising their profitability per unit of own capital. Moreover, the securitization of mortgage loans has depended on banks deploying complex computationally intensive models of risk. The result was that information collection and risk management by banks lost much of its substantive content. In short, the bubble of 2001–2007 represents systemic failure of private banking in the US in the fundamental sense of banks failing to deliver their presumed functions in a capitalist economy, as is discussed in more detail below.

The bubble bursts, general crisis follows: 2007–2009

In 2006–2007 subprime mortgage holders started to default in large numbers in the US. As a result tradable securities created by the financial system on the back of household mortgages became gradually illiquid; consequently, banks began to face difficulties in accessing fresh funds in the money market; hence holders of financial liabilities associated with banks started to withdraw from the markets. A systemic banking crisis of liquidity and solvency gradually emerged.

The immediate causes of the banking crisis in the US have been extensively discussed in the economic literature, attention being paid to the emergence of the 'shadow' banking system associated with money market funds and derivatives markets.[31] Briefly

---

31 The most prominent exponent of the view that the crisis has been caused primarily by the practices of 'shadow' banking has been Gary Gorton; see 'The Subprime Panic', Yale ICF Working Paper No. 08–25, 30 September 2008; and 'Information, Liquidity, and the (Ongoing)

put, money market mutual funds (MMMF) operating in the money markets diverted retail deposits away from 'traditional' banks; commercial banks securitized assets and moved them off the balance sheet; repurchase agreements (repos) were widely deployed to give liquidity to securitized bonds. Traditional banking stands in contrast to securitized banking; the former is the business of making and holding loans, with insured demand deposits as the main source of funds; the latter is the business of packaging and reselling loans, with repurchase agreements as the main source of funds.

In this light, the financial crisis of 2007–2008 was a system-wide bank run which, however, did not occur in the traditional but in the securitized banking sector. While a traditional bank run amounts to the mass withdrawal of deposits, a securitized bank run amounts to the mass withdrawal of repurchase agreements (repos). The cause of the run was concern about the liquidity of the bonds used as collateral for repos, particularly when these bonds were related to the subprime market. The result was that the US financial system became insolvent since it could not service its debts.

The causes of the US banking crisis have also been attributed to the emergence of banks that are 'too big to fail'. This issue is directly related to the regulation of the financial system – and is thus discussed in Chapter 10 – but it also has a bearing on the unfolding of the crisis. Lisa DeFerrari and David Palmer recognized the dominant role of a few financial institutions already in the early 2000s, coining the term 'large complex banking organizations'. Large banks have turned toward derivatives trading. They transact heavily with non-bank financial institutions and continually expand their global reach, requiring risk-focused supervision. For Viral Acharya and Matthew Richardson, this kind of large bank has been able to repackage loans (typically mortgages) into asset-backed securities, held both on and off the balance sheet. The aim has been to reduce the amount of capital kept against loans, thus increasing the ability of the large bank to make further loans. Hence banks became 'overleveraged' and took on greatly enlarged risks. Darrell Duffie has also stressed the problematic role of large banks arguing that the collapse of a 'dealer' bank could result from the flight of short-term secured creditors, hedge-fund clients, derivatives counterparties, leading to devastating loss of clearing and settlement services.[32]

Panic of 2007', *American Economic Review* 99:2, May 2009. See also Gary Gorton and Andrew Metrick, 'Regulating the Shadow Banking System', *Brookings Papers on Economic Activity* 41:2, Fall 2010; and Gorton and Metrick, 'Securitized Banking and the Run on Repo', *Journal of Financial Economics* 104:3, 2012. The importance of the 'shadow' banking system to the US crisis was immediately appreciated by practitioners, such as Paul McCulley, focusing on 'the whole alphabet soup of levered up non-bank investment conduits, vehicles, and structures'. See McCulley, 'Teton Reflections', Global Central Bank Focus, September 2007.

32 Lisa DeFerrari and David E. Palmer, 'Supervision of Large Complex Banking Organizations', *Federal Reserve Bulletin,* February 2001; Viral V. Acharya and Matthew Richardson,

There is little doubt that the first signal of impending crisis was a shortage of liquidity for securitized assets in the interbank money market in August 2007.[33] US and other banks held large volumes of mortgage-backed securities, or were in practice obliged to support financial institutions that actually held such securities. As mortgage failures rose in the US, mortgaged-based securities became progressively illiquid (unsaleable) because banks preferred to hoard liquid funds instead of lending to other banks. As bank liquidity declined, however, bank solvency also became increasingly doubtful. Compounding the worsening of solvency was the steady decline of stock markets after December 2007, as equity buyers eventually began to grasp the underlying weakness of banks. Falling share prices meant that banks had difficulties in obtaining private capital to support losses in mortgage-backed and other securities, thereby exacerbating the solvency problem.

The burst of the bubble thus led to the apparent contradiction of financial institutions being awash with loanable capital but extremely short of liquidity. In this regard, Marx's fundamental remark about capitalist crises was confirmed: financial institutions were in urgent need to hold value in the form of money, but they could not obtain it commercially because liquidity was hoarded. The typical hoarders of liquidity were financial institutions that were worried about meeting their own obligations. This condition has characterized the global financial system at several junctures since the outbreak of crisis in 2007.

Predictably, central banks swung into action to confront the shortage of liquidity. The Federal Reserve and other central banks deployed a range of methods of extraordinary liquidity provision, including open market operations, discount window lending, term auction facilities, direct lending to investment banks, swapping mortgage-backed for public securities, and purchasing commercial paper from industrial and commercial corporations. At the same time, central banks cut interest rates, on occasion even approaching zero percent, including in the US in 2008. Central bank policies in effect operated as subsidy to banks by lowering the cost of bank liabilities. Advancing this subsidy to banks has been possible mostly because of the command exercised by central banks over contemporary money. It is notable, and will be discussed in more detail in the rest of this chapter, that the liquidity advance has often been undertaken against

---

'Causes of the Financial Crisis', *Critical Review* 21:2, 2009; Darrell Darrell Duffie, *How Big Banks Fail and What to Do About It,* Princeton, NJ: Princeton University Press, 2011. Note that Gary Dymski has offered a critical perspective on 'too big to fail' banks, arguing that their emergence has placed a constraint on the ability of the authorities to adopt radical measures to resolve a crisis. 'Megabanks' have a hold on financial and regulatory policy, shaping it according to their own preferences. Gary Dymski, 'Genie out of the Bottle: The Evolution of Too-Big-to-Fail Policy and Banking Strategy in the US', 8 June 2011, at postkeynesian.net.

33 The following account of the crisis draws heavily on Costas Lapavitsas, 'Financialised Capitalism: Crisis and Financial Expropriation', *Historical Materialism* 17:2, 2009, pp. 114–48.

weak collateral provided by the banks. In effect, central banks provided extraordinary liquidity to commercial banks, while also taking some of the credit risk accumulated by banks in the course of the bubble.

The crisis went through two major peaks in 2008 resulting from the interaction between liquidity and solvency in the financial system. The first was the collapse of Bear Stearns in March 2008, a giant US investment bank that found it impossible to obtain funds privately in the money market, while its holdings of problematic mortgage-backed assets made it insolvent. The Federal Reserve together with the US Treasury managed the collapse of Bear Stearns by forcing a take-over by the investment bank JP Morgan, which received a concessionary public loan for the purpose.

The second peak occurred in August–October 2008, representing a rare episode in the history of banking. As conditions in the US housing market worsened, two giant Government Sponsored Enterprises ('Fannie Mae' and 'Freddie Mac') that partook of roughly half the annual transactions of mortgage-backed securities in the US, and typically bought only prime quality, came close to collapse. During the bubble both had engaged in riskier investment banking, including subprime mortgages, thus becoming weaker and forcing the US state to intervene to support them. At the same time, Lehman Brothers, another giant US investment bank, found itself in a similar position to Bear Stearns. Unlike Bear Stearns, however, the US authorities allowed Lehman Brothers to go bankrupt, entailing losses for both shareholders and creditors. This was a colossal blunder because it showed that the state was not consistent in dealing with banks in difficulties: Lehman Brothers's creditors faced losses whereas Bear Stearns's creditors were spared this predicament. Differential treatment by the state destroyed all remaining vestiges of trust among banks in the money markets, leading to a freeze in lending.

In September–October 2008, liquidity disappeared completely, bank shares collapsed and genuine panic spread across financial markets. The US state was forced rapidly to alter its stance and effectively to guarantee banks against further failure. A decisive step was to advance public funds to deal with the underlying problem of bank solvency, typically under the Troubled Asset Relief Program (TARP) which is further discussed below. Despite state intervention, by the end of 2008 a major recession began to unfold across the world. Constriction of the supply of credit by banks and markets forced enterprises to cut back on output and employment; consumption declined as worried and over-indebted households rearranged expenditure; export markets collapsed, particularly for automobiles and consumer electronics. Developing countries also suffered as capital flows became problematic, necessitating emergency borrowing.

The global turmoil that broke out in 2008 was thus spurred by a banking crisis and the ensuing tightening of credit. Pools of credit completely disappeared as financial institutions abandoned securitization; banks tightened credit provision in an attempt to improve liquidity and solvency; laden with debt and confronted with falling housing markets, households drastically reduced borrowing; aggregate demand declined, impacting on firm inventories, output and employment; investment collapsed across mature capitalist countries; international trade fell, contributing to a general recession.

The worst was avoided through extensive and systematic state intervention in 2008–2009. However, a contradictory result of state intervention was the appearance of a sovereign debt crisis after 2009 which took a particularly vicious form in Europe. Before considering the eurozone crisis, it is necessary to examine analytically the forms of intervention adopted by the US state in 2008–2009, casting further light on the content of financialization.

The state intervenes to prevent the worst; US leads the way, 2008–2009

The pivotal role played by the state in financialization has become apparent during the turmoil that began in 2007. State policy has focused primarily on three underlying weaknesses of finance in the course of the crisis: liquidity shortages, bad assets held by financial institutions, and recapitalization of institutions holding insufficient own capital. It is notable that the US state has been bolder and more decisive in confronting the crisis than the states comprising the European Union. The response of the US is considered immediately below, in contrast to the response of EU states, considered in subsequent sections.

Liquidity provision

During the initial phases of the crisis interbank liquidity vanished for reasons primarily associated with the transformation of banks in the course of financialization, including securitization of mortgages and other assets as well as heavy reliance on the money market to obtain necessary liquidity.[34] Banks and other financial institutions were unable to obtain fresh liquidity as the purchasers of short-term assets began to withdraw from the money market. The disappearance of liquidity reflected fundamentally the loss of trust of banks in each other but also the loss of confidence by holders of bank and non-bank financial liabilities. The equivalent of a bank run began to emerge in the 'shadow' banking sector, threatening to bring collapse of finance in the US and elsewhere.[35]

The state in the US and the UK, consequently, had to re-affirm the guarantee of ordinary deposits with banks to prevent a full-scale bank run. Deposit insurance guarantees by the state are a decisive form of intervention in contemporary finance altering the costs and the rates of return for financial institutions. The implications of deposit insurance for banking and finance in general are further considered in Chapter 10, but

---

34   Markus Brunnermeier and Lasse Heje Pedersen have distinguished between 'funding' and 'market' liquidity in the context of the crisis ('Market Liquidity and Funding Liquidity', *Review of Financial Studies* 22:6, 2009). The former broadly refers to the ability of an institution to make payments promptly, the latter to the ease of selling an asset in the market. Clearly the two are related: their interplay contributed to the generalized disappearance of liquidity in the course of the crisis.

35   As the mainstream literature mentioned in note 26 has established.

there can be little doubt that, in its absence, it would have been extremely difficult to restore liquidity provision to banks during the recent crisis.

With private deposits under guarantee, liquidity intervention entailed two inter-related policies by the central bank: first, reducing interest rates and, second, providing banks with liquid funds under public guarantee. A template for both had already been established by the actions of the Bank of Japan during the crisis that followed the bubble of the 1980s. Perhaps the most fundamental step by central banks in the US, the UK, and even the EU, was effectively to drive nominal interest rates toward zero, following BoJ practice in the 1990s. This policy amounted to a public subsidy to banks since it reduced the cost of bank liabilities, and hence raised the profitability of banking, particularly as banks simultaneously acquired public sector debt that carried a low risk of default.

In addition to lowering interest rates, and again following the practice of the BoJ in the 1990s and 2000s, central banks supplied public liquidity directly to commercial banks. Both the US and UK central banks adopted quantitative easing after the collapse of Lehman Brothers, and further deployed this policy in subsequent years. Quantitative easing implies the systematic over-expansion of reserves held by banks with the central bank, as was shown in Chapter 4. Unlike the BoJ, however, the Federal Reserve and the Bank of England did not adopt quantitative targets for the reserves of commercial banks. Quantitative easing has also included the announcement of intent by the central bank to drive down long-term interest rates.[36] Whether as quantitative easing or as plain lending to commercial banks, liquidity provision by central banks also represents a public subsidy to banks since it replaces risky private with safe public credit.

Quantitative easing stands for the abandonment of independent central banking as well as inflation targeting, the hallmarks of the period of Great Moderation discussed in Chapter 7. For, quantitative easing reflects the overlapping of fiscal and monetary policy as the central bank acquires state bonds, thus financing state expenditure. The abandonment of the central banking shibboleths of the 1990s and 2000s has been quietly acknowledged by the mainstream literature as attention has shifted to the effectiveness of central bank policy.[37] Effectiveness in this context appears to refer, first and foremost, to the impact of quantitative easing on interest rates. Bernanke, Reinhart, and Sack observed several years before the crisis that such 'non-standard' measures could be effective, a view that has gradually become

---

36   It is notable that the European Central Bank has not formally adopted 'quantitative easing', though it has substantially expanded lending to private banks, signifying its unusual character as a central bank, discussed in the rest of this chapter.

37   Richhild Moessner and Philip Turner, 'Threat of Fiscal Dominance? Workshop Summary', BIS Papers No. 65, Bank for International Settlements, 2012.

prevalent.[38] There has, however, been debate on the relative importance of the channels through which quantitative easing operates, including the rebalancing of the portfolios of financial institutions and the direct impact of holding reserves. Both the Federal Reserve and the Bank of England consider that quantitative easing has a significant effect on interest rates in the asset markets; the effect on long-term rates, however, might decline with successive expansion programmes.[39]

The effectiveness of quantitative easing in influencing asset markets is an empirical issue which remains unclear. Of greater theoretical interest is that liquidity provision by central banks in the course of the crisis has followed Walter Bagehot's long-standing advice in *Lombard Street* – to lend freely and settle accounts later.[40] It is equally notable, however, that key parts of Bagehot's prescription have been ignored – to lend to commercial banks only on excellent collateral and at punitive interest rates. Instead, central banks have lent at extraordinarily low interest rates, while systematically lowering the quality of collateral acceptable for lending. In short, the public sector has not only subsidized private banks but has also absorbed bad private risks.

The state in the US and elsewhere has thus overcome the worst of liquidity shortages essentially by deploying the central bank's command over money to engulf the frozen interbank market. Note, however, that emergency liquidity provision is a short-term response that cannot deal with the underlying causes of loss of trust toward private banks, which ultimately account for the destruction of liquidity. Note also that the state cannot permanently take over the money market, if the nature of the financial system is to remain fundamentally private. Liquidity provision is inherently a short-term emergency measure that cannot resolve a deep crisis. Despite state intervention, private liquidity provision among banks has remained persistently irregular in international money

---

38   Ben Bernanke, Vincent Reinhart, and Brian Sack, 'Monetary Policy Alternatives at the Zero Bound: An Empirical Assessment', *Brookings Papers on Economic Activity* 2, 2004.

39   The relevant literature is already sizeable and expanding; see C.A.E. Goodhart, 'Monetary Policy and Public Debt', *Financial Stability Review* 16, April 2012; Arvind Krishnamurthy and Annette Vissing-Jorgensen, 'The Effects of Quantitative Easing on Interest Rates', NBER Working Paper No. 17555, October 2011; Stafania D'Amico and Thomas B. King, 'Flow and stock effects of large-scale treasury purchases', *Federal Reserve Board Finance and Economics Discussion Series* 52, 2010; Michael Joyce et al., 'The Financial Market Impact of Quantitative Easing', *Bank of England Working Papers* 393, 2010; James D. Hamilton and Jing Cynthia Wu, 'The Effectiveness of Alternative Monetary Policy Tools in a Zero Lower Bound Environment', NBER Working Paper No. 16956, April 2011; Eric T. Swanson, 'Let's Twist Again: A High-Frequency Event-Study Analysis of Operation Twist and Its Implications for QE2', *Brookings Papers on Economic Activity* 42:1, Spring 2011; and Jack Meaning and Feng Zhu, 'The Impact of Recent Central Bank Asset Purchase Programmes', *BIS Quarterly Review*, December 2011, pp. 73–83.

40   Walter Bagehot, *Lombard Street*, in *The Collected Works of Walter Bagehot*, vol. 9, ed. Norman St John-Stevas, London: The Economist, 1978, pp. 74–5.

markets following the outbreak of turmoil in 2007. This is a reflection of the structural character of the crisis of financialization, explored further in the following sections.

Dealing with bad assets held by banks

Liquidity shortages have been associated with weakened solvency due to problematic securities and other loans accumulated by banks. The combination of liquidity shortages and weak solvency naturally disrupted the lending activities of banks, since banks refused to roll over loans and raised the threshold of creditworthiness for new loans. Credit shortages hampered investment and consumption, reducing aggregate demand and intensifying recession. Consequently, there emerged the need for state intervention to remove bad assets from bank balance sheets and to improve bank solvency. But removing bad assets from bank balance sheets has proven far from easy in view of the economic and social interests involved, as was demonstrated in the case of the US.

The first problem was lack of transparency. Since commercial banks are private and competitive capitalist enterprises, they have an incentive to conceal the extent of problematic loans on their books to prevent loss of trust among counterparties. Even when several banks hold bad assets, the first bank to reveal the full extent of the problem would suffer disproportionately in terms of access to liquidity, share price, inflow of deposits, and so on. An immediate difficulty for state intervention, consequently, was to deal with the opacity surrounding the bad assets of private banks.

More complex than revelation, however, was the problem of the price at which bad assets would be removed from the balance sheet of banks, since that would determine the incidence of inevitable losses. If the price was high – at the limit equal to the full price of the removed assets – losses would be shifted disproportionately onto the new holder; if the price was low, the incidence would weigh more heavily on the banks. In the first case, it would be difficult to find new private holders, and hence bad assets would probably end up with the public sector; in the second, banks would perhaps become intractably insolvent and face bankruptcy.

Note also that, if resolution of the bad debt problem was simply postponed in the hope that banks would be able to deal with bad assets individually – or in the hope that the original issuers would be able to repay according to contract – even worse difficulties could emerge. Bank balance sheets would have remained illiquid for a long time, preventing resumption of normal banking functions. The longer that the normal supply of banking credit would have been disturbed, the greater the disruption to accumulation would have become, perhaps resulting in an even larger volume of bad assets on the books of banks. Mere passage of time cannot be a cure for the problem of bad assets held by banks.

Under presumed conditions of competitive capitalism the expected course of action would have been to impose the losses from bad assets onto private banks, even to the point of forcing bankruptcy. After all, banks are supposed to specialize in information gathering and processing, including the tasks of screening and monitoring loans. If bad assets have accumulated on balance sheets, banks should bear the costs and consequences of their decisions and actions. Under conditions of financialization, however, things unfolded very differently for large banks.

For one thing, small depositors were protected by state guarantees; potential losses, therefore, would have to be borne by equity, bond holders and large depositors. Shareholders have an ownership claim on the bank and its profits, and are supposed to take the risk of loss of equity invested; bondholders and other creditors have a legal claim to interest and repayment of principal, but inevitably carry some risk of loss of loanable capital. In principle, bad assets could have been confronted by wiping out the value of shareholdings as well as by imposing losses on bondholders and large depositors – a 'haircut'. However, equity, bondholders and large depositors typically include institutional investors of developed countries as well as large public and semi-public institutions of developing countries. Banks gather loanable capital and spare money across society, as was discussed in Chapter 5. Imposing losses on banks, therefore, would require ranking shareholders, bond holders and large depositors according to non-economic as well as economic criteria.

It is intuitive that such criteria must have a social dimension. On what grounds should bank losses be imposed, for instance, on households that have placed pension savings with institutional investors, which must accept losses as holders of bank liabilities? Why should bank failure in developed countries impinge upon the savings of workers in developing countries? Questions of this nature arise from the role of banks as large-scale social organizers of production and circulation in contemporary capitalism. They further reflect the tension between private ownership and social functioning of large banks.

The difficulties of ranking potential loss-bearers are apparent in the method that has often been deployed in recent decades to resolve the problem of bad assets – namely creating a 'bad bank', or equivalently, 'good banks'. Accordingly, for the current crisis, Willem Buiter proposed the establishment of new public banks that would aggregate the sound assets of stricken banks. The public banks would be able to resume lending, while leaving failed banks to cope with bad assets over time. Jeremy Bulow and Paul Klemperer, in contrast, proposed creating 'good' private banks by taking over all the assets but only the most senior liabilities of stricken banks (including deposits). The remaining liabilities would continue to be held by the failed old banks, which would also hold the equity of the new banks.[41] However, in practice the typical policy adopted after the outbreak of crisis in 2007 has been to pass the cost of bad assets as far as pos-

---

41   There are several technical ways of ring-fencing bad assets available from the long experience of bank failures during the last three decades – see Gerard Caprio and Daniela Klingebiel, 'Bank Insolvencies: Cross-country Experience', World Bank Policy Research Working Paper 1620, 1996; but a 'bad bank' is perhaps the mainstay. See also William Buiter, 'The "Good Bank" Solution', *Financial Times* (online), 2009 January 29; and Jeremy Bulow and Paul Klemperer, 'Reorganising the Banks: Focus on the Liabilities, Not the Assets', VoxEU.org, 21 March 2009.

sible onto the public sector, allowing share and bond holders to escape with minimal damage. This has been the spirit in which the US state has dealt with the problem, particularly after the bankruptcy of Lehman Brothers which did impose costs onto equity and bond holders, but resulted in panic conditions in financial markets.

Removing bad assets from the balance sheet of banks was proclaimed a priority of the Troubled Asset Relief Program in September 2008 that came to command $700bn of public funds. In March 2009 the Geithner Plan was put forth, in similar spirit to TARP. The underlying assumption of that plan was that bad assets reflected the drying up of liquidity, rather than bad credit decisions.[42] The objective, therefore, was to remove bad assets by restarting the market for securitized securities, while obtaining for the banks the highest possible price. The aim was to appear to solve the problem of bad assets by relying on private capital and without imposing costs on the public purse. To this purpose the Geithner Plan proposed that banks should engage in auctions thereby removing bad assets from their balance sheets.

By 2009, however, the policy of liquidity provision had already succeeded in shoring up bank profits in the US since it had provided banks with large public subsidies. Moreover, banks had also begun to receive substantial capital injections from the state on highly favourable terms, as is shown in the next section. Consequently, banks had little incentive to engage in auctioning bad assets at a loss. From their perspective it was better to wait until maturity, dealing with losses out of recovering profits, or via restored capital. That was the path eventually taken by US banks after 2009. The inevitable implication was that for a significant length of time provision of fresh bank credit remained problematic, particularly as the housing market continued to be weak thus further damaging the value of bank assets. The prospects for demand and output were correspondingly negative.

Injecting capital into banks

As losses from bad assets gradually accrued for US banks, the state was forced to shift the emphasis of its intervention toward replenishing the capital of banks. By early 2009 US commercial banks and other financial institutions had received more than $300bn of capital injections from TARP, typically as preferred stock with guaranteed interest payments. Capital injections into troubled banks raised issues that went to the heart of the functioning of banks in financialized capitalism: what would be the ultimate source of the additional capital, and what implications would capital injections have for owning and managing banks?

In a crisis as deep as that commencing in 2007 the US state inevitably veered toward injecting capital into banks directly from public funds in the first instance; private sources of capital would have hardly been forthcoming in view of pervasive doubts

---

42   Lucian A. Bebchuk, 'How to Make TARP II Work', Harvard Law and Economics Discussion Paper No. 626, Harvard Law School, February 2009.

about the solvency of banks. Consequently, the issue of public ownership and control over banks came to the forefront. For state functionaries in the US, the UK and elsewhere this development created severe difficulties in view of the ideological dominance of neoliberalism in recent years. It was imperative to make public injections of capital look like a temporary measure that would not lead to permanent public ownership and control over banks. Even more important was to avoid any suggestion that public was superior to private management, even though the latter had self-evidently proven deficient.

The first step for the US state, therefore, was to overcome the opacity created by private banks and to acquire a better grasp of the problem of capital shortage. The natural method to improve transparency would have been for independent auditors, preferably public employees, to take charge of banks, opening the books and establishing the true extent of the solvency problem as well as searching for illegality or malfeasance. However, such action would have resembled purposeful nationalization. Consequently, the method adopted by the US government was to introduce the Supervisory Capital Assessment Program in March 2009; the program amounted to 'stress tests' of several of the largest banks, to be conducted by US regulatory authorities on the basis of information requested from the banks.

Specifically, banks were asked to make their own assessment of bad debts using a 'baseline' and a 'more adverse' scenario of the behaviour of the economy as a whole. The assessments were subsequently examined and adjusted by the authorities, always in close contact with the banks. The 'stress tests' merely assessed the likely losses on loans maturing to 2010. This was a very different exercise to attempting to ascertain the value of bad assets carried by the banks, and thus the likely magnitude of losses, if banks were forced to clean up their balance sheets. Still, the tests led to an estimate of the additional capital needs by banks at only $75bn, bearing in mind that banks had already received substantial sums from TARP and had been building up their capital since the end of 2008, particularly as bank profitability rose in 2009.[43]

Stress tests coupled with state guarantees of meeting capital shortfalls contributed to the restoration of confidence in US banks. Confidence was also restored on account of public provision of liquidity, and the reassertion of public insurance for deposits. Furthermore, banks were able to restore profitability helped by the receipt of public subsidies. Consequently, already from the middle of 2009, US banks were again able to raise capital privately through fresh issues of equity. The result was that the largest banks could start to repay funds that had been received through TARP in 2008–2009.

Quick repayment of TARP funds was important to banks, even though the funds had been provided by the state without significant direct implications for ownership

---

43   Federal Reserve Bank, 'The Supervisory Capital Assessment Program: Design and Implementation', 24 April 2009. Federal Reserve Bank, 'The Supervisory Capital Assessment Program: Overview of Results', 7 May 2009.

and control over banks. Only relatively minor, and highly contested, conditions were applied, requiring banks to maintain the level of their lending, while limiting the exceptional remuneration of management. In effect, the US state treated the public rescue of failed private banks as a temporary measure undertaken reluctantly and resembling public investment in bank stock. As long as bank shares did not fall in price, the public interest would be presumably protected. Even so, private banks were fully aware of the potential risk to ownership and control posed by public ownership of shares as well as by passive reliance on the public purse. They were also keen to shake off the mild restrictions imposed for receipt of TARP funds. Barely nine months after the Lehman shock the largest US banks started to repay TARP, while taking steps to restore management remuneration to pre-crisis levels.

In sum, US state intervention injected public funds into failed private banks in 2008–2009, thus protecting shareholders and bondholders from losses arising out of loans in the course of the bubble. Furthermore, liquidity was supplied under public guarantee, driving interest rates down and improving bank profitability. Implicit and explicit guarantees against failure were also offered to banks and their depositors. Supported by public largesse, US banks were able to hoard liquidity, minimize losses from bad assets, and improve profitability. However, credit creation by banks inevitably suffered, prolonging the disruption of productive accumulation.

In effect, US society was forced to bear the brunt of the banking crisis as state intervention aimed at protecting private banks without bringing them under public control. The unspoken objective of the US and other states was to defend the underlying relations of financialization from the shock of the crisis. The implications became clear in 2010–11 as the crisis took a further and even more dangerous turn.

The crisis becomes fiscal: The eurozone in turmoil

The global recession of 2008–2009 had grave implications for public finance, in view especially of state intervention to rescue banks. Tax revenue declined and government budget deficits increased in the US, the UK and elsewhere. A crisis that had begun due to the exposure of banks to the US real estate market eventually produced a major disruption of public finance, and therefore of sovereign debt. The impact of the new phase of the crisis was particularly severe in the eurozone, initially in the peripheral countries of Greece, Ireland, Portugal, and Spain, but increasingly in countries of the core.

By late 2011 the crisis posed a threat to the existence of the euro, and thus to the stability of the international monetary system; meanwhile, European and other banks faced renewed problems of liquidity and solvency. State intervention in 2008–2009 had not decisively resolved even the financial component of the crisis, which threatened to engulf banks again perhaps in even more acute form. It gradually became clear that financialization had given rise to a systemic crisis capable of disrupting the monetary and financial components of capitalist accumulation across the world. To grasp the complex twist taken by the crisis after 2009 it is thus necessary to undertake a short detour on the eurozone.

Emergence of core and periphery within the eurozone

Economic and financial development in the European Union in the 2000s has been shaped by the mechanisms and institutions of the European Monetary Union, which have also determined the form of the crisis after 2009.[44] The euro has never been a simple means of value measurement and payment in Europe; rather, it has been a form of world money designed to serve the interests of large financial, industrial and commercial capital in Europe as well as the interests of the most powerful states within the European Monetary Union.[45] The character of state intervention in the eurozone crisis, particularly in contrast to the US state, reflects the peculiar role of the euro as world money under conditions of financialized capitalism.

From the perspective of Marxist political economy, and as was discussed in Chapter 4, world money is a form of the universal equivalent associated with the tendencies and requirements of the world market. A characteristic feature of the world market is lack of homogeneity in laws, accounting practices, trade practices and norms, payment customs, and even weights and measures; a further characteristic feature is the absence of an integrated credit system to provide credit and liquidity. Put otherwise, the world market lacks both a world state and a world central bank. Therefore, its functioning relies on the organizing role of a world money capable of acting reliably as a means of hoarding (international reserves) and a means of payment for international operations, provided that it already acts as a means of value measurement (unit of account). Furthermore, the hierarchy of capitalist states is also partially determined by command over world money which ultimately acts as a weapon of imperial power.

The historic form of world money has been that of precious metals, but for most of the twentieth century gold has been reduced to a hoard-of-last-resort. The role of world money under conditions of financialization in particular has been undertaken by national currencies, above all, the US dollar. By this token, the imperial power of the US has come partly to depend on world money that is produced by the US state. However, in view of its nature, the dollar has faced continuous competition from other national currencies. The euro has been established in the context of competing against the dollar, and this has lent to it a contradictory and discriminatory character.

It cannot be overemphasized that the euro is a *sui generis* form of world money. Unlike the dollar, the euro is not a pre-existing national money that has been catapulted into a world role because of the intrinsic strength of its economy and state. Equally important is that the euro has not attained its role as world money through the organic development of the financial and commercial spheres in Europe. Rather,

---

44   Analysis in this section draws heavily on three reports on the eurozone crisis produced by Research on Money and Finance in London in 2010–11. The reports can be found in book form in Costas Lapavitsas et al., *Crisis in the Eurozone*, London: Verso, 2012.

45   The significance of the euro as world money is also analysed in ibid.

the euro has been created *ex nihilo* by an alliance of European states that took into account the interests of large European banks and other monopoly capitals.

For this reason the institutional mechanisms of the eurozone reflect the interests of the large banks that have set the pace of financialization in Europe. Thus, an independent central bank was established to support a homogeneous money market with the explicit mandate of keeping inflation low; the Stability and Growth Pact was introduced, aimed at fiscal discipline to keep inflation under control, even though compliance was left to each sovereign state; competitiveness in the internal market, meanwhile, came to depend on productivity growth and on the fluctuations of nominal unit labour costs in each country.[46]

The institutional mechanisms of the eurozone have further reflected hierarchical relations among its member states. Core countries – particularly Germany – have deployed the euro as a means of control over lesser states in the union.[47] German industrial capital has gained competitive advantages from the lowering of transaction costs across the internal market, and from the opportunity to outsource productive capacity. For other member states the euro has implied loss of the weapon of currency

---

46 The social and political interests represented by, and promoted through, the establishment of the euro are well understood within heterodox literature. Guglielmo Carchedi has stressed that the euro might be able to deliver the broader international functions that the Deutschmark was unable to perform, thus benefiting German capital ('The EMU, Monetary Crisis, and the Single European Currency', *Capital and Class* 19:63, 1997). Werner Bonefeld has emphasized the political dimension of establishing the euro as a means of fostering bourgeois class domination in Europe that would also restrict the scope for democracy ('Politics of European Monetary Union: Class, Ideology and Critique', *Economic and Political Weekly* 33:35, 1998; 'Europe, the Market and the Transformation of Democracy', *Journal of Contemporary European Studies* 13:1, 2005). John Grahl had made similar points earlier (*After Maastricht*, London: Lawrence and Wishart, 1997).

47—It matters not at all whether Germany or France played the main role in setting up the eurozone in the 1990s. The point is that by the end of the 2000s Germany had emerged as the dominant country of the eurozone, fully conscious of its place. The drive to create a monetary union in Europe, after all, goes back at least to the Werner Report of 1970 which was followed by several, essentially failed, attempts to fix exchange rates during the next two decades. The thinking behind the creation of the euro can perhaps be seen in the report by the Committee for the Study of Economic and Monetary Union, the so-called Delors Report (*Report on Economic and Monetary Union in the European Community*, CB-56-89-401-EN-C, 1989). The document makes clear the need for the European Union to respond to the unstable international conditions created after the end of the Bretton Woods Agreement. It also makes clear the politically driven – and strictly speaking unnecessary – nature of the decision to make the euro the common domestic currency of member states. The combination of these two aspects has contributed to the tremendous crisis of the euro.

FIG. 5 Evolution of nominal unit labour costs in the eurozone

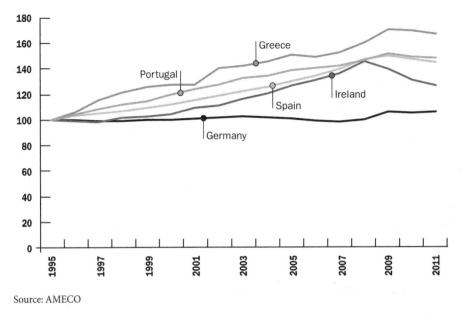

Source: AMECO

depreciation in the face of German exporting prowess. German financial capital has, meanwhile, benefited from the homogeneity of the money market within the European Monetary Union and from the global role of the euro as reserve currency. The euro has facilitated bank borrowing in international markets, lending across the world, and engaging in financial transactions. In particular, the tendency of the euro to rise against the dollar in the 2000s has benefited the German financial sector but also German industrial capital by facilitating its relocation across Europe.[48]

A striking feature of the development of the eurozone has been the emergence of a division between core and periphery, the latter including at least Spain, Portugal, Ireland, and Greece.[49] The split between core and periphery has emanated from a 'race to the bottom' in eurozone labour markets. Member countries have been obliged to adopt a common monetary policy determined by the European Central Bank, while the exercise of fiscal policy has been severely restricted by the Stability and Growth Pact, setting limits on budget deficits at 3 percent of GDP and national debt at 60 percent of GDP. Even though the pact has been frequently breached, it has still operated as a

---

48 Huw Macartney, 'Variegated neo-liberalism: Transnationally oriented fractions of capital in EU financial market integration', *Review of International Studies* 35, 2009.

49 There is also an external periphery of the eurozone, mostly in Eastern Europe, but by definition it is not subject to the same pressures as the internal periphery. It is the latter that has played the pivotal role in the crisis.

FIG. 6 Eurozone current account balances as percentage of GDP

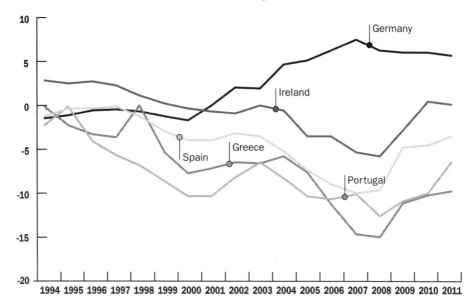

Source: BoPS Yearbook (BPM5)

straitjacket on fiscal policy. Given the rigidity of monetary and fiscal policy, member countries have been encouraged to apply pressure on labour wages and conditions in order to generate competitiveness in the internal eurozone market.

The 'race to the bottom' has been won by German capitalists who have succeeded in keeping wage growth low as well as creating entire areas devoid of trade union organization in both the old East and West Germany. The diverging paths of nominal unit labour costs in figure 5 show the gains in competitiveness made by Germany compared to peripheral countries.

The roots of the disturbance in the eurozone as well as the particular form taken by the crisis of financialization in Europe are evident in figure 5. German levels of competitiveness were already higher than those of the periphery when the euro was introduced; but as nominal unit labour costs in the periphery moved upwards, the German lead in competitiveness has been significantly exacerbated. It is important to stress that the German advance has been overwhelmingly due to keeping the nominal cost of labour low. Productivity growth in Germany throughout this period has been poor, and in fact weaker than in peripheral countries, with the exception of Spain. Germany has emerged as the leading country of the eurozone on the back of systematic pressure on the pay and conditions of German workers.[50]

50   See Costas Lapavitsas et al., *Crisis in the Eurozone*, London: Verso, 2012, part 1.

FIG. 7 Net saving in the eurozone, percentage of GDP

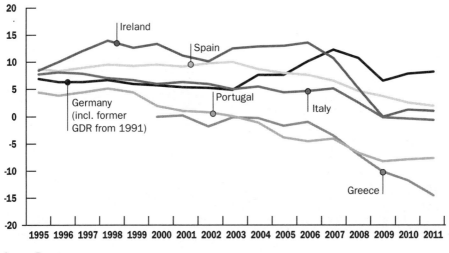

Source: Eurostat

The steady widening of the gap in competitiveness has brought persistent imbalances to current accounts within the eurozone: the periphery has registered large deficits, while Germany has made substantial surpluses, as is shown in figure 6. It is notable that the bulk of German surpluses have originated within the eurozone, of which the periphery is only a small part. The euro has effectively turned the eurozone into an internal market for German capital, allowing limited success to peripheral capitals.

Rising current account deficits for the periphery have naturally meant that peripheral net saving has been a downward path; current account surpluses for Germany, on the other hand, have implied rising German net saving, as is shown in figure 7.

Even in this regard financialization has followed a different path in Germany compared to the US, since German saving has registered substantial increases after the early 2000s. Peripheral saving has meanwhile declined, collapsing entirely in Portugal and Greece. This is a measure of the malfunctioning of domestic accumulation in the periphery and of the difficulty of future recovery.

Debt accumulation in the periphery

The establishment of a core periphery division in the eurozone has led to enormous indebtedness among peripheral countries, giving a particular form to peripheral financialization. To be specific, while peripheral countries were losing competitiveness and registering current account deficits, the European Central Bank (ECB) kept interest rates across the eurozone at very low levels. Low interest rates have had the following two important implications with regard to peripheral debt.

First, peripheral countries were able easily to finance international deficits, thus accumulating external debt, both private and public. The external debt of peripheral

FIG. 8 Core bank exposure to eurozone periphery, US $mn

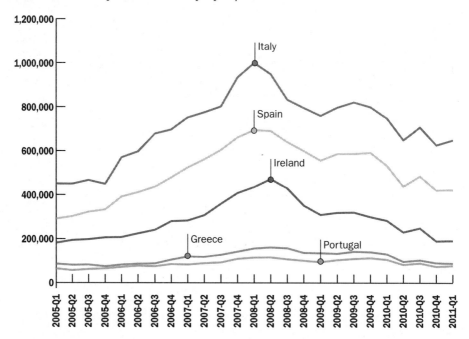

Source: BIS Consolidated Banking Statistics; RMF reports

countries which has subsequently played a destructive role in the eurozone crisis has been closely related to the loss of competitiveness. The lenders to the periphery were primarily the banks of core countries, mostly German and French, which were in effect recycling the surpluses made by core countries on current account. Figure 8 shows the rising exposure of German, French, Belgian, and Dutch banks, taken as proxy for core banks, to the periphery; it also shows the substantial exposure of these banks to Italy. Note further that core bank lending to peripheral countries rose in late 2008, following the bankruptcy of Lehman Brothers. In effect, core banks advanced loans to peripheral states in 2008–2009 on the wrong assumption that such lending was safe as sovereign default was impossible within the European Monetary Union.

Second, low interest rates allowed banks to obtain euro-denominated liquidity cheaply in the interbank market. Given the availability of cheap funding, peripheral banks were able to expand their lending rapidly, particularly after 2005, as is shown in figure 9.[51] In short, peripheral banks incurred debt externally which they proceeded to transform into domestic lending; they also took the opportunity to expand their activities internationally.

---

51   Irish banks expanded much more than other peripheral banks, partly reflecting the Irish policy of privileging foreign capital inflows for more than two decades.

FIG. 9 Peripheral eurozone bank assets as proportion of GDP

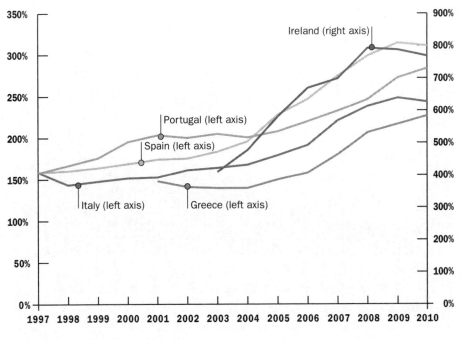

Source: National Central Banks; RMF reports

Financialization of peripheral countries in the context of the eurozone has thus entailed an enormous accumulation of debt domestically as well as internationally. As the international competitiveness of peripheral countries declined resulting in current account deficits, the periphery boosted domestic credit on the basis of low ECB interest rates, the bulk of which went to households and real estate investment; domestic saving, meanwhile, remained on a downward path. Important aspects of the US bubble were thus reproduced in the periphery of the eurozone, but under different institutional arrangements, and hence without the prominent growth of 'shadow' banking, or securitization, characteristic of the US. The heaviest growth of indebtedness in the periphery has been due to private debt, as is shown in figures 10, 11, and 12 for Spain, Portugal, and Greece, respectively.

It cannot be overstressed that the primary cause of peripheral indebtedness has not been the accumulation of sovereign debt. Even in Greece, which has carried a proportionately greater weight of sovereign debt already since the 1980s, the bulk of additional indebtedness since the late 1990s has been due to debt incurred by households and banks. Spain and Portugal have exhibited broadly similar patterns, though the burden of public debt has been considerably lower than Greece. The remarkable feature of peripheral sovereign debt during this period has been the change in its composition, rather than its growth. By the end of the 2000s, for instance, two-thirds of Greek sov-

FIG. 10 Spanish debt by sector of issuer

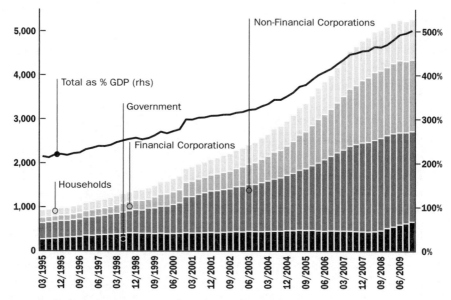

Source: Bank of Spain RMF reports

Note: Debt is adjusted for ECB operations, includes trade credit

FIG. 11 Portuguese debt by sector of issuer

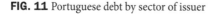

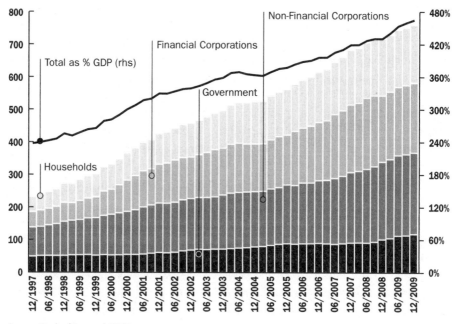

Source: Bank of Portugal; RMF reports

Note: Debt is adjusted for ECB operations, includes trade credit

FIG. 12 Greek debt by sector of issuer

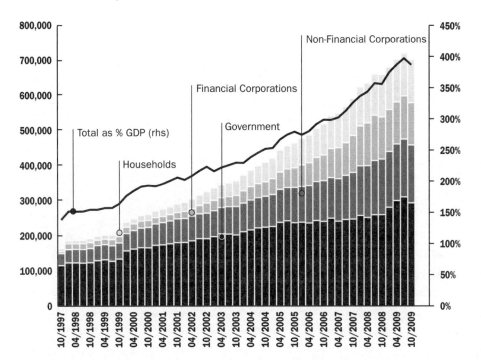

Source: Bank of Greece, Quarterly External Dedt Statistics, World Bank; IMF; RMF reports.

ereign debt was owed to foreigners, and a similar proportion held for Portugal.

In sum, as domestic saving collapsed, peripheral states changed the composition of sovereign debt by borrowing internationally. For much of the 2000s it appeared that peripheral countries had benefited enormously from membership of the eurozone since sovereign borrowing was denominated in euro, that is, presumably in the domestic currency, and for exceptionally low interest rates. In practice peripheral countries were borrowing in a currency that would in the end behave as foreign money to them, even if it was legally domestic. Peripheral states were soon to realize their error, which was only matched by the error of core banks in assuming that lending to the periphery was equivalent to lending to core states of the eurozone.

A fiscal, banking, and monetary crisis in Europe

The global recession that followed the bankruptcy of Lehman Brothers in 2008 led to falling tax revenues for eurozone states and therefore to increased budget deficits, as is shown in figure 13. Fiscal imbalances in the periphery of the eurozone were the result and not the cause of the crisis, even in Greece.

Escalating budget deficits as the recession unfolded led to rapid growth of sovereign debt in the periphery, shown in figure 14.

FIG. 13 Eurozone government primary balances as percentage of GDP

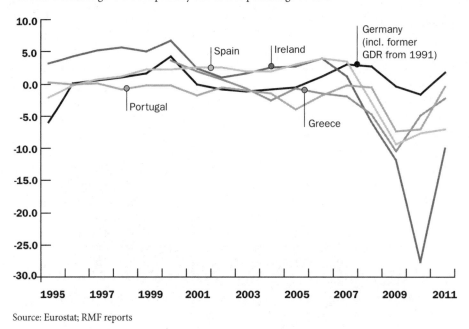

Source: Eurostat; RMF reports

As peripheral sovereign debt began to escalate, bond markets came to realize that the debt of peripheral states was not of the same quality as the debt of core states. Even worse, in late 2009 it became clear that core eurozone countries were not prepared to honour peripheral public debt. Consequently, the states of Greece, Ireland, and Portugal were progressively shut out of international bond markets in 2010–11; moreover, the states of both Spain and Italy were placed in an increasingly precarious position. The crisis of financialization had become a crisis of sovereign debt primarily because peripheral states had borrowed in a currency – the euro – which appeared to be domestic but was in effect foreign.[52]

---

52 It is understood in both heterodox and mainstream literature that the institutional structures of the eurozone imply that peripheral debt is effectively denominated in a foreign currency. Thus, L. Randall Wray, commenting on the constraints imposed by ECB monetary policy independence, argued that: 'It will be as if each EMU member country were to attempt to operate fiscal policy in a foreign currency; deficit spending will require borrowing in that foreign currency according to the dictates of private markets.' (*Understanding Modern Money*, Cheltenham: Edward Elgar, 1998, p. 92; see aslo Dmitri Papadimitriou and L. Randall Wray, 'Euroland's Original Sin', Levy Economics Institute Policy Note 2012/8, 2012) More recently, Giancarlo Corsetti has compared the fate of periphery countries to the 'original sin' of developing countries ('The "Original Sin" in the Eurozone', VoxEU.org, 9 May 2010). This concept was introduced by Barry

FIG. 14 Ratio of public debt to GDP in the periphery of the eurozone

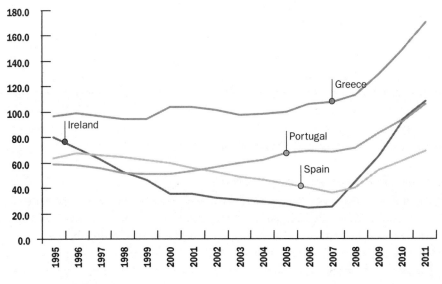

Source: Eurostat; RMF reports

The accumulation of peripheral sovereign debt and the gradual exclusion of peripheral countries from bond markets posed substantial risks for the banks of both core and periphery since banks had acquired a large exposure to public and private debt in the previous period, as was shown above. More specifically, the threat of sovereign default in peripheral countries implied that European banks faced dangers of both insolvency and illiquidity. The sovereign debt crisis meant that a banking crisis could re-emerge, first in

---

Eichengreen and Ricardo Hausmann to emphasize the pressures of servicing foreign debt for countries that are unable to borrow in their domestic currency and have to rely on some form of world money ('Exchange Rates and Financial Fragility', Federal Reserve Bank of Kansas City, 1999). Along similar lines Paul De Grauwe and Yuemei Ji have contrasted eurozone countries to non-member countries that have kept full control of their domestic currency: the latter cannot easily be forced into default as they are protected from self-fulfilling liquidity and solvency crisis (De Grauwe, 'The Governance of a Fragile Eurozone', CEPS Working Document No. 346, May 2011; De Grauwe, 'The European Central Bank: Lender of Last Resort in the Government Bond Markets?', CESifo Working Paper No. 3569, September 2011; De Grauwe, 'The ECB as a Lender of Last Resort', VoxEU, October 2011; De Grauwe and Ji, 'Mispricing of Sovereign Risk and Multiple Equilibria in the Eurozone', CEPS Working Document No. 361, January 2012). Daniel Gros has also emphasized the significance of national debt in the eurozone being owned by non-resident investors whom member-states lack the legal jurisdiction to tax ('External versus Domestic Debt in the Euro Crisis', CEPS Policy Brief No. 243, 25 May 2011).

Europe and perhaps subsequently in the US, the UK and elsewhere. The pacification of banking unrest that had occurred in 2009 mostly through intervention by the US state was at the risk of being undone by peripheral eurozone sovereign indebtedness. If the banking system of Europe was plunged into crisis, the survival of the euro could be put in question as peripheral and other countries might be forced to exit the monetary union.

By 2010–11, consequently, the crisis of financialization began to acquire an even more severe form capable of directly undermining the global monetary order. Core countries of the eurozone found themselves obliged to respond urgently. Their response to the crisis reflected the contradictory and hierarchical nature of the monetary union, while casting further light on financialization.

European states intervene with limited results

Intervention by the state has been fundamental to confronting the eurozone turmoil, but both outlook and methods have been quite different to those in the US. The reasons ultimately lie in the political and social relations underpinning the euro. As has been mentioned above, monetary union in Europe essentially represents a hierarchical alliance of sovereign states giving rise to a new form of world money. To support the nascent reserve currency the eurozone has had to institute a single central bank, proclaiming its liabilities to be legal tender as well as creating a homogeneous money market to provide liquidity to the banks of the monetary union. However, eurozone banks have remained largely national with regard to regulation and to solvency. Moreover, none of the allied states possesses the right to tax across the entire eurozone area, and none is large and powerful enough to act as ultimate guarantor of the liabilities of the European Central Bank. Finally, core states have refused responsibility for the debts of peripheral states, particularly as no mechanisms exist to regulate fiscal affairs across the monetary union. The result has been fumbling state intervention which has even exacerbated the crisis.

The limits of liquidity provision

The most urgent task of state intervention was to meet liquidity shortages among eurozone banks, which has naturally been delegated to the ECB. However, the ECB is an unusual central bank since it cannot rely on the backing of either a unitary or a federal state. Since its inception in 1998 the ECB has operated as an independent central bank, with command over monetary policy and an explicit mandate to control inflation. Its capital has been provided by all member states in proportions that reflect the hierarchical nature of the eurozone, each state carrying individual responsibility for its share. Under no circumstances was the ECB to finance public borrowing by member states since that would effectively mean that some states would take responsibility for the debt of others.[53] By this token, the ECB has supported its euro liabilities primarily

---

53   Clearly stated in Article 104 of the Maastricht Treaty.

with privately issued securities, while also holding substantial quantities of gold as hoard of last resort.

At various points during the crisis the ECB has supplied liquidity to private banks thus acting as lender of last resort on a large scale. The previously noted discrepancy from Bagehot's historic prescription has once again emerged: liquidity has been provided to banks on poor collateral and at a very low rate of interest. ECB liquidity intervention has in effect meant that private banks have been provided with a substantial subsidy, similarly to the liquidity interventions of the Federal Reserve. Large advances took place in August 2007 as the financial crisis first burst out; in 2008 following the collapse of Lehman Brothers; and at the end of 2011 as the sovereign debt crisis emerged in full earnest.[54]

The fundamental difference with the earlier phase of the crisis, however, was that at the end of 2009 liquidity shortages also affected peripheral states, which began to face increasing difficulties in issuing bonds in financial markets worried about the risk of sovereign default. By implication, banks also began to come under pressure in obtaining liquidity and ensuring solvency since they were exposed to sovereign debt. The ECB, consequently, faced pressure to meet the borrowing needs of weaker eurozone states, and thus indirectly to support banks. Meeting the borrowing needs of states, however, contravenes the statutes of the ECB and poses profound problems for the central bank. The reason is obvious and integral to the make-up of the eurozone: unlike the central banks of the US, the UK and Japan, the ECB is not backed by a single state, whose debt it would have been buying under the explicit or implicit guarantee of the same state. If the ECB bought the debt of peripheral states, it would be relying on the backing of core states. In effect core states would be accepting responsibility for the debt of peripheral states, which they have refused to do from the beginning since this action contradicts the fiscal basis of the monetary union.

Nonetheless, since 2010 the ECB has had to relent to some extent as the sovereign crisis took a turn for the worse and Greece was forcibly excluded from bond markets. The ECB has thus introduced the Securities Market Programme and started purchasing sovereign debt instruments in the secondary markets, providing banks and other sellers of public bonds with liquidity, while also trying to keep interest rates on public debt low. In effect, the ECB took action to homogenize public borrowing in the monetary union by substituting itself for the missing unitary or federal state in the eurozone. By implication the ECB has acquired significant credit risk from the public bonds of states that faced default. This risk could not be ultimately guaranteed by a state power since the ECB has been substituting itself precisely for this missing state. This absurd outcome has reflected the contradictory and unsustainable nature of the monetary union.

The difficulty of mounting effective state intervention in the eurozone has thus originated in the particular form of the solvency problem after 2009, which has also shaped

---

54   Lapavitsas et al., *Crisis in the Eurozone*, part 2.

the liquidity problem of the financial system – namely, the main risk of insolvency has applied to states, which has exacerbated the risk of insolvency for banks, and hence has worsened liquidity shortages for both states and banks. A central bank is not the appropriate agent to deal either with insolvent states, or with insolvent banks. Both of these tasks require intervention by a sovereign entity that has direct access to tax revenue. In the absence of a suitable state institution, the ECB has found itself under increasing pressure to play a role for which it has not been equipped. It has thus faced considerable risks to its own credibility as well as to the acceptability of its liabilities – to the international standing of the euro as world money.

The complexity of the solvency problem

Solvency has been particularly difficult to deal with in the context of the eurozone for two interrelated reasons. First, and as has already been mentioned, the risk to banks has arisen in large part because of the risk to states. Second, despite the existence of a common monetary policy and a homogeneous money market in the eurozone, banks have remained resolutely national. When solvency is at stake, banks can only turn to their own nation state. Indeed, in the course of the crisis European banks have become even more national than before since they have proportionately increased their lending to their respective national states.[55] The deeper problem this poses for the eurozone is apparent: the backbone of the monetary union is the homogeneous space created for banks to borrow on similar terms from the ECB, thus also lending at comparable rates. If the banking space is losing its homogeneity and is becoming more national, it follows that the eurozone is breaking up from within and national interest rates would begin to diverge significantly. The more immediate problem is equally apparent: how could a peripheral state, whose debt constituted a threat to banks, also act as rescuer of the same banks? More broadly, on what grounds could a state be expected to act as rescuer of the banks of another state?

The problem nonetheless remained that, with bank solvency at risk, the entire structure of the monetary union was threatened with collapse. The eurozone was consequently obliged to provide funding for states that were shut out of bond markets, thus preventing sovereign default and by extension protecting the solvency of banks. A complex mechanism of 'bail outs' was devised, ostensibly to rescue peripheral states that faced default, but in essence to support European banks. A temporary European Financial Stability Facility (EFSF) was established in 2010, to be replaced by a more permanent European Stability Mechanism (ESM) in 2013. The EFSF was essentially a special-purpose vehicle, similar to those active in the US bubble of 2001–2007. It issued its own bonds in order to be able to lend to states in distress, but stuck to the principle of individual responsibility for the debt of each guarantor state. It could also make funds directly available to banks in distress.[56]

---

55   Ibid., part 3.
56   Ibid., part 2.

Greece, Ireland, and Portugal received 'bail outs' from the EFSF, supplemented by the International Monetary Fund, in 2010–11. The funds were essentially loans guaranteed on an intergovernmental basis, pro rata to each state's contribution to the capital of the ECB. The loans were initially advanced at punitively expensive rates of interest presumably to teach a moral lesson to delinquent sovereign borrowers, in sharp contrast to subsidized liquidity available to banks from the ECB. Above all, loans were advanced on condition of tough austerity policies to be imposed on peripheral countries, designed and supervised by the IMF.

The inadequacy and contradictoriness of this response to the solvency problem became apparent in late 2011 as the sovereign crisis deepened exacerbating the risk to banks. The capacity of the EFSF to borrow and thus to lend had been limited by the contributions and guarantees of eurozone states at around EUR440bn, a sum that was manifestly inadequate to support both states and banks. But in order to expand its resources, the EFSF would need either to function on the basis of joint and several (rather than individual) liability for its debts, or it would have to draw directly on the guarantees of core states to rescue the banks of peripheral states. In both cases the EFSF would have to transgress the fiscal basis of the eurozone – that one state should not accept responsibility for the deficits or debts of another.

EFSF intervention, consequently, proved ineffectual in tackling the solvency problem of either states, or banks. Faced with EFSF weakness, pressure increased to find another method of dealing with the solvency problem of states, and the suggestion most heavily proposed has been to issue Eurobonds. Several different plans have been mooted but the core idea has been in common: public bonds guaranteed jointly and severally by all eurozone members would be used to meet the borrowing needs of peripheral and other states. If weak states were able to borrow cheaply on this basis, the risk of default would be ameliorated.[57] Yet, the suggestion also implied that core

---

57   Eurobonds were already discussed in the Giovannini Group Report (2000) the idea essentially being to issue bonds by a single authority which would borrow on behalf of the member states allowing individual states to meet funding shortfalls. In the course of the crisis economists have proposed several variants of Eurobonds. Thus, Paul De Grauwe and Wim Moesen proposed a commonly issued Eurobond whereby each participating member state would guarantee only its share of the joint instrument ('Gains for All: A Proposal for a Common Euro Bond', *Intereconomics* 44:3, 2009). Wim Boonstra, Jacques Delpla, and Jakob von Weizsäcker proposed a different instrument issued by a group of euro-area member states backed by several and joint guarantees, making it an indivisible legal object (Boonstra, 'How EMU Can Be Strengthened by Central Funding of Public Deficits', in *The Creation of a Common European Bond Market*, March 2010; Delpla and Von Weizsäcker, 'The Blue Bond Proposal', Bruegel Policy Brief 2010/13, May 2010). Finally, Daniel Gros and Stefano Micossi proposed a still further Eurobond issued by an EU institution that would lend the funds raised member states ('A Bond-Issuing EU Stability Fund Could Rescue Europe', *Europe's World*, Spring 2009). The instrument would be backed

states would have to accept higher interest rates for their own borrowing as well as carrying some residual risk from peripheral default. In effect, Eurobonds would lead to a sharing of sovereign risk among member states, thus violating directly the Maastricht Treaty. More than that, the mutualization of risk contravened the underlying fiscal logic of the EMU and thus led to arguments about loss of fiscal discipline and imposing an inequitable sharing of benefits and costs among member states.[58] Core states, with Germany in the lead, have persistently refused to adopt the idea.

Failure to deal decisively with the solvency problem meant that the eurozone remained in severe danger from the risk of sovereign default throughout 2011–2012, threatening to result in exit by one or more peripheral states. The risk became even greater due to the policy of austerity that has accompanied the 'bail out' programmes.

Austerity

The precondition for receipt of 'bail out' funds has been the imposition of austerity packages coupled with liberalization and privatization. Across the periphery, but also increasingly in the core, public spending has been cut, taxes have been increased, wages have been reduced, markets have been further deregulated, and public enterprises have been lined up for privatization. These policies have aimed at shifting the costs of adjustment onto workers in the periphery as well as protecting the interests of industrial capital by changing the balance of power against labour.

The original cause of the eurozone crisis was not fiscal profligacy but loss of competitiveness and the accumulation of debt by the periphery, as was shown above. By this token, austerity and additional pressure on labour in the periphery were unlikely to assuage the crisis in the short run, if at all. Figure 6 shows that German nominal unit labour costs have risen gently as the German economy recovered from the initial shock of the global crisis in 2008–2009. In contrast, Greek and Irish costs have collapsed, while Spanish and Portuguese costs have declined more gradually. Thus, the policy of crushing labour costs would take several years before significantly reducing the gap of competitiveness. By extension, and as is clear from figure 7, it would be several years before the imbalances in current accounts were successfully confronted on this basis.

Even worse, public expenditure cuts and tax increases together with credit shortages due to persistent difficulties of banks have exacerbated the tendency to recession in the periphery. Conditions in Greece, in particular, have been particularly grave since

---

by several and joint guarantees of all members states, not explicitly but deriving from the EU legal order.

58   See Otmar Issing, 'Why a Common Eurozone Bond Isn't Such a Good Idea', *Europe's World*, Summer 2009; and Wim Kösters, 'Common Eurobonds: No Appropriated Instrument', *Intereconomics* 44:3, pp. 135–8, 2009; but see also Carlo A. Favero and Alessandro Missale, 'EU Public Debt Management and Eurobonds', in *Euro Area Governance – Ideas for Crisis Management Reform*, Brussels: European Parliament, 2010.

2010, leading to collapsing GDP as the country has entered the most severe contraction in its post-war history. Other peripheral countries have also faced a re-emergence of recession, with the attendant rise in unemployment, especially among the young, particularly in Spain and Greece.

Austerity has been particularly destructive in the periphery of the eurozone in view of the inability to devalue, thus regaining competitiveness decisively. The contraction of aggregate demand caused by cuts in public expenditure and reductions in wages has been barely offset by the narrowing of the current account deficits. In effect, peripheral countries have found themselves trapped within the eurozone, facing austerity and high unemployment for years. As GDP has contracted, the burden of sovereign debt has become even heavier, thus exacerbating the prospect of insolvency and default for peripheral states.

The fumbling intervention by the EU in the course of the crisis has aimed at protecting the interests of large financial and industrial capital, but has also undermined these interests. As recession in the periphery deepened and insolvency became worse, the banks of both core and periphery have faced greater risks. The creditworthiness of Italy and other large countries in the eurozone has also been affected since they held substantial volumes of public and private debt. By 2013 the crisis of financialization had led Europe deeper into crisis creating greater risks of breaking up for the euro. If that eventuality occurred, a deeper and more general crisis would follow across the world.

10. CONTROLLING FINANCE

The crisis of the 2000s has raised profound questions regarding financial regulation as well as the performance and role of private banks, including their ability to undertake information collection and risk management. It has also raised the issue of confronting financialization and dealing with its implications. This chapter considers the broad parameters of financial regulation since the end of the Second World War focusing on the scope of and prospects for regulation in the context of financialization. To engage in analysis, it proposes two important distinctions; first, the distinction between market-conforming and market-negating regulation; second, the distinction between generic and systemic market-negating regulation. In this light, the chapter also briefly discusses confronting financialization from the perspective of working people.

The dominant form of regulation during the last three decades has been market-conforming regulation – regulation shaped by private financial institutions, operated by semi-public bodies, and largely focused on the practices of individual financial institutions. The threatened collapse of private banking at several junctures since the outbreak of the crisis has flagged the ineffectiveness of this form of regulation. However, the crisis has also indicated that a more deeply embedded form of regulation has continued to thrive in the years of financialization: generic market-negating regulation that includes lender of last resort, deposit protection, and implicit guarantees of large financial institutions by the state.

Financial regulation tends generally to influence the returns to capital employed in the sphere of finance, and thus has a market-negating aspect. However, in the years of financialization, generic market-negating regulation has explicitly supported the profitability of private financial institutions. It has also been sharply different from regulation during the three decades after the Second World War, which was also market-negating but had the specific aim of controlling finance as a system. To this purpose systemic market-negating regulation included an array of mutually interacting measures, such as price and quantity controls, functional specialization of institutions, and capital controls. The underlying assumption was that the untrammelled operation of financial markets could potentially destabilize capitalist accumulation, and hence finance had to be controlled as a system.

With the rise of financialization, systemic market-negating regulation has gone into retreat to be replaced by market-conforming regulation; during the same period, however, generic market-negating regulation has also become stronger, buttressing the private returns of finance. The crisis of the 2000s has cast a harsh light on market-conforming regulation, while posing again the issue of market-negating regulation aiming to control finance as a system. Nonetheless, re-instating systemic market negation in finance is far from easy under conditions of financialization, in view of the structural transformation of non-financial enterprises and banks but also of the nature of contemporary world money.

The difficulty of imposing regulatory controls over finance under conditions of financialization has raised afresh the prospect of expanding public ownership in finance. Publicly owned financial institutions and mechanisms would offer fresh scope both to control finance and to reverse financialization. Needless to say, however, confronting financialization would be far more complex than merely introducing public banking on a large scale. Financialization is a deeply rooted transformation of contemporary capitalism. Opposing it would require profound social and political changes, including public provision of basic goods and services for households. Not least, it would also require an ideological challenge to neoliberalism. In short, confronting financialization would ultimately lead to confronting the capitalist character of society as a whole.

The trajectory of regulation after the Second World War: Market-negating regulation

From the end of the Second World War to the mid-1970s – a period of unprecedented growth of real accumulation – a range of regulations and controls applied to the financial systems of mature economies as well as to the international operations of finance. The theoretical and ideological justification for tight controls over finance was provided by Keynes's damning verdict on financial excess in the *General Theory*, calling for the 'the euthanasia of the rentier' as a valid aim of monetary and financial policy that would strengthen the role of productive capitalists.[1] The regulation of finance was an integral part of the dominant Keynesianism of the period, summed up as 'financial repression'.[2]

The system of financial repression had its roots in the great crisis of the 1930s which ushered in major regulatory changes with the aim of placing finance under control. The major institutional and legal change of the era took place in the US with the introduction of the Glass–Steagall Act in 1933, which separated commercial from investment banking as well as setting administrative limits on bank interest rates (under the so-called Regulation Q) and limits on the volume of bank lending against securities.[3] The Glass–Steagall Act encapsulated the dominant approach to financial regulation until the gradual emergence of financialization had signalled the second great wave of financial ascendancy. Financial repression was also spurred by the vast accumulation

---

1   John Maynard Keynes, *The General Theory of Employment, Interest and Money*, London: Macmillan, 1973, ch. 24.

2   The term is typically associated with Ronald McKinnon and Edward Shaw – both highly critical of it – although Raymond Goldsmith had covered the main ideas earlier. Ronald McKinnon, *Money and Capital in Economic Development*, Washington: The Brookings Institution, 1973. Edward S. Shaw, *Financial Deepening in Economic Development*, New York: Oxford University Press, 1973. Raymond Goldsmith, *Financial Structure and Development*, New Haven, CT: Yale University Press, 1969.

3   Franklin R. Edwards, *The New Finance: Regulation and Financial Stability*, Washington, DC: AEI Press, 1996.

of public debt by mature countries in the course of the Second World War. The leading states of the world market, confronted with public debts that were held by both financial institutions and households, adopted administrative measures regulating interest rates, often forcing real interest rates into negative territory. Financial repression effectively worked as a subsidy to states allowing for the gradual reduction of public debt.

The system of regulation applied to both money and finance, domestically as well as internationally. It relied, on the one hand, on the role of the dollar as world money under the Bretton Woods Agreement and, on the other, on administrative controls on prices, quantities and functions within the domestic financial system. Three elements characterized financial regulation generally across mature capitalist countries, although the distinction between market-based (Anglo-Saxon) versus bank-based (German–Japanese) financial systems never ceased to apply. In spite of the prominent role played by the Glass–Steagall Act, these elements were most vividly apparent in Japan, a late developer that finally joined the ranks of mature capitalist countries in the three decades after the Second World War.[4]

First, there were controls on interest rates, received by and paid to, financial institutions. Rates on assets were frequently determined administratively, based on the lending rate of the central bank, and were kept deliberately low in nominal terms with the (spoken or unspoken) aim of supporting productive capitalists. Rates on liabilities, primarily on deposits, were even more tightly controlled, often being zero for a range of deposits. Further, there were also controls on the quantities of credit and the direction of credit flows generated by financial institutions. Several ratios on bank balance sheets were administratively set, including reserves to deposits, and credit was often directed to selected industries and areas of economic activity. Thus, the backbone of financial repression was provided by controls over prices and quantities of credit, even if there were significant variations among developed countries.

Second, there were controls on the range of functions that financial institutions were allowed to undertake. This aspect of financial repression again varied according to the historical and institutional trajectory of particular countries, but several features were in common across both mature and developing countries. Commercial banking was generally kept separate from investment banking through legislation – the Glass–Steagall Act in the US and its equivalent, Article 65, in Japan – or through monopoly practices and informal 'clubbing' exclusivity (as in the UK and elsewhere). Banks that provided long-term investment funds were also generally kept separate from other banks, through special privileges in obtaining liabilities (for instance, issuing long-term bonds) or even through direct state ownership. Typically, financial institutions that engaged in providing credit for international trade, agriculture, housing, and consumption were kept separate from each other.

Third, there were controls on international capital flows, operating as a necessary

---

4   Yoshio Suzuki, *The Japanese Financial System*, Oxford: Clarendon Press, 1987.

supplement to the Bretton Woods Agreement that guaranteed convertibility of the US dollar into gold at $35 to the ounce. In effect, gold still functioned as the global means of ultimate hoarding among states, even though the dollar was used in practice for payments as well as for hoarding value internationally. International monetary transactions, consequently, occurred at largely fixed exchange rates. To support fixed exchange rates, it was necessary to regulate international capital flows, which meant controls on the capital account, including outright prohibition on acquiring foreign assets, applying differential exchange rates to financial as opposed to commercial transactions, and taxing foreign financial returns.

The content of financial repression was particularly clear in the context of developing countries. Countries in Asia and Africa that emerged from colonialism in the 1950s rapidly acquired national financial systems with the aim of replacing the imperial commercial banks and severing the links with the financial and monetary networks of the metropolis.[5] National commercial banks were created, often publicly owned, and central banks were established to act as arms of the state, even in the absence of a domestic money market. Financial repression was the norm across developing countries, including controls on interest rates, credit flows and functional specialization of financial institutions. Financial systems, furthermore, tended to be bank-based, assigning a weak role to stock markets, or often lacking stock markets altogether.

Theoretical justification for financial repression in developing countries was typically sought in the dominant Keynesianism of the time but also reflected the particular evolution of development economics. More generally, and even within international organizations such as the World Bank, economic development was perceived as a matter of planning domestic investment in the face of shortages of domestic saving. Consequently, development was thought to necessitate regular financial flows from abroad, often to be officially provided. The dominant approach among policymakers was that financial prices and quantities ought to be regulated in order to attain planned growth objectives.

Regulation of prices, quantities and functions self-evidently altered the normal profit-making activities of financial institutions. Therefore, the type of regulation characteristic of the immediate post-war period can be called market-negating: it affected the equalization of returns between finance and the rest of the economy, particularly as ceilings were administratively imposed on interest rates. Market-negating regulation also created risks for financial institutions since credit was directed to selected sectors and often had a long-term character. Furthermore, market-negating regulation affected

---

5   For a historical discussion in the context of Africa, for instance, see Martin Brownbridge and Charles Harvey, *Banking in Africa*, Oxford: Currey, 1998. For institutional and economic analysis of both repression and deregulation in Africa, see Machiko Nissanke and Erenest Aryeetey, *Financial Integration and Development: Liberalization and Reform in Sub-Saharan Africa*, London: Routledge, 1998.

maturity transformation since it typically lengthened the maturity of the assets of com-mercial banks and other financial institutions. In sum, the system of market-negating regulation after the Second World War transformed the returns of financial institutions partly into rents that had state backing.[6]

Financial repression in both developed and developing countries began to unravel in the late 1960s and collapsed in the 1970s as the ascendancy of Keynesianism came to an end. Two fundamental reasons contributed to its decline and prepared the ground for the emergence of financialization. First, in the 1950s and 1960s there gradually emerged financial processes that lay outside the system of controls both internationally and domestically. In the international sphere arose the so-called 'Euromarkets', that is, financial markets in which internationally active corporations and banks could hold and trade assets beyond the regulatory reach of the authorities. London provided a hospitable venue for such activities, while British banks and US multinationals were among the first to take advantage.[7] In the domestic sphere, a multiplicity of equal-ly important, if less noticeable, financial processes also emerged bypassing domestic repression. In Japan, for instance, there arose the *gensaki* market, an unregulated mar-ket in which corporations were able to trade temporarily idle funds.[8]

Unregulated financial processes, both international and domestic, gradually allowed financial institutions to bypass regulatory controls, thus undermining regu-lation as a whole. A fundamental reason in this respect was that unregulated financial activities disrupted competition among financial institutions since some transactions generated market-determined returns, while others generated controlled (hence lower) returns. Pressures to change the regulatory regime thus began to emerge spontaneously within the financial system.

From the perspective of Marxist theory of finance discussed in Chapter 4, it is hardly surprising that financial repression eventually undermined itself. The financial system is an outgrowth of capitalist accumulation mobilizing idle money and organ-

---

6   The rent-like character of financial returns was evident in Japan, where banks drew low but fairly secure returns, backed by the state. In effect, committees were created at various levels involving the leading representatives of sections of the capitalist class and leading state bureau-crats. These committees supervised returns and competition within the financial system and other sectors of the economy, while also overseeing the interaction between finance and the rest of the economy; see Keiichiro Inaba, 'The Transformation of Japanese Commercial Banking: Information Gathering and Assessing', unpublished PhD thesis, University of London, 2008.

7   Eric Helleiner, *States and the Re-emergence of Global Finance: From Bretton Woods to the 1990s*, Ithaca, NY: Cornell University Press, 1994. Soviet institutions were among the first to hold Euromarket assets, attracted by the lack of US authority controls. The Federal Reserve attempted to control the Euromarkets by introducing reserve requirements, but failed. Ibid., pp. 135–68.

8   Yoshio Suzuki, 'Financial Reform in Japan – Developments and Prospects', *Monetary and Economic Studies* 5:3, December 1987.

izing trade credit. The imposition of controls on prices, quantities and functions cannot obviate the intrinsic tendencies of capitalist accumulation to create trade credit relations as well as generate idle money capital available for lending. Other things equal, these tendencies would create scope for new and uncontrolled institutions and practices which would sit uneasily with controlled existing structures. The result would be tension among financial institutions pivoting in the first instance on systematic divergences in returns.

The second reason for the decline of financial repression was the collapse of the Bretton Woods Agreement in 1971–73. Its demise was due in part to the accumulation of US dollars abroad which propelled the growth of 'Euromarkets'. International dollar hoards increased as the US economy registered persistent trade deficits, leading to growing inability of US authorities to honour the pledge of converting the dollar into gold at a fixed price. The accumulation of dollars became even greater after the first oil shock of 1973, thus catapulting the Euromarkets toward further growth.[9] The failure of Bretton Woods was a reflection of the changing balance in the world market as the relative weight of the US economy declined. For our purposes, however, what matters is that the collapse of Bretton Woods eventually led to lifting controls on the capital account. Once the pledge of convertibility had been dishonoured by the US, a series of developments followed, including the disappearance of the gold anchor, the impossibility of maintaining fixed exchange rates, the introduction of flexible exchange rates, and the eventual lifting of controls on international capital flows.

The period that followed the demise of Bretton Woods has been characterized by great volatility of exchange rates; moreover, inflation rose sharply in the 1970s contributing to volatility of interest rates. For financial institutions active in the world market it became important to remove controls on international capital flows precisely to confront the risks generated by the new volatilities.[10] Rising volatility of exchange rates and interest rates as well as the gradual lifting of financial controls encouraged financial innovation, a process that has transformed the conduct of banks in the period of financialization.

Removing international capital controls and abolishing domestic regulations laid the ground for financial liberalization. An important step was the partial abolition of regulation Q in the US in the 1960s, thus freeing some interest rates on bank liabilities. Equally important was the introduction of Competition and Credit Control legislation in the UK in 1970s which began to dismantle international regulations constraining British banks. Financial deregulation accelerated in the 1970s and became the norm

---

9   Helleiner, *States and the Re-emergence of Global Finance*, pp. 101–14; and Paul Langley, *World Financial Orders: An Historical International Political Economy*, London: Routledge, 2002, p. 86.

10   John Eatwell and Lance Taylor, *Global Finance at Risk*, Cambridge: Polity Press, 2000.

in the 1980s.[11] The end result was substantial disappearance of controls on financial prices, quantities, and functions – thus of the very substance of systemic market-negating regulation.

Financial liberalization also spread to developing countries in the 1970s mostly on the grounds that low interest rates had failed to encourage investment by productive capitalists. Funds for development could presumably be internally generated as domestic saving would respond positively to rising (decontrolled) interest rates. These ideas and policies began a trend in development finance that eventually led to the Washington Consensus in the late 1980s the underlying principle of which is that financial repression is counterproductive not least because it leads to weak and inefficient investment. From this perspective, the appropriate approach to finance in developing countries is to allow interest rates and all attendant financial magnitudes to be determined freely by financial markets.[12]

It is important to note that financial liberalization in developing countries has always had a derivative character. Unlike developed countries, liberalized finance has been partly imposed on developing countries through pressure by multilateral organizations, including the World Bank and the IMF. To be sure, in all instances of financial liberalization there has been a domestic constituency favouring the abolition of financial repression; however, the driving force has often come from the outside. The lever for the imposition of financial liberalization has typically been conditionality attached to international loans given by multilateral organizations and developed countries to developing countries caught up in the repeated crises of the last three decades. The path was thus laid for subordinate financialization to emerge in developing countries.

Regulation under conditions of financialization: Market-conforming regulation and persistent market negation

The ascendancy of financial liberalization during the decades of financialization should not be confused with the absence of regulation. Finance has continued to be heavily regulated, both domestically and internationally, but regulation has been of a very

---

11 For discussion of the adoption of financial deregulation, see Helleiner, *States and the Re-emergence of Global Finance*.

12 The literature on financial liberalization is enormous, emanating from Ronald McKinnon, *Money and Capital in Economic Development*, Brookings Institution, 1973; and Edward S. Shaw, *Financial Deepening in Economic Development*, Oxford: Oxford University Press, 1973. A further key contribution was made in Ronald McKinnon, *The Order of Economic Liberalization*, London: Johns Hopkins University Press, 1991. For an accessible condensation of the fundamental ideas, see Maxwell Fry, *Money, Interest and Banking in Economic Development*, London: Johns Hopkins University Press, 1988. For a devastating and prescient critique, see Carlos Diaz-Alejandro, 'Good-Bye Financial Repression, Hello Financial Crash', *Journal of Development Economics* 19:1–2, 1985.

different type than that of the period immediately after the Second World War. The prevalent approach can be characterized as market-conforming regulation in contrast to the systemic market-negating regulation that had set financial prices, quantities and functions during the previous period. The dominant agents of regulation, furthermore, have been public bodies that are closely, and even organically, connected to the financial system.[13]

Before discussing the broad outline of market-conforming regulation, however, it is vital to note that market-negating regulation has far from disappeared in the period of financialization. On the contrary, a generic type of market-negating regulation – some aspects of which have already been discussed in Chapter 9 in connection with the role of the state in the course of crises – has thrived. Financialization has been underpinned by market-negating regulation which long predates the great crisis of the 1930s and the subsequent rise of Keynesianism. The following three components are fundamental to it.

The first and classic component has been the function of the 'lender of last resort' for the central bank, which emerged in the British financial system in the second half of the nineteenth century.[14] The experience of regular decennial crises, capped by the collapse of Overend, Gurney, and Co. in 1866, contributed to the realization that the central bank ought to provide liquidity freely in a crisis. It has become conventional wisdom in mature capitalism that the central bank functions as lender of last resort, a view summed up by Bagehot already in the early 1870s, as was noted in Chapter 9. Lender of last resort, needless to say, negates market processes by ensuring the viability of financial institutions in the face of liquidity shortages. Participants in capitalist

---

13   Both the shift to a different regime of financial regulation and the proliferation of market-conforming practices are well appreciated in the critical literature. In a series of books, Susan Strange has proposed the notion of 'Casino Capitalism' based on the self-regulating financial market (*Casino Capitalism*, Oxford: Basil Blackwell, 1986; *States and Markets*, London: Continuum, 1994; *The Retreat of the State*, Cambridge: Cambridge University Press, 1996). For Strange the financial sector possesses power because of the structures of credit, but also because of the structures of international money and the flows of global finance; the global markets are gradually prevailing over national states. Picciotto and Haines have similarly called the new regime 'self-authorized self-regulation' ('Regulating Global Financial Markets', *Journal of Law and Society* 26:3, 1999, pp. 360); the bodies that exercise regulation are seen as inherently undemocratic public-private hybrids (Sol Picciotto, 'International Transformations of the Capitalist State', *Antipode* 43:1, 2011).

14   General policy intervention in the sphere of money and finance had emerged considerably earlier. Already in the 1830s the Bank of England operated the 'Palmer Rule' regulating its gold reserves relative to its liabilities, which then took a rigid form in the Bank Act of 1844, see Makoto Itoh and Costas Lapavitsas, *Political Economy of Money and Finance*, London: Macmillan, 1999, ch. 1.

markets presumably have to bear the consequences of their own decisions. If it is necessary for financial markets occasionally to receive wholesale provision of liquidity from the state, it follows that markets produce suboptimal results, while participants are protected from their own actions by publicly backed liquidity. Consequently, moral hazard is an inherent outcome of the function of lender of last resort.

The second component of generic market-negating regulation is deposit insurance guarantees. The practice emerged already in the late nineteenth century, and can take a variety of legal forms – private and public as well as explicit and implicit. Contemporary financial systems are characterized by implicit guarantees of deposits offered by the state, the need for which arises from the transformation of extremely short-term liabilities into longer-term assets inherent to commercial banking. If deposit holders converged on a bank demanding cash, the bank would go bankrupt irrespective of its profitability, of the quality of its assets, and so on. Public guarantees prevent or ameliorate bank runs by re-establishing trust in banks among the public. It is apparent that public deposit insurance guarantees represent market-negating regulation since they effectively lower the cost of liabilities for banks. But they also create moral hazard since, on the one hand, some of the liabilities of banks are publicly protected and, on the other, deposit holders need not ultimately monitor the performance of banks. By this token, deposit insurance guarantees raise the profitability of banks, other things equal.

The third and most striking aspect of market-negating regulation in the course of financialization, however, has been the gradual prevalence of the principle of 'too big to fail' among financial institutions. Banks considered 'too big to fail' have often been effectively (if tacitly) protected against failure on the grounds that failure would have severe externalities, including the possibility of generalized collapse of the financial system. Intervention has, therefore, focused on avoiding the putative 'systemic' risk by protecting the solvency of banks, rather than simply providing liquidity; public funds have frequently been made available to financial institutions for this purpose. The principle of 'too big to fail' clearly poses moral hazard problems since it protects bank shareholders and bondholders from the consequences of failure. Moreover, the implicit state guarantees of solvency keep the cost of capital artificially low for banks and other financial institutions, thus increasing profitability.[15]

---

15 Even Lord Turner of the UK's Financial Services Agency has wondered aloud about the social usefulness of bloated finance, while Mervyn King, Governor of the Bank of England, has been concerned about some banks being 'too big'; see Adair Turner, 'Adair Turner Roundtable: How to Tame Global Finance', *Prospect*, September 2009, pp. 34–41; and Mervyn King, 'Speech by Mervyn King, Governor of the Bank of England, at the Lord Mayor's Banquet for Bankers and Merchants of the City of London at the Mansion House', 17 June 2009. The Governor of the Federal Reserve, Ben Bernanke, meanwhile, was pleased that a legal framework to 'wind down' 'systemically critical firms' had been developed by 2012; see Ben Bernanke, 'Some Reflections on the Crisis and the Policy Response', 13 April 2012, at federalreserve.gov.

Summing up, generic market-negating regulation in the course of financialization has operated as a set of – implicit or explicit – public mechanisms that boost the returns to finance amidst generalized ideological promotion of free markets. Financial institutions have been protected and supported by the state in terms of liquidity and solvency, thus securing higher profits, while losses and risks have been passed to the public. These fundamental features of the contemporary regulation of finance have been vital to the handling of the crisis that broke out in 2007.

Nonetheless, the characteristic form of regulation in the years of financialization has been market-conforming.[16] This type of regulation has tended to apply primarily to individual financial institutions, rather than to the financial system as a whole, with the aim of facilitating delivery of their putative tasks. It has often focused on the balance sheet of banks seeking to affect operations through quantitative or qualitative changes. Note that market-negating regulation after the Second World War also affected the balance sheet of banks, including the asset side. Thus, both loans and reserves were subjected to controls to ensure the direction of credit as well as the availability of adequate liquidity for banks. In contrast, market-conforming regulation in the years of financialization has shifted regulatory attention to the liability side of the balance sheet, above all, to the adequacy of own capital with a view to ensuring bank solvency.

Market-conforming regulation of finance has drawn ideological sustenance from the new microeconomics of finance stressing information-theoretic, principal–agent analysis of financial institutions, discussed in Chapter 5 and elsewhere in this book. Information asymmetries between lender and borrower could presumably lead to problems of adverse selection and moral hazard, thus resulting in suboptimal results in financial markets, including failure of markets to clear. Consequently, they provide grounds for market-conforming regulation of finance, advocated even by some who have been generally critical of financial liberalization.[17]

Contrary to the practices of the immediate post-war years, market-conforming regulation has not been based on the assumption that freely operating financial markets could be inimical to growth and accumulation. The assumption has been, rather, that financial markets occasionally face difficulties in delivering optimal results due to

---

16   In the rest of this chapter, restrictions applying to financial institutions with regard to obtaining a license (entry), branching, setting up holding companies, and so on, are ignored. These are powerful instruments of state intervention, but are different from regulation of prices and quantities, which is the main concern of this chapter.

17   See, for instance, Joseph Stiglitz, 'Markets, Market Failures and Development', *American Economic Review* 79:2, 1989, pp. 197–202; and Joseph Stiglitz, 'More Instruments and Broader Goals: Moving Toward the Post Washington Consensus', WIDER Annual Lecture, Helsinki, 7 January 1998. A further justification for regulation might be that financial failure has significant externalities on economic activity, but the theoretical foundations of this view are not nearly as well developed.

informational and other institutional weaknesses. Therefore, regulation could – and even should – take place to ameliorate problems of market failure. Such regulation would be market-conforming, in the sense that it would assuage the functioning of financial institutions by improving the ability to monitor borrowers but also bolstering the assurances offered to the holders of the liabilities of institutions.

Equally fundamental to market-conforming regulation has been the ascendancy of the concept of risk in analysing banking coupled with increasing technical sophistication in its measurement. Banks have historically deployed conventional wisdom in managing assets and liabilities, deriving from practical experience. Banks typically accumulate customary and practical knowledge in handling loanable capital as well as in managing trade credit according to the specific historical, political and even physical conditions of a country. In the years of financialization the conventional wisdom of banks has been given a computationally intensive scientific veneer, often with the use of mathematical formulae borrowed from physics.[18] Regulatory changes in accounting systems, including mark-to-market, have reinforced the practice of continuous quantitative measurement of risk on bank balance sheets, thus determining required levels of bank capital.

This approach to regulation has been institutionalized in the accords known as Basel I and II, which have been under review to form Basel III. The Basel Accords are instances of market-conforming regulation, essentially formed by banks for banks and promulgated internationally by bodies that have only loose connections with nation states.[19] The Accords have been the product of the Bank for International Settlements (BIS) a body established to promote cooperation among central banks through a variety of institutional methods, including regular meetings. Within the BIS regulatory power resides in good measure with the Basel Committee for Banking Supervision (BCBS) the members of which are nation states represented by their central bank; the BCBS issued the Basel I Accord in 1988. The accords do not have legal force but the nation states participating in BCBS have agreed to enforce the supervisory standards specified in the accords.

The Basel Accords have been explicitly based on the incorporation of the concept of risk in specifying regulatory practice. Thus, Basel I was primarily concerned with credit risk arising from loans made by banks, and consequently attempted to forestall

---

18   Costas Lapavitsas and Paulo Dos Santos, 'Globalization and Contemporary Banking: On the Impact of New Technology', *Contributions to Political Economy* 27, 2008, pp. 31–56.

19   This point has been well established in the literature; see, for instance, Geoffrey Underhill, 'Markets Beyond Politics?', *European Journal of Political Research* 19:2–3, 1991, pp. 197–225. For Underhill, the relationship between markets and the state constitutes a whole in which the interests of the market can be integrated with the state. Geoffrey Underhill, 'Global Money and the Decline of State Power', in *Strange Power: Shaping the Parameters of International Relations and International Political Economy*, ed. Thomas Lawton et al., Burlington, VT: Ashgate, 2000.

it by setting a minimum level of own capital at 8 percent of bank assets which were appropriately risk-weighted ('capital adequacy'). It was clear to those who drafted the accord that banks faced several other risks in addition to credit risk, but agreement was postponed on how to confront these.[20] Perhaps the crudest aspect of the accord, however, was the adoption of only five weight classes for bank assets applying across international banks – 0 percent for cash and claims on government, 0 percent, 10 percent, 20 percent or 50 percent for claims on other public entities, 20 percent for claims on certain categories of 'secure' bank, 50 percent for mortgages, and 100 percent for a broad range of other claims on the private sector.[21]

The unwieldy and arbitrary aspect of the original capital adequacy regulation became apparent as the turn of banks toward mediation in open markets continued to develop apace in the 1990s, including derivatives trading. Heavy involvement of banks in financial transactions meant new dangers of losses due to changes in asset prices; these gave rise to 'market risk'. A key step in the development of the Basel Accords, therefore, was the introduction of the Amendment of 1996 which made provision for market risk.[22] For the largest banks this meant the introduction of advanced models of calculating risk based on value at risk (VaR). The VaR approach simulates changes in the market value of a bank's portfolio and calculates a capital requirement based upon possible mark-to-market losses.[23] Bank balance sheets thus began continually to reflect the movement of securities prices in the open markets, a factor that proved important in the unfolding of the crisis of 2007.

As banks continued to grow and to become increasingly involved in trading in open markets, a still further risk emerged – operational risk. The transformation of banks wrought significant changes in the internal organization of the institutions, changing the balance and nature of tasks between front desk and back office. With the increase in bureaucratic complexity, it became more likely that errors – or deliberate malpractice – would occur in trading, thus creating the possibility of substantial losses. Operational risk covers a wide variety of areas, from delays in finalizing legal documentation, to not sending cash payments in time, and even fraud. The collapse of Barings, the British investment bank, in 1995 partly as a result of the actions of a 'rogue trader' cast light on this danger, which has only become larger with the passage of time,

---

20   BIS, 'Risk Management for Electronic Banking and Electronic Money Activities', Basel Committee on Banking Supervision, March 1998, pp. 8–9.

21   Ibid., appendix 2.

22   BIS, 'Amendment to the Capital Accord to Incorporate Market Risks', January 1996.

23   For standard analysis, see Anthony Saunders and Linda Allen, *Credit Risk Measurement*, 2nd ed., New York: John Wiley and Sons, 2002, pp. 84–106; and Darrell Duffie and Kenneth Singleton, *Credit Risk: Pricing, Measurement, and Management*, Princeton, NJ: Princeton University Press, 2003, pp. 31–42.

including the use of rogue algorithms in computer-based high speed trading.[24] Operational risk, consequently, has become a focal point of market-conforming regulation. The characteristic feature of Basel II introduced in 2004 but receiving a comprehensive form in 2006 was to incorporate both market and operational risk in its stipulations.[25]

The crisis of 2007, irrespective of its origins, is prima facie evidence of the failure of Basel II. One consequence, therefore, has been the further development of the regulatory framework through the Basel III Accord that began to take shape in 2010–2011. The underlying logic of Basel III is similar to that of the previous two accords: market-conducive regulation designed by the financial system and aiming to strengthen the solvency of individual financial institutions by improving capital adequacy. One important difference, however, is the stronger emphasis on risk deriving from open market trading particularly in connection with derivatives.

In the course of the crisis of 2007 it became apparent that heavy use of credit default swaps by banks and other financial institutions created new sources of credit risk arising out of market trading. The integration of derivative instruments into the accounting practices of banks has been instrumental in creating these new risks, a development that has become gradually evident in the 2000s. The change has been codified through the credit valuation adjustment desks which use mark-to-market practices to simulate changes in the value of the entire portfolio of trades for each counterparty to transactions, and including correlations between risk factors.[26] Basel III has included credit valuation adjustment considerations directly in the accord with the aim of further improving capital adequacy.[27] Irrespective of the eventual effectiveness of the new accord, the outcome will be the further legitimation of mark-to-market practices and thus the strengthening of the turn of banks toward trading in open markets.

The failure of private banking and the difficulty of re-introducing market-negating regulation

Market-conforming regulation in the years of financialization has focused heavily on banks, as is only appropriate in view of the continued preponderance of banks in the financial system. The crisis of 2007, however, has raised the spectre of mass failure of private banks in several mature capitalist countries, an unprecedented occurrence

---

24   David Easley et al., 'The Microstructure of the Flash Crash: Flow Toxicity, Liquidity Crashes, and the Probability of Informed Trading', *The Journal of Portfolio Management* 37:2, 2011.

25   BIS, 'International Convergence of Capital Measurement and Capital Standards: A Revised Framework', Comprehensive Version', June 2006.

26   For further discussion, see Steven Zhu and Michael Pykhtin, 'Measuring Counterparty Risk for Trading Products under Basel II', in *The Basel Handbook: A Guide for Financial Practitioners*, 2nd ed., ed. Michael Ong, London: Risk Books, 2007.

27   BIS, 'Basel III: A Global Regulatory Framework for More Resilient Banks and Banking Systems', December 2010 (revised June 2011), pp. 29–37.

since the 1930s. The expansion of banks in the course of financialization has led to an accumulation of private and public debt as well as to weak solvency and liquidity for banks, as has been shown in previous chapters. In the absence of sustained state intervention, it is probable that there would have been large scale collapse of international banks in recent years, also signalling the failure of market-conforming regulation.

The failure of regulation but, even more important, the prospect of mass banking collapse have posed profound questions about the role of banks and regulation in financialized capitalism. For Marxist political economy, the banking system is an integrating mechanism of the capitalist economy collecting information, transferring resources across society via the flows of loanable capital, and facilitating the equalization of the rate of profit. Mainstream analysis of finance, on the other hand, treats banks as specialists in gathering and assessing information as well as monitoring borrowers and managing risks; financial markets, more generally, are also assumed to price and distribute risk. The transformation of banks in the course of financialization and the vast crisis that commenced in 2007 have put a different complexion on these issues.

For one thing, securitization has directly undermined the notion that banks reliably gather and assess information about borrowers. Securitization presumably compartmentalizes risk, rendering its various components more susceptible to assessment assigned to other specialists, including ratings organizations, credit enhancers, and so on.[28] For a short period of time in the early 2000s, securitization appeared to be the pinnacle of 'modern' finance in handling risk. In practice, securitization led to effective abandonment of assessment and monitoring across the chain of constitutive transactions. The assignment of risk assessment to others created gaps and omissions resulting in misjudgement of the creditworthiness of securities. Banks acquired assets often without even a perfunctory examination of their quality on the expectation that these assets would be rapidly taken off the balance sheet through securitization.

The self-evident failure of banks to manage risk bespeaks of the deeper transformation of banking in the course of financialization.[29] For mainstream economics, banks acquire information in qualitative ('soft') ways, including regular contact with borrowers, personal relations, visiting the site of borrower operations, and placing

---

28 For an analysis of this point from a political economy perspective see Sherif Hesham Elkholy, *Political Economy of Securitization and Development: The Case of Egypt*, unpublished PhD thesis, University of London, 2010.

29 Andrew Haldane considers the mismanagement of risk by banks to be a market failure, and attributes it to 'disaster myopia' as well as to network externalities and misaligned incentives. But there must also be a historically specific element to this gigantic failure, which Haldane does not discuss. See Andrew Haldane, 'Why Banks Failed the Stress Test', basis for a speech given at the Marcus-Evans Conference on Stress-Testing, 9–10 February 2009, available at bankengland. co.uk.

staff on company boards; banks also acquire information in quantitative ('hard') ways involving analysis of company, market and general economic data.[30] Financialization has thus shifted the focus of banks from 'soft', 'relational' methods towards 'hard', statistically driven techniques.

Arm's-length assessment of borrowers, for instance, has been deployed in judging the risk of mortgages in the US, including 'credit scoring' of individuals based on numerical information (income, age, assets, etc) that could be manipulated statistically.[31] The risk of default on assets has been more generally assessed via quantitative models that utilize historical rates of default; estimates were largely extrapolations from past trends, stress-tested within limits indicated by data. Banks, as was discussed in the previous section, have also deployed value-at-risk methods to assess the probability that the value of their assets would decline below a certain level, relying on correlations between asset prices and volatility. VaR methods have made it imperative to adopt the accounting practice of 'marking to market' – to use current market valuations rather than historic prices. These practices have become officially incorporated in market-conforming regulation, thus gaining further influence among banks.

Historically, banks were able to arrive at a socially valid assessment of borrower creditworthiness partly through 'relational' interactions with other agents in the financial system.[32] It appears that the adoption of 'hard' and computationally intensive techniques has led to loss of capacity by banks to collect information and assess risk on a 'relational' basis. Meanwhile, the new techniques have contributed to the failure of banks and of the financial system as a whole to assess risk in the 2000s.[33] The use of past prices to calculate correlations hardly works in times of the unprecedented

---

30   These are clumsy terms, but their meaning is clear; see Allen Berger and Gregory Udell, 'Relationship Lending and Lines of Credit in Small Firm Finance', *Journal of Business* 68:3, 1995; Allen Berger and Gregory Udell, 'Small Business Credit Availability and Relationship Lending: The Importance of Bank Organisational Structure', *Economic Journal* 112, February 2002; Allen Berger and Gregory Udell, 'Small Business and Debt Finance', in *Handbook of Entrepreneurship Research*, ed. Zoltán J. Ács and David Audretsch, Boston: Kluwer Academic Publishers, 2003; 'The Ability of Banks to Lend to Informationally Opaque Small Businesses', *Journal of Banking and Finance* 25, 2001; and Allen Berger et al., 'Does Function Follow Organizational Form? Evidence From the Lending Practices of Large and Small Banks', *Journal of Financial Economics* 76, 2005.

31   Loretta J. Mester, 'What is the Point of Credit Scoring?', *Federal Reserve Bank of Philadephia Business Review*, September–October 1997.

32   Costas Lapavitsas, *Social Foundations of Markets, Money and Credit*, London: Routledge, 2003, ch. 4.

33   To call this 'mispricing of risk' is uncharacteristically lame of Charles Goodhart; the real issue is systemic failure to apprehend risk altogether. See C.A.E. Goodhart, 'The Background to the 2007 Financial Crisis', *International Economics and Economic Policy* 4, 2008.

co-movements of prices. The 'hard' techniques may have even increased the homogeneity of decisions by financial intermediaries, thus exacerbating price swings and general instability.[34]Yet, if banks have lost capacity reliably to collect information and assess risk, what is their social and economic function in financialized capitalism? As was shown in chapters 8 and 9, the mediating role of banks in the flows of loanable capital is now less important for large corporations, and has proven problematic for households. Banks certainly play a vital role in creating money and operating the payments mechanism in mature economies, but these are not functions that are specific to banking capital and could be taken over by other institutions, for instance, by the post office. What, then, is the social purpose of private banks in financialized capitalism?

The problem has been compounded by the systematic bypassing of Basel II regulations by banks in the course of the bubble of 2001–2007. As was discussed in Chapter 8, securitization has involved setting up new institutions, such as Structured Investment Vehicles, that issued asset-backed liabilities. Bank assets were moved off-balance-sheet and thus capital adequacy requirements were not infringed. In short, market-conforming regulation actively encouraged large banks to securitize assets in order to 'churn' regulatory capital. Banks were able to continuing lending and making profits while appearing to meet capital adequacy requirements.

This process has been referred to as 'regulatory arbitrage', often implying that it was due either to the inadequacy of the regulators, or to a temporary lapse in bank operating practice.[35] However, the bypassing of Basel II is merely an instance of the spontaneous tendency of the financial system to undermine regulation by creating new activities with higher returns, which was briefly discussed above. Basel II created opportunities for large banks to engage in 'regulatory arbitrage' since it placed emphasis on 'hard' techniques of risk measurement to set the precise level of capital adequacy. But it is misleading to assume that market-conforming regulation could ever be designed permanently to avoid the danger of 'regulatory arbitrage'. The best that could be hoped for would be continually to revise the regulatory framework to contest the efforts of financial institutions to bypass existing regulations.

The failures associated with market-conforming regulation in the context of financialization have led to a search for new approaches to 'systemic' regulation. Ideas have been put forth of treating the financial system as a 'network' or as a biological system, but these have not led to concrete suggestions regarding regulation. There have also been attempts to explore 'macroprudential' regulation, but they have hardly amounted

---

34　Avinash Persaud, 'Liquidity Black Holes', WIDER Discussion Paper No. 2002/31, World Institute for Development Economics Research, March 2002.

35　Acharya and Richardson, for instance, effectively claim that regulatory arbitrage arose from design faults and lack of foresight on the part of regulatory authorities, or because of abandonment of sensible 'business models' by banks. Viral V. Acharya and Matthew Richardson, 'Repairing a Failed System: An Introduction', New York University Stern White Papers, August 2008.

to anything more than establishing a range of early warning signals, or of discretionary levers of intervention, to help regulators deal with crises.[36] Others, finally, have proposed the re-establishment of institutional barriers between investment and commercial banking.[37] Amidst this debate, however, Basel III has reaffirmed the basic principles of market-conforming regulation, designed by banks for banks, focusing on capital adequacy and treating banks largely as participants in open market transactions.

It has proven difficult to re-institute even basic elements of systemic market-negating regulation capable of limiting the tendency toward instability and crises. This difficulty is not merely the result of the paucity of new ideas. The structural basis for systemic market-negating regulation is far from apparent within financialized capitalism. After all, the three pillars of post-war regulation would be extremely hard to reinstate under conditions of financialization. First and foremost, there is no prospect of introducing a form of world money that could stabilize exchange rates. Substantial

---

36 For 'network' analysis of finance, see Andrew Haldane, 'Small Lessons from a Big Crisis', 8 May 2009, at bis.org; Andrew Haldane, 'Rethinking the Financial Network', April 2009, at bankofengland.co.uk. For macroprudential regulation, see Claudio Borio, 'The Macroprudential Approach to Regulation and Supervision', VoxEU.org, 14 April 2009.

37 This is a view that has made considerable headway in the UK, see, for instance, John Kay, 'Narrow Banking: The Reform of Banking Regulation', Centre for the Study of Financial Innovation, 2009. Kay has called the approach 'narrow' banking but this is a misnomer which confuses 100% reserve banking (the traditional meaning of 'narrow' banking) with commercial banking in general. The original proposal for 'narrow' banking occurred in the US and is associated with the Chicago School, notably Henry Simons et al., 'Banking and Currency Reform', in *Research in the History of Economic Thought and Methodology, Archival Supplement 4*, ed. Warren J. Samuels, Greenwich, CT: JAI Press, 1933; and Irving Fisher, '100% Money and the Public Debt', *Economic Forum*, April–June 1936. In the post-war period, the idea received strong support from Milton Friedman ('A Program for Monetary Stability', New York: Fordham University Press, 1960). In a nutshell, if commercial banks operated with 100% reserves formed out of state fiat money, there would be no bank runs, the supply of money would be fully controlled, the capacity of banks to create credit would be curtailed, and public debt would be dramatically reduced as the state would acquire fiat claims on circulation. This notion has been recently revived in an IMF paper that curiously combines the monetarism of the Chicago School with the chartalism of radical anthropology; see Jaromir Benes and Michael Kumhof, 'The Chicago Plan Revisited', IMF Working Paper WP/12/202, International Monetary Fund, August 2012. 'Narrow' banking profoundly contradicts the nature of both money and banking in advanced capitalism. If the state did indeed transform the vast bulk of modern money into fiat along the lines suggested by Benes and Kumhof, capitalist banking as it has been known for centuries would come to an end; the state would also emerge as the arbiter of circulation in command of vast stocks of fiat money. It is bizarre that this vast empowerment of the state could be considered as strengthening free markets and competitive capitalism.

volatility of exchange rates is likely to remain for the foreseeable future, sustaining the growth of international financial markets. Moreover, large international financial markets would resist attempts to control the movement of loanable capital through the capital account.[38] They would also make it far from easy to re-introduce functional specialization of banks, including the rigid separation of commercial from investment banking. Contemporary international banks tend to generate liquidity through securities transactions in open markets precisely because they have turned to open markets with the aim of earning returns. Investment banking functions are no longer an optional extra for commercial banks but an integral part of their functioning.[39] Under such conditions, it would take profound social and political change to re-introduce generalized administrative controls of prices and quantities of credit.

Confronting financialization: Some concluding remarks

The travails of regulation reflect the deeply rooted character of financialization, its structural and historic place in the development of capitalism. Financialization is not the outcome of policy; it has not resulted from the lifting of financial regulation; it is not a tendency that could be dealt with through regulatory change alone. The crisis of 2007 and its aftermath, furthermore, indicate that financialization is persistent. Confronting it and dealing with its problematic outcomes from the standpoint of working people will take more than merely intervening in the regulatory framework of finance.

The main thesis of this book is that financialization represents a transformation of mature capitalism resting on the altered conduct of non-financial enterprises, banks and households. The transformation has taken place during the last four decades within a 'channel of accumulation' determined by neoliberal ideology and shaped through deregulation of labour and financial markets. Financialization also has a subordinate dimension in developing countries reflecting the hierarchical nature of the world market and world money.

Market-conforming regulation poses no obstacle to financialization; indeed it is consistent with it, even if it has also failed at critical junctures. Generic market-negating regulation, on the other hand, including lender of last resort, deposit insurance guarantees and the application of 'too big to fail', has been fundamental to promoting

---

38   That is not to say that capital account controls are not desirable, particularly controls over short-term flows. The post-Keynesian literature has long established the beneficial impact that controls would have on growth, particularly with regard to capital flight (Grabel 2003, 2006). It is remarkable that even the IMF has recently begun to realize that a degree of capital controls might be desirable (Ostry et al., 2010). Nonetheless, the feasibility of generalized capital control in the absence of reliable world money remains a moot point.

39   A point that Kregel notes in connection with the difficulty of returning to Glass-Steagall. Jan Kregel, 'No Going Back: Why We Cannot Restore Glass-Steagall's Segregation of Banking and Finance', *Public Policy Brief* 107, Levy Economics Institute of Bard College, 2010

financialization, while imposing costs on society. Systemic market-negating regulation, finally, requires profound social and political change, if it is to be re-imposed, not least resolving the problem of a reliable world money. Therefore, there are no clear paths of regulatory change to confront financialization. This is without even considering the enormous social and political power of finance which will certainly be mobilized to block reform nationally and internationally.

The poor prospects of regulatory control and the failure of private banking have brought to the fore the issue of private property over financial institutions. If it is necessary to adopt a more interventionist attitude toward finance than merely setting a regulatory framework, then property rights over financial institutions ought to be considered directly. Controlling finance as a system would acquire a different complexion, if public ownership and control over banks were re-introduced systematically. Note that public ownership of banks and other major financial institutions is not an unusual occurrence in financialized capitalism. After the collapse of Lehman Brothers, the extension of public ownership over stricken banks was publicly discussed even in the US.[40] Capital injections in the period that followed, in both the US and the UK, effectively established a strong public ownership stake in banking.

However, public ownership has typically been treated as a temporary counter-crisis measure aimed at restoring the solvency of banks with the aim of returning them to private ownership. Governments have consistently refused to exercise effective control over banks in which they hold a dominant ownership stake. The aim of nationalization has typically been to return banks to private hands, while avoiding outright losses on capital injected. Finance has been treated as a sector that periodically requires public ownership to deal with losses and to prevent collapse, only to be returned to private ownership when the conditions of profitability would have been stabilized.

Public property rights and active public control over banks, however, allow for much more than merely dealing with the problems created by private ownership and control. For one thing, public banks could support the provision of banking services to real accumulation as well as to households. As has been established in previous chapters, private banks have performed badly in these respects in the decades of financialization. It has already been suggested in the literature that provision of this type of credit should be considered as similar to a public utility, for instance, transport, electricity and water.[41] Needless to say, there can be no simple analogy between the provision of credit and the operation of a public utility, since credit in not a normal commodity but a set of economic relations based on trust and anticipation of returns. Yet, in principle, there would be no intrinsic difficulty in publicly managing the flow of

---

40   See, for instance, Adam S. Posen, 'A Proven Framework to End the US Banking Crisis Including Some Temporary Nationalizations', 26 February 2009, at piie.com.

41   Ismail Erturk et al., Memorandum from CRESC to the House of Commons – Treasury, January 2009, at www.publications.parliament.uk.

credit to households and to non-financial enterprises to achieve socially set objectives as well as to eliminate financial expropriation.

Public credit could be supplied to non-financial enterprises to buttress circulating capital and to facilitate the flows of trade credit. It could further be supplied to households for housing, education, and health as well as for smoothing general consumption. The supply of public credit would typically be on condition of regular repayment at publicly determined rates of interest. Interest payments would represent a public charge for the service that would cover costs as well as expanding the scope for future provision. The rate of interest and the general terms of repayment could vary among borrowers according to the broader objectives of social policy. It would thus be possible for public banks to deploy the techniques of information collection for income, employment, and personal conditions, including credit scoring and quantitative risk management. There is no reason why public banks could not provide a full range of monetary services to non-financial enterprises and households, including payments, safekeeping and value transfers.

More broadly, public banks could also enter the field of longer-term lending for large-scale investment. Funding could be secured in a variety of ways, including preferential access to deposits and issuing publicly guaranteed bonds. After all, private banks have been able to grow enormously in the years of financialization by relying on explicit and implicit deposit insurance guarantees by the state; the result has been to exacerbate moral hazard and to boost private returns. If public guarantees were removed, public banks would benefit from a steady supply of funding as deposits would migrate from private banks. Public banks would thus be able to adopt a longer-term horizon in lending, helping to strengthen the productive sector and to reverse financialization.

General re-introduction of public banking should not be confused with simple bank nationalization, which has already effectively happened under conditions of financialization on several occasions; it would be even less the replacement of failed private managers by state bureaucrats. Rather, public banks ought to have a social and collective remit as well as adopting transparent decision making and full accountability to elected bodies. Public banks ought to operate as levers for the re-strengthening of the social and the collective at the expense of the private and the individual across the economy. If the public interest was fully represented and democratically expressed within finance, it could help re-establish public service as a superior motive compared to private gain across the economy in general. A re-strengthened spirit of public service would be a vital step to reversing the ascendancy of finance in recent decades, while also laying foundations from a broader transformation of the economy in the interests of the many.

Re-establishing public property and control over banks would also create fresh space for regulatory intervention in the realm of finance and in the rest of the economy. Financialization reflects the increasing involvement of non-financial corporations in financial markets as well as the systematic turn of banks toward financial markets. Financial profits have been generated through transacting in loanable capital, including through the expropriation of transacting parties. The growth of financial markets, moreover, has severe implications for the internal organization and performance of non-financial corporations as well as for economic policy. An important regulatory step in confronting financialization, therefore, could be to impose a tax on financial transactions, widely known as a 'Tobin tax'.[42]

Tobin taxes were originally conceived as currency transactions taxes. However, they could be considered more broadly as taxes on financial transactions in general with the aim of dissuading short-term speculative flows of loanable capital hoping to make financial profit. The 'churning' of loanable capital in financial markets could be reduced as could the ceaseless invention of new ways to transact in loanable capital by banks and other financial institutions. Effective Tobin taxes would probably require international coordination among states, though there is scope in practice for introduction at a national or regional level.

If public property and control were widely re-established in the sphere of finance, the introduction of Tobin taxes would probably become easier. Public banks operating in a spirit of public service would more easily refrain from regulatory arbitrage and would more naturally accept restricted trading in open financial markets. A weightier presence for public banks in the financial system, moreover, would reduce the ability of private banks to influence the policymaking environment. In short, regulatory change would benefit from changes in the property relations within the financial system. Public regulation and public property over finance could reinforce each other.

Financialization, however, has also drawn strength from the increasing involvement of households in the realm of finance. The retreat of public provision across a range of fields associated with the livelihood of working people – housing, health, education, pensions, and so on – has created space for private provision. Private finance has emerged as the mediator of private provision across these fields, even though it has no evident skills in delivering such services and even if its performance has often been predatory and crisis-prone. Confronting financialization, therefore, cannot simply involve the regulation of private financial practices and nor even the establishment of public financial institutions to provide requisite services to households as utility, or

---

42   James Tobin's proposal was to impose a small tax on foreign exchange transactions to dissuade speculative, short-term inflows into the foreign exchange markets ('A Proposal for International Monetary Reform', *Eastern Economic Journal* 4, 1978). The intention was to reduce the risk of a sudden withdrawal of speculative funds, and thus of interest rate escalation. The original idea of a transactions tax imposed on foreign exchange markets can actually be found in Chapter XII of Keynes's *General Theory*. Note that Tobin's proposal has had a very different life to the one intended by its instigator. It was adopted by anti-globalization activists, the focus was shifted onto the potential income from the tax and emphasis was placed on the possible uses of the putative funds by government. But for the purposes of confronting financialization, Tobin's own intention is more important.

otherwise. It must also involve re-establishing public provision of goods and services that constitute the real income of working people.

Consequently, confronting financialization includes reasserting the importance of public housing, health, education, pensions, and consumption more generally. It entails the re-imposition of a public spirit across these fields and the ascendancy of the notion of a public right to access basic goods and services. The expanded rule of money over the livelihood of households and individuals would thus be reversed. Room to engage in policies of public provision is afforded by the rise of new technologies and by the spontaneous opposition of working people to the monetization of life. Needless to say, there can be no return to the years prior to the rise of neoliberalism. Fresh approaches to public provision, incorporating democratic and communal practices, are required. However, there is no doubt about the need to strengthen public provision, if financialization is to be opposed.

It is evident, in this light, that countering neoliberalism is integral to confronting financialization. The ideas of neoliberalism – above all, on markets and tax – have set the terrain for financialization and for the broader transformation of capitalism during the last four decades. Financialization cannot be confronted without re-establishing the ideological primacy of the collective over the individual, and of the public over the private. It cannot be opposed without re-asserting the superiority of the public interest over the profits and benefits of the individual. It cannot be reversed without accepting that public authorities have the right and the obligation to intervene in the economy in the interests of the many. Only on this basis would it be possible to devise policies that could re-establish control over capital domestically and internationally. Confronting financialization, in other words, is inherently a stance that leads to anti-capitalist ideas, policies and practices, and for this reason it should be part of the struggle for socialism.

BIBLIOGRAPHY

Aalbers, Manuel B., 'The Financialization of Home and the Mortgage Market Crisis', *Competition and Change* 12:2, 2008, pp. 148–66.

Acemoglu, Daron, and David Autor, 'What Does Human Capital Do? A Review of Goldin and Katz's *The Race Between Education and Technology*', NBER Working Paper No. 17820, National Bureau of Economic Research, February 2012.

Acharya, Viral V., and Matthew Richardson, 'Causes of the Financial Crisis', *Critical Review* 21:2, 2009, pp. 195–210.

Acharya, Viral V., and Matthew Richardson, 'Repairing a Failed System: An Introduction', New York University Stern White Papers, August 2008.

Adrian, Tobias, and Adam Ashcraft, *Shadow Banking Regulation*, Staff Report No. 559, Federal Reserve Bank of New York, 2012.

Adrian, Tobias, and Hyon Song Shin, 'The Changing Nature of Financial Intermediation and the Financial Crisis of 2007–09', *Annual Review of Economics* 2, 2010, pp. 603–18.

Adrian, Tobias, and Hyon Song Shin, 'The Shadow Banking System: Implications for Financial Regulation', *Banque de France Financial Stability Review* 13, 2009, pp. 1–10.

Aglietta, Michel, 'Into the New Growth Regime', *New Left Review* 54, 2008, pp. 61–74.

Aglietta, Michel, 'Shareholder Value and Corporate Governance: Some Tricky Questions', *Economy and Society* 29:1, 2000, pp. 146–59.

Aglietta, Michel, and Antoine Rebérioux, *Dérives du capitalisme financier*, Paris: Albin Michel, 2004.

Aglietta, Michel, and Régis Breton, 'Financial Systems, Corporate Control and Capital Accumulation', *Economy and Society* 30:4, 2001, pp. 433–66.

Aizenman, Joshua, and Jaewoo Lee, 'International Reserves: Precautionary Versus Mercantilist Views: Hypothesis and Evidence', *Open Economies Review* 18, 2007, pp. 191–214.

Aizenman, Joshua, and Jaewoo Lee, 'International Reserves: Precautionary Versus Mercantilist Views: Theory and Evidence', IMF Working Paper WP/05/198, International Monetary Fund, October 2005.

Aizenman, Joshua, and Kenta Inoue, 'Central Banks and Gold Puzzles', NBER Working Paper No. 17894, National Bureau of Economic Research, 2012.

Aizenman, Joshua, and Reuven Glick, 'Pegged Exchange Rate Regimes: A Trap?', *Journal of Money, Credit and Banking* 40:4, 2008, pp. 817–35.

Aizenman, Joshua, and Reuven Glick, 'Sterilization, Monetary Policy, and Global Financial Integration', NBER Working Paper No. 13902, National Bureau of Economic Research, 2008.

Akyüz, Yılmaz, 'Managing Financial Instability in Emerging Markets: a Keynesian Perspective', TWN Global Economy Series No. 12, pp. 1–48, Penang: Third World Network; first published in *METU Studies in Development*, 35:1, 2008.

Albert, Michel, *Capitalism vs. Capitalism: How America's Obsession with Individual Achievement and Short-Term Profit has led it to the Brink of Collapse*, New York: Four Walls Eight Windows, 1993.

Albert, Michel, *Capitalisme Contre Capitalisme*, Paris: Editions Le Seuil, 1991.

Albritton, Robert, Makoto Itoh, Richard Westra, and Alan Zuege (eds), *Phases of Capitalist Development: Booms, Crisis and Globalizations*, New York: Palgrave, 2001.

Alesina, Alberto, and Guido Tabellini, 'Rules and Discretion with Non-Coordinated Monetary Policies', *Economic Enquiry* 25:4, 1987, pp. 619–30.

Allen, Franklin, and Anthony M. Santomero, 'The Theory of Financial Intermediation', *Journal of Banking and Finance* 21, 1998, pp. 1461–85.

Allen, Franklin, and Anthony M. Santomero, 'What Do Financial Intermediaries Do?', *Journal of Banking and Finance* 25, 2001, pp. 271–94.

Allen, Franklin, and Douglas Gale, 'Comparative Financial Systems: A Survey', Working Paper 01–15, Center for Financial Institutions, Wharton, 2001.

Allen, Franklin, and Douglas Gale, *Comparing Financial Systems*, Cambridge, MA: MIT Press, 2000.

Allen, Helen, 'Innovations in Retail Payments: E-Payments', *Bank of England Quarterly Bulletin*, Winter 2003, pp. 428–38.

Alvaredo, Facundo, and Emmanuel Saez, 'Income and Wealth Concentration in Spain from a Historical and Fiscal Perspective', *Journal of the European Economic Association* 7:5, 2009, pp. 1140–67.

Amable, Bruno, *The Diversity of Modern Capitalism*, Oxford: Oxford University Press, 2003.

Amin, Samir, *Accumulation on a World Scale*, vols 1 and 2, New York: Monthly Review Press, 1974.

Amin, Samir, *Unequal Development*, Hassocks: Harvester, 1976.

Amiti, Mary, and Kevin J. Stiroh, 'Is the United States Losing its Productivity Advantage?', *Current Issues in Economics and Finance* 13:8, 2007, pp. 1–7.

Amromin, Gene, and Sujit Chakravorti, 'Debit Card and Cash Usage: A Cross-Country Analysis', WP 2007–04, Federal Reserve bank of Chicago, 2007.

Anderson, Edward, 'Openness and Inequality in Developing Countries: A Review of Theory and Recent Evidence', *World Development* 33:7, 2005, pp. 1045–63.

Aoki Masahiko, *Information, Incentives and Bargaining in the Japanese Economy*, Cambridge: Cambridge University Press, 1988.

Aoki Masahiko, 'The Japanese Firm as a System of Attributes: A Survey and Research Agenda', in *The Japanese Firm: Sources of Competitive Strength*, ed. Mashiko Aoki and Ronald Dore, Oxford: Clarendon Press, 1994, pp. 11–40.

Aoki Masahiko, 'Toward and Economic Model of the Japanese Firm', *Journal of Economic Literature* 28, 1990, pp. 1–27.

Aoki Masahiko, and Gregory Jackson, 'Understanding an Emergent Diversity of Non-Financial Governance and Organizational Architecture: An Essentiality-Based Analysis', *Industrial and Non-Financial Change* 17, 2008, pp. 1–27.

Aoki Masahiko, and Hugh Patrick (eds), *The Japanese Main Bank System: Its Relevance for Developing and Transforming Economies*, New York: Oxford University Press, 1994.

Arestis, Philip, and Malcolm Sawyer, 'Can Monetary Policy Affect the Real Economy?', Working Paper No. 355, The Levy Economics Institute, 2002.

Arestis, Philip, and Malcolm Sawyer, 'Inflation Targeting: A Critical Appraisal', Working Paper No. 388, The Levy Economics Institute, 2003.

Aristotle, *Nicomachean Ethics*, Cambridge, MA: Harvard University Press, 1926.

Aristotle, *Politics*, Cambridge, MA: Harvard University Press, 1932.

Arrighi, Giovanni, *Adam Smith in Beijing: Lineages of the Twenty-First Century*, London: Verso, 2007.

Arrighi, Giovanni, 'Financial Expansions in World Historical Perspective: A Reply to Robert Pollin', *New Left Review* 224, 1997, pp. 154–9.

Arrighi, Giovanni, *The Long Twentieth Century: Money, Power, and the Origins of Our Times*, London: Verso, 1994.

Arrighi, Giovanni, 'The Social and Political Economy of Global Turbulence', *New Left Review* 20, 2003, pp. 5–71.

Arrighi, Giovanni, and Jason W. Moore, 'Capitalist Development in World Historical Perspective', in *Phases of Capitalist Development: Booms, Crises and Globalization*, ed. Robert Albritton, Makoto Itoh, Richard Westra, and Alan Zuege, London: Palgrave Macmillan, 2001.

Arrighi, Giovanni, and Beverly J. Silver, *Chaos and Governance in the Modern World System*, Minneapolis: University of Minnesota Press, 1999.

Arthur, Christopher J., 'Money and Exchange', *Capital and Class* 30:3, 2006, pp. 7–35.

Arthur, Christopher J., 'Money and the form of value', in *The Constitution of Capital*, ed. Riccardo Bellofiore and Nicola Taylor, New York: Palgrave Macmillan, 2004.

Atkinson, Anthony, Thomas Piketty, and Emmanuel Saez, 'Top Incomes in the Long Run of History', *Journal of Economic Literature* 49:1, 2011, pp. 3–71.

Autor, David, and David Dorn, 'The Growth of Low Skill Service Jobs and the Polarization of the US Labor Market', Cambridge, MA: MIT Department of Economics, 2012.

Autor, David, Lawrence Katz, and Melissa Kearney, 'The Polarization of the US Labor Market', *American Economic Review* 96:2, 2006, pp. 189–94.

Autor, David, Frank Levy, and Richard Murnane, 'The Skill Content of Recent Technological Innovation: An Empirical Investigation', *Quarterly Journal of Economics*, 118:4, 2003, pp. 1279–333.

Autor, David, Frank Levy, and Richard Murnane, 'Upstairs, Downstairs: Computer-Skill Complementarity and Computer-Labor Substitution on Two Floors of a Large Bank', NBER Working Paper No. 7890, National Bureau of Economic Research, 2000.

Bagehot, Walter, *Lombard Street*, in *The Collected Works of Walter Bagehot*, vol. 9, ed. Norman St John-Stevas, London: The Economist, 1978.

Bairoch, Paul, *Economics and World History*, Hemel Hempstead: Harvester Wheatsheaf, 1993.

Bairoch, Paul, and Richard Kozul-Wright, 'Globalization Myths: Some Historical Reflections on Integration, Industrialization and Growth in the World Economy', UNCTAD Discussion Papers No. 113, March 1996.

Baker, Dean, Gerald Epstein, and Robert Pollin, *Globalization and Progressive Economic Policy*, Cambridge: Cambridge University Press, 1998.

Banaji, Jairus, *Agrarian Change in Late Antiquity: Gold, Labour, and Aristocratic Dominance*, Oxford: Oxford University Press, 2001.

Bank for International Settlements (BIS), 'Amendment to the Capital Accord to Incorporate Market Risks', January 1996, at bis.org.

Bank for International Settlements (BIS), 'Basel III: A Global Regulatory Framework for More Resilient Banks and Banking Systems', December 2010 (revised June 2011).

Bank for International Settlements (BIS), 'Implications for Central Banks of the Development of Electronic Money', October 1996.

Bank for International Settlements (BIS), 'International Convergence of Capital Measurement and Capital Standards', July 1988.

Bank for International Settlements (BIS), 'International Convergence of Capital Measurement and Capital Standards: A Revised Framework', Comprehensive Version', June 2006.

Bank for International Settlements (BIS), 'Risk Management for Electronic Banking and Electronic Money Activities', Basel Committee on Banking Supervision, March 1998.

Bank for International Settlements (BIS), 'Security of Electronic Money', Report by the Committee on Payment and Settlement Systems and the Group of Computer Experts of the Central Banks of the Group of Ten Countries, August 1996.

Bank for International Settlements (BIS), 'Semiannual OTC Derivatives Statistics at End-June 2011', 2011.

Bank for International Settlements (BIS), 'Statistics on Payment and Settlement Systems in Selected Countries', Committee on Payment and Settlement Systems, July 2002.

Bank for International Settlements (BIS), 'Statistics on Payment and Settlement Systems in Selected Countries', Committee on Payment and Settlement Systems, March 2007.

Bank for International Settlements (BIS), 'Survey of Developments in Electronic Money and Internet and Mobile Payments', March 2004.

Bank for International Settlements (BIS), 'Triennial Central Bank Survey of Foreign Exchange and Derivatives Market Activity in 2010 – Final Results', December 2010.

Baran, Paul A., and Paul M. Sweezy, *Monopoly Capital*, New York: Monthly Review Press, 1966.

Barro, Robert, and David Gordon, 'A Positive Theory of Monetary Policy in a Natural-Rate Model', *Journal of Political Economy* 91:4, 1983, pp. 589–610.

Barro, Robert, and David Gordon, 'Rules, Discretion and Reputation in a Model of Monetary Policy', *Journal of Monetary Economics* 12:1, 1983, pp. 101–21.

Barshay, Andrew, *The Social Sciences in Modern Japan: The Marxian and Modernist Traditions*, Berkeley: University of California Press, 2004.

Barratt Brown, Michael, *After Imperialism*, 2nd ed., New York: Humanities, 1970, p. 322.

Barratt Brown, Michael, *The Economics of Imperialism*, Harmondsworth: Penguin, 1974.

Barratt Brown, Michael, *Essays on Imperialism*, Nottingham: Spokesman, 1972.

Basu, Susanto, John Fernald, and Matthew Shapiro, 'Productivity Growth in the 1990s: Techology, Utilization, or Adjustment', *Carnegie-Rochester Conference Series on Public Policy* 55, 2001, pp. 117–65.

Basu, Susanto, John Fernald, Nicholas Oulton, and Sylaja Srinivasan, 'The Case of the Missing Productivity Growth: Or, Does Information Technology Explain why Productivity Accelerated in the United States but not the United Kingdom?', Working Paper 2003–08, Federal Reserve Bank of Chicago, 2003.

Bauer, Otto, *The Question of Nationalities and Social Democracy*, Minneapolis: University of Minnesota Press, 2000.

Bean, Charles, 'Asset Prices, Financial Imbalances and Monetary Policy: Are Inflation Targets Enough?', *Revue d'Economie Politique* 110:6, 2003, pp. 787–807.

Bebchuk, Lucian A., 'How to Make TARP II Work', Harvard Law and Economics Discussion Paper No. 626, Harvard Law School, February 2009.

Becker, David, and Richard Sklar, *Postimperialism and World Politics*, London: Praeger, 1999.

Becker, David, Jeff Frieden, and Sayre Schatz, and Richard Sklar, *Postimperialism: International Capitalism and Development in the Late Twentieth Century*, Boulder, CO: Rienner Publishers, 1987.

Becker, Joachim, and Johannes Jaeger, 'Development Trajectories in the Crisis in Europe', *Debate: Journal of Contemporary Central and Eastern Europe* 18:1, 2010, pp. 5–27.

Becker, Joachim, Johannes Jaeger, Bernhard Leubolt, and Rudy Weissenbacher, 'Peripheral Financialization and Vulnerability to Crisis: A Regulationist Perspective', *Competition and Change* 14:3/4, 2010, pp. 225–47.

Benes, Jaromir, and Michael Kumhof, 'The Chicago Plan Revisited', IMF Working Paper WP/12/202, International Monetary Fund, August 2012.

Berger, Allen, and Gregory Udell, 'Relationship Lending and Lines of Credit in Small Firm Finance', *Journal of Business* 68:3, 1995, pp. 351–81.

Berger, Allen, and Gregory Udell, 'Small Business Credit Availability and Relationship Lending: The Importance of Bank Organisational Structure', *Economic Journal* 112, February 2002, pp. 32–53.

Berger, Allen, and Gregory Udell, 'Small Business and Debt Finance', in *Handbook of Entrepreneurship Research*, ed. Zoltán J. Ács and David Audretsch, Boston: Kluwer Academic Publishers, 2003.

Berger, Allen, Leora Klapper, and Gregory Udell, 'The Ability of Banks to Lend to Informationally Opaque Small Businesses', *Journal of Banking and Finance* 25, 2001, pp. 2127–67.

Berger, Allen, Nathan Miller, Mitchell Petersen, Raghuram Rajan, and Jeremy Stein, 'Does Function Follow Organizational Form? Evidence From the Lending Practices of Large and Small Banks', *Journal of Financial Economics* 76, 2005, pp. 237–69.

Berle, Adolph, and Gardiner Means, *The Modern Corporation and Private Property*, New York: Macmillan, 1932.

Bernanke, Ben, 'The Global Saving Glut and the U.S. Current Account Deficit', remarks at the Sandridge Lecture, Virginia Association of Economists, Richmond, VA, 10 March 2005, available at federalreserve.gov.

Bernanke, Ben, 'The Great Moderation', remarks at the meeting of the Eastern Economic Association, Washington, DC, 20 February 2004, at federalreserve.gov.

Bernanke, Ben, 'Some Reflections on the Crisis and the Policy Response', speech delivered at the Russell Sage Foundation and the Century Foundation conference on 'Rethinking Finance', New York, 13 April 2012, available at federalreserve.gov.

Bernanke, Ben, 'The Subprime Mortgage Market', speech at the Federal Reserve Bank of Chicago's 43rd Annual Conference on Bank Structure and Competition, Chicago, 17 May 2007, at federalreserve.gov.

Bernanke, Ben, and Mark Gertler, 'Monetary Policy and Asset Price Volatility', *Economic Review* 4, 1999, pp. 18–51.

Bernanke, Ben, Thomas Laubach, Frederic S. Mishkin, and Adam Posen, *Inflation Targeting: Lessons from the International Experience*, Princeton, NJ: Princeton University Press, 1999.

Bernanke, Ben, Vincent Reinhart, and Brian Sack, 'Monetary Policy Alternatives at the Zero Bound: An Empirical Assessment', *Brookings Papers on Economic Activity* 2, 2004, pp. 1–78.

Bernstein, Eduard, *Evolutionary Socialism*, New York: Schocken, 1961.

Biccheti, David, and Nicolas Maystre, 'The Synchronized and Long-Lasting Structural Change on Commodity Markets: Evidence from High-Frequency Data', MPRA Paper No. 37486, UNCTAD, 2012.

Blackburn, Robin, *Age Shock: How Finance Is Failing Us*, London: Verso, 2007.

Blackburn, Robin, *Banking on Death, or Investing in Life: The History and Future of Pensions*, London: Verso, 2002.

Blackburn, Robin, 'Finance and the Fourth Dimension', *New Left Review* 39, 2006, pp. 39–70.

Blackburn, Robin, 'How to Rescue a Failing Pension Regime: The British Case', *New Political Economy* 9:4, 2004, pp. 559–79.

Bloom, Nick, Raffaella Sadun, and John van Reenen, 'It Ain't What You Do It's The Way That You Do I.T.: Testing Explanations of Productivity Growth Using US Affiliates', Centre for Economic Performance, London School of Economics, 2005.

Boeschoten, Willem, and Gerrit E. Hebbink, 'Electronic Money, Currency Demand and Seignorage Loss in the G10 Countries', Econometric Research and Special Studies Department, De Nederlandsche Bank, NV, 1996.

Bonefeld, Werner, 'Europe, the Market and the Transformation of Democracy', *Journal of Contemporary European Studies* 13:1, 2005, pp. 93–106.

Bonefeld, Werner, 'Politics of European Monetary Union: Class, Ideology and Critique', *Economic and Political Weekly* 33:35, 1998, pp. 55–69.

Bonefeld, Werner, and John Holloway, *Global Capital, National State and the Politics of Money*, London: Macmillan, 1995.

Boonstra, Wim, 'How EMU Can Be Strengthened by Central Funding of Public Deficits', in *The Creation of a Common European Bond Market*, Cahier Comte, Boel, No.14, ELEC, March 2010.

Boot, Arnold, and Anjan Thakor, 'Financial System Architecture', *Review of Financial Studies* 10:3, 1997, pp. 693–733.

Bordo, Michael, and David Wheelock, 'Price Stability and Financial Stability: The Historical Record', *The Federal Reserve Bank of St. Louis Review* 80:4, 1998, pp. 41–62.

Bordo, Michael, Michael J. Dueker, and David Wheelock, 'Aggregate Price Shocks and Financial Instability: A Historical Analysis', Working Paper 2000–005B, Federal Reserve Bank of St. Louis, 2000.

Borio, Claudio, 'The Macroprudential Approach to Regulation and Supervision', VoxEU.org, 14 April 2009.

Boron, Atilio A., *Empire and Imperialism: A Critical Reading of Michael Hardt and Antonio Negri*, London: Zed Books, 2005.

Bowring, Finn, 'From the Mass Worker to the Multitude: A Theoretical Contextualisation of Hardt and Negri's *Empire*', *Capital and Class* 83, Summer 2004, pp. 101–32.

Boyd, John H., and Edward C. Prescott, 'Financial Intermediary-Coalitions', *Journal of Economic Theory* 38, 1986, pp. 211–32.

Boyer, Robert, 'Feu le régime d'accumulation tiré par la finance: La crise des subprimes en perspective historique', *Revue de la régulation* 5, Spring 2009.

Boyer, Robert, 'Is a Finance-Led Growth Regime a Viable Alternative to Fordism? A Preliminary Analysis', *Economy and Society* 29:1, 2000, pp. 111–45.

Braudel, Fernand, *Civilization and Capitalism, 15th–18th Century: The Wheels of Commerce*, trans. Sian Reynolds, Berkeley: University of California Press, 1982.

Braverman, Harry, *Labor and Monopoly Capital: The Degradation of Work in the Twentieth Century*, New York: Monthly Review Press, 1974.

Brenner, Robert, *The Boom and the Bubble: The US in the World Economy*, London: Verso, 2002.

Brenner, Robert, 'The Economics of Global Turbulence', *New Left Review* 229, 1998, pp. 1–264.

Brenner, Robert, *The Economics of Global Turbulence*, London: Verso, 2006.

Brenner, Robert, 'New Boom or New Bubble', *New Left Review* 25, 2004, pp. 57–100.

Brenner, Robert, 'What Is Good for Goldman Sachs: The Origins of the Current Crisis', new introduction to 2009 edition of Brenner, *The Economics of Global Turbulance*, London: Verso.

Brenner, Robert, and Mark Glick, 'The Regulation Approach: Theory and History', *New Left Review* 188, 1991, pp. 45–119.

Bresnahan, Timothy, and Manuel Trajtenberg, 'General Purpose Technologies: "Engines of Growth?"', NBER Working Paper No. 4148, National Bureau of Economic Research, 1992.

Bresnahan, Timothy, Erik Brynjolfsson, and Loren Hitt, 'Information Technology, Workplace Organization, and the Demand for Skilled Labor: Firm-Level Evidence', *Quarterly Journal of Economics* 117:1, 2002, pp. 339–76.

Brewer, Anthony, *Marxist Theories of Imperialism*, 2nd ed., London: Routledge, 1990.

Brownbridge, Martin, and Charles Harvey, *Banking in Africa*, Oxford: Currey, 1998.

Bruegel, Irene, and Diane Perrons, 'Deregulation and Women's Employment: The Diverse Experiences of Women in Britain', *Feminist Economics* 4:1, 1998, pp. 71–101.

Brunnermeier, Markus K., and Lasse Heje Pedersen, 'Market Liquidity and Funding Liquidity', *Review of Financial Studies* 22:6, 2009, pp. 2201–38.

Bryan, Dick, and Michael Rafferty, *Capitalism with Derivatives: A Political Economy of Financial Derivatives, Capital and Class*, Basingstoke: Palgrave Macmillan, 2006.

Bryant, John, 'A Model of Reserves, Bank Runs, and Deposit Insurance', *Journal of Banking and Finance* 4, 1980, pp. 335–44.

Brynjolfsson, Erik, and Lorin Hitt, 'Beyond Computation: Information Technology, Organizational Transformation and Business Performance', *Journal of Economic Perspectives* 14:4, 2000, pp. 23–48.

Brynjolfsson, Erik, and Lorin Hitt, 'Computing Productivity: Firm-Level Evidence', MIT-Sloan Working Paper 4210–01, 2003.

Brynjolfsson, Erik, Lorin Hitt, and Shinkyu Yang, 'Intangible Assets: Computers and Organizational Capital', *Brookings Papers on Economic Activity: Macroeconomics*, vol. 1, 2002, pp. 137–99.

Buiter, Willem, and Anne Sibert, 'The Central Bank as the Market-Maker of Last Resort: From Lender of Last Resort to Market-Maker of Last Resort', in *The First Global Financial Crisis of the 21st Century*, ed. Andrew Felton and Carmen Reinhart, London: Center for Economic Policy Research (CERP), 2007; available at VoxEU.org.

Buiter, Willem, 'New Developments in Monetary Economics: Two Ghosts, Two Eccentricities, a Fallacy, a Mirage and a Mythos', *Economic Journal*, 115, 2005, pp. C1–C31.

Buiter, William, 'The "Good Bank" Solution', *Financial Times* (online), 29 January 2009.

Bukharin, Nikolai, *The Economics of the Transformation Period (with Lenin's critical remarks)*, first published in Russian, New York: Bergman; also published as *The Politics and Economics of the Transition Period*, 1979, London: Routledge & Kegan Paul, 1971 (1920).

Bukharin, Nikolai, *Imperialism and World Economy*, London: Merlin, 1972 (1915).

Bulow, Jeremy, and Paul Klemperer, 'Reorganising the Banks: Focus on the Liabilities, Not the Assets', VoxEU.org, 21 March 2009.

Burawoy, Michael, *Manufacturing Consent: Changes in the Labor Process Under Capitalism*, Chicago: University of Chicago Press, 1979.

Bussiere, Matthieu, and Christian Mulder, 'External Vulnerability in Emerging Market Economies: How High Liquidity Can Offset Weak Fundamentals and the Effects of Contagion', IMF Working Paper WP/99/88, International Monetary Fund, July 1999.

Cable, John, 'Capital Market Information and Industrial Performance: The Role of West German Banks', *Economic Journal* 95:377, 1985, pp. 118–32.

Callinicos, Alex, *Bonfire of Illusions*, New York: John Wiley, 2010.

Cameron, Rondo (ed.), *Banking in the Early Stages of Industrialisation: A Study in Comparative Economic History*, New York: Oxford University Press, 1967.

Cameron, Rondo, and V.I. Bovykin (eds), *International Banking*, New York: Oxford University Press, 1991.

Campbell, Martha, 'The Credit System', in *The Culmination of Capital: Essays on Volume III of Marx's Capital*, ed. Martha Campbell and Geert Reuten, London: Palgrave, 2002.

Caprio, Gerard, and Daniela Klingebiel, 'Bank Insolvencies: Cross-Country Experience', Policy Research Working Paper 1620, Washington, DC: World Bank, 1996.

Carchedi, Guglielmo, 'The EMU, Monetary Crisis, and the Single European Currency', *Capital and Class* 19:63, 1997, pp. 85–112.

Card, David, and Thomas Lemieux, 'Can Falling Supply Explain the Rising Return to College for Younger Men? A Cohort-Based Analysis', *Quarterly Journal of Economics* 116:2, 2001, pp. 705–46.

Case, Karl, and Robert Shiller, 'Is There a Bubble in the Housing Market?', *Brookings Papers on Economic Activity* 2, 2003, pp. 299–362.

Castells, Manuel, *End of Millenium*, 2nd ed., vol. 3 of *The Information Age: Economy, Society and Culture*, Oxford: Blackwell, 2000.

Castells, Manuel, *The Internet Galaxy*, Oxford: Oxford University Press, 2001.

Castells, Manuel, *The Power of Identity*, vol. 2 of *The Information Age: Economy, Society and Culture*, Oxford: Blackwell, 1997.

Castells, Manuel, *The Rise of the Network Society*, 2nd ed., vol. 1 of *The Information Age: Economy, Society and Culture*, Oxford: Blackwell, 2000.

Chandrasekhar, C.P., 'Finance and the Real Economy: The Global Conjuncture', paper delivered at ERC/METU International Conference in Economics VI, Ankara, Turkey, 11–12 September 2002.

Chandrasekhar, C.P., 'Global Liquidity and Financial Flows to Developing Countries: New Trends in Emerging Markets and Their Implications', G24 Discussion Paper Series No. 52, UNCTAD, 2008.

Chesnais, François, 'The Economic Foundations of Contemporary Imperialism', *Historical Materialism* 15:3, 2007, pp. 121–42.

Chesnais, François, 'Mondialisation du capital et régime d'accumulation à dominante financiére', *Agone* 16, 1996; also in *Hermès*, 29 November 2009.

Chesnais, François (ed.), *La mondalisation financière: Genèse, enjeux et coûts*. Paris: Syros, 1996.

Chesnais, François, 'La théorie du régime d'accumulation financiarisé: contenu, portée et interrogations', Forum de la regulation, Paris, 11–12 Octobre 2001.

Claessens, Stijn, and Tom Glaessner, 'The Internationalization of Financial Services in Asia', Policy Research Working Paper, 1911, Washington, DC: World Bank, 1998.

Claessens, Stijn, Tom Glaessner, and Daniela Klingebiel, 'Electronic Finance: Reshaping the Financial Landscape Around the World', *Journal of Financial Research* 22: 2002, pp. 29–61.

Claessens, Stijns, Asli Demirgüç-Kunt, and Harry Huizinga, 'How Does Foreign Bank Entry Affect Domestic Banking Markets?', *Journal of Banking and Finance* 25, 2001, pp. 891–911.

Clark, Gordon L., *Pension Fund Capitalism*, Oxford: Oxford University Press, 2000.

Clark, Ian, 'Owners and Managers: Disconnecting Managerial Capitalism? Understanding the Private-Equity Business Model', *Work, Employment and Society* 23: 2009, pp. 775–86.

Clarke, George, Robert Cull, Maria Peria, and Susana Sanchez, 'Foreign Bank Entry: Experience, Implications for Developing Economies and Agenda for Further Research' *The World Bank Research Observer* 18:1, 2003, pp. 25–59.

Coates, David (ed.), *Varieties of Capitalism, Varieties of Approaches*, Basingstoke: Palgrave Macmillan, 2005.

Cohen, Benjamin J., 'Electronic Money: New Day or False Dawn?', *Review of International Political Economy* 8:2, Summer 2001, pp. 197–225.

Cohen, Edward E., *Athenian Economy and Society: A Banking Perspective*, Princeton: Princeton University Press, 1992.

Committee for the Study of Economic and Monetary Union, *Report on Economic and Monetary Union in the European Community*, CB-56-89-401-EN-C, Luxembourg: Office for Official Publications of the European Communities, 1989.

Corbett, Jenny, and Tim Jenkinson, 'The Financing of Industry, 1970–1989: An International Comparison', *Journal of the Japanese and International Economies* 10:1, 1996, pp. 71–96.

Corbett, Jenny, and Tim Jenkinson, 'How Is Investment Financed? A Study of Germany, Japan, the United Kingdom and the United States', *The Manchester School* 65, supplement, 1997, pp. 69–93.

Corpataux, José, Olivier Crevoisier, and Thierry Theurillat, 'The Expansion of the

Finance Industry and Its Impact on the Economy: A Territorial Approach Based on Swiss Pension Funds', *Economic Geography* 85:3, 2009, pp. 313–34.

Corrigan, E. Gerald, 'Are Banks Special? – A Revisitation', *The Region*, The Federal Reserve Bank of Minneapolis, March 2000, at minneapolisfed.org.

Corsetti, Giancarlo, 'The "Original Sin" in the Eurozone', VoxEU.org, 9 May 2010.

Cox, Robert, 'Democracy in Hard Times: Economic Globalization and the Limits to Liberal Democracy' in *The Transformation of Democracy? Globalization and Territorial Democracy*, ed. Anthony McGrew, Malden, MA: Blackwell, 1997, pp. 49–72.

Cox, Robert, 'Globalization, Multilateralism, and Democracy', in *Approaches to World Order*, ed. Richard Cox and Timothy Sinclair, New York: Cambridge University Press, 1996, pp. 524–36.

Crompton, Rosemary, and Fiona Harris, 'Explaining Women's Employment Patterns', *British Journal of Sociology* 49:1, 1998, pp. 118–36.

Crotty, James, 'Owner-Manager Conflict and Financial Theory of Investment Stability: A Critical Asessment of Keynes, Tobin, and Minsky', *Journal of Post Keynesian Economics* 12:4, 1990, pp. 519–42.

Crotty, James, 'Profound Structural Flaws in the US Financial System That Helped Cause the Financial Crisis', *Economic and Political Weekly* 44:13, 2009, pp. 127–35.

Crotty, James, 'Structural Causes of the Global Financial Crisis: A Critical Assessment of the "New Financial Architecture"', Working Paper 180, Political Economy Research Institute, 2008.

Crotty, James, and Gerald Epstein, 'Proposals for Effectively Regulating the US Financial System to Avoid yet Another Meltdown', Working Paper 181, Political Economy Research Institute, 2008.

Crotty, James, and Gerald Epstein, 'Regulating the US Financial System to Avoid Another Meltdown', *Economic and Political Weekly* 44:13, 2009, pp. 87–93.

D'Amico, Stafania, and Thomas B. King, 'Flow and Stock Effects of Large-Scale Treasury Purchases', *Federal Reserve Board Finance and Economics Discussion Series* 52, 2010.

Dallery, Thomas, 'Post-Keynesian Theories of the Firm under Financialization', *Review of Radical Political Economics* 41:4, 2009, pp. 492–515.

Dalton, George, 'Primitive Money', *American Anthropologist* 67:1, Feb. 1965, pp. 44–65.

David, Paul A., 'The Dynamo and the Computer: An Historical Perspective on the Modern Productivity Paradox', *American Economic Review* 80:2, 1990, pp. 355–61.

Day, Richard B., *The Crisis and the 'Crash'*, London: NLB, 1981.

De Brunhoff, Suzanne, *Marx on Money*, New York: Urizen Books, 1976.

De Grauwe, Paul, 'The ECB as a Lender of Last Resort', *VoxEU*, October 2011.

De Grauwe, Paul, 'The European Central Bank: Lender of Last Resort in the Government Bond Markets?', CESifo Working Paper No. 3569, September 2011.

De Grauwe, Paul, 'The Governance of a Fragile Eurozone', CEPS Working Document No. 346, Centre for European Policy Studies, May 2011.

De Grauwe, Paul, 'There is More to Central Banking Than Inflation Targeting', in *The*

First Global Financial Crisis of the 21st Century, ed. Andrew Felton and Carmen Reinhart, VoxEU–Center for Economic Policy Research, 2007.

De Grauwe, Paul, and Wim Moesen, 'Gains for All: A Proposal for a Common Euro Bond', *Intereconomics* 44:3, 2009, pp. 132–5.

De Grauwe, Paul, and Yuemei Ji, 'Mispricing of Sovereign Risk and Multiple Equilibria in the Eurozone', CEPS Working Document No. 361, Centre for European Policy Studies, January 2012.

De Paula, João Antonio, Hugo E. A. da Gama Cerqueira, Alexandre Mendes Cunha, Carlos Eduardo Suprinyak, Leonardo Gomes de Deus, Eduardo da Motta e Albuquerque, Guilherme Habib Santos Curi, and Marco Túlio Vieira, 'Marx in 1869: Notebook B113, The Economist and The Money Market Review', Discussion Paper No. 417, Cedeplar, Universidade Federal de Minas Gerais, 2011.

De Roover, Raymond, *L'Evolution de la Lettre de Change*, Librairie Armand Colin: Paris, 1953.

De Roover, Raymond, *The Medici Bank: Its Organization, Management, Operations, and Decline*, New York: New York University Press, 1948.

De Roover, Raymond, *The Rise and Decline of the Medici Bank*, Cambridge, MA: Harvard University Press, 1963.

De Ste. Croix, Geoffrey Ernest Maurice, 'Ancient Greek and Roman Maritime Loans', in *Debits, Credits, Finance and Profits*, ed. Harold Edey and Basil Yamey, London: Sweet and Maxwell, 1974.

DeFerrari, Lisa, and David E. Palmer, 'Supervision of Large Complex Banking Organizations', *Federal Reserve Bulletin*, February 2001, pp. 47–57.

Delpla, Jacques, and Jakob von Weizsäcker, 'The Blue Bond Proposal', Bruegel Policy Brief 2010/13, May 2010.

Demirgüç-Kunt, Asli, and Ross Levine, 'Bank Based and Market Based Financial Systems: Cross Country Comparisons', World Bank Policy Research Working Paper No. 2143, 1999.

Demirgüç-Kunt, Asli, and Ross Levine, 'Stock Markets, Corporate Finance and Economic Growth: An Overview', *The World Bank Economic Review* 10:2, 1996, pp. 223–39.

Detragiache, Enrica, Thierry Tressel, and Poonam Gupta, 'Foreign Banks in Poor Countries: Theory and Evidence,' IMF Working Paper No. 06/18, International Monetary Fund, 2006.

Dew-Becker, Ian, and Robert J. Gordon, 'Where Did the Productivity Growth Go? Inflation Dynamics and the Distribution of Income', NBER Working Paper No. 11842, National Bureau of Economic Research, 2005.

Diamond, Douglas, 'Financial Intermediation and Delegated Monitoring', *Review of Economic Studies* 51, 1984, pp. 393–414.

Diamond, Douglas, and Philip Dybvig, 'Bank Runs, Deposit Insurance and Liquidity', *Journal of Political Economy* 91, 1983, pp. 401–19.

Diamond, Douglas, and Raghuram Rajan, 'Liquidity Risk, Liquidity Creation, and

Financial Fragility: A Theory of Banking', *Journal of Political Economy* 109:2, 2001, pp. 287–327.

Diaz-Alejandro, Carlos, 'Good-Bye Financial Repression, Hello Financial Crash', *Journal of Development Economics* 19:1–2, 1985, pp. 1–24.

Dixon, Adam D., 'The Rise of Pension Fund Capitalism in Europe: An Unseen Revolution?', *New Political Economy* 13:3, 2008, pp. 249–70.

Dobb, Maurice, *Political Economy and Capitalism*, London: Routledge and Kegan Paul, 1937.

Dobb, Maurice, *Studies in the Development of Capitalism*, London: Routledge and Kegan Paul, 1946.

Dobb, Maurice, *Theories of Value and Distribution*, Cambridge: Cambridge University Press, 1973.

Dodd, Randall, 'Subprime: Tentacles of a Crisis', *Finance and Development*, December 2007, pp. 15–19.

Dooley, Michael P., David Folkerts-Landau, and Peter Garber, 'An Essay on the Revived Bretton Woods System', NBER Working Paper No. 9971, National Bureau of Economic Research, 2003.

Dore, Ronald, 'Financialization of the Global Economy', *Industrial and Corporate Change* 17:6, 2008, pp. 1097–1112.

Dore, Ronald, *Stock Market Capitalism: Welfare Capitalism*, Oxford: Oxford University Press, 1998.

Dorn, James A. (ed.), *The Future of Money in the Information Age*, Washington, DC: The Cato Institute, 1996.

Dos Santos, Paulo, 'Foreign Capital and Familial Control in Philippine Banking: Essays on Method, Accommodation and Competition', unpublished PhD thesis, University of London, 2007.

Dos Santos, Paulo, 'On the Content of Banking in Contemporary Capitalism', *Historical Materialism* 17:2, 2009, pp. 180–213; also published in Lapavitsas (ed.), *Financialisation in Crisis*, pp. 83–118.

Drehmann, Mathias, Charles Goodhart, and Malte Krueger, 'Challenges to Currency', *Economic Policy*, April 2002, pp. 195–227.

Duffie, Darrell, *How Big Banks Fail and What to Do About It*, Princeton, NJ: Princeton University Press, 2011.

Duffie, Darrell, and Kenneth Singleton, *Credit Risk: Pricing, Measurement, and Management*, Princeton, NJ: Princeton University Press, 2003.

Duménil, Gérard, and Dominique Lévy, *Capital Resurgent: Roots of the Neoliberal Revolution*, Cambridge, MA: Harvard University Press, 2004.

Duménil, Gérard, and Dominique Lévy, 'Costs and Benefits of Neoliberalism: A Class Analysis', *Review of International Political Economy* 8:4, 2001, pp. 578–607.

Duménil, Gérard, and Dominique Lévy, *The Crisis of Neoliberalism*, Cambridge, MA: Harvard University Press, 2011.

Duménil, Gérard, and Dominique Lévy, 'Finance and Management in the Dynamics of Social Change (Contrasting Two Trajectories: United States and France)', 26 June 2006, at www.jourdan.ens.fr/levy.

Duménil, Gérard, and Dominique Lévy, 'The Real and Financial Components of Profitability (United States, 1952–2000)', *Review of Radical Political Economics* 36:1, 2004, pp. 82–110.

Dupuy, Claude, Stéphanie Lavigne, and Dalia Nicet-Chenaf, 'Does Geography Still Matter? Evidence on the Portfolio Turnover of Large Equity Investors and Varieties of Capitalism', *Economic Geography* 81:1, 2010, pp. 75–98.

Dutt, Amitava Krishna, 'Maturity, Stagnation and Consumer Debt: A Steindlian Approach', *Metroeconomica* 57, 2005, pp. 339–64.

Dymski, Gary, 'Genie out of the Bottle: The Evolution of Too-Big-to-Fail Policy and Banking Strategy in the US', paper presented at the Post-Keynesian Studies Group meeting at SOAS, University of London, 8 June 2011; available at post-keynesian.net.

Dymski, Gary, 'Racial Exclusion and the Political Economy of the Sub-Prime Crisis', *Historical Materialism* 17:2, 2009, pp. 149–79; also published in Lapavitsas (ed.), *Financialisation in Crisis*, pp. 51–82.

Easley, David, Marcos Lopez de Prado, and Marueen O'Hara, 'The Microstructure of the Flash Crash: Flow Toxicity, Liquidity Crashes, and the Probability of Informed Trading', *The Journal of Portfolio Management* 37:2, 2011, pp. 118–28.

Eatwell, John, and Lance Taylor, *Global Finance at Risk*, Cambridge: Polity Press, 2000.

Edwards, Franklin R., *The New Finance: Regulation and Financial Stability*, Washington, DC: AEI Press, 1996.

Edwards, Jeremy, and Sheilagh Ogilvie, 'Universal Banks and German Industrialization: A Reappraisal', *Economic History Review* 49:3, 1996, pp. 427–46.

Edwards, Richard, *Contested Terrain: The Transformation of the Workplace in the Twentieth Century*, New York: Basic Books, 1979.

Eichengreen, Barry, and Ricardo Hausmann, 'Exchange Rates and Financial Fragility', from the proceedings of the symposium 'New Challenges for Monetary Policy', Federal Reserve Bank of Kansas City, 1999, pp. 329–68.

Einaudi, Luigi, 'The Medieval Practice of Managed Currency', in *The Lessons of Monetary Experience: Essays in Honor of Irving Fisher*, ed. Arthur David Gayer, London: George Allen & Unwin, 1970.

Einaudi, Luigi, 'The Theory of Imaginary Money from Charlemagne to the French Revolution' in *Enterprise and Secular Change*, ed. Frederic Lane and Jelle Riemersma, Homewood, IL: Richard Irwin, 1953. Translation of 'Teoria della moneta immaginaria nel tempo del Carlomagno alla rivoluzione francese', *Rivista di storia economia* I, 1936, pp. 1–35.

Elkholy, Sherif Hesham, 'Political Economy of Securitization and Development: The Case of Egypt', unpublished PhD thesis, University of London, 2010.

Engelen, Ewald, Martijn Konings, and Rodrigo Fernandez, 'Geographies of Financialization in Disarray: The Dutch Case in Comparative Perspective', *Economic Geography* 86:1, 2010, pp. 53–73.

Engelen, Ewald, 'The Case for Financialization', *Competition and Change* 12, 2008, pp. 111–19.

Engelen, Ewald, 'The Logic of Funding European Pension Restructuring and the Dangers of Financialiation', *Environment and Planning A* 35, 2003, pp. 1357–72.

Epstein, Gerald (ed.), *Financialization and the World Economy.* Cheltenham: Edward Elgar, 2005.

Epstein, Gerald, and Arjun Jayadev, 'The Rise of Rentier Incomes in OECD Countries: Financialization, Central Bank Policy and Labor Solidarity', in *Financialization and the World Economy*, ed. Gerald Epstein, Cheltenham: Edward Elgar, 2005, pp. 46–74.

Ergüneş, Nuray, 'Global Integration of the Turkish Economy in the Era of Financialisation', RMF Discussion Paper 7, 2009; also published in Lapavitsas (ed.), *Financialisation in Crisis.*

Erturk, Ismail, Julie Froud, Sukhdev Johal, Adam Leaver, and Karel Williams (eds), *Financialization at Work*, London: Routledge, 2008.

Erturk, Ismail, Julie Froud, Sukhdev Johal, Adam Leaver, and Karel Williams, Memorandum from CRESC to the House of Commons – Treasury, January 2009, at www.publications.parliament.uk.

European Central Bank, *Electronic Money System Security Objectives*, May, 2003.

European Central Bank, 'Electronification of Payments in Europe', *Monthly Bulletin*, May 2003, pp. 61–72.

European Central Bank, 'Issues Arising from the Emergence of Electronic Money', *Monthly Bulletin*, November 2000, pp. 49–60.

European Commission, 'Evaluation of the E-Money Directive (2000/46/EC)', submitted by the Evaluation Partnership for the DG Internal Market, February 2006.

European Monetary Institute (EMI) Directive, 'Directive 2000/28/EC of the European Parliament and of the Council of 18 September, Amending Directive 2000/12/EC Relating to the Taking Up and Pursuit of the Business of Credit Institutions', *Official Journal of the European Union*, L 275, 27 October 2000, pp. 37–8.

European Monetary Institute (EMI) Directive, 'Directive 2000/46/EC of the European Parliament and of the Council of 18 September 2000 on the Taking Up, Pursuit of and Prudential Supervision of the Business of Electronic Money Institutions', *Official Journal of the European Union*, L 275, 27 October 2000, pp. 39–43.

European Monetary Institute (EMI) Report, 'Report to the Council of the European Monetary Institute on Prepaid Cards by the Working Group on EU Payment Systems', May 1994.

Evans, Trevor, 'The 2002–7 of US Economic Expansion and Limits of Finance-Led Capitalism', *Studies in Political Economy* 83, 2009, pp. 33–59.

Fama, Eugene, and Kenneth French, 'Testing Trade-Off and Pecking Order Predictions About Dividends and Debt', *Review of Financial Studies* 15:1, 2002, pp. 1–33.

Favero, Carlo A., and Alessandro Missale, 'EU Public Debt Management and

Eurobonds', in *Euro Area Governance – Ideas for Crisis Management Reform*, Brussels: European Parliament, 2010, ch. 4.

Federal Reserve Bank, 'The Supervisory Capital Assessment Program: Design and Implementation', 24 April 2009.

Federal Reserve Bank, 'The Supervisory Capital Assessment Program: Overview of Results', 7 May 2009.

Federal Reserve Bulletin, 'Trends in the Use of Payment Instruments in the United States', Spring 2005, pp. 180–201.

Federal Reserve Bulletin, 'The Use of Checks and Other Noncash Payment Instruments in the United States', December 2002, pp. 360–74.

Federal Reserve, 'The Future of Retail Electronic Payments Systems: Industry Interviews and Analysis', Staff Study 175, Federal Reserve Staff for the Payments System Development Committee, December 2002.

Fernhald, John, and Shanthi Ramnath, 'The Acceleration in US Total Factor Productivity After 1995: The Role of Information Technology', *Economic Perspectives* 28:1, First Quarter 2004, pp. 52–67.

Fieldhouse, David, *The West and the Third World*, Oxford: Blackwell, 1999.

Financial Services Authority, *The Regulation of Electronic Money Issuers*, Consultation Paper 117, December 2001.

Fine, Ben, 'Banking Capital and the Theory of Interest', *Science and Society* 49:4, 1985–86, pp. 387–413.

Fine, Ben, 'Examining the Ideas of Globalisation and Development Critically: What Role for Political Economy', *New Political Economy* 9:2, 2004, pp. 213–31.

Fine, Ben, 'From Capital in Production to Capital in Exchange', *Science and Society* 52:3, Fall 1988, pp. 326–37.

Fine, Ben, and Alfredo Saad-Filho, *Marx's Capital*, London: Pluto Press, 2004.

Fine, Ben, and Costas Lapavitsas, 'Markets and Money in Social Science: What Role for Economics?', *Economy and Society* 29:3, 2000, pp. 357–82.

Fine, Ben, Costas Lapavitsas, and Dimitris Milonakis, 'Analysing the World Economy: Two Steps Back', *Capital and Class* 67, Spring 1999, pp. 21–47.

Fine, Ben, Costas Lapavitsas, and Alfredo Saad-Filho, 'Transforming the Transformation Problem: Why the New Solution is a Wrong Turning', *Review of Radical Political Economics*, 36:1 Winter, 2004, pp. 3–19.

Fine, Ben, Costas Lapavitsas, and Jonathan Pincus (eds), *Development Policy in the Twenty-First Century: Beyond the Post-Washington Consensus*, London: Routledge, 2001.

Finley, Moses I., 'Aristotle and Economic Analysis', *Past and Present* 47, May 1970, pp. 3–25.

Fisher, Irving, '100% Money and the Public Debt', *Economic Forum*, April–June 1936, pp. 406–20.

Fohlin, Caroline, 'Relationship Banking, Liquidity, and Investment in the German Industrialization', *The Journal of Finance* 53:5, 1998, pp. 1737–58.

Foley, Duncan, 'Marx's Theory of Money in Historical Perspective', in *Marx's Theory of Money: Modern Appraisals*, ed. Fred Moseley, London: Palgrave Macmillan, 2004.

Foley, Duncan, *Money, Accumulation and Crisis*, London: Harwood Academic Publishers, 1986.

Foley, Duncan, 'On Marx's Theory of Money', *Social Concept* 1:1, 1983, pp. 5–19.

Foley, Duncan, 'Realization and Accumulation in a Marxian Model of the Circuit of Capital', *Journal of Economic Theory* 28, 1982, pp. 300–19.

Foley, Duncan, *Understanding Capital*, Cambridge, MA: Harvard University Press, 1986.

Foley, Duncan, 'The Value of Money, the Value of Labour Power and the Marxian Transformation Problem', *Review of Radical Political Economics* 14:2, 1982, pp. 37–47.

Foster, John Bellamy, 'The Financialization of Accumulation', *Monthly Review* 62:5, 2010.

Foster, John Bellamy, 'The Financialization of Capital and the Crisis', *Monthly Review* 59:11, 2008.

Foster, John Bellamy, 'The Financialization of Capitalism', *Monthly Review* 58:11, 2007

Foster, John Bellamy, and Fred Magdoff, *The Great Financial Crisis: Causes and Consequences*, New York: Monthly Review Press, 2009.

Foster, John Bellamy, and Robert W. McChesney, 'Monopoly-Finance Capital and the Paradox of Accumulation', *Monthly Review* 61:5, 2009.

Frank, Andre Gunder, *Capitalism and Underdevelopment in Latin America*, 2nd ed. revised, New York: Monthly Review Press, 1969.

Frank, Andre Gunder, *Dependent Accumulation and Underdevelopment*, New York: Monthly Review Press, 1979.

Frank, Andre Gunder, *Lumpenbourgeoisie: Lumpendevelopment*, New York: Monthly Review Press, 1972.

Frank, Andre Gunder, *World Accumulation, 1492–1789*, London: Macmillan, 1978.

Frank, Murray, and Vidhan Goyal, 'Tradeoff and Pecking Order Theories of Debt', in *The Handbook of Empirical Corporate Finance*, ed. B. Espen Ecko, Amsterdam: Elsevier, 2008, pp. 135–97.

Franks, Julian, Colin Mayer, and Hannes Wagner, 'The Origins of the German Corporation – Finance, Ownership and Control', Discussion Paper 65, SFB/TR15, Government and the Efficiency of Economic Systems, 2005.

Freedman, Charles, 'Monetary Policy Implementation: Past, Present and Future – Will Electronic Money Lead to the Eventual Demise of Central Banking?', *International Finance* 3:2, 2000, pp. 211–27.

Freixas, Xavier, and Jean-Charles Rochet, *Microeconomics of Banking*, Cambridge, MA: MIT Press, 2008.

Friedman, Benjamin, 'Decoupling at the Margin: The Threat of Monetary Policy from the Electronic Revolution in Banking', *International Finance* 2:3, 2000, pp. 261–72.

Friedman, Benjamin, 'The Future of Monetary Policy: The Central Bank as an Army with Only a Signal Corps?', *International Finance* 2:3, 1999, pp. 321–38.

Friedman, Milton, 'A Monetary and Fiscal Framework for Economic Stability', *American Economic Review* 38:3, 1948, pp. 245–64.

Friedman, Milton, 'A Program for Monetary Stability', New York: Fordham University Press, 1960.

Froud, Julie, Colin Haslam, Sukhdev Johal, and Karel Williams, 'Financialisation and the Coupon Pool', *Capital and Class* 78, Autumn 2002, pp. 119–51.

Froud, Julie, Colin Haslam, Sukhdev Johal, and Karel Williams, 'Shareholder Value and Financialization: Consultancy Promises, Management Moves', *Economy and Society* 29, 2000, pp. 80–110.

Froud, Julie, Sukhdev Johal, Adam Lever, and Karel Williams, *Financialization and Strategy: Narrative and Numbers*, London: Routledge, 2006.

Fry, Maxwell, *Money, Interest and Banking in Economic Development*, London: Johns Hopkins University Press, 1988.

Fullarton, John, *On the Regulation of Currencies*, London: John Murray, 1845.

Gallagher, John, and Ronald Robinson, 'The Imperialism of Free Trade', *Economic History Review* 6:1, 1953, pp. 1–15.

Gavin, Michael, and Ricardo Hausmann, 'Securing Stability and Growth in a Shock-Prone Region: The Policy Challenge for Latin America', in *Securing Stability and Growth in Latin America: Policy Issues and Prospects for Shock-Prone Economies*, ed. Ricardo Hausmann and Helmut Reisen, Paris: Organisation for Economic Co-operation and Development, 1996.

Germer, Claus, *The Commodity Nature of Money in Marx's Theory*, London: Routledge, 2004.

Gerschenkron, Alexander, *Economic Backwardness in Historical Perspective*, Cambridge MA: Harvard University Press, 1962.

Gertler, Mark, and John H. Boyd, 'U.S. Commercial Banking: Trends, Cycles and Policy', in *NBER Macroeconomics Annual*, ed. O. Blanchard and S. Fischer, Cambridge, MA: MIT Press, 1993.

Gherity, James A., 'The Evolution of Adam Smith's Theory of Banking', *History of Political Economy* 26:3, 1994, pp. 423–41.

Ghosh, Atish, and Steven Phillips, 'Warning: Inflation May be Harmful to Your Growth', *IMF Staff Papers* 45:4, 1998, pp. 672–710.

Ghosh, Jayati, 'The Economic and Social Effects of Financial Liberalization: A Primer for Developing Countries', DESA Working Paper No. 4, October 2005.

Giddens, Anthony, *The Consequences of Modernity*, Cambridge: Polity Press, 1991.

Gilbert, Neil, *Transformation of the Welfare State: The Silent Surrender of Public Responsibility*, Oxford: Oxford University Press, 2002.

Glyn, Andrew, *Capitalism Unleashed*, Oxford: Oxford University Press, 2006.

Goldin, Claudia, and Lawrence F. Katz, *The Race between Education and Technology*, Cambridge, MA: Belknap Press of Harvard University Press, 2008.

Goldsmith, Raymond, *Financial Structure and Development*, New Haven, CT: Yale University Press, 1969.

Goode, Patrick, *Karl Kautsky: Selected Political Writings*, London: Macmillan, 1983.

Goodhart, C.A.E., 'The Background to the 2007 Financial Crisis', *International Economics and Economic Policy* 4, 2008, pp. 331–46.

Goodhart, C.A.E., 'Can Central Banking Survive the IT Revolution?', *International Finance* 3:2, 2000, pp. 189–209.

Goodhart, C.A.E., 'Monetary Policy and Public Debt', *Financial Stability Review* 16, April 2012, pp. 123–30.

Gordon, Robert J., 'Does the "New Economy" Measure up to the Great Inventions of the Past?', *The Journal of Economic Perspectives* 14:4, 2000, pp. 49–74.

Gordon, Robert J., 'The Evolution of Okun's Law and of Cyclical Productivity Fluctuations in the United States and in the EU-15', presentation at the EES/IAB workshop, 'Labor, Market Institutions and the Macroeconomy', Nuremberg, 17–18 June 2011.

Gordon, Robert J., 'Exploding Productivity Growth: Context, Causes and Implications', *Brookings Papers on Economic Activity* 2, 2003, pp. 207–79.

Gordon, Robert J., 'Has the "New Economy" Rendered the Productivity Slow-Down Obsolete?', working paper, Northwestern University, mimeo, 1999.

Gordon, Robert J., 'Is U.S. Economic Growth Over? Faltering Innovation Confronts the Six Headwinds', NBER Working Paper No. 18315, National Bureau of Economic Research, 2012.

Gordon, Robert J., 'Monetary Policy in the Age of Information Technology', Discussion Paper no. 99-E-12, Institute for Monetary and Economic Studies, Bank of Japan, 1999.

Gordon, Robert J., 'Revisiting the US Productivity Growth over the Past Century with a View of the Future', NBER Working Paper No. 15834, National Bureau of Economic Research, March 2010.

Gordon, Robert J., 'The Time-Varying NAIRU and its Implications for Economic Policy', *Journal of Economic Perspectives* 11:1, 1997, pp. 11–32.

Gordon, Robert J., 'Why Was Europe Left at the Station when America's Productivity Locomotive Departed?', NBER Working Paper No. 10661, National Bureau of Economic Research, 2004.

Gorton, Gary, 'Information, Liquidity, and the (Ongoing) Panic of 2007', *American Economic Review* 99:2, May 2009, pp. 567–72.

Gorton, Gary, 'The Subprime Panic', Yale ICF Working Paper No. 08–25, 30 September 2008, pp. 1–40.

Gorton, Gary, and Andrew Metrick, 'Regulating the Shadow Banking System', *Brookings Papers on Economic Activity* 41:2, Fall 2010, pp. 261–312.

Gorton, Gary, and Andrew Metrick, 'Securitized Banking and the Run on Repo', *Journal of Financial Economics* 104:3, 2012, pp. 421–560.

Gowan, Peter, 'Crisis in the Heartland', *New Left Review* 55, 2009, pp. 5–29.

Gowan, Peter, *The Global Gamble: Washington's Faustian Bid for World Dominance*, London: Verso, 1999.

Grabel, Ilene, 'Averting Crisis? Assessing Measures to Manage Financial Integration in Emerging Economies', *Cambridge Journal of Economics* 27:3, 2003, pp. 317–36.

Grabel, Ilene, 'A Post-Keynesian Analysis of Financial Crisis in the Developing World and Directions for Reform', in *A Handbook of Alternative Monetary Economics*, ed. Philip Arestis and Malcolm Sawyer, Cheltenham: Edward Elgar, 2006, pp. 403–19.

Graeber, David, *Debt: The First 5000 Years*, New York: Melville House, 2011.

Grahl, John, *After Maastricht: A Guide to the European Monetary Union*, London: Lawrence and Wishart, 1997.

Grahl, John, and Paul Teague, 'The *Régulation* School, the Employment Relation and Financialization', *Economy and Society* 29:1, 2000, pp. 160–78.

Green, Francis, *Demanding Work: The Paradox of Job Quality in the Affluent Economy*, Princeton: Princeton University Press, 2006.

Green, Francis, and Nicholas Tsitsianis, 'Can the Changing Nature of Jobs Account for National Trends in Job Satisfaction?', Studies in Economics No. 0406, Department of Economics, University of Kent, 2004.

Green, Francis, and Nicholas Tsitsianis, 'An Investigation of National Trends in Job Satisfaction', *British Journal of Industrial Relations* 43:3, 2005, pp. 401–29.

Greenspan, Alan, 'Currency Reserves and Debt', Remarks Before the World Bank Conference on Recent Trends in Reserves Management, Washington, DC, 29 April 1999.

Grierson, Philip, *The Origin of Money*, London: Athlone Press, 1977.

Griliches, Zvi, 'Productivity, R&D, and the Data Constraint', *American Economic Review* 84:1, 1994, pp. 1–23.

Gros, Daniel, 'External versus Domestic Debt in the Euro Crisis', CEPS Policy Brief No. 243, Centre for European Policy Studies, 25 May 2011.

Gros, Daniel, and Stefano Micossi, 'A Bond-Issuing EU Stability Fund Could Rescue Europe', *Europe's World*, Spring 2009.

Grossman, Henryk, *Law of the Accumulation and Breakdown of the Capitalist System*, trans. and abridged by Jairus Banaji, Leipzig: Hirschfeld, 1929.

Gurley, John, and Edward Shaw, *Money in a Theory of Finance*, Washington, DC: Brookings Institute, 1960.

Guttmann, Robert, 'A Primer on Finance-Led Capitalism and Its Crisis', *Revue de la régulation* 3/4, Autumn 2008.

Hackethal, Andreas, and Reinhard Schmidt, 'Financing Patterns: Measurement Concepts and Empirical Results', Working Paper Series: Finance and Accounting, No. 125, Goethe University Frankfurt, January 2004.

Hahn, Frank, *Money and Inflation*, Blackwell: Oxford, 1982.

Haldane, Andrew, 'Rethinking the Financial Network', speech delivered at the Financial Student Association, Amsterdam, April 2009, available at bankofengland.co.uk.

Haldane, Andrew, 'Small Lessons from a Big Crisis', remarks at the Federal Reserve Bank of Chicago 45th Annual Conference 'Reforming Financial Regulation', Chicago, 8 May 2009, available at bis.org.

Haldane, Andrew, 'Why Banks Failed the Stress Test', basis for a speech given at the

Marcus-Evans Conference on Stress-Testing, 9–10 February 2009, available at bankengland.co.uk.

Hall, Peter A., and David Soskice (eds), *Varieties of Capitalism: The Institutional Foundations of Comparative Advantage,* Oxford: Oxford University Press, 2001.

Hall, Robert Ernest, 'E-Capital: The Link Between the Stock Market and the Labor Market in the 1990s', *Brookings Papers on Economic Activity* 2, 2000, pp. 73–102.

Hall, Robert Ernest, 'The Stock Market and Capital Accumulation', *American Economic Review* 91:5, 2001, pp. 1185–202.

Hamilton, James D., and Jing Cynthia Wu, 'The Effectiveness of Alternative Monetary Policy Tools in a Zero Lower Bound Environment', NBER Working Paper No. 16956, National Bureau of Economic Research, April 2011.

Hancké, Bob, Martin Rhodes, and Mark Thatcher (eds), *Beyond Varieties of Capitalism: Contradictions and Complementarities in the European Economy,* Oxford: Oxford University Press, 2007.

Hardt, Michael, and Antonio Negri, *Empire,* Cambridge, MA: Harvard University Press, 2000.

Harman, Chris, 'Not All Marxism Is Dogmatism: A Reply to Michel Husson', *International Socialism Journal* 125, Winter 2010.

Harman, Chris, *Zombie Capitalism,* London: Bookmarks, 2009.

Harris, Laurence, 'On Interest, Credit and Capital', *Economy and Society* 5:2, 1976, pp. 145–77.

Harris, Milton, and Artur Raviv, 'The Theory of Optimal Capital Structure', *Journal of Finance* 48, 1991, pp. 297–356.

Harrison, Ann, John McLaren, and Margaret McMillan, 'Recent Perspectives on Trade and Inequality', *Annual Review of Economics* 3, 2011, pp. 261–89.

Harvey, David, *The Condition of Postmodernity: An Enquiry into the Origins of Cultural Change,* Oxford: Blackwell, 1989.

Harvey, David, *Justice, Nature and the Geography of Difference,* Oxford: Blackwell, 1996.

Harvey, David, *The Limits to Capital,* 3rd ed., Oxford: Blackwell, 2007.

Harvey, David, *The New Imperialism,* New York: Oxford University Press, 2003.

Harvey, David, *Spaces of Hope,* Edinburgh: Edinburgh University Press, 2000.

Heffernan, Shelagh, *Modern Banking in Theory and Practice,* New York: Wiley, 1996.

Hein, Eckhard, *The Macroeconomics of Finance-Dominated Capitalism – and Its Crisis,* Cheltenham: Edward Elgar, 2012.

Hein, Eckhard, 'A (Post-)Keynesian Perspective on Financialisation', IMK Working Paper No. 01-2009, Macroeconomic Policy Institute at the Hans Boeckler Foundation, 2009.

Hein, Eckhard, and Till Van Treeck, 'Financialisation and Rising Shareholder Power in Kaleckian/Post-Kaleckian Models of Distribution and Growth', *Review of Political Economy* 22, 2010, pp. 205–33.

Hein, Eckhard, Torsten Niechoj, Peter Spahn, and Achim Truger (eds), *Finance-Led Capitalism?,* Marburg: Metropolis Verlag, 2008.

Helleiner, Eric, *States and the Re-emergence of Global Finance: From Bretton Woods to the 1990s*, Ithaca, NY: Cornell University Press, 1994.

Henderson, Dale, and Warwick McKibbin, 'A Comparison of Some Basic Monetary Policy Regimes for Open Economies: Implications of Different Degrees of Instrument Adjustment and Wage Persistence', *Carnegie-Rochester Conference Series on Public Policy* 39:1, 1993, pp. 221–318.

Herman, Edward S., 'Do Bankers Control Corporations?', *Monthly Review* 25:2, 1973, pp. 12–29.

Herman, Edward S., 'Kotz on Banker Control', *Monthly Review* 31:4, 1979, pp. 46–57.

Hicks, John, *Critical Essays in Monetary Theory*, Oxford: Clarendon Press, 1967.

Hilferding, Rudolf, *Finance Capital*, London: Routledge & Kegan Paul, 1981 (1910).

Himmelweit, Susan, 'The Discovery of "Unpaid Work"', *Feminist Economics* 1:2, 1995, pp. 1–20.

Hirschman, Albert O., *Exit, Voice, and Loyalty: Responses to Decline in Firms, Organizations, and States*, Cambridge, MA: Harvard University Press, 1970.

Hirst, Paul, and Grahame Thompson, *Globalization in Question*, 2nd ed. rev., Cambridge: Polity, 1999.

Hobson, John A., *Imperialism*, 3rd ed., London: George Allen & Unwin, 1938 (1902).

Hoca, Bülent, 'A Suggestion for a New Definition of the Concept of Finance Capital Using Marx's Notion of "Capital as Commodity"', *Cambridge Journal of Economics* 36, 2012, pp. 419–34.

Hoogvelt, Ankie, *Globalisation and the Postcolonial World*, 2nd ed. rev., Basingstoke: Palgrave, 2001.

Höpner, M. 'What Connects Industrial Relations and Corporate Governance? Explaining Institutional Complementarity', *Socio-Economic Review*, 3, 2005, pp. 331–58.

Horwitz, Steven, 'Complementary Non-Quantity Theory Approaches to Money: Hilferding's *Finance Capital* and Free-Banking Theory', *History of Political Economy* 26:2, 1994, pp. 221–38.

Husson, Michel, 'L'ecole de la regulation, de Marx à la Fondation Saint-Simon: un aller sans retour?', in *Dictionnaire Marx Contemporain*, ed. Jacques Bidet and Eustache Kouvélakis, Paris: PUF, 2001.

Inaba, Keiichiro, 'The Transformation of Japanese Commercial Banking: Information Gathering and Assessing', unpublished PhD Thesis, University of London, 2008.

Ingham, Geoffrey, "Babylonian Madness": On the Historical and Sociological Origins of Money', in *What Is Money?*, ed. John Smithin, London: Routledge, 2000.

Ingham, Geoffrey, 'Fundamentals of a Theory of Money: Untangling Fine, Lapavitsas and Zelizer', *Economy and Society* 30:3, 2001, pp. 304–23.

Ingham, Geoffrey, 'Further Reflections on the Ontology of Money: Responses to Lapavitsas and Dodd', *Economy and Society* 35:2, 2006, pp. 259–78.

Ingham, Geoffrey, *The Nature of Money*, Cambridge: Polity Press, 2004.

International Monetary Fund (IMF), *Global Financial Stability Report – Statistical Appendix*, Washington, DC: International Monetary Fund, 2011.

Issing, Otmar, 'Hayek, Currency Competition and European Monetary Union', Annual Hayek Memorial Lecture delivered at the Institute of Economic Affairs, 27 May 1999.

Issing, Otmar, 'New Technologies in Payments: A Challenge to Monetary Policy', lecture delivered at the Center for Financial Studies Frankfurt am Main, European Central Bank, June 2000.

Issing, Otmar, 'Why a Common Eurozone Bond Isn't Such a Good Idea', *Europe's World*, Summer 2009.

Itoh Makoto, *The Basic Theory of Capitalism*, London: Macmillan, 1988.

Itoh Makoto, 'The Historical Significance of the Social Costs of the Subprime Crisis: Drawing on the Japanese Experience', in *Financialisation in Crisis*, ed. Costas Lapavitsas, Leiden: Brill, 2012, pp. 145–60.

Itoh Makoto, 'A Study of Marx's Theory of Value', in *Value and Crisis*, London: Pluto, 1980.

Itoh Makoto, and Costas Lapavitsas, *Political Economy of Money and Finance*, London: Macmillan, 1999.

Itoh Makoto, and K. Mori, *Kahei Sinyou no Kihon Riron* (The basic theory of money and credit), Tokyo: Hyouronsha, 1978.

Ivatury, Gautam, and Mark Pickens, *Mobile Phone Banking and Low-Income Customers: Evidence from South Africa*, Consultative Group to Assist the Poor; World Bank; United Nations Foundation, 2006.

Jack, William, and Tavneet Suri, 'The Economics of M-PESA', NBER Working Paper No. 16721, National Bureau of Economic Research, 2011.

Jackson, Gregory, and Richard Deeg, 'From Comparing Capitalisms to the Politics of Institutional Change', *Review of International Political Economy* 15, 2008, pp. 680–709.

Jensen, Michael C., and William H. Meckling, 'Theory of the Firm: Managerial Behavior, Agency Costs and Ownership Structure', *Journal of Financial Economics* 3:4, 1976, pp. 305–60.

Jones, Robert A., 'The Origin and Development of Media of Exchange', *Journal of Political Economy* 84, 1976, pp. 757–6.

Jorgenson, Dale, and Kevin Stiroh, 'Raising the Speed Limit: US Economic Growth in the Information Age', *Brookings Papers on Economic Activity* 1, 2000, pp. 125–211.

Jorgenson, Dale, Mun S. Ho, and Kevin Stiroh, 'Projecting Productivity Growth: Lessons from the US Growth Resurgence', *Federal Reserve Bank of Atlanta Economic Review*, 3rd Quarter 2002, pp. 1–13.

Jorgenson, Dale, Mun S. Ho, and Kevin Stiroh, 'A Retrospective Look at the US Productivity Growth Resurgence', *Journal of Economic Perspectives* 22:1, 2008, pp. 3–24.

Jorgenson, Dale, Mun S. Ho, and Kevin Stiroh, 'Will the US Productivity Resurgence Continue?', *FRBNY Current Issues in Economics and Finance* 10:13, 2004, pp. 1–7.

Joyce, Michael, Ana Lasaosa, Ibrahim Stevens, and Matthew Tong, 'The Financial Market Impact of Quantitative Easing', *Bank of England Working Papers* 393, 2010.

Karacimen, Elif, 'Political Economy of Consumer Debt in Developing Countries: Evidence from Turkey', unpublished PhD thesis, University of London, 2013.

Karshenas, Massoud, 'The Impact of the Global Financial and Economic Crisis on LDC Economies', United Nations Office of the High Representative for the Least Developed Countries, Landlocked Developed Countries and Small Island Developing States, 2009.

Kautsky, Karl, 'Ultra-Imperialism', New Left Review 59, Jan–Feb 1970, pp. 41–6; fraction of original 'Der Imperialismus', Die Neue Zeit, Sept. 1914.

Kay, John, 'Narrow Banking: The Reform of Banking Regulation', Centre for the Study of Financial Innovation, 2009.

Keynes, John Maynard, The Economic Consequences of the Peace, London: Macmillan, 1919.

Keynes, John Maynard, The General Theory of Employment, Interest and Money, London: Macmillan, 1973 (1936).

King, Mervyn, 'Challenges for Monetary Policy: New and Old', in New Challenges for Monetary Policy, Kansas City: Federal Reserve Bank of Kansas City, 1999.

King, Mervyn, 'Speech by Mervyn King, Governor of the Bank of England, at the Lord Mayor's Banquet for Bankers and Merchants of the City of London at the Mansion House', 17 June 2009; available at bankofengland.co.uk.

King, Robert G., and Ross Levine, 'Finance and Growth: Schumpeter Might be Right', Quarterly Journal of Economics 153, 1993, pp. 717–38.

Kiyotaki, Nobuhiro, and John Moore, 'Credit Cycles', Journal of Political Economy 105:2, 1997, pp. 211–48.

Klein, Michael W., and Giovanni Olivei, 'Capital Account Liberalization, Financial Depth, and Economic Growth', Journal of International Money and Finance 27:6, Ocotober 2008, pp. 861–76.

Knapp, Georg Friedrich, The State Theory of Money, London: Macmillan, 1924.

Kösters, Wim, 'Common Eurobonds: No Appropriated Instrument', Intereconomics 44:3, pp. 135–8, 2009.

Kotz, David M., Bank Control of Large Corporations in the United States, Berkeley: University of California Press, 1978.

Kraus, Alan, and Robert H. Litzenberger, 'A State-Preference Model of Optimal Financial Leverage', Journal of Finance 33, pp. 911–22, 1973.

Kregel, Jan, 'No Going Back: Why We Cannot Restore Glass-Steagall's Segregation of Banking and Finance', Public Policy Brief 107, Levy Economics Institute of Bard College, 2010.

Krippner, Greta, Capitalizing on Crisis: The Political Origins of the Rise of Finance, Cambridge, MA: Harvard University Press, 2011.

Krippner, Greta, 'The Financialization of the American Economy', Socio-Economic Review 3, 2005, pp. 173–208.

Krishnamurthy, Arvind, and Annette Vissing-Jorgensen, 'The Effects of Quantitative Easing on Interest Rates: Channels and Implications for Policy', NBER Working

Paper No. 17555, National Bureau of Economic Research, October 2011.

Kroszner, Randall S., 'Currency Competition in the Digital Age', in *Evolution and Procedures in Central Banking*, ed. David Altig and Bruce D. Smith, Cambridge: Cambridge University Press, 2003, pp. 275–305.

Krueger, Malte, 'E-Money Regulation in the EU', in *E-Money and Payment Systems Review*, ed. Pringle R. and Robinson M., London: Central Banking, 2002, pp. 239–51.

Kurata, Minoru, *Wakaki Hirufadingu* (The Young Hilferding), Mitaka: Okashobo, 1984.

Kuznets, Simon, 'Economic Growth and Income Inequality', *American Economic Review* 45:1, 1955, pp. 1–28.

Kydland, Finn E., and Edward C. Prescott, 'Rules Rather than Discretion: The Inconsistency of Optimal Plans', *Journal of Political Economy* 85:3, 1977, pp. 473–92.

La Porta, Rafael, Florencio Lopez-de-Silanes, Andrei Shleifer, and Robert Vishny, 'Law and Finance', *Journal of Political Economy*, vol. 106. No. 6, 1998, pp. 1113–55.

Lamoreaux, Naomi, 'The Great Merger Movement in American Business, 1895–1904', Cambridge: Cambridge University Press, 1985.

Lamoreaux, Naomi, *Insider Lending*, NBER, Cambridge: Cambridge University Press, 1994.

Lane, Frederic, and Reinhold Mueller, *Money and Banking in Medieval and Renaissance Venice*, vols 1 and 2, Baltimore: Johns Hopkins University Press, 1985.

Langley, Paul, *The Everyday Life of Global Finance: Saving and Borrowing in America*, Oxford: Oxford University Press, 2008.

Langley, Paul, 'Financialization and the Consumer Credit Boom', *Competition and Change* 12:2, pp. 133–47, 2008.

Langley, Paul, 'In the Eye of the "Perfect Storm": The Final Salary Pensions Crisis and the Financialization of Anglo-American Capitalism', *New Political Economy* 9:4, 2004, pp. 539–58.

Langley, Paul, *World Financial Orders: An Historical International Political Economy*, London: Routledge, 2002.

Lapavitsas, Costas, 'The Banking School and the Monetary Thought of Karl Marx', *Cambridge Journal of Economics* 18:5, 1994, pp. 447–61.

Lapavitsas, Costas, 'The Classical Adjustment Mechanism of International Balances: Marx's Critique', *Contributions to Political Economy* 15:1, 1996, pp. 63–79.

Lapavitsas, Costas, 'The Emergence of Money in Commodity Exchange, or Money as Monopolist of the Ability to Buy', *Review of Political Economy* 17:4, 2005, pp. 549–69.

Lapavitsas, Costas, 'The Eurozone Crisis Through the Prism of World Money', in *The Handbook of the Political Economy of Financial Crises*, ed. Gerald Epstein and Martin Wolfson, Oxford: Oxford University Press, 2012.

Lapavitsas, Costas (ed.), *Financialisation in Crisis*, Leiden: Brill, 2012.

Lapavitsas, Costas, 'Financialised Capitalism: Crisis and Financial Expropriation', *Historical Materialism* 17:2, 2009, pp. 114–48; also published in Lapavitsas (ed.), *Financialisation in Crisis*, pp. 15–50.

Lapavitsas, Costas, 'Hilferding's Theory of Banking in the Light of Steuart and Smith', *Research in Political Economy*, 21, pp. 161–80, 2004.

Lapavitsas, Costas, 'Money and the Analysis of Capitalism: The Significance of Commodity Money', *Review of Radical Political Economics* 32:4, 2000, pp. 631–56.

Lapavitsas, Costas, 'Money as Monopolist of the Ability to Buy', in *Marx's Theory of Money: Modern Appraisals*, ed. Fred Moseley, London: Palgrave Macmillan, 2004.

Lapavitsas, Costas, 'On Marx's Analysis of Money Hoarding in the Turnover of Capital', *Review of Political Economy* 12:2, 2000, pp. 219–35.

Lapavitsas, Costas, 'The Political Economy of Central Banks: Agents of Stability or Source of Instability?', *International Papers in Political Economy* 4:3, 1997, pp. 1–52.

Lapavitsas, Costas, 'Power and Trust as Constituents of Money and Credit', *Historical Materialism* 14:1, 2006, pp. 129–54.

Lapavitsas, Costas, *Social Foundations of Markets, Money and Credit*, London: Routledge, 2003.

Lapavitsas, Costas, 'The Social Relations Of Money as Universal Equivalent: A Response to Ingham', *Economy and Society* 34:3, 2005, pp. 384–403.

Lapavitsas, Costas, 'The Theory of Credit Money: A Structural Analysis', *Science and Society* 55:3, 1991, pp. 291–322.

Lapavitsas, Costas, 'Two Approaches to the Concept of Interest-Bearing Capital', *International Journal of Political Economy* 27:1, Spring 1997, pp. 85–106.

Lapavitsas, Costas, A. Kaltenbrunner, G. Lambrinidis, D. Lindo, J. Meadway, J. Michell, J.P. Painceira, J. Powell, E. Pires, A. Stenfors, N. Teles, and L. Vatikiotis, *Crisis in the Eurozone*, London: Verso, 2012.

Lapavitsas, Costas, and Paulo Dos Santos, 'Globalization and Contemporary Banking: On the Impact of New Technology', *Contributions to Political Economy* 27, 2008, pp. 31–56.

Lapavitsas, Costas, and Iren Levina, 'Financial Profit: Profit from Production and Profit Upon Alienation', Discussion Paper No. 24, Research on Money and Finance, May 2011.

Lapavitsas, Costas, and Makoto Noguchi (eds), *Beyond Market-Driven Development: Drawing on the Experience of Asia and Latin America*, London: Routledge, 2005.

Latzer, Michael, and Stefan Schmitz, *Carl Menger and the Evolution of Payments Systems*, Cheltenham: Edward Elgar, 2002.

Lavoie, Don, 'Marx, the Quantity Theory, and the Theory of Value', *History of Political Economy* 18:1, 1986, pp. 155–70.

Lazonick, William, 'Controlling the Market for Corporate Control: The Historical Significance of Managerial Capitalism', *Industrial and Corporate Change* 1:3, 1992, pp. 445–88.

Lazonick, William, 'Financial Commitment and Economic Performance: Ownership and Control in the American Industrial Corporation', *Business and Economic History*, second series, 17, 1988, pp. 115–28.

Lazonick, William, 'The Fragility of the US Economy: The Financialized Corporation and the Disappearing Middle Class', in *The Third Globalization*, ed. Dan Breznitz and John Zysman, Oxford: Oxford University Press, 2013.

Lazonick, William, 'Innovative Business Models and Varieties of Capitalism: Financialization of the US corporation', *Business History Review* 84, 2010, pp. 675–802.

Lazonick, William, and Mary O'Sullivan, 'Maximizing Shareholder Value: A New Ideology for Corporate Governance', *Economy and Society* 29:1, 2000, pp. 13–35.

Leary, Mark T., and Michael R. Roberts, 'Do Firms Rebalance Their Capital Structures?', *Journal of Finance* 60:6, December 2005, pp. 2575–619.

Lee, Roger, Gordon L. Clark, Jane S. Pollard, and Andrew Leyshon, 'The Remit of Financial Geography – Before and After the Crisis', *Journal of Economic Geography* 9, 2009, pp. 723–47.

Leland, Hayne, and David H. Pyle, 'Informational Asymmetries, Financial Structure and Financial Intermediation', *The Journal of Finance* 32, 1977, pp. 371–87.

Lenin, V.I., *The Collapse of the Second International*, in *Collected Works*, vol. 21, Moscow: Progress Publishers, 1964 (1917), pp. 205–59.

Lenin, V.I., *Imperialism, the Highest Stage of Capitalism*, in *Collected Works*, vol. 22, Moscow: Progress Publishers, 1964 (1917), pp. 185–304.

Lenin, V.I., *Imperialism and the Split of Socialism*, in *Collected Works*, vol. 23, Moscow: Progress Publishers, 1964 (1916), pp. 105–20.

Lenin, V.I., *The Question of Peace*, in *Collected Works*, vol. 21, Moscow: Progress Publishers, 1964 (1915), pp. 290–94.

Lenin, V.I., *Socialism and War*, in *Collected Works*, vol. 21, Moscow: Progress Publishers, 1964 (1915), pp. 297–338.

Lenin, V.I., *Under a False Flag*, in *Collected Works*, vol. 21, Moscow: Progress Publishers, 1964 (1917), pp. 135–57.

Levine, Ross, 'Financial Development and Economic Growth', *Journal of Economic Literature* 35:2, 1997, pp. 688–726.

Levine, Ross, and Sara Zervos, 'Stock Market Development and Long-Run Growth', *The World Bank Economic Review* 10:2, 1996, pp. 323–39.

Levine, Ross, and Sara Zervos, 'Stock Markets, Banks, and Economic Development', *American Economic Review* 88, 1998, pp. 537–88.

Levine, Ross, Norman Loyaza, and Thorsten Beck, 'Financial Intermediation and Growth: Causality and Causes', *Journal of Monetary Economics* 46, 2000, pp. 31–77.

Leyshon, Andrew, and Nigel Thrift, 'The Capitalization of Almost Everything: The Future of Finance and Capitalism', *Theory, Culture and Society* 24, 2009, pp. 97–115.

Leyshon, Andrew, and Nigel Thrift, *Money/Space: Geographies of Monetary Transformation*, London: Routledge, 1997.

Lindo, Duncan, 'Political Economy of Financial Derivatives: The Role and Evolution of Banking', unpublished PhD dissertation, School of Oriental and African Studies, University of London, 2013.

LiPuma, Edward, and Benjamin Lee, 'Financial Derivatives and the Rise of Circulation', *Economy and Society* 34:3, 2005, pp. 404–27.

Lordon, Frédéric, 'Après la crise financière: "regular" ou refondre?', *Revue de la regulation* 5, 2009.

Lordon, Frédéric, *Fonds de pension, piège à cons? Mirage de la démocratie actionnariale*, Paris: Raisons d'Agir, 2000.

Lordon, Frédéric, 'Le nouvel agenda de la politique economique en régime d'accumulation financiarisé', in *Le triangle infernal: Crise, mondialisation, financiarisation*, ed. Gérard Duménil and Dominique Lévy, Paris: PUF, 1999.

Lucas, Robert E., 'Why Doesn't Capital Flow from Rich to Poor Countries?', *American Economic Review* 80:2, 1990, pp. 92–6.

Luxemburg, Rosa, *The Accumulation of Capital*, London: Routledge & Kegan Paul, 1968 (1913).

Luxemburg, Rosa, 'Reform or Revolution', in *Rosa Luxemburg Speaks*, New York: Pathfinder Press, 1970.

Lysandrou, Photis, 'Global Inequality, Wealth Concentration and the Subprime Crisis: A Marxian Commodity Analysis', *Development and Change* 42:1, 2011, pp. 183–208.

Maastricht Treaty, 'Treaty on European Union', *Official Journal of the European Union* C 191, 29 July 1992.

Macartney, Huw, 'Variegated Neo-Liberalism: Transnationally Oriented Fractions of Capital in EU Financial Market Integration', *Review of International Studies* 35, 2009, pp. 451–80.

MacKenzie, Donald, *An Engine, Not a Camera: How Financial Models Shape Markets*, Cambridge, MA: MIT, 2006.

MacKenzie, Donald, and Yuval Millo, 'Constructing a Market, Performing Theory: The Historical Sociology of a Financial Derivatives Exchange', *American Journal of Sociology* 109:1, 2003, pp. 107–45.

Magdoff, Harry, and Paul M. Sweezy, *Stagnation and the Financial Explosion*, New York: Monthly Review Press, 1987.

Mandel, Ernest, *Marxist Economic Theory*, London: Merlin, 1968.

Markose, Sheri, and Yiing Jia Loke, 'Network Effects on Cash-Card Substitution in Transactions and Low Interest Rate Regimes', *Economic Journal* 113, April 2003, pp. 456–76.

Martin, Randy, *Financialization of Daily Life*, Philadelphia: Temple University Press, 2002.

Martin, Ron, *Money and the Space Economy*, London: Wiley, 1999.

Marx, Karl, *Capital*, vol. 1, London: Penguin/NLR, 1976 (1867).

Marx, Karl, *Capital*, vol. 2, London: Penguin/NLR, 1978 (1885).

Marx, Karl, *Capital*, vol. 3, London: Penguin/NLR, 1981 (1894).

Marx, Karl, *A Contribution to the Critique of Political Economy*, Moscow: Progress Publishers, 1970 (1859).

Marx, Karl, *Grundrisse*, London: Penguin/NLR, 1973 (1939).

Marx, Karl, *Karl Marx and Frederick Engels: Collected Works*, vol. 40, *Correspondence, 1856–1859*, London: Lawrence and Wishart, 1983.

Marx, Karl, *Theories of Surplus Value*, part 1, London: Lawrence & Wishart, 1969 (1905–10).

Marx, Karl, *Theories of Surplus Value*, part 3, London: Lawrence & Wishart, 1972 (1905–10).

Mattick, Paul, *Economic Crisis and Crisis Theories*, Armonk, NY: M.E. Sharpe, 1981.

Mayer, Colin, 'The Assessment: Financial Systems and Corporate Investment', *Oxford Review of Economic Policy* 3:4, 1987, pp. i–xvi.

McCallum, Bennett T., 'Crucial Issues Concerning Central Bank Independence', *Journal of Monetary Economics* 39:1, 1997, pp. 99–112.

McCallum, Bennett, 'The Present and Future of Monetary Policy Rules', *International Finance*, 3:2, (2000), pp. 273–286.

McCallum, Bennett T., 'Two Fallacies Concerning Central Bank Independence', *American Economic Review* 85:2, May 1995, pp. 207–11.

McCloud, Scott, 'Misunderstanding Micropayments', 11 September 2003, at scottmccloud.com.

McCulley, Paul A., 'Teton Reflections', Global Central Bank Focus, September 2007, at pimco.com.

McGee, Robert, 'What Should a Central Bank Do?', Department of Economics, Florida State University, mimeo, 2000.

McKinnon, Ronald, *Money and Capital in Economic Development*, Washington: The Brookings Institution, 1973.

McKinnon, Ronald, *The Order of Economic Liberalization: Financial Control in the Transition to a Market Economy*, Baltimore: Johns Hopkins University Press, 1991.

Meaning, Jack, and Feng Zhu, 'The Impact of Recent Central Bank Asset Purchase Programmes', *BIS Quarterly Review*, December 2011, pp. 73–83.

Meek, Ronald L., *Studies in the Labor Theory of Value*, New York: Monthly Review Press, 1975.

Meikle, Scott, 'Aristotle on Business', *The Classical Quarterly*, New Series 46:1, 1996, pp. 138–51.

Meikle, Scott, 'Aristotle on Money', *Phronesis* 39:1, 1994, pp. 26–44.

Meiksins Wood, Ellen, *Empire of Capital*, London: Verso, 2003.

Menger, Carl, 'On the Origin of Money', *Economic Journal* 2, 1892, pp. 239–55.

Menger, Carl, *Principles of Economics*, New York: New York University Press, 1981.

Messori, Marcello, 'Credit and Money in Schumpeter's Theory', in *Essays in Honour of Augusto Graziani*, ed. Richard Arena and Neri Salvadori, Aldershot, Hants: Ashgate, 2004.

Mester, Loretta J., 'What is the Point of Credit Scoring?', *Federal Reserve Bank of Philadephia Business Review*, September–October 1997, pp. 3–16.

Meyer, Peter B., and Michael J. Harper, 'Preliminary Estimates of Multifactor Productivity Growth', *Monthly Labour Review* 125:6, June 2005.

Milanovic, Branko, 'Global Income Inequality: What Is It and Why It Matters?', DESA Working Paper No. 26, ST/ESA/2006/DWP/26, United Nations Department of Economic and Social Affairs, 2006.

Milanovic, Branko, *Worlds Apart: Measuring International and Global Inequality*, Princeton, NJ: Princeton University Press, 2005.

Milberg, William, 'Shifting Sources and Uses of Profits: Sustaining US Financialization with Global Value Chains', *Economy and Society* 37:3, 2008, pp. 420–51.

Milberg, William, and Deborah Winkler, 'Financialisation and the Dynamics of Off-shoring in the USA', *Cambridge Journal of Economics* 34, 2010, pp. 275–93.

Milgrom, Paul, and John Roberts, 'The Economics of Modern Manufacturing: Technology, Strategy and Organization', *American Economic Review* 80, 1990, pp. 511–28.

Milgrom, Paul, and John Roberts, *Economics, Organization and Management*, Englewood Cliffs, NJ: Prentice Hall, 1992.

Millett, Paul, *Lending and Borrowing in Ancient Athens*, Cambridge: Cambridge University Press, 1991.

Minns, Richard, 'The Political Economy of Pensions', *New Political Economy* 1:3, 1996, pp. 375–91.

Minsky, Hyman, *Can "It" Happen Again? Essays on Instability and Finance*, Armonk, NY: M.E. Sharpe, 1982.

Minsky, Hyman, *John Maynard Keynes*, New York: Columbia University Press, 1975.

Minsky, Hyman, *Stabilizing an Unstable Economy*, New Haven, CT: Yale University Press, 1986.

Minsky, Hyman, 'Uncertainty and the Institutional Structure of Capitalist Economies', Working Paper No. 155, Levy Economics Institute of Bard College, April 1996.

Minsky, Hyman, and Charles Whalen, 'Economic Insecurity and the Institutional Prerequisites for Successful Capitalism', Working Paper No. 165, Levy Economics Institute of Bard College, 1996.

Mishel, Lawrence, and Kar-Fai Gee, 'Why Aren't Workers Benefiting from Labour Productivity Growth in the United States?', *International Productivity Monitor* 23, Spring 2012, pp. 34–43.

Mitchell-Innes, A., 'The Credit Theory of Money', *Banking Law Journal*, January 1914, pp. 151–68; reprinted in Wray, *State and Credit Theories of Money*.

Mitchell-Innes, A., 'What Is Money?', *Banking Law Journal*, May 1913, pp. 377–408; reprinted in Wray, *State and Credit Theories of Money*.

Modigliani, Franco, and M.H. Miller, 'The Cost of Capital, Corporate Finance and the Theory of Investment', *American Economic Review* 48, 1958, pp. 201–97.

Moessner, Richhild, and Philip Turner, 'Threat of Fiscal Dominance? Workshop Summary', BIS Papers No. 65, Bank for International Settlements, 2012.

Moore, Basil J., *Horizontalists and Verticalists: The Macroeconomics of Credit Money*, Cambridge: Cambridge University Press, 1988.

Morawcynski, Olga, and Gianluca Miscione, 'Examining Trust in Mobile Banking Transactions: The Case of M-PESA in Kenya', in *Social Dimensions of Information and Telecommunications Policy*, ed. Chrisanthi Avgerou, Matthew L. Smith, and Peter van den Besselaar, New York: Springer, 2008, pp. 287–98.

Morera Camacho, Carlos, and Jose Antonio Rojas Nieto, 'The Globalisation of Financial Capital, 1997–2008', RMF Discussion Paper 6, 2009; also published in Lapavitsas (ed.), *Financialisation in Crisis*, pp. 161–84.

Morin, François, 'Le capitalisme de marché financier et l'asservissement du cognitif', *Cahiers du GRES*, May 2006.

Morin, François, A Transformation in the French model of Shareholding and Management. *Economy and Society* 29, 2000, pp. 36–53.

Morris-Suzuki, Tessa, *A History of Japanese Economic Thought*, London: Routledge, 1991.

Moseley, Fred (ed.), *Marx's Theory of Money: Modern Appraisals*, London: Palgrave Macmillan, 2004.

Murray, Patrick, 'Money as Displaced Social Form: Why Value cannot be Independent of Price', in *Marx's Theory of Money: Modern Appraisals*, ed. Fred Moseley, London: Palgrave Macmillan, 2004.

Myers, Stewart C., 'The Capital Structure Puzzle', *Journal of Finance* 39:3, July 1984, pp. 575–92.

Myers, Stewart C., 'Capital Structure', *Journal of Economic Perspectives* 15:2, 2001, pp. 81–102.

Myers, Stewart C., and Nicholas S. Majluf, 'Corporate Financing and Investment Decisions When Firms Have Information That Investors Do Not Have', *Journal of Financial Economics* 13:2, 1984, pp. 187–221.

Neikirk, William, *Volcker: Portrait of the Money Man*, New York and Chicago: Congdon & Weed, 1987

Nelson, Anitra, *Marx's Concept of Money: The God of Commodities*, London: Routledge, 1999.

Neumann, Manfred J.M., and Jürgen von Hagen, 'Does Inflation Targeting Matter?', *Federal Reserve Bank of St. Louis Review* 84:4, July/August 2002, pp. 127–48.

Nissanke, Machiko, and Erenest Aryeetey, *Financial Integration and Development: Liberalization and Reform in Sub-Saharan Africa*, London: Routledge, 1998.

Nordhaus, William D., 'Productivity Growth and the New Economy', NBER Working Paper No. 8096, National Bureau of Economic Research, January 2001.

North, Peter, *Alternative Currencies as a Challenge to Globalisation? A Case Study of Manchester's Local Currency Networks*, London: Ashgate, 2006.

North, Peter, *Money and Liberation: The Micropolitics of Alternative Currency Movements*, Minneapolis: University of Minnesota Press, 2007.

O'Mahony, Mary, and Bart van Ark (eds), *EU Productivity and Competitiveness: An Industry Perspective*, Luxemburg: Office for Official Publications of the European Communities, 2003.

Ohmae, Kenichi, *The Borderless World*, London: HarperCollins, 1990.

Oliner, Stephen, and Daniel Sichel, 'Information Technology and Productivity: Where are we Now and Where are we Going?', *Economic Review*, Federal Reserve Bank of Atlanta, Third Quarter, 2002, pp. 15–44.

Oliner, Stephen, and Daniel Sichel, 'The Resurgence of Growth in the Late 1990s: Is

Information Technology the Story?', *Journal of Economic Perspectives* 14:4, 2000, pp. 3–22.

Onaran, Özlem, Engelbert Stockhammer, and Lucas Grafl, 'Financialization, Income Distribution and Aggregate Demand in the USA', in *Cambridge Journal of Economics* 35, 2011, pp. 637–61.

Orhangazi, Özgür, 'Financialization and Capital Accumulation in the Non-Financial Corporate Sector: A Theoretical and Empirical Investigation of the US Economy, 1973–2004', *Cambridge Journal of Economics*, 32, 2008, pp. 863–86.

Orhangazi, Özgür, *Financialization and the US Economy*, Northampton: Edward Elgar, 2007.

Orléan, André, *Le pouvoir de la finance*, Paris: Odile Jacob, 1999.

Ostry, Jonathan, Atish Ghosh, Karl Habermeier, Marcos Chamon, Mahvash Qureshi, and Dennis Reinhardt, 'Capital Inflows: The Role of Controls', IMF Staff Position Note, SPN/10/04, International Monetary Fund, 19 February 2010.

Owen, Roger, and Bob Sutcliffe (eds), *Studies in the Theory of Imperialism*, London: Longman, 1972.

Painceira, Juan Pablo, 'Central Banking in Middle Income Countries in the Course of Financialisation: A Study with Special Reference to Brazil and Korea', unpublished PhD thesis, University of London, 2011.

Painceira, Juan Pablo, 'Central Banking in Middle Income Countries in the Course of Financialisation: A Study with Special Reference to Brazil and Korea', unpublished PhD thesis, University of London, 2011.

Painceira, Juan Pablo, 'Developing Countries in the Era of Financialisation: From Deficit Accumulation to Reserve Accumulation', RMF Discussion Papers 4, February 2009; also published in Lapavitsas (ed.), *Financialisation in Crisis*, pp. 185–216.

Palley, Frederick A., and John E. Sandys, *Select Private Orations of Demosthenes*, Cambridge: Cambridge University Press, 1874.

Palley, Thomas I., 'A Post Keynesian Framework for Monetary Policy: Why Interest Rate Operating Procedures are Not Enough', Presented to the Conference on *Economic Policies: Perspectives from Keynesian Heterodoxy*, Dijon, France, 14–16 November, 2002, revised March 2003.

Panico, Carlo, Interest and Profit in the Theories of Value and Distribution, London: Macmillan, 1987.

Panico, Carlo, 'Marx on the Banking Sector and the Interest Rate: Some Initial Notes for a Discussion', *Science and Society* 52:3, Fall 1988, pp. 310–25.

Panico, Carlo, 'Marx's Analysis of the Relationship Between the Rate of Interest and the Rate of Profit', *Cambridge Journal of Economics* 4, 1980, pp. 363–78.

Panitch, Leo, and Sam Gindin, 'American Imperialism and EuroCapitalism: The Making of Neoliberal Globalization', *Studies in Political Economy* 71/72, 2003, pp. 7–38.

Panitch, Leo, and Sam Gindin, 'The Current Crisis: A Socialist Perspective', *Studies in Political Economy* 83, 2009, pp. 7–31.

Panitch, Leo, and Sam Gindin, 'Finance and American Empire', in *American Empire and the Political Economy of Global Finance*, ed. Leo Panitch and Martijn Konings, New York: Palgrave Macmillan, 2009, pp. 17–47.

Panitch, Leo, and Sam Gindin, *Global Capitalism and American Empire*, London: Merlin Press, 2004.

Panitch, Leo, and Sam Gindin, *The Making of Global Capitalism*, London: Verso Books, 2012.

Papadimitriou, Dmitri, and L. Randall Wray, 'Euroland's Original Sin', Policy Note 2012/8, Levy Economics Institute of Bard College, 2012.

Patnaik, Prabhat, 'The Economics of the New Phase of Imperialism', paper presented at IDEAS conference on The Economics of the New Imperialism, 22–24 January 2004, Jawaharlal Nehru University, New Delhi, 2005.

Patnaik, Prabhat, 'Globalization of Capital and the Theory of Imperialism', *Social Scientist* 24:11/12, 1996, pp. 5–17.

Patnaik, Prabhat, 'The Humbug of Finance' in *The Retreat to Unfreedom*, Delhi: Tulika, 2003.

Patnaik, Prabhat (ed.), *Lenin and Imperialism*, London: Sangham, 1986.

Patnaik, Prabhat, 'The Theory of Money and World Capitalism', paper presented at IDEAS conference on International Money and Developing Countries, Muttukadu, Tamil Nadu, India, 19 December 2002.

Patnaik, Prabhat, *The Value of Money*, New York: Columbia University Press, 2009.

Pauly, Louis, 'Capital Mobility, State Autonomy and Political Legitimacy', *Journal of International Affairs* 48:2, 1995, pp. 369–88.

Pauly, Louis, *Who Elected the Bankers? Surveillance and Control in the World Economy*, Ithaca, NY: Cornell University Press, 1997.

Peck, Jamie, and Nik Theodore, 'Variegated Capitalism', *Progress in Human Geography* 31:6, 2007, pp. 731–72.

Persaud, Avinash, 'Liquidity Black Holes', WIDER Discussion Paper No. 2002/31, World Institute for Development Economics Research, March 2002.

Picciotto, Sol, 'International Transformations of the Capitalist State', *Antipode* 43:1, 2011, pp. 87–107.

Picciotto, Sol, and Jason Haines, 'Regulating Global Financial Markets', *Journal of Law and Society* 26:3, 1999, pp. 351–68.

Pike, Andy, and Jane Pollard, 'Economic Geographies of Financialization', *Economic Geography* 86:1, 2010, pp. 29–51.

Piketty, Thomas, 'Income Inequality in France, 1901–1998.' *Journal of Political Economy* 111:5, 2003, pp. 1004–42.

Piketty, Thomas, 'Top Incomes over the Twentieth Century: A Summary of Main Findings', in *Top Incomes over the Twentieth Century: A Contrast between Continental European and English-Speaking Countries*, ed. A.B. Atkinson and Thomas Piketty, Oxford: Oxford University Press, 2007, pp. 1–17.

Piketty, Thomas, and Emmanuel Saez, 'The Evolution of Top Incomes: A Historical and International Perspective.' *American Economic Review* 96:2, 2006, pp. 200–5.

Piketty, Thomas, and Emmanuel Saez, 'Income Inequality in the United States, 1913–1998.' *Quarterly Journal of Economics* 118:1, 2003, pp. 1–39.

Plihon, Dominique, *Le nouveau capitalisme*, 3rd edition, Paris: Éditions La Découverte, 2009.

Polak, Jacques J., and Peter B. Clark, 'Reducing the Costs of Holding Reserves: A New Perspective on Special Drawing Rights', *The New Public Finance: Responding to Global Challenges*, ed. Inge Kaul and Pedro Conceição, Oxford: Oxford University Press, 2006, pp. 549–63.

Polanyi, Karl, 'The Economy as Instituted Process', in *Trade and Markets in Early Empires*, ed. Karl Polanyi, Conrad Arensberg, and Harry Pearson, Glencoe, IL: Free Press, 1957.

Polanyi, Karl, *The Great Transformation*, Boston: Beacon Press, 1944.

Pollin, Robert, 'Contemporary Economic Stagnation in World Historical Perspective', *New Left Review* 219, 1996, pp. 109–18.

Pollin, Robert, 'Remembering Paul Sweezy', *Counterpunch*, 6/7 March 2004.

Pollin, Robert, 'The Resurrection of the Rentier', *New Left Review* 46, 2007, pp. 140–53.

Porteous, David, *The Enabling Environment for Mobile Banking in Africa*, Department for International Development (DFID), 2006, at bankablefrontier.com.

Posen, Adam S., 'A Proven Framework to End the US Banking Crisis Including Some Temporary Nationalizations', testimony before the joint committee of the US Congress hearing on 'Restoring the Economy: Strategies for Short-Term and Long-Term Change', 26 February 2009, at piie.com.

Pozsar, Zoltan, Tobias Adrian, Adam Ashcraft, and Hayley Boesky, 'Shadow Banking', Staff Report 458, Federal Reserve Bank of New York, July 2010, rev. February 2012, pp. 1–35.

Prasad, Eswar, Rajan Raghuram and Arvind Subramanian, 'Foreign Capital and Economic Growth', *Brookings Papers on Economic Activity* 38, 2007, pp. 153–230.

Pryke, Michael, and Paul du Gay, 'Take an Issue: Cultural Economy and Finance', *Economy and Society* 36:3, 2007, pp. 339–54.

Radner, Roy, 'The Organization of Decentralized Information Processing', *Econometrica* 61:5, 1993, pp. 1109–46.

Redlich, Fritz, *The Molding of American Banking*, vols 1 and 2, New York: Johnson Reprint Corporation, 1951, reprinted 1968.

Reed, C.M., *Maritime Traders in the Ancient Greek World*, Cambridge: Cambridge University Press, 2003.

Reuten, Geert, and Michael Williams, *Value Form and the State*, London: Routledge, 1989.

Ricardo, David, *The High Price of Bullion*, in *The Works and Correspondence of David Ricardo*, vol. 3, ed. Piero Sraffa and Maurice Dobb, Cambridge: Cambridge University Press, 1951 (1810).

Ricardo, David, *Letters*, in *The Works and Correspondence of David Ricardo*, vol. 6, ed. Piero Sraffa and Maurice Dobb, Cambridge: Cambridge University Press, 1951 (1810).

Ricardo, David, *On the Principles of Political Economy and Taxation*, in *The Works and Correspondence of David Ricardo*, vol. 1, ed. Piero Sraffa and Maurice Dobb, Cambridge: Cambridge University Press, 1951 (1817).

Rodrik, Dani, 'The Social Cost of Foreign Exchange Reserves', NBER Working Paper No. 11952, National Bureau of Economic Research, January 2006.

Rogoff, Kenneth, 'Blessing or Curse? Foreign and Underground Demand for Euro Notes', *Economic Policy* 13:26, April 1998, pp. 263–303.

Rogoff, Kenneth, 'The Optimal Degree of Commitment to an Intermediate Monetary Target', *Quarterly Journal of Economics* 100:4, 1985, pp. 1169–90.

Rogoff, Kenneth, 'Reputational Constraints on Monetary Policy' in *Carnegie-Rochester Conference Series on Public Policy* 26, Spring 1987, pp. 141–81. Revised and reprinted as 'Reputation, Coordination and Monetary Policy', in *Modern Business Cycle Theory*, ed. Robert J. Barro, Cambridge, MA: Harvard University Press, 1989.

Rosdolsky, Roman, *The Making of Marx's 'Capital'*, London: Pluto Press, 1977.

Rubery, Jill, 'Part-Time Work: A Threat to Labour Standards', in *Part-Time Prospects: An International Comparison of Part-Time Work in Europe, North America and the Pacific Rim*, ed. Jacqueline O'Reilly and Colette Fagan, New York: Routledge, 1998, pp. 137–55.

Rubery, Jill, Mark Smith, and Colette Fagan, 'National Working-Time Regimes and Equal Opportunities', *Feminist Economics* 4:1, 1998, pp. 71–101.

Rubin, Isaak I., *Essays in Marx's Theory of Value*, Detroit: Black and Red, 1972.

Saad-Filho, Alfredo, Elmer Altvater, and Gregroy Albo, 'Neoliberalism and the Left: A Symposium', in *Socialist Register 2008*, ed. Leo Panitch and Colin Leys, London: Merlin Press, 2007.

Saad-Filho, Alfredo, and Deborah Johnston (eds), *Neoliberalism: A Critical Reader*, London: Pluto Press, 2005.

Sadun, Raffaella, and John Van Reenen, 'Information Technology and Productivity: It Ain't What You Do It's the Way That You Do I.T.', EDS Innovation Research Programme, Discussion Paper No. 002, London School of Economics, October 2005.

Saez, Emmanuel, 'Income and Wealth Concentration in a Historical and International Perspective', in *Public Policy and the Income Distribution*, ed. Alan Auerbach, David Card, and John M. Quigley, NY: Russell Sage Foundation, 2006, pp. 221–58.

Saunders, Anthony, and Linda Allen, *Credit Risk Measurement: New Approaches to Value at Risk and Other Paradigms*, 2nd ed., New York: John Wiley and Sons, 2002.

Savage, Mike, and Karel Williams (eds), *Remembering Elites*, London: John Wiley and Sons, 2008.

Sawyer, Malcolm, 'The NAIRU: A Critical Appraisal', *International Papers in Political Economy* 6:2, 1999, pp. 1–40; reprinted in *Money, Finance and Capitalist Development*, ed. Philip Arestis and Malcolm Sawyer, Aldershot: Edward Elgar, 2001, pp. 220–54.

Sayers, R.S., *Modern Banking*, Oxford: Oxford University Press, 1938.

Schaps, David, *The Invention of Coinage and the Monetization of Ancient Greece*, Ann Arbor: The University of Michigan Press, 2004.

Schmitz, Stefan W., and Geoffrey Wood (eds), *Institutional Change in the Payments System and Monetary Policy*, London: Routledge, 2006.

Schor, Juliet, *The Overworked American: The Unexpected Decline of Leisure*, New York: Basic Books, 1992.

Schumpeter, Joseph A., *Capitalism, Socialism and Democracy*, 5th ed., London: George Allen & Unwin, 1976.

Schumpeter, Joseph A., *History of Economic Analysis*, New York: Oxford University Press, 1954.

Schumpeter, Joseph A., *Imperialism and Social Classes*, New York: Augustus Kelly, 1951.

Schumpeter, Joseph A., *The Theory of Economic Development*, Cambridge, MA: Harvard University Press, 1934 (1912).

Schwartz, Anna, 'Financial Stability and the Safety Net', in *Restructuring Banking and Financial Services in America*, ed. William S. Haraf and Rose Marie Kushmeider, Washington, DC: American Enterprise Institute For Public Policy and Research, 1988, pp. 34–62.

Schwartz, Anna, 'Why Financial Stability Depends on Price Stability', in *Money, Prices and the Real Economy*, ed. Geoffrey Wood, Northampton: Edward Elgar, 1998, pp. 34–41.

Schweikart, Larry, *Banking in the American South: From the Age of Jackson to Reconstruction*, Baton Rouge: Louisiana State University Press, 1987.

Sekine, Thomas, 'Arthur on Money and Exchange', *Capital and Class* 33:3, 2009, pp. 33–57.

Sekine, Thomas, *The Dialectic of Capital*, vols. 1 and 2, Tokyo: Toshindo, 1986.

Sekine, Thomas, 'Marxian Theory of Value: An Unoist Approach', *Chiiki Bunseki, Aichi Gakuin* 37:2, 1999, pp. 99–136.

Sekine, Thomas, *An Outline of the Dialectic of Capital*, London: Macmillan, 1997.

Serfati, Claude, 'Financial Dimensions of Transnational Corporations, Global Value Chains and Technological Innovations', *Journal of Innovation Economics* 2:2, 2008, pp. 35–61.

Serfati, Claude, 'Le role actif de groupes à dominante industrielle dans la financiarisation de l'économie', in *La mondialisation financière : genèse, coût et enjeux*, ed. François Chesnais, Paris: Syros, 1996, pp. 142–82.

Serfati, Claude, 'Transnational Corporations as Financial Groups', *Work Organisation, Labour and Globalisation* 5:1, 2011, pp. 10–38.

Shaikh, Anwar, 'Explaining Inflation and Unemployment: An Alternative to Neoliberal Economic Theory' in *Contemporary Economic Theory*, ed. Andriana Vlachou, London: Macmillan, 1999.

Shaikh, Anwar, 'Explaining the Global Economic Crisis', *Historical Materialism* 5, Winter 1999, pp. 103–44.

Shaikh, Anwar, 'The Falling Rate of Profit and Long Waves in Accumulation: Theory and Evidence', in *New Findings in Long Wave Research*, ed. Alfred Kleinknech, Ernest Mandel, and Immanuel Wallerstein, London: Macmillan, 1992.

Shaikh, Anwar, 'The Falling Rate of Profit and the Economic Crisis in the US', in *The Imperiled Economy*, book 1, ed. Robert D. Cherry, New York: Union of Radical Political Economics, 1987.

Shaikh, Anwar, 'An Introduction to the History of Crisis Theories', in *US Capitalism in Crisis*, ed. Bruce Steinberg and Union for Radical Political Economics, New York: Monthly Review Press, 1978.

Shaikh, Anwar, 'Political Economy and Capitalism: Notes on Dobb's Theory of Crisis', *Cambridge Journal of Economics* 2:2, 1978, pp. 223–51.

Shaikh, Anwar, 'The Transformation from Marx to Sraffa: Prelude to a Critique of the Neo-Ricardians' in *Marx, Ricardo, Sraffa*, ed. Ernest Mandel, London: Verso, 1984.

Shaikh, Anwar, and E. Tonak, *Measuring the Wealth of Nations: The Political Economy of National Accounts*, Cambridge: Cambridge University Press, 1994.

Shaw, Edward S., *Financial Deepening in Economic Development*, New York: Oxford University Press, 1973.

Shirky, Clay, 'Fame vs Fortune: Micropayments and Free Content', 5 September 2003, at shirky.com.

Silvennoinen, Annastiina, and Susan Thorp, 'Financialization, Crisis and Commodity Correlation Dynamics', Research Paper 267, Quantitative Finance Research Centre, University of Technology Sydney, 2010.

Simons, Henry et al., 'Banking and Currency Reform', in *Research in the History of Economic Thought and Methodology, Archival Supplement 4*, ed. Warren J. Samuels, Greenwich, CT: JAI Press, 1933.

Sklair, Leslie, *Capitalism and Its Alternatives*, 3rd ed. rev. and retitled, Oxford: Oxford University Press, 2002.

Sklair, Leslie, *The Transnational Capitalist Class*, Oxford: Blackwell, 2001.

Skott, Peter, and Soon Ryoo, 'Macroeconomic Implications of Financialization', *Cambridge Journal of Economics* 32:6, 2008, pp. 827–62.

Smaldone, William, *Rudolf Hilferding*, Dekalb, IL: Northern Illinois University Press, 1998.

Smith, Adam, *The Wealth of Nations*, ed. Edwin E. Cannan, London: Methuen, 1904 (1776).

Solow, Robert, 'We'd Better Watch Out', review of *Manufacturing Matters*, by Stephen S. Cohen and John Zysman, *New York Times*, 12 July 1987.

Spufford, Peter, *Money and Its Use in Mediaeval Europe*, Cambridge: Cambridge University Press, 1988.

Spufford, Peter, *Power and Profit: The Merchant in Medieval Europe*, New York: Thames & Hudson, 2002.

Standing, Guy, 'Global Feminization Through Flexible Labor: A Theme Revisited', *World Development* 27:3, 1999, pp. 583–602.

Standing, Guy, 'Global Feminization Through Flexible Labor', *World Development* 17:7, 1989, pp. 1077–95.

Stenfors, Alexis, 'LIBOR as a Keynesian Beauty Contest: A Process of Endogenous

Deception', Discussion Paper no. 40, Research on Money and Finance, 2012.

Stenfors, Alexis, 'LIBOR Games: Means, Opportunities and Incentives to Deceive', Discussion Paper no. 39, Research on Money and Finance, 2012.

Steuart, James, *An Inquiry into the Principles of Political Economy*, vols 1–4, in *Works, Political, Metaphysical, and Chronological, of the Late Sir James Steuart*, London: Routledge, 1995 (1767).

Stiglitz, Joseph, 'Markets, Market Failures and Development', *American Economic Review* 79:2, 1989, pp. 197–202.

Stiglitz, Joseph, 'More Instruments and Broader Goals: Moving Toward the Post Washington Consensus', WIDER Annual Lecture, Helsinki, 7 January 1998.

Stiglitz, Joseph, 'Whither Reform? Ten Years Of The Transition', World Bank, Annual Bank Conference On Development Economics, 28–30 April 1999.

Stiglitz, Joseph, 'Why Financial Structure Matters', *Journal of Economic Perspectives* 2:4, Fall 1988.

Stiglitz, Joseph, and Andrew Weiss, 'Credit Rationing in Markets with Imperfect Information', *American Economic Review* 71:3, 1981, pp. 393–410.

Stiroh, Kevin, 'Is IT Driving the US Productivity Revival?', *International Productivity Monitor*, vol. 2, 2001, pp. 31–6.

Stix, Helmut, 'How Do Debit Cards Affect Cash Demand? Survey Data Evidence', Working Paper 82, Oesterreichische Nationalbank, 2003.

Stockhammer, Engelbert, 'Financialization and the Slowdown of Accumulation', *Cambridge Journal of Economics*, 28, 2004, pp. 719–41.

Stockhammer, Engelbert, 'Neoliberalism, Income Distribution and the Causes of the Crisis', RMF Discussion Paper No. 19, 2010.

Stockhammer, Engelbert, 'Some Stylized Facts on the Finance-Dominated Accumulation Regime', *Competition and Change* 12:2, 2008, pp. 184–202.

Strange, Susan, *Casino Capitalism*, Oxford: Basil Blackwell, 1986.

Strange, Susan, 'Finance, Information and Power', *Review of International Studies* 16:3, 1990, pp. 259–74.

Strange, Susan, *The Retreat of the State*, Cambridge: Cambridge University Press, 1996.

Strange, Susan, *States and Markets*, London: Continuum, 1994.

Strange, Susan, 'Still an Extraordinary Power: America's Role in a Global Market System', in *The Political Economy of International and Domestic Monetary Relations*, ed. Raymond Lombra and Willard Witte, Ames: Iowa State University Press, 1982.

Suzuki, Yoshio, 'Financial Reform in Japan – Developments and Prospects', *Monetary and Economic Studies* 5:3, December 1987.

Suzuki, Yoshio, *The Japanese Financial System*, Oxford: Clarendon Press, 1987.

Svensson, Lars, 'What Is Wrong with Taylor Rules? Using Judgement in Monetary Policy Through Targeting Rules', *Journal of Economic Literature* 41:2, 2003, pp. 426–77.

Swanson, Eric T., 'Let's Twist Again: A High-Frequency Event-Study Analysis of Operation Twist and Its Implications for QE2', *Brookings Papers on Economic Activity* 42:1, Spring 2011, pp. 151–88.

Sweezy, Paul M. (ed.), *Karl Marx and the Close of His System, by Eugen von Böhm-Bawerk. Böhm-Bawerk's Criticism of Marx, by Rudolf Hilferding; Together with an Appendix Consisting of an Article by Ladislaus von Bortkiewicz on the Transformation of Values into Prices of Production in the Marxian System*, New York: A.M. Kelley, 1949.

Sweezy, Paul M., 'More (or Less) on Globalization', *Monthly Review* 49:4, 1997.

Sweezy, Paul M., *The Theory of Capitalist Development*, New York: Monthly Review Press, 1942.

Sweezy, Paul M., 'The Triumph of Financial Capital', *Monthly Review* 46:2, 1994.

Szymanski, Albert, *The Logic of Imperialism*, New York: Praeger, 1981.

Takumi, M., 'Hilferding', in *Marukusu Keizaigaku Kogi (Discourses in Marxian Economics)*, ed. K. Suzuki, Tokyo: Seirinshoin-shinsa, 1972.

Tang, Ke, and Wei Xiong, 'Index Investment and Financialization of Commodities', mimeo, Princeton University, March 2011.

Taylor, John B., 'Discretion Versus Policy Rules in Practice', *Carnegie-Rochester Conference Series on Public Policy* 39:1, 1993, pp. 195–214.

Thakor, Anjan V., 'The Design of Financial Systems: An Overview', *Journal of Banking and Finance* 20, 1996, pp. 917–48.

Thompson, Paul, 'Disconnected Capitalism: Or Why Employers Can't Keep Their Side of the Bargain', *Work, Employment and Society* 17, 2003, pp. 359–78.

Thompson, Paul, 'Foundation and Empire: A Critique of Hardt and Negri', *Capital and Class* 86, Summer 2005, pp. 73–98.

Tobin, James, 'A Proposal for International Monetary Reform', *Eastern Economic Journal* 4, 1978, pp. 153–9.

Toniolo, Gianni, *Central Bank Cooperation at the Bank of International Settlements, 1930–1973*, Cambridge: Cambridge University Press, 2005.

Tooke, Thomas, *An Inquiry into the Currency Principle*, London: LSE Reprint Series, 1959 (1844).

Toporowski, Jan, 'The Economics and Culture of Financial Inflation', *Competition and Change* 13:2, 2009, pp. 145–56.

Toporowski, Jan, *The End of Finance: The Theory of Capital Market Inflation, Financial Derivatives and Pension Fund Capitalism*, London: Routledge, 2000.

Torrens, Robert, *The Principles and Practical Operation of Sir Robert Peel's Act of 1844 Explained and Defended*, 2nd ed. London: Longman, Brown, Green, Longmans and Roberts, 1857.

Tougan-Baranowsky, Michel (Mikhail Tugan-Baranovsky), *Les Crises industrielles en Angleterre*, Paris: M. Giard & E. Brière, 1913.

Townsend, Robert M., 'Optimal Contracts and Competitive Markets with Costly State Verification', *Journal of Economic Theory* 22, 1979, pp. 265–93.

Triplett, Jack, 'High-Tech Industry Productivity and Hedonic Price Indices', *OECD Proceedings: Industry Productivity, International Comparison and Measurement Issues*, OECD, 1996, pp. 119–42.

Triplett, Jack, and Barry Bosworth, 'Productivity in the Services Sector', *Brookings Economics Papers*, January 2000.

Triplett, Jack, and Barry Bosworth, 'What's New About the New Economy? IT, Economic Growth and Productivity', *International Productivity Monitor*, vol. 2, 2001, pp. 19–30.

Trotsky, Leon, 'The Curve of Capitalist Development', originally published in Russian, *Fourth International* 2:4, 1941 (1923), pp. 111–14.

Turner, Adair, 'Adair Turner Roundtable: How to Tame Global Finance', *Prospect*, September 2009, pp. 34–41.

UNCTAD, *World Investment Report 1999: Foreign Direct Investment and the Challenge of Development*, New York: UN, 1999.

UNCTAD, *World Investment Report 2002: Transnational Corporations and Export Competitiveness*, New York: UN, 2002.

UNCTAD, *World Investment Report 2003: FDI Policies for Development. National and International Perspectives*, New York: UN, 2003.

UNCTAD, *World Investment Report 2005: Transnational Corporations and the Internationalization of R&D*, New York: UN, 2005.

UNCTAD, *World Investment Report 2006: FDI from Developing and Transition Economies. Implications for Development*, New York: UN, 2006.

Underhill, Geoffrey, 'Global Money and the Decline of State Power', in *Strange Power: Shaping the Parameters of International Relations and International Political Economy*, ed. Thomas Lawton, James Rosenau, and Amy Verdun, Burlington, VT: Ashgate, 2000.

Underhill, Geoffrey, 'Markets Beyond Politics? The State and the Internationalisation of Financial Markets', *European Journal of Political Research* 19:2–3, 1991, pp. 197–225.

Uno Kozo, *Keizai Genron* (Principles of Political Economy), Vol. 1, Tokyo: Iwanami Shoten, 1950.

Uno Kozo, *Keizai Genron* (Principles of Political Economy), Vol. 2, Tokyo: Iwanami Shoten, 1952.

Uno Kozo, *Keizai Seisakuron*, Tokyo: Kobundo Shobo, 1936. A translation in English by T. Sekine is available in mimeo under the title *The Types of Economic Policy under Capitalism*.

Uno Kozo, *Kyoukouron* (Theory of Crisis), Tokyo: Iwanami Shoten, 1953.

Uno Kozo, *Principles of Political Economy*, translated by T. Sekine, Brighton: Harvester Press, 1980.

Usher, Abbott, 'The Early History of Deposit Banking in Mediterranean Europe', Cambridge, MA: Harvard University Press, 1943.

Usher, Abbott, 'The Origins of Banking: The Primitive Bank of Deposit, 1200–1600' in *Enterprise and Secular Change*, ed. Frederic Lane and Jelle Riemersma, Homewood, IL: Richard Irwin. Originally published in *Economic History Review*, 1934, IV, pp. 399–428, 1953.

Van Alstyne, Marshall, and Erik Brynjolfsson, 'Global Village or Cyber-Balkans: Modeling and Measuring the Integration of Electronic Communities', *Management Science*, 2004.

Van Els, Peter, Alberto Locarno, Julian Morgan, and Jean-Pierre Villetelle, 'Monetary Policy Transmission in the Euro Area: What Do Aggregate and National Structural Models Tell Us?', Working Paper No. 94, European Central Bank, December 2001.

Van Werveke, Hans, 'Monnaie de Compte et Monnaie Réelle', *Revue Belge de Philologie et d' Histoire* 13: 1–2, 1934, pp. 123–52.

Vilar, Pierre, *A History of Gold and Money*, 1450–1920, London: Verso, 2011.

Volcker, Paul, 'The Role of Private Capital in the World Economy', in *Private Enterprise and the New Economic Challenge*, ed. Stephen Guisinger, Indianapolis: Bobbs-Merrill, 1979.

Volcker, Paul, and Toyoo Gyohten, *Changing Fortunes: The World's Money and the Threat of American Leadership*, New York: Times Books, 1992.

Wagner, F. Peter, *Rudolf Hilferding: Theory and Politics of Democratic Socialism*, Atlantic Highlands, NJ: Humanities Press, 1996.

Walras, Léon, *Elements of Pure Economics*, London: Allen & Unwin, 1954.

Warren, Bill, *Imperialism Pioneer of Capitalism*, 2nd ed., London: Verso, 1980.

Weber, Max, *Economy and Society: An Outline of Interpretive Sociology*, in two volumes, ed. Guenther Roth and Claus Wittich, New York: Bedminster Press, 1968.

Weeks, John, 'Surfing the Troubled Waters of 'Global Turbulence': A Comment', *Historical Materialism* 5, Winter 1999, pp. 211–30.

Weiss, Linda, 'Globalization and the Myth of the Powerless State', *New Left Review* 225, 1997, pp. 3–27.

Whalen, Charles, 'The U.S. Credit Crunch of 2007: A Minsky Moment', Public Policy Brief No. 92, Annandale-on-Hudson, NY: Levy Economics Institute, 2007.

White, William R., 'Is Price Stability Enough?', Working Paper No. 205, Bank for International Settlements, 2006.

White, William R., 'Procyclicality in the Financial System: Do We Need a New Macrofinancial Stabilisation Framework?', Working Paper No. 193, Bank for International Settlements, 2006.

Wicksell, Knut, 'The Influence of the Rate of Interest on Commodity Prices', in *Selected Papers on Economic Activity*, New York: Augustus M. Kelley Publishers, 1969 (1898).

Wigan, Duncan, 'Financialisation and Derivatives: Constructing an Artifice of Indifference', *Competition and Change* 13:2, 2009, pp. 157–72.

Wijnholds, J. Onno de Beaufort, and Lars Søndergaard, 'Reserve Accumulation: Objective or By-Product?', European Central Bank, Occasional Paper Series, No 73, 2007.

Williams, Karel, 'From Shareholder Value to Present-Day Capitalism', *Economy and Society* 29:1, 2000, pp. 1–12.

Williamson, John, 'The Washington Consensus Revisited', in *Economic and Social Development into the XXI Century*, ed. Louis Emmerij, Washington: Inter-American Development Bank, 1997.

Williamson, John, 'What Washington Means by Policy Reform', in *Latin American*

Readjustment: How Much has Happened?, ed. John Williamson, Washington: Institute for International Economics, 1990.

Woodford, Michael, *Interest and Prices: Foundations of a Theory of Monetary Policy*, Princeton: Princeton University Press, 2003.

Woodford, Michael, 'Monetary Policy in a World without Money', *International Finance*, 2:3, 2000, pp. 229-60.

Woodford, Michael, 'Monetary Policy in the Information Economy', *Economic Policy for the Information Economy*, Jackson Hole, Wyoming: Federal Reserve Bank of Kansas City, 2001, pp. 297-371,

Wray, L. Randall, 'Financial Markets Meltdown: What Can We Learn from Minsky?', Public Policy Brief No. 94, Annandale-on-Hudson, NY: Levy Economics Institute, April 2008.

Wray, L. Randall, 'Lessons from the Subprime Meltdown', Working Paper No. 552, The Levy Economics Institute, 2007.

Wray, L. Randall, 'Minsky's Money Manager Capitalism and the Global Financial Crisis', Working Paper 661, Annandale-on- Hudson, NY: Levy Economics Institute of Bard College, 2011.

Wray, L. Randall, 'Modern Money', in *What Is Money?*, ed. John Smithin, London: Routledge, 2000.

Wray, L. Randall, *Money and Credit in Capitalist Economies*, Aldershot and Brookfield: Edward Elgar, 1990.

Wray, L. Randall (ed.), *State and Credit Theories of Money: The Contributions of A. Mitchell Innes*, Cheltenham: Edward Elgar, 2004.

Wray, L. Randall, *Understanding Modern Money: The Key to Full Employment and Price Stability*, Cheltenham: Edward Elgar, 1998.

Yamaguchi, Shigekatsu., *Kinyuu Kikou no Riron* (Theory of the Structure of Finance), Tokyo: Tokyo Daigaku Shuppansha, 1984.

Zelizer, Viviana, 'Fine Tuning the Zelizer View', *Economy and Society* 29:3, 2000, pp. 383-9.

Zelizer, Viviana, 'Pasts and Futures of Economics Sociology', *American Behavioral Scientist* 50:8, 2007, pp. 1056-69.

Zhu, Steven, and Michael Pykhtin, 'Measuring Counterparty Risk for Trading Products under Basel II', in *The Basel Handbook: A Guide for Financial Practitioners*, 2nd ed., ed. Michael Ong, London: Risk Books, 2007.

Zysman, John, *Governments, Markets and Growth: Financial Systems and the Politics of Industrial Change*, Ithaca: Cornell University Press, 1983.

INDEX

Page numbers in **bold** refer to figures, page numbers in *italic* refer to tables